STANDING WITH STANDING ROCK

INDIGENOUS AMERICAS
Robert Warrior, Series Editor

STANDING WITH STANDING ROCK

Voices from the #NoDAPL Movement

NICK ESTES AND JASKIRAN DHILLON
EDITORS

INDIGENOUS AMERICAS

University of Minnesota Press
Minneapolis
London

Published by the University of Minnesota Press
111 Third Avenue South, Suite 290
Minneapolis, MN 55401-2520
http://www.upress.umn.edu

ISBN 978-1-5179-0536-1 (pb) — ISBN 978-1-5179-0535-4 (hc)

A Cataloging-in-Publication record for this book is available from the Library of Congress.

Printed in the United States of America on acid-free paper

The University of Minnesota is an equal-opportunity educator and employer.

25 24 23 22 21 20   10 9 8 7 6 5 4 3 2

Contents

PART V. EDUCATION AND CRITICAL PEDAGOGIES

PART VI. INDIGENOUS ORGANIZING AND SOLIDARITY IN MOVEMENT BUILDING

Prologue

One evening in October 2016, before the violent eviction of the 1851 Treaty Camp on Highway 1806 on October 27, Nick Estes was invited to a strategy session at Prairie Knights Casino, near Cannon Ball, North Dakota. Phyllis Young, a former Standing Rock councilwoman and a longtime member of the American Indian Movement, led the meeting. She played an audio recording from a meeting on September 30, 2014, between the Standing Rock Council and representatives of Energy Transfer Partners and the Dakota Access Pipeline. The meeting took place when the Oceti Sakowin, the Great Sioux Nation, led historic resistance against the Keystone XL Pipeline, which cut through the heart of the 1868 Fort Laramie Treaty territory. At that time, the focus was on defeating KXL; few had heard of DAPL. Those who had took it seriously as an existential threat to Indigenous sovereignty and the future of not just Standing Rock but also the downriver Indigenous nations, non-Native peoples, non-Native life, and other-than-human life.

The audio clip played at the meeting begins with Tribal Chairman David Archambault II unequivocally declaring that Standing Rock opposed DAPL and all pipelines trespassing through the 1868 treaty territory and concludes with Phyllis Young's prophetic words and warning to DAPL. Her words have informed the spirit of #NoDAPL and this book. We share them here in honor and respect for this Standing Rock elder and dignitary. As history was being told, history was unfolding. And it has not stopped.

> We will put our best warriors in the front. We are the vanguard. We are Hunkpapa Lakota. That means the horn of the buffalo. That's who we are. We are protectors of our nation of Oceti Sakowin, the Seven Council Fires. Know who we are. We will put forward our young people, our young lawyers who understand the weasel words of the English language, who know one word can mean seven things. We understand the forked tongue that our grandfathers talked about. We know about talking out both sides of your mouth, smiling with one side of your face. We know all about the tricks of the wasicu [the fat-taker, the capitalist] world. Our young people have mastered it. I have mastered your language. I can speak eloquently in the English language. My grandmother taught me. But I also know the genetic psyche, and I also have the collective memory of the damages that have occurred to my people. I will never submit to any pipeline to go through my homeland. Mitakuye Oyasin.

"Fist Up." Photograph by Jaida Grey Eagle.

Introduction

THE BLACK SNAKE, #NoDAPL, AND THE RISE OF A PEOPLE'S MOVEMENT

Nick Estes and Jaskiran Dhillon

It is prophecy. A great Black Snake, Zuzeca Sapa, will spread itself across the land bringing destruction to the land, the water, and the people. The Black Snake is the Dakota Access Pipeline (DAPL), a $3.8 billion, 1,172-mile pipeline that transports half a million barrels of oil a day across four states (North Dakota, South Dakota, Iowa, and Illinois) and under the Missouri River twice and under the Mississippi River once. A rupture jeopardizes the drinking water of millions of human souls and countless other-than-humans who depend on the river for life. While the Black Snake prophecy portends doom, it also sparks hope. Indigenous nations will have to unite with non-Indigenous allies to protect Unci Maka, Grandmother Earth. Few could have imagined it would happen in their lifetimes, except for, perhaps, the visionaries themselves who kept the dream alive; and yet it happened, in the isolated, rural geography of dirt roads, farmlands, and the lush shorelines of the Mni Sose, the Missouri River. The Oceti Sakowin, the Nation of the Seven Council Fires of the Lakota-, Dakota-, and Nakota-speaking peoples, was reborn. No one could have predicted the movement would spread like wildfire across Turtle Island and the world, moving millions to rise up, speak out, and take action. That's how revolutionary moments, and the movements within those moments, come about. Freedom and victory are never preordained. A new world at first inhabits the shell of the old. In the colonial context, it's the old world that came before, an Indigenous world that never went away, that inhabits the imprisoning shell of the new world, waiting to break free. The dream that became one of the largest Indigenous uprisings in recent history had been nurtured and carefully brought into existence to save the water. It started with the youth.

Youth runners from Standing Rock led grueling hundred-mile and then thousand-mile runs to spread the word of the Black Snake threatening their homelands. Thousands, and then millions, answered the call. "City by city, block by block, we stand with Standing Rock!" "Tell me what the prophecy looks like, this is what the prophecy looks like!" "Mni Wiconi! Water is life!" These were the chants that rang through city streets across the world and on the isolated county and state highways of what is currently North Dakota. Like the #IdleNoMore movement in Canada that began in December 2012 that connected First Nations' sovereignty to protection of the environment, #NoDAPL emerged as an Indigenous- and women-led movement. #NoDAPL, however, was not a departure from so much as it was a continuation—a moment within a longer movement, but also a movement within a moment—of long traditions of Indigenous resistance deeply grounded in place and history. (Those histories and struggles include but are not limited to Alcatraz 1969, the Trail of Broken Treaties 1972, Wounded Knee 1973, the so-called Oka Crisis of 1990, #IdleNoMore 2013, and Unist'ot'en.) Thousands tuned in via social media livestreams for minute-by-minute updates whether in urban centers or in rural locations of North Dakota, often when mainstream media failed to take notice. Because of this critical link connecting this otherwise rural geography to the world, the tempo of the camps constructed north of Standing Rock kept pace with the massive solidarity organizing elsewhere. It was, and still is, a truly grassroots movement.

More than three hundred Native nations and countless allied movements planted their flags in solidarity at Oceti Sakowin Camp, the largest of several camps. Other camps included Sacred Stone Camp, Rosebud Camp, and Red Warrior Camp. Oceti Sakowin Camp was north of the Standing Rock Indian Reservation at the confluences of the Cannonball and Missouri Rivers, within the boundaries of the 1851 and 1868 Fort Laramie Treaties. Oceti Sakowin Camp was situated on the Missouri shoreline, treaty and ancestral land now claimed by the U.S. Army Corps of Engineers after it was flooded in the 1960s by Oahe Dam. Oahe was one of the five earthen-rolled Pick-Sloan dams on the Missouri River that flooded seven Indian reservations, forcefully dislocating a third of their populations. The treaties guarantee the Oceti Sakowin sole jurisdiction of Mni Sose's waterways. The Water Protectors, as they call themselves, vowed to defend the treaties and to stop the trespass of DAPL. In doing so, they challenged and redefined the ambit of legal jurisdiction that legitimates the settler state's claim to lands, waters, and peoples not entirely its own. Water Protectors became criminal precisely because they were generating and upholding a different kind of law contrary to settler law (one that places relations with nonhumans, the land, and water equal to, or sometimes surpassing, human-made laws), while also reminding the United States of its own obligations to uphold its own treaties—its original agreements—with the Oceti Sakowin.

In this volume, Craig Howe, Tyler Young, Edward Valandra, LaDonna Bravebull Allard, Marcella Gilbert, and Kim TallBear poignantly remind us that the Mni Sose, and water in general, is not a thing that is quantifiable according to possessive logics. Mni Sose is a relative: the Mni Oyate, the Water Nation. She is alive. Nothing owns her. Thus, the popular Lakotayapi assertion "Mni Wiconi": water is life or, more accurately, water is alive. You do not sell your relative, Water Protectors vow. To be a good relative mandates protecting Mni Oyate from the DAPL's inevitable contamination. This is the practice of Wotakuye (kinship), a recognition of the place-based, decolonial practice of being in relation to the land and water.

Mni Wiconi embodies the strength and wisdom of ancestral anticolonial struggles imprinted on the land and Mni Sose. It is also situated in the power and leadership of Indigenous youth and Indigenous women, who are foregrounding the way that colonialism functions through race, class, gender, and sexuality to create interlocking systems of oppression. Mni Wiconi simultaneously speaks to the past, present, and future—catapulting us into a moment of critical, radical reflection about the colonial wounds and wounding in the spaces between calls to save planet Earth and the everyday sociopolitical realities facing Indigenous peoples.

The largest Indigenous uprising in North America in recent memory also announced itself at a critical historical conjuncture, not only for Indigenous peoples but for the entire planet. Few could have predicted a humble, Indigenous-led movement marching under the banners of #NoDAPL and Mni Wiconi would mark the end of the first African American U.S. president's eight-year legacy. What optimism remained for a drastic change of course from business as usual—mitigating cataclysmic human-caused climate change and the earth's sixth mass extinction event—seemed to be shattered by Obama's successor. An open racist and misogynist running on the slogans "Build the Wall!" and "Make America Great Again" was elected president. Empowered by this rhetoric, Nazis and white supremacists openly marched in major U.S. cities and strong-armed their way onto college campuses, meeting little opposition from authorities and meeting frequent resistance from organized antifascists. Many progressive reforms and gains for Indigenous and marginalized peoples have been reversed since Trump's election. Millions of acres of lands, like those at Bears Ears National Monument, a sacred site to five Indigenous nations, have been opened up for private industry, specifically uranium mining.[1] More than a billion acres off the Atlantic, Pacific, and Arctic coasts have been opened for oil and gas drilling.[2] And the new president began aggressively expanding Obama-era domestic energy production policies, which were initiated to drill the United States out of the Great Recession of 2008 primarily at the expense of Indigenous lands and lives.[3] Days after his January inauguration, Trump signed two executive orders fast-tracking DAPL and the all-but-dead Keystone XL Pipeline. Weeks later the Army Corps, with the help of Morton County and the North Dakota National Guard, carried out a mandatory, forceful eviction of Oceti Sakowin, and Sacred Stone Camp was also cleared out. The profound backlash against the momentous upsurge at Standing Rock tends to overshadow the movement's importance, within that particular moment in time, a moment that deserves to be remembered and reflected upon for generations to come.

If there is a lesson to be learned from the historic movement that began at the Standing Rock Indian Reservation to halt DAPL, it is that great men don't make history. Presidents at the helm of a white supremacist empire will not save us or the planet. That much is sure. Nor do they, as individual men, doom our collective fate. The good people of the earth have always been the vanguards of history and radical social change. Such was the case at Standing Rock: everyday people taking control of their lives. As Marcella Gilbert, LaDonna Bravebull Allard, Lewis Grassrope, and Zaysha Grinnell remind us in the volume, it is a deeply intergenerational struggle, with grandparents organizing alongside grandchildren and sometimes great-grandchildren. Each drew from centuries of Indigenous resistance that didn't necessarily begin or end at Standing Rock but connected to it in profound ways. Likewise, as the diversity of contributors to this collection demonstrates, those connections cut across many movements and distinct geographies. Thus #NoDAPL's mass appeal. That historic character of the struggle, however, also made it the target of widespread state repression.

As rapidly as the movement gained steam, so too did the forces to undermine it. On August 19, 2016, North Dakota governor Jack Dalrymple declared a state of emergency, fearful an Indigenous uprising would imperil oil companies and their profits and thus negatively impact the state's oil-dependent economy. Under the powers of the Emergency Management Assistance Compact (EMAC), a federal program that allows states to solicit aid from other states during natural disasters or during "community disorders, insurgency, or enemy attack," North Dakota enlisted equipment and personnel from more than seventy-five law enforcement agencies from around the country, as well as the North Dakota National Guard, Border Patrol, and Homeland Security. In 2015, the state of Maryland made a similar EMAC request to crush the Black-led uprisings in Baltimore after police murdered Freddie Gray, a young Black man. In total, the state of North Dakota spent roughly $38 million alone in pipeline security expenses, a bill that was later reimbursed to the state by federal tax dollars. Chokepoints, armed checkpoints, concrete barricades, armored personnel carriers, and miles and miles of concertina wire dotted what was otherwise a rural landscape. As a result of the intensification of police and military, more than eight hundred Water Protectors were arrested.

The Intercept later revealed that DAPL hired a murky private security firm, TigerSwan, to protect its investments. The firm cut its teeth on counterinsurgency campaigns waged against militants and civilians in the Middle East as a contractor in the United States' "war on terror," and now imported that model to a "domestic" counterinsurgency campaign against people praying with water in order to protect it. The lines between corporate and state interests were further blurred when it was exposed that TigerSwan provided intelligence briefings to the Morton County sheriff's department, the law enforcement agency in charge of policing the #NoDAPL protests. This corporate-state collaboration and the counterintelligence campaign it waged against the Standing Rock Sioux Tribe and unarmed, nonviolent Water Protectors was devastatingly effective. Critics are quick to cite the inevitability of "progress" as the reason for DAPL's completion. Indians just happened to be in the way of that progress—once again. But there was nothing inevitable about DAPL. The most powerful state in the history of the world, with its military and police hand-in-hand with private security forces, waged a heavily armed, one-sided battle against some of the poorest people in North America to guarantee a pipeline's trespass. That Water Protectors held out against the ritualistic brutality of tear gas, pepper spray, dog attacks, water cannons, disinformation campaigns, and twenty-four-hour surveillance is a pure miracle and a testament to the powerful resolve of the Oceti Sakowin, Indigenous peoples, and their allies. Yet the wounds inflicted are long-lasting and descend from a longer history of colonial violence.

In this way, the #NoDAPL struggle is a continuation of the Indian wars of extermination. Such a massive militarized mobilization had not been seen in what is currently North Dakota since the nineteenth century. Morton County, for instance, descends from the infamous Seventh Cavalry and the notorious Colonel George Armstrong Custer. In 1873, Custer and his regiment were stationed at Fort Abraham Lincoln near what is currently the town of Mandan, the county seat of Morton County. The Northern Pacific Railroad threatened to trespass through Oceti Sakowin territory crossing the Missouri River at Bismarck, and it met heavy Indigenous resistance, much like the current pipeline. The fort took its name from the so-called Great Emancipator. The same week Lincoln signed the Emancipation Proclamation he also ordered the hanging of thirty-eight Dakota men as punishment for the 1862 Dakota Uprising, which remains the largest mass execution in U.S. history. From Fort Lincoln Custer led several expeditions into He Sapa, the Black Hills, in search of gold and in blatant violation of the 1868 Fort Laramie Treaty. His last sortie to the Little Bighorn Mountains in 1876 aimed to wipe out a supposedly hostile Native camp numbering in the thousands. On June 25, 1876, just days before the centennial celebrations of U.S. Independence Day, Custer's Seventh Cavalry met its demise at the hands of a Cheyenne, Arapaho, and Oceti Sakowin confederacy at the Battle of Greasy Grass. Custer was posthumously promoted to general for his courage.

Whether railroads, gold mines, or oil pipelines, in each instance the Oceti Sakowin stood between settlers and unrestricted capital accumulation. Put simply, the Indian Problem is out of control precisely when Indians stand between capitalists and their money. North Dakota, its white-dominated border towns, and state authorities simply carry on the legacy of flagrant anti-Indianism, trespass, and retributive violence. While this volume illuminates the sober reality of endemic police violence as a tool of corporate plunder, it also points to the political possibilities of imagining and reimagining Indigenous decolonization and the political project of getting free—freedom for ourselves and the planet. In this sense, #NoDAPL wasn't a failure because DAPL was ultimately built. The movement reignited the fire of Indigenous liberation and reminded us that it is a fire that cannot be quelled. It provided, for a brief moment in time, a collective vision of what the future could be.

Why This Book? Why Now?

This collection offers a series of radical engagements with the political resistance at Standing Rock—both in the movement's specificity as an anticolonial, Indigenous-led struggle for liberation from pervasive, ongoing colonial violence, which includes the reclamation of Indigenous land/life/authority, and in its ability to transcend the borders of U.S. empire and speak to transnational movements for decolonization. As Linda Tuhiwai-Smith importantly articulates, "decolonization is a process which engages with imperialism and colonialism at multiple levels."[4] The angles of vision, intellectualism, and architecture of critical resistance reflected at Standing Rock are tied to a complex politics of decolonization situated and embodied in the theories and practices of rising local, national, and transnational movements for revolutionary social change. It is our intention for this book to be taken up with this wider context in mind. As many of the contributors aptly point out, we must collectively shift our attention to the linkages among respective battles even though the frontiers of these struggles may exist thousands of miles apart.

Our curatorial approach for this edited collection is explicitly informed by such a practice of decolonial politics. It is also underpinned by a desire to showcase multiple lines of sight, stories emerging from a range of entry points, and a plurality of perspectives on the resistance effort. The work presented by the contributors sharpens critiques of settler colonialism in the past and present to be sure, but it also brings into relief new avenues of political organizing against forms of racial capitalism that are highly gendered, colonial state violence, and the destruction of land, water, air, humans, and other-than-humans. Through poetry and prose, essays, photography, interviews, and politicized intellectual interventions, these writers, thinkers, artists, and activists compel us to resurrect colonial history not simply as lessons learned but as essential guideposts into current and future radical political organizing and popular, political education efforts. They prompt us to step back and critically examine the intersections among Indigenous, Palestinian, and Black struggles for freedom and justice and migrant justice struggles against the violence of colonial borders, to view these movements, and a host of others, in relation to one another. And they push us to dive deep into ourselves—our own epistemologies and social histories, relationships to colonial power, and radical possibilities for environmental and social justice that are seeded in our collective imaginations and materially rooted in everyday practices of decolonization.

Numerous lines of inquiry stitch the pieces in this collection together. Among the most salient that factored into our thinking were these: How do we situate Standing Rock within a social, political, cultural, and historical context of Indigenous anticolonial resistance against occupation and various forms of state violence inherent to settler colonialism? How do we understand Indigenous resurgence as making discursive and theoretical interventions in the dominant environmental justice movement by foregrounding relationality to land, water, and air through

Indigenous epistemologies and ontologies? How does the pivotal leadership of Indigenous youth and the convergence of allied struggles inform transformative political possibilities for decolonization? How are social movements and academic fields of study accountable to Indigenous nations in the #NoDAPL movement with respect to research agendas, advocacy strategies, and education-based interventions? And finally, how does Standing Rock speak to similar movements across the globe, and where are the points of convergence and divergence?

It is also important to emphasize that the curatorial scope of this book was guided, first and foremost, by the inclusion of Lakota and Dakota scholars and many nonacademic contributors whose work is often excluded from edited collections circulating within the academy. The book retains intellectual and political rigor and at the same time refuses to adhere to academic publishing standards that have historically policed the boundaries of what constitutes "valid" knowledge and/or truth claims about our shared world; knowledge, Macarena Gómez-Barris reminds us, is also a site of conquest.[5] We intended for this book to be widely read, to be used within university classrooms but accessible and broad-ranging enough that it will be utilized in secondary schools, community settings, youth organizations, social justice collectives, movement building, and on the front lines of resistance camps.

Organization of the Book

Standing with Standing Rock: Voices from the #NoDAPL Movement is organized around six thematic parts, each bringing a different dimension of the political resistance at Standing Rock to the fore. As editors we tried to be extensive and as far-reaching as possible in our scope, but a single book can't do it all. We hope this is one of many projects focusing on the movement that took off at Standing Rock; we know it will be a movement that will resonate for generations. With this in mind, each part has been crafted around specific areas, while each individual piece may cut across numerous subjects, histories, and geographies. Throughout this volume there are pictures from Indigenous photographers—Jaida Grey Eagle, Michelle Latimer, Vanessa Bowen, and Nick Estes—that offer visual engagement with the camp and the many actions in support of Standing Rock's historic struggle.

The first part, "Leading the Resistance," begins with a series of meditations on the dynamics of leadership in the #NoDAPL movement. Kim TallBear, Mark K. Tilsen, Zaysha Grinnell, Lewis Grassrope, and David Archambault II each reflect on the dynamics of leadership concerning the reunification of the Oceti Sakowin, formal leadership from the Standing Rock Sioux Tribe, grassroots direct action against pipeline construction, the central role of Indigenous youth, and the importance of challenging heteropatriarchy. Notably, this part highlights the leadership of Indigenous youth and women in #NoDAPL and explores how their unique knowledge and strategies as leaders strengthened and informed everyday life on the front lines and the broader political goals of the movement. The role of Indigenous leadership and traditional governance as they intersect with #NoDAPL is also taken up within this first theme.

#NoDAPL is a product of a collective history of struggle and should be placed within the larger context of Indigenous resistance, treaties, and relationality to the land and water. Part II, "Living Histories," explores Oceti Sakowin and Indigenous histories from multiple vantage points as told through oral histories, histories of place, and the histories of treaties. LaDonna Bravebull Allard, Craig Howe and Tyler Young, Edward Valandra, Roxanne Dunbar-Ortiz, and Jeffrey Ostler and Nick Estes explore, in various ways, the long arc of historical and cultural knowledge about the land and water that are the foundations for the #NoDAPL movement. To destroy the land is also to destroy the histories of the land, and thus limit the possibilities of a livable future. "Our people and our histories have a right to live," LaDonna Bravebull Allard reminds us in this volume. "We have a right to share that history with the next generation." This part considers the philosophy of Mni Wiconi (Water Is Life) as it relates to the profound responsibilities to the river, the land, and its people; it underscores how this relationship tells the history of a people but also how it narrates the possibility of a future when our collective memory is reconfigured.

Questions of "legality"—who has the right to build a pipeline and who has the right to protect water—were at the heart of the DAPL struggle. In the third part, "Legal and Sociopolitical Landscapes and State Violence," Michelle L. Cook, Andrew Curley, Layli Long Soldier, Elizabeth Ellis, and Alleen Brown, Will Parish, and Alice Speri examine the multiple levels of jurisdiction and the broad array of tactics to halt pipeline construction. These range from high-risk direct action, to divestment from the financial institutions backing DAPL and other fossil-fuel projects, to mobilizing Indigenous sovereignty in defense of the land, the water, and the people. A number of the writers also explore how the police, military, and private security are integral to the settler state's management of the Indian Problem and how state violence against Indigenous bodies works in tandem with state and capitalist exploitation of Indigenous lands.

Further mapping how #NoDAPL is interlinked with strategic pushback against metastatic capitalist accumulation that is intertwined with the exploitation of land and the people inhabiting those lands, the fourth thematic focus, "Environmental Colonization," takes us to discussions of colonialism and finance, as well as to dialogues about how resistance efforts like #NoDAPL must be framed as struggles against colonialism. In an interview with Freda Huson, Anne Spice charts the history of the Unist'ot'en resistance to pipeline construction and settler-state violence, as well as the encampment's role in promoting Indigenous resurgence through land-based cultural practice and intergenerational healing. Shiri Pasternak, Katie Mazer, and D. T. Cochrane highlight the enduring continental character and political and economic implications of the #NoDAPL movement in terms of capital reorganization and questions of Indigenous jurisdiction. Jaskiran Dhillon circles back to the ways that Standing Rock defies purely localized analysis and highlights key points for consideration within the context of organizing for environmental justice. This part brings the notion of "multiple front lines" into sharp relief by showcasing the widespread social, political, and economic practices of environmental colonization and the colonial racism that fuels the violence of infrastructure projects.

Educational spaces, both formal and informal, as well as community-based teaching and learning centers are central players in popular, political education and public awareness campaigns for any social movement. The #NoDAPL movement was no different in this regard. The fifth part of the collection, "Education and Critical Pedagogies," with essays by Sandy Grande, Natalie Avalos, Jason Mancini, Christopher Newell, and endawnis Spears, by Tomoki Mari Birkett and Teresa Montoya, by Marcella Gilbert, by Sarah Sunshine Manning, and by the New York City Stands with Standing Rock Collective, takes up a robust exploration of the multiple forms of political and popular education that surfaced during #NoDAPL. It provides insight about the myriad forms of cultural production (music and artistry) that fueled the movement and communicated important political messages (often counter to mainstream media) to a broad public as well as youth leaders. As Sarah Sunshine Manning importantly explains in her essay, "compared to the standard classrooms of contemporary American education, the camps at Standing Rock produced an environment substantially and holistically more supportive for Native youth." Questions of accountability, as they pertain to academic fields of study (research agendas, advocacy strategies, and education-based interventions) and institutions of higher education, are discussed by the New York City Stands with Standing Rock Collective in its discussion of the creation of the Standing Rock Syllabus Project.

Finally, the edited collection closes with a distinct focus on Indigenous organizing and solidarity building. Indeed, one of the most powerful aspects of the #NoDAPL movement was its ability to garner support from organizations and collectives engaged in related, but distinct, social movements. Part VI, "Indigenous Organizing and Solidarity in Movement Building," foregrounds the importance of intersectional struggles in the fight against DAPL. Michelle Latimer, Kevin Bruyneel, David Uahikeaikalei'ohu Maile, Amin Husain and Nitasha Dhillon, Joel Waters, and Katie Mazer, Martin Danyluk, Elise Hunchuck, and Deborah Cowen speak to the ways that #NoDAPL aligns with the Movement for Black Lives, struggles against the occupation of Palestine, Kanaka Maoli struggles to protect Mauna Kea from the Thirty Meter Telescope, and, perhaps more obviously, a growing movement for environmental justice that is being fostered and carried forward by an explicit centering of questions of colonialism and occupation. The writing in Part VI also does the hard work of opening the door to a much-needed conversation about the ways those fighting for justice and freedom, against the endemic violence of the settler state past, present, and future, must join forces while being attentive to the specificities of distinctive struggles. These are battles that require us to stand together, to find ways to build coalitions across variant political histories and contemporary life experience, and to remain unified against the colonial structures and forces that ultimately threaten the future of everything.

In conclusion, the scope of this book is neither conclusive nor definitive. But it should be read as a roadmap of a longer movement within a moment of uprising. Instead of just informing our understanding of that recent past, it should also provide lessons, visions, and dreams of a deeper history that precedes and exists in spite of violent white supremacist empires like the United States. These histories and coming Indigenous futures are not settled or defeated but always on the horizon, always emerging. This book is simply the wind that stokes the embers of past and forthcoming Indigenous resistance, allied struggles, and a decolonial future for all things that make life possible.

NOTES

1. See Angelo Baca, "Bears Ears Is Here to Stay," *New York Times*, December 8, 2017, https://www.nytimes.com.

2. See "Trump Expands Offshore Drilling in 'Assault' on Biodiversity and Coastal and Indigenous Communities," *Democracy Now!*, January 11, 2018, https://www.democracynow.org.

3. See Robert Rapier, "The Irony of President Obama's Oil Legacy," *Forbes*, January 15, 2016.

4. Linda Tuhiwai-Smith, *Decolonizing Methodologies: Research and Indigenous Peoples* (New York: Zed Books, 1999), 20.

5. Macarena Gómez-Barris, *Extractive Zone: Social Ecologies and Decolonial Perspectives* (Durham, N.C.: Duke University Press, 2017), 11.

I.

LEADING THE RESISTANCE

"Two-Spirit Camp Grand Entry." Photograph by Nick Estes.

1

BADASS INDIGENOUS WOMEN CARETAKE RELATIONS
#STANDINGROCK, #IDLENOMORE, #BLACKLIVESMATTER

Kim TallBear

*This is an expanded and revised version of an essay that was originally published
December 22, 2016, on the* Cultural Anthropology *website as part of the Hot Spots series.*

Women of the Oceti Sakowin, or the Seven Council Fires, are at the center of the
movement at Standing Rock. Our peoples are also known as Dakota, Lakota, and
Nakota. With allies from around the world, the Oceti Sakowin work to protect
the water and land from the Dakota Access Pipeline (DAPL). Rerouted from an
original path near North Dakota's capital city of Bismarck, DAPL cuts through
Oceti Sakowin treaty lands at the edge of the Standing Rock Sioux Reservation,
and beneath Mni Sose, the Missouri River. The Oceti Sakowin Camp, a "unified
encampment of Water Protectors," has a mission to not only protect "land and
water against the Dakota Access Pipeline," but to assure "the welfare of all people
by honoring human rights, treaties, agreements, and cultures" and "to peacefully
and prayerfully defend our rights, and rise up as one to sustain Mother Earth and
her inhabitants."[1]

Standing Rock Shares Ground with Idle No More, Berta Cáceres

The Standing Rock movement continues the momentum of Indigenous and other
women-led social and environmental movements. Idle No More (INM), for example, was founded in 2012 in Saskatoon, Canada, by four women—three Indigenous (Jessica Gordon, Sylvia McAdam, Nina Wilson) and one non-Indigenous
ally (Sheelah McLean).[2] INM connected Bill C-45, introduced by the Conservative Harper government, which attacked environmental protections, to violations
of Indigenous land and treaty rights in Canada. In January 2013, INM articulated
a vision for their movement focused on "Indigenous ways of knowing rooted
in Indigenous sovereignty to protect water, air, land and all creation for future

generations."[3] It organized peaceful round dances in public spaces and blockades of rail lines and highways to bring attention to fossil-fuel and other industry injustices and infringements on Indigenous land rights. Indigenous peoples' recognition that our lives and treaty rights are also dependent upon the well-being of our other-than-human relatives, water, and land sparked both INM and Standing Rock into being. The view is that Indigenous movements do this not only for Indigenous peoples, but for everyone. The work of renowned Lenca environmental activist Berta Cáceres of Honduras also comes to mind. Her activism combined defense of Indigenous rights with defense of the environment. Tragically, she was assassinated in her home on March 3, 2016, after repeated threats on her life.

LaDonna Bravebull Allard, Standing Rock Sioux Tribe's historic preservation officer and founder of the movement's Sacred Stone Camp (one of several #NoDAPL camps at Standing Rock), speaks explicitly to settler colonialism and Indigenous genocide. Indigenous people have been killed outright, but another tactic to eliminate us is to sever our relations with the land and our other-than-human relatives. Bravebull Allard writes about police violence committed against nonviolent, prayerful Standing Rock Water Protectors while the all-White, heavily armed Bundy militia was acquitted of charges after its armed takeover in early 2016 of federal land. But this is not strictly an issue of racially disparate treatment of human beings. Bravebull Allard ties the fate of Indigenous peoples to the fate of the land and to nonhumans: "The land they claimed to take back was cleared of our relatives and the buffalo nation so that white ranchers like the Bundys could graze their cattle there."[4] In earlier centuries, and still today, the U.S. colonial state and its White supremacist citizens, be they armed ranchers or oil industry executives and their private security henchmen, work to eliminate Indigenous peoples from these lands and they work to eliminate our relations with these lands and waters in order to ensure White occupation and profit. The tied oppressions and fates of Indigenous peoples and our other-than-human relations is a key ethic undergirding both Standing Rock's and Idle No More's actions.

Faith Spotted Eagle, Ihanktonwan Dakota elder and a founder of the Brave Heart Society, which links environmental assaults to sexual violence against Indigenous women, also explains the entangled lives of Indigenous people and the land upon which our peoplehoods depend:

> I think it's the rebirth of a Nation, and I think that all of these young people dreamed that one day they would live in a camp like this because they heard the old people tell the stories of living along the river. They heard them talking about the campfires and the Horse Nation. And they're actually living it. . . . Resistance is demonstrated by the fact that we're alive. Because when you look at the genocide that has happened to our people we shouldn't even be here. . . . No matter what they do to us, no matter what that pipeline does, at some point in the future these prayers are going to take power and that pipeline is going to be destroyed.[5]

The English words "Nation" or "People" are translations for the word "Oyate" in our Indigenous language. I hear Spotted Eagle referring to the rebirth not of a better U.S. nation-state, but to the resurgence of nations—both human and other-than-human—living in good relation. Her English name "Faith" reminds me that it is not Barack Obama's U.S. exceptionalist "hope" or "progress" for redeeming a nation-state built on a foundation of White supremacy that spurs us to action. Rather, it is faith in these Indigenous women-led movements that provide alternative visions for being better relatives with each other and with the planet. I also know younger women who are doing physically, intellectually, and emotionally difficult organizing work at Standing Rock. I won't name them. I don't have published comments to draw from. I have instead private emails, Skype and Facebook message conversations. But like our elders whom I have cited, they too lead and teach our peoples and others everyday with their strength and vision for living in better relation as Oceti Sakowin, as humans. The work of these women preceded and will go beyond the important historical moment that is these camps. I have faith in the vision of these women.

Two Spirit leadership has also been key to both Standing Rock and Idle No More. Alex Wilson—Idle No More activist, University of Saskatchewan professor, and Two Spirit scholar—explains that Two Spirit people "can encourage political and personal transformation." Wilson and Melody McKiver—a Two Spirit videographer with Idle No More—agree that "Although two-spirit people have different roles depending on the particular Indigenous community they belong to, a general understanding is that they encourage open-mindedness. . . . They are necessary for a community to be balanced."[6] A Two Spirit camp was established at Standing Rock, and Indigenous people there have organized under the banner of the Two Spirit Nation.[7] Oglala Lakota tribal member and trans and queer health care specialist Candi Brings Plenty has been a visible Two Spirit advocate in the Standing Rock movement. The Indigenous rights and environmental justice work of Berta Cáceres also linked LGBTQ oppression to the oppression of Indigenous peoples by the same powerful interests who also assault the planet.[8]

Black Lives Matter

I must also recognize Black Lives Matter that was founded by three Black women: Alicia Garza, Patrisse Cullors, and Opal Tometi. #BlackLivesMatter emerged as a hashtag and movement in 2013 after the acquittal of George Zimmerman, killer of seventeen-year-old Trayvon Martin in Florida. Black Lives Matter also responded to multiple heartbreaking incidents of police brutality against Black people nationwide. In November 2015, Yvonne S. Marquez published an article on Autostraddle.com: "Badass Black Queer Women Paved the Way for the Mizzou Movement." Marquez explained that students demonstrating against structural racism on the University of Missouri campus, including Black male athletes who brought the university to its knees by refusing to play ball, were "inspired by the Black Lives Matter movement. . . . And just like the Black Lives Matter movement, the #ConcernedStudent1950 group was led and organized by queer black women."[9] Black Lives Matter activists have also worked on behalf of other vulnerable communities, for criminal justice reform broadly, for the rights of trans and gender nonconforming people, for domestic workers, for immigrant justice, and for human rights. I see their social justice organizing as powerful acts of (queer) women-led governance.

As a Dakota feminist, and observer and supporter of Black Lives Matter, I also see Black women who lead the movement as sharing ground with Indigenous women from Standing Rock and Idle No More. I see all of these women caretaking their peoples and kin, and I watch closely the conceptual, emotional, and organizing work their movements for change take. I will clarify two points: (1) I use "kin" in ways that contradict patriarchal White settler ideas of it. I do not refer only to close biological or even human relatives alone. Standing Rock and Idle No More link the protection of Indigenous peoples and Indigenous treaty rights to the protection of the earth and our other-than-human relatives. Black Lives Matter activists also seem to caretake and make what I as a Dakota would call kin as they defend bodies marginalized in a brutal anti-Black, antitrans, anti-immigrant, antiworker, etc., world. (2) When I speak of these women-led movements as a form of caretaking, I do not view this as the domain alone of cisgendered, biologically reproductive women. Nor do I view women period as being the only members of our communities who caretake. Men clearly play important caretaking roles. Standing Rock Sioux Tribe Chairman Dave Archambault II is strategically working the federal-tribal government-to-government legal channels to resist DAPL's intrusion into Oceti Sakowin territory. We see young men on horseback and on foot at the frontlines of the #NoDAPL movement. Men, like women, are cultural knowledge holders and teachers. In all of these movements, men as well as gender nonconforming people and brave youth (they deserve a special shout-out) caretake our peoples, make and caretake relations, and add to our collective strength. But the women-led condition of these movements is striking.[10]

Not Indigenous Rights versus "the Environment"

Despite the clarity of the vision at Standing Rock, their core analytical framework and ethical approach to #NoDAPL is missed by some observers. As I hope I have made clear, this is not a movement in which there are two separate issues that just happen to align around the Oceti Sakowin resistance to the Dakota Access Pipeline. I have seen commentators in the press and on social media—Indigenous and non-Indigenous alike—describe #NoDAPL as bringing together two separate struggles: Indigenous rights, Indigenous sovereignty, and human rights on the one hand; and climate change or defense of "the environment" on the other. Such observers understandably worry about the hijacking of the Indigenous rights struct by opportunistic environmental activists who are not sufficiently invested in our survival as Indigenous peoples. But I also suspect that hierarchical Western binaries that assert human needs as a priority—as somehow not always already intimately entangled with the fate of other-than-human communities—also taints some Indigenous thinking. The culture/nature or human/animal divide misses the point of the Oceti Sakowin and their allies at Standing Rock identifying themselves as "Water Protectors." It is a fundamental misunderstanding of the core ethical framework that guides the Oceti Sakowin resistance to DAPL. The human beings gathered there stand with their other-than-human relations—with the water, the land, and the many other nonhuman nations who reside within Oceti Sakowin historic lands—a place with which the Oceti Sakowin is coconstituted. LaDonna Bravebull Allard makes beautifully plain this human-place coconstitution:

> Erasing our footprint from the world erases us as a people. These sites must be protected, or our world will end; it is that simple. If we allow an oil company to dig through and destroy our histories, our ancestors, our hearts and souls as a people, is that not genocide?[11]

NOTES

1. Oceti Sakowin Camp, http://www.ocetisakowincamp.org/about (site discontinued).
2. Idle No More, http://www.idlenomore.ca; "Idle No More", Wikipedia, https://en.wikipedia.org/wiki/Idle_No_More.
3. Idle No More, http://www.idlenomore.ca/about-us/press-releases/item/83-press-release-january-10–2013-for-immediate-release (page discontinued).
4. LaDonna Bravebull Allard, "Why Do We Punish Dakota Pipeline Protestors but Exonerate the Bundys?" November 2, 2016, *The Guardian*, https://www.theguardian.com/.
5. "Protester: 'It will be a battle'" (interview with Faith Spotted Eagle), CNN, November 1, 2016, http://www.cnn.com.
6. Alex Wilson and Melody McKiver in Laura Zahody, "Idle No More Organizers Reach Out to Queer Community," in *The Winter We Danced: Voices from the Past, the Future, and the Idle No More Movement*, ed. the Kino-nda-niimi Collective (Winnipeg: ARP Books, 2014), 289, 288.
7. Samuel White Swan-Perkins, "Two Spirit Nation to Hold Grand Entry at Standing Rock," *Huffington Post*, October 14, 2016.
8. David Kaimowitz, "The Work of Indigenous Rights Activist Berta Cáceres Does Not End with Her Death," Ford Foundation, March 3, 2016, https://www.fordfoundation.org.
9. See Yvonne S. Marquez, "Badass Black Queer Women Paved the Way for the Mizzou Movement," Autostraddle, November 10, 2015, http://www.autostraddle.com.

10. Alexandria Wilson, "Afterword. A Steadily Beating Heart: Persistence, Resistance and Resurgence," in *More Will Sing Their Way to Freedom: Indigenous Resistance and Resurgence*, ed. Elaine Coburn (Winnipeg: Fernwood Press, 2015).

11. See Allard, "Why Do We Punish Dakota Pipeline Protestors but Exonerate the Bundys?"

2

IN THE BEGINNING

Mark K. Tilsen

We sleep to peyote songs and raucous laughter
Young men stretching their first war whoops
and mocking rooster crows answer from the tipis
We wake to geese calls,
before sunrise the loud yapping of packs of coyotes
that always remind of a small horde of freshmen jostling one another in the
hallways
The Bros of the animal world
If we win
These sounds will greet our great grandchildren
and one day
I'll be there on the hill with white hair
on the microphone hologram
Talking about these mad days when the
Hunkpapa called
and We answered.
I might even embellish how brave I was
Or important
If we fail
only silence
I ask all my grandmothers and grandfathers
living and dead
Be with us now
Bear witness
Help us find the will
to do what needs to be done
I am not going to die here

I don't want to be arrested
And I am too big to run
But I am not a fighter, not really
I don't see what lies ahead
There is so much that could've been done
We ought to have reached out to our Black brothers and sisters to stand with us
Sent out our most respectable to every
Mayor's office, city council meeting
PTA, School board, and town hall
on the Missouri, every town and farming community that drinks this water or
the pipeline crosses
And
Doesn't really matter now.
We are here
They are coming
All I ask of myself is to live these next few days well
The Camp is waking up
Hoka.

"Water Protector." Photograph by Nick Estes.

3

"THIS FIGHT HAS BECOME MY LIFE, AND IT'S NOT OVER"
AN INTERVIEW WITH ZAYSHA GRINNELL

Jaskiran Dhillon

A version of this interview was first published on December 22, 2016, on the Cultural Anthropology *website as part of the* Hot Spots *series.*

JASKIRAN DHILLON: I'm here with Zaysha Grinnell, a fifteen-year-old Indigenous young woman (and a sophomore in high school) who is an enrolled member of the Mandan, Hidatsa, and Arikara Nations located in northwestern North Dakota. Zaysha lives on the Fort Berthold Reservation and is one of many courageous Indigenous youth who have been leaders in the struggle against the Dakota Access Pipeline (DAPL). Zaysha, can you explain what prompted you to become involved with the resistance against DAPL?

ZAYSHA GRINNELL: In the recent years my reservation, Fort Berthold, has become known as part of the "oil boom." As a young person I noticed the differences all around me due to this extraction project—in the environment, the lands, the people. I saw the lands that I had grown up on getting destroyed little by little, drill by drill. The people I grew up to love and care for were being sexually abused and sexually harassed on a daily basis. When these oil companies come in they bring in the men. These men bring with them the man camps and with that comes violence and sex trafficking. Indigenous women and girls near the camps are really affected by this, and we are not going to put up with it. Making more girls into leaders, because we witness it firsthand, is so important. As a young Indigenous woman, I can feel the suffering of my people. I always remember this feeling; even speaking to you about it right now I remember it—the hurt in my heart seeing this happening to my people. I vowed to myself that I would never let myself feel this way again.

When I heard about the Dakota Access Pipeline and how they wanted to run it through our Missouri River, the very water we depend on for so many things,

I knew it was time to stand up to protect it. When this pipeline breaks, it would not only affect us, as people, but the animals and aquatic life would be impacted too. Basically everything that my people value and care for is at great risk of being harmed.

JD: How did you decide to take action or "stand up" as you say?

ZG: In May 2016 I created a youth group called the Modern Day Warriors in opposition to the Dakota Access Pipeline. The Modern Day Warriors vowed to not only protect our lands from this pipeline, but to protect our Mother Earth, Ihcca Awahe. Since the beginning of this struggle, this group has stood with Standing Rock and the Sacred Stones Camp. And we created a petition to stop the pipeline, which now has over eight thousand signatures. We also helped out in the rallies and spoke to members of my tribe to get them to support Standing Rock. There are other youth besides me doing this too. We have the Oceti Sakowin youth runners and runners from Rezpect Our Water who have run thousands of miles to raise awareness about the pipeline, and there are more and more youth groups being created all over to fight against DAPL. The Standing Rock International Youth Council helps a lot within the camp, and they work closely with the elders too. We know how to get information out there, and we are spreading it through social media. The elders pass on their wisdom to us so we are able to do these things, and we will keep going until our lands are permanently protected against the destruction. The more youth that come and join us the more power we have, and we are reclaiming the resistance that comes from our ancestors.

JD: Your last comment leads directly to my next question: How is your leadership as an Indigenous young woman guided by the history of resistance led by Indigenous Nations across Turtle Island?

ZG: Our ancestors protected and honored this earth, and every day I try to walk in their footsteps the best I can. And I'm going to continue to do that. Everyone at Standing Rock is going to continue to do that. Our ancestors are known for their strength and resilience because of the things they went through for us to be here today, and that same thing is within us because we carry it in our DNA. When we are on the front lines, that's when that strength and resilience is pumping through our veins the most. This fight isn't just about one pipeline. It's about protecting Mother Earth, Ihcca Awahe. It's about caring for our land and water. This is the time of the seventh generation, a time when the young take a stand for the future. We are leading everyone in a good way and showing people how to live a better life.

JD: If you could leave the readers of this interview with one final message, what would it be?

ZG: This is a historical time, not just because of how much of an impact we're making at Standing Rock but because everything we are fighting for is about the future of our generations to come. I want my children to know what it's like to drink clean water and breathe clean air. There have to be other alternatives for the resources we need; we can't afford to continue destroying the earth just to put money in our pockets. When Mother Earth comes crashing down will the money matter? It won't, because we'll be busy just trying to survive. There is no alternative to water. There is no alternative to this Earth. This fight has become my life, and it's not over. I think this is only the beginning for me, for all of us. Do you want a future for your children and grandchildren? If you want them to have a future then stand with Standing Rock because this is just the beginning of a revolution.

4

TRADITIONAL LEADERSHIP AND THE OCETI SAKOWIN
AN INTERVIEW WITH LEWIS GRASSROPE

Nick Estes

This interview was conducted on January 14, 2018.

NICK ESTES: I'm here with Lewis Grassrope, from Kul Wicasa Oyate, the Lower Brule Sioux Tribe. Lewis, can you introduce yourself?

LEWIS GRASSROPE: My name is Lewis Grassrope. That's my English name, but my Lakota name is Wicahpi Ksapa. I come from the Kul Wicasa Ospaye, but I also come from the Peji Wakan Tiospaye.

NE: Lewis, one thing that a lot of people know about the camps is that they were named after our nation, Oceti Sakowin. Can you give a little background on where the name Oceti Sakowin comes from and its significance?

LG: That's a big question itself. There's some discussion about it. But either way Oceti Sakowin and Peta Ga Sakowin all mean the same thing in the end. One means stoves and the other means fires. But it's all basically the same. The true meaning is the actual Seven Council Fires. The Tintonwan, the Lakotas, are also made of Seven Council Fires, which is where the Kul Wicasa or the Sicangus come from. There are many nations, many tribes that are just a little clannish or smaller but they're all part of the original council fires. There's the Mdewakantonwan, Sissintonwan, Wahpekute, and Wahpetonwan who are the Dakota people. Then there are the Ihanktonwan and Ihanktonwanna. That's seven.

Those are the ones that consist of the original traditional governments that we all have in our nation. This makes one great big nation. That's how we come together and that's why we are considered the Oceti Sakowin. . . .

NE: At the camps in the Standing Rock, the name of the larger camp was Oceti Sakowin, but they also had the camp horn to show the reunification. Can you explain that significance of uniting or reuniting the nations?

LG: For a brief history, the last time that the Oceti Sakowin was ever together was before and during the encroachment of white people or Europeans onto our lands. We united to resist this initial encroachment. Then it was reunited during Standing Rock. The intention was to unite our tribes, to unite the clans and all the different types of nations, different dialects, to come together. But we were actually brought together to resist the same thing—encroachment again! *[laughs]*

NE: *[laughs]* How were each of the leaders from each of the nations or the different bands selected traditionally and how are they selected today?

LG: We're still trying to figure that out. Usually every tribe has their own Naca, and there's many Itancans underneath him. There's not just one chief, there are many. But there's usually one that will stand out, and that will probably be your elder, one of your elders that have been through a lot in their life and has earned every feather that they wear. He would be the representative. That's the way that they were chosen. But they were never seen as the *actual* leader of their nations or their respective Tiospayes or Ospayes. They were just representatives. They were picked or chosen for negotiations and everything that comes with that. It was about being a negotiator, about being a politician, but then they're also not considered politicians as we understand politicians today. They were considered to be very ikce men, very common men. They were known for their values and how they earned their feathers. They would come together to speak on behalf of their tribes, but they would never make a decision without consulting with the rest of the tribe first.

How they were chosen is a good question because we are still trying to figure that out. When it came to Standing Rock, they picked, they chose who was there at camp. We were just there for the camp. We were there for the people. We were asked to represent our tribes or chosen to represent an unci, a grandma. That's how we were chosen for kind of the same reason as before. It had even more to do with who had a camp, which camps were represented, and bringing them together to come together to stand against DAPL.

NE: The Oceti Sakowin has multiple levels beginning at the Tiospaye level, going up to the Ospaye level, and then finally the Oyate. Tiospaye means family or extended family. Ospaye means something like the larger band of families. Then Oyate means the people or the larger nation. But even Oyate is kind of difficult because it means many things. You could say Oyate to mean a smaller nation, or you could say Oyate to mean a larger nation. . . .

LG: That's like I said, it's the majority of what we talk about. We can't go back to Tiospayes because the way that we are in this time and age. You can't go to Oyate because you're falling underneath the same thing that the modern tribal reservation governments are actually based on. So you have Kul Wicasa, Rosebud, Oglala, etc. They're all underneath Oyate. But we would have to fall back into Ospaye because Ospaye means that we're all kind of part of each tribe. In all reality, when we talk about actual relatives we actually mean it. We're all related! *[laughs]*

NE: Yeah. *[laughs]* No one is *the* nation, *the* Oyate. We're all the Oyate.

LG: We're part of those tribes, those Ospayes, but we're all one nation. We're not separate nations. We're all part of the—and I don't even like using the word Sioux— the Great Sioux Nation. But the larger nation is Sioux itself. We're a part of the Sioux Nation. There's no difference between Lakota, Dakota, and Nakota. Those are just the dialects that were spoken at the time. So we all come from one big tribe, one big Oyate. *[laughs]*

NE: One big nation.

LG: Yeah.

NE: The difficulty that you're talking about is that people identify based on reservation, and they don't identify based on Tiospaye, or family, or even, to some degree, Ospaye because in a place like Standing Rock, for example, you have Dakota and Lakota people. There, you have Hunkpapa as well as Ihanktonwan. So what you're saying is that there has been a move to think of more broadly in terms of Oyate, one nation, versus thinking specifically about these kind of smaller, reservation-based political divisions. Is that something that's a result of this organizing? This idea of the Oceti Sakowin?

LG: Well it's not really the ideal, it's the way that it works. The reason why I would say I want to separate from Oyate because Oyate is tied in with the IRA governments.[1] We don't want to use that because that's what their government is already labeling us, as something separate. So when you talk about Ospaye because the fact is we all come from different places. That is what I mean by the Ospaye. Our families are all from different places, you know. Some of us may have Ihanktonwan blood. Some of us may have Ihanktonwanna blood. Some of us may have Hunkpapa blood. Some of us may have Oglala blood. Due to the way that the government has set us up into pedigree law, basically saying that we're all from different places but in all reality we're all bands, bands of the same nation, you know? So that's where it comes from there.

NE: Yeah, so there's a lot of, there's a lot of complexity and just saying Oceti Sakowin because it means so many different things. The idea of being Lakota, Dakota, or Nakota is very complicated is what you're saying. When you say that the Oceti Sakowin is reuniting then people have to figure out what does that actually mean and what does it actually look like.

LG: Yeah, that's where we're at because like I explained earlier is that it's been over a hundred something years since it's actually been done. And a lot of it has to go back to our oral history with the people that are actually keepers of those old stories and the keepers of our ways, especially our ceremonies. We had to go through a lot of searching and a lot of knowledge-finding to actually figure how we would put up the horn, or how you would form the actual encampment of Oceti Sakowin. We call it the horn because it's shaped like a buffalo horn.

NE: At the same time, there's also a broader political consciousness around that we, for lack of a better word, Sioux people, hold much more in common. This brings up another question. You talked about the Indian Reorganization Act governments. Prior to their formation there were the treaty councils, which kind of came out of this older political organization, or traditional organization of the Oceti Sakowin. The treaty councils were based on people who had signed the 1868 Fort Laramie Treaty. Can you talk about the significance of the treaty councils?

LG: The Indian Reorganization Act was actually given to us, actually imposed on us as a mockery. It's just a mockery type of government of the corporation of what the United States actually is. It was imposed onto our tribes, but they would not recognize our traditional government. The reason being, in layman's terms, is that it's like during a war or in a military action. They want to know who the leader is. In our traditional governments we really have no leader. We had *leaders* but we didn't have them out in the front, as we see now. Today's politicians want to be out in the limelight. We had people that didn't have anything like that. It was kind of like a republic. It came from the people, the decisions. But those are the things that the U.S. government disliked. The reason being is because some people, some of our greatest leaders in our history, did not agree with some people, went off on their own, and went on the warpath. That was the basis of why they didn't accept any of our governments because we were allowed to leave if we didn't agree with something.

Then it led to the actual 1868 Fort Laramie Treaty in which we asked respectful Nacas of the time to act in accordance for their people to come to terms of peace with the United States and to stop the war that the United States imposed on us. It was done in that way, and it was basically a peace treaty. After that happened there came the 1889 [Indian Appropriation] Act or the Sioux Agreement . . . and then it became these councils, these old men that were a part of the '68 treaty and then their families carried it on. It was kind of like a hereditary thing. But they carried on the way of sitting on these councils to keep trying to hold the United States accountable to that treaty that was made. There's a long history of it, but treaty councils came way after. I think it was in the 1920s and during the time of the Indian Reorganization Act.

Treaty councils came from respectful people from our tribes. They were chosen to represent the tribes, to go out and report back, and to go see what's going on in Indian Country and within our lands so that we could take it back to our people. . . . I could sit here talking for hours. *[laughs]* But what it all comes down to is the treaty councils are basically kind of forms of old traditional government. They were a part of the IRA at one time when they first started. When they found out that they were blockaded because they basically said you have to go to your IRA government rather than the traditional government, they stepped away from the IRA because they didn't want to remain in that type of government. They wanted to be their own traditional government, which is what a lot of people are fighting to get back today. But like I said it's a long history. Treaty councils are there on the grassroots level. They are there to keep the traditions alive and there to be a reminder of some of the things, such as we aren't tied down by any government or bound by any government to act in their accordance versus an IRA government where they're actually confined to it, they have to abide by what their U.S. government says.

NE: The IRA government system is set up so that the federal government has the final say, whereas in the traditional governance system the everyday people had the final say. That brings up a question about gender and leadership. Men weren't historically the *only* leaders of the Oceti Sakowin. Yet, when Europeans first arrived who came from male-dominated societies, of course they wouldn't talk to Native women when they saw women as inferior. That's why they created treaty systems where only Native men were consulted. What was the role of women in traditional leadership?

LG: That question is being pondered right now. What a majority of us are trying to do is bring back a traditional government where women always had a say. They never didn't have a say. After the treaty was signed, a lot of the men during that time were warriors, and leaders stepped back from being out in the front. Some of them took the ceremonies and all this knowledge to the underground, so that it wouldn't disappear into history. When we look into that now, women played an important role. If you look at history and the pictures that are out there, even from Sahiyela, our Cheyenne relatives, you see that there were women that *did* wear headdresses. There were women that actually had societies, women societies that were warrior societies. And there were a lot more societies out there where women played an important role. In our traditional governments, it wasn't a patriarchy or it wasn't a matriarchy or a matriarchal society, it was actually complementary and an egalitarian society where we worked hand in hand with each other, collaboratively and collectively so that way women had the say so, too.

The reason you bring up this question is because, yeah, today what we're hearing is women can't be in these meetings, because these are men's meetings. And that's kind of a tradition, but it's also a way of saying that, letting people know because people think that when men go into the meeting they make a decision that's it, it's done, it's over. But in reality, in most, in the final, that traditional government they never did. They would sit in there and listen and take everything in. I mean, these meetings would take probably three, four days, maybe even weeks. They would go back to their Tiospaye then and talk and listen to their women and their men that were there. If the women said no, that was no. If men took it into a meeting and were trying to make decisions on their own and a woman came in and threw a rock into the middle of that meeting, that ended the meeting. This goes back to actually creating traditional governance. The old teachings of it are that women have to have had their part. There was a women's society actually involved in the traditional government. Women played a big role just as much as the men. . . .

NE: So it wasn't just men making decisions behind closed doors but it was actually a very democratic, open process. If somebody didn't agree with someone else or a decision that was being made they could say so. It sounds like what you're saying is that women also had the ultimate veto power. They could throw a rock into a meeting and just end it right there. But also if people didn't like a decision or the direction that a certain camp was going, they could just leave. The reservation system created conditions where if people disagree with each other there is nowhere to go. It's created a different dynamic around how all of these sorts of political and social relations work out.

Wiconi Un Tipi at Lower Brule wasn't a camp that started because of the #NoDAPL protest, but it began with the Keystone XL Pipeline protest. Can you talk about that particular history?

LG: That's a good history in itself. *[laughs]* For Wiconi Un Tipi, we had no knowledge or prior knowledge of things that were going on within our IRA tribal governments, so some of us went to a treaty meeting to go find out what was going on. That process informed us that our tribe was in a working relationship with TransCanada, the owner of Keystone XL Pipeline. From there we had to go face the music with our other relatives in Sicangu land and throughout Oceti Sakowin where we were told that we were sellouts, since everyone else opposed the pipeline. But in the end they knew that we didn't know so they helped us to start a camp. It was right after Rosebud had their camp up. After their camp was made we started ours and went forward to fight against our Indian Reorganization Act council because they were still in cahoots with TransCanada.

We gained a lot of camaraderie and rebuilding old kinships within the tribe, and a lot of it had to do with just coming together in unity. From that point on we went forward the best we could. We made it through the first round of Keystone XL Pipeline and ended up beating it. After that was done we all kind of sat back, relaxed, thinking we were done doing our work. But Standing Rock happened. Then we were asked to go up there. Some of us felt it in our heart because we had fought against a big pipeline that we should go up there. But we also felt the spiritual calling of what Standing Rock was about, so we went. We went up there and stayed the duration, as long as we could until the end. Then we came back here to Lower Brule, taking the majority of our camp that we had in Standing Rock. We've been going ever since then and now we're standing back in opposition to Keystone XL.

NE: Right, because Trump fast-tracked the Dakota Access Pipeline the second week he was in office and then fast-tracked Keystone XL. Right now, Keystone XL is in limbo about whether or not it's financially doable.

LG: That's the big question right now. That's where it's at. Our camp was put up to keep the movement going forward from Oceti Sakowin, from everything that happened at Standing Rock, and still go forward to try to reestablish that old traditional governance, to go forward in the best way we can for our nation's survival. We're also here to oppose what Trump may have coming down the pipe for all nations, not just Lakota, Dakota, Nakota, for all tribal nations. I know there are things that we're looking at in this camp, trying to figure out how can we go forward the best way we can. As you can see in the news headlines, we aren't the only ones. There's a lot of them trying to do the same.

NE: Right. It's important to point out too that it's not just Trump because the majority of the #NoDAPL movement happened under the Obama administration. Trump accelerated that process of oil and gas development, but a lot of that happened under Obama's administration as well. It's not so much a question about who's in charge. It's a question of how the ikce wicasa, the humble people, the common people, take matters into their own hands. That's what moved me and a lot of others from Kul Wicasa about Wiconi Un Tipi. It was in 2013 that we had the community town hall meeting about Keystone XL about what we were going to do. As far as I know, those kind of town hall meetings hadn't happened for decades, you know?

LG: A lot of those meetings are still going on. I just came back from one recently.

NE: Right.

LG: And it's still carrying on so . . . I mean you're right on that.

NE: This fire has been lit and it's still continuing to burn. This gets into the broader vision of not just Oceti Sakowin and not just Lakota, Dakota, and Nakota people. This movement wasn't *just* about us and our lands, even though it *very* much was. But it was about other people. No one was really turned away from camp. And people ask, what would happen if we actually upheld the treaties? People think that we would do the same to them as they did to us which means kick them off their land and genocide them, but that didn't happen. You had a bunch of people show up because they knew those treaties were important. Can you kind of talk about that larger vision?

LG: Well, that kind of thing happened in Standing Rock. A lot of people came together. It was like our people had been sleeping for so long and living the way that we have, and then we woke up! We didn't step away from our way of life, but we are finding the way back to it. Like you said, it's just not our people, it's every-one. And it's awakening people to see that they have a power within themselves rather than in a politician or anybody else that has a higher say. Because they're the ones that are being affected, and I think that's what the movement was really about, the little Joe Shmoes or the little people. For us to uphold our treaty, declare our sovereignty, and hold the U.S. government accountable for honoring our trea-ties and staying true to them, we had to open the eyes of a lot of our other sister nations around. Sister, brother nations from all over Turtle Island were willing to have stand up in the same way because they knew that if anybody is going to help save this world or bring back some type of restorative balance it's going to be the Native people and it's going to be helping the very people who are the cause of traumatic history. But we still hold that value of being a good relative or practic-ing kinship and showing people a different way to get out of capitalist thinking.

The bigger picture is about trying to restore things without the way everybody always thinking that we have to rely on our government to supply for us or we have to do this. The movement is bringing back the way of being self-sustainable, self-sufficient. This is due to the prior administrations and the many administra-tions that have wanted to get out of the treaty business. A lot of us Native people are coming out of that silence, have been voicing their concerns more, and getting people to actually see that if we don't change, Mother Nature will. It comes down to man-made law versus spiritual law, which we know spiritual law or natural law will win. But the whole movement was based off of Mother Earth. For us, it has always been about that direction and the spirits that have come to us and showed us there's a direction that we must follow. The funny thing about—not really the funny thing but the touchy thing about it, what happened in Standing Rock, it's bringing every ethnicity, different walks and ways of life together because they were called there for the same reason too. Now the majority of the people are wanting to go back to being who they really are and working with each other as any religion basically tells us in their books or their scribes or however they see it. But it all comes down to the same thing, a sense of freedom.

NE: We do have the mechanisms within our belief systems but also within our traditions and our long history of resistance that aren't just for Indigenous peoples. There are aspects of that that are incredibly pertinent and relevant to this particular day and age. What you were talking about when you were saying, Mitakuye Oyasin, or we are all related, we really believe in a really profound way that what you do to the land, or what you do to your nonhuman relatives such as the plants, the animals, and the birds, you also do to yourself, because those are your relations. People take that and think it's some kind of like mystical thing, but we're seeing it now. We've been saying it for so long and people now are coming around to it. Maybe can you talk a little bit more about Mitakuye Oyasin?

LG: When I talk about that, it's like the word itself is self-explanatory. It says we're all related. But even for our own people you have to open their eyes to see that's not what the word actually means. When we say we're all related, it's like us standing in a big group and saying "oh, we're all related!" But they don't get it. What it means is actual restoration of connections to all life. To understand that, we need to work, even us as humans, we play our role in this, into this natural balance of beings, along with plants, birds, trees, every life that's out there. When you see an old grandma and grandpa sometimes—I've seen it a couple of times—where you would see them pull off alongside the road and take off their shoes and stand out in the wide open prairie just with their bare feet. That's them just restoring that connection that they want to feel that because for us, especially living in tipis, and that's what our people used to live in, tipis, we would be able to see and feel because sometimes those connections would help us know what's coming.

For us Lakota people, we were a migrant people. We migrated with the buffalo and followed the herd. We followed everything that we can. But also everywhere we went we prayed to creation, to the Creation, to Tunkasila, to forgive us for wherever we may set down a camp, because we have to pray and ask for that. So that we have that asking permission to stay there and take things that are around there, take a life, or anything we needed to live in our daily lives. So the word Mitakuye Oyasin hits the heart, for me anyways, because that means we truly are connected to everything. But people just don't see it that way.

We're actually seeing through Standing Rock that we *are* all related. I've sat down with people from Iraq, Iran, and Egypt. I've met some from the Philippines. Their stories are all pretty interesting when you hear about it because we think that we're not really truly related to all people from different continents. But why would people from Africa bring over a necklace that has a piece of our pipestone in it and say that they needed to come here because of this gathering? Then you have people that have dreams that were from Egypt, saying that they had a dream that they were told they needed to come. And they showed up. A lot of these people are still out here fighting, still trying to do the awakening.

The whole world is always the same. It is like we are all truly related to all beings. It's part of the Great Mystery I guess. *[laughs]* That's the basis of where everything is at. We're starting to find out more as mortal people, as mortal men, mortal women, that we tend to think that we can control everything. Let's say we didn't go pray where we were going to build a road, and we put up a road. People say, "ahh, that's an awesome road." The next thing you know here comes natural law to destroy that road. Maybe that's because we didn't actually ask for permission to set that road there. Maybe there was something there, you know? There are a lot of things that we can't interrupt and a lot of things we shouldn't do but as I said us as mortal men, we think we can control everything. Then natural law comes and shows us it supersedes us. People tend to think, "that's just the weather." But that's actual Mother Nature or the spirits of those other realms that are actually telling us that we shouldn't have done that.

I think of Standing Rock, when I just sat there and said, there's Iranian people there. There were Iraqi people there; there were Egyptian people there. You had many people from different European countries that came to Standing Rock. Different walks of life. Filipinos. You have every walk of life there. And they were told to come there. Why were they told to come there? Here we are in this day and age thinking that we have to talk on cell phones all the time. We really think we need to get the message out to each other, but when we call each other up, we're already on the same page. For us, it's like going into a sweat lodge. That open line of communication isn't a cell phone. It's actually our spirits intertwining with everything. That's what it means when we say Mitakuye Oyasin. Our message does go out. The message goes out everywhere, to everyone, and they're thinking the same thing. It's crazy because everybody's like "oh I didn't think of it so." Who says we need a cell phone to call Creator to sit there and say "What do we do now"? But in all reality he's already showing us. He's been showing us for quite a while, but it took an awakening like Standing Rock and a lot of other major things that are going on within, around the world to wake people up, to see that we have forgotten the true meaning of practicing of being good relatives, of being and practicing kinship.

In today's society we build a house, put a white picket fence around it, and that's the American dream, right? But once you go past that white picket fence, nothing matters. But once you come back in that white picket fence, to anybody inside that white picket fence you say, "Get out of here! What are you doing here?" We're so quick to kill each other. We're not even being good relatives and not really trying to take care of nature, your surroundings, or anything. We're just sitting there saying, "I'm gonna take this. I'm gonna take that." And we're not giving back. That's also about what you were saying about our relations, calling them our nonhuman relations. I'm talking about all of our spirit and animal spirit, and I mean all these animal relatives and all these tree relatives, all of them are all saying the same thing. And Unci Maka herself has showed herself and said the same thing that it's time to start giving back and start doing the best we can to try to save her along with saving our own humanity and be practicing the actual kinship that we're supposed to be following.

NE: I was thinking about that metaphor you used of the white picket fence and the case of Standing Rock. North Dakota built its house on our land and built a white picket fence around it. When we said, "Hey, don't do that!" they called the cops on us. *[laughs]*

This notion of relationality, I was thinking of Standing Rock and the context we found ourselves in. The one you're talking about is about connections, relationships, reciprocity, and giving back not just to our human relations but also our nonhuman relations. If you went outside of that, just one hundred yards to the front line, you had one of the largest militarized police presences in the Dakotas in one and a half centuries since the Indian wars and four decades since Wounded Knee II. This kind of living and thinking, of being in relation to the land and water, represents a threat. Can you talk about the police presence at the camps? In the aftermath, states like South Dakota and North Dakota have been preparing for another possible uprising by passing antiprotesting laws and by scaring people in the media. In your experience returning to Lower Brule, how have relations changed with non-Natives?

LG: Being in this camp we're in now, we have different people here who are from our Ska Oyate, from our white nation people. *[both laugh]* They're here residing with us, too. Living in Standing Rock everyday seeing the massive military buildup and massive police presence that was called in for people praying to stop a pipeline, but there was no actual militarized action from people who were there wanting to pray in front of them and to stop them from building. That became something feared for society in itself. Christianity is used as fear-based religion to say that you can't do this because you're going to go to hell. What happened in Standing Rock was that you had many ways and walks of life and different ways of praying that came together. That showed them that no matter what people said or what people did, or whoever is in control or whoever thinks they're in control of any situation, they weren't and something else was in control. They found that through that strong prayer that was there—that's what really scared the heck out of everyone, especially knowing there were people there who had no guns and were willing to stand up against the military to stop a pipeline.

It's a funny thing when you think about it. It comes down to history repeating itself. For me, that military and those people were afraid of a nation that actually went to war with the United States and never lost. We lost a lot of people, but we never lost. They came to us and asked us to sign a treaty of peace with them. So we did. That's what happened at Standing Rock. We had all these people gathering up again fighting the fights our ancestors had fought before in the past. That's what they were truly scared of, they didn't want another big Indian uprising. But we're not all Indian this time! *[both laugh]* The basis of that alone—the spirituality, the faith, the belief that people had—in the end wasn't about anything else but each other. That comes back to what we were talking about with Mitakuye Oyasin. After a while, it didn't matter what race or what color you were. You were there to protect each other. That scared the shit out of people standing on the other side! Because even they questioned their faith. They questioned their belief. And some of them quit. Some of them didn't even want to be there because they didn't want to take life. That was their biggest fear. How can they take people's lives that are praying for the people?

From the time our ancestors were at Greasy Grass, you know how that fight turned out. That's what the U.S. government was afraid of happening again. This time it was on a larger scale because not only did we unite the tribes, we also united every nation within Turtle Island and our relatives from South America. A lot of them were here just to stand, not to take up arms but stand. That scared them and it scares a lot of people because we're not even considered people in our homelands. We as Lakota people are part of the Sioux Nation. But we're trying to establish something for all brown people, for all Indian nations. They call us Indian but, you know, we're not Indian. We're fighting for our survival and our identity. People can say we have an identity. But we were placed under the Department of War before the treaty was signed and then we were switched over to the Department of Interior, the department that manages cattle! So where does that put us? *[laughs]* That's our fight. Even though other ethnicities came to the United States, they got more recognition than we ever did for living here on this continent before they even arrived. We're still not recognized in that way. We're still looked down upon. With everything that happened in Standing Rock, however, there was a lot of healing. We thank Wes Clark Jr. for coming and doing what he did.[2] That was a big step for our veterans. A lot of men were affected by military service. It really comes down to we were here first and people who stood for our way of life. That's what happened in Standing Rock. We wanted to keep our way of life going and we're willing to give our lives for that.

That brings us back to the whole basis of traditional governance and bringing back old societies that still exist today, but they're not out in the front. No one really knows that. I'm talking about Tokala societies. I'm talking about Akicita societies. I'm talking about Red Hand societies. There are all kinds of societies out there that played their specific role within a camp. Those are the things—from my perspective, living in a camp right now—that the U.S. government doesn't want us to go back to being what they considered uncivilized, pagan, and savage Indians. That's what scares them the most. It's not about what's more powerful. It's that our people believed in all creation. They believed in nothing else. They didn't even believe in themselves because they put their lives on the line for their own people and even for our buffalo's sake—and for *everything* to protect it. At Standing Rock, we were there to protect not only the people possibly affected if that pipeline breaks along the river, but we were there to protect all of our animal nations, all of our wildlife, all of our plant life, all of the ecosystems that exist.

I was in a recent argument where I was told that the oil doesn't affect the land as much as people think. I was like, "Well, it doesn't matter what you think. I'm not worried about that. I'm a hunter. I survive. That's what warriors do. They provide for their families. What am I going to hunt if there's nothing there? What am I going to protect if I can't even teach my kids about all the traditional medicines that we use to help heal ourselves? What are we going to do when those don't exist?" The European societies that came here don't want to hear that. But it's crazy how they have taken a lot of our traditional governance as their own. Look at the U.S. Constitution. It's based off us uncivilized tribes, you know? *[laughs]*

They've taken a lot from us and learned a lot from us, but we're the ones that suffer the most. What happened at Standing Rock showed the people that it's not just Natives that suffer. It's all races and minorities. You had people quitting their jobs out of nowhere just to be at Standing Rock. That should have been an eye-opener to the rest of the world that this means something to everybody. This is everyone's fight.

NOTES

1. The IRA, or Indian Reorganization Act, was first introduced in 1935 during the so-called Indian New Deal. Tribes had the option of drafting constitutions modeled after the U.S. Constitution. The process and legacy of creating IRA governments has drawn criticism from grassroots and traditional leadership because it adopts a Western model of adversarial politics and undermines historic kinship relations.
2. Wes Clark Jr. led a group of veterans to stand with Water Protectors and to apologize to Indigenous nations for the crimes that the U.S. military perpetrated against Indigenous peoples.

5

TAKING A STAND AT STANDING ROCK

David Archambault II

The New York Times *originally published this essay on August 24, 2016, days before the arrest of Chairman Archambault and the release of attack dogs on Water Protectors by private security guards at a construction site over Labor Day weekend.*

It is a spectacular sight: thousands of Indians camped on the banks of the Cannonball River, on the edge of the Standing Rock Sioux Reservation in North Dakota. Our elders of the Seven Council Fires, as the Oceti Sakowin, or Great Sioux Nation, is known, sit in deliberation and prayer, awaiting a federal court decision on whether construction of a $3.7 billion oil pipeline from the Bakken region to southern Illinois will be halted.

The Sioux tribes have come together to oppose this project, which was approved by the state of North Dakota and the U.S. Army Corps of Engineers. The nearly 1,200-mile pipeline, owned by a Texas oil company named Energy Transfer Partners, would snake across our treaty lands and through our ancestral burial grounds. Just a half mile from our reservation boundary, the proposed route crosses the Missouri River, which provides drinking water for millions of Americans and irrigation water for thousands of acres of farming and ranching lands.

Our tribe has opposed the Dakota Access Pipeline since we first learned about it in 2014. Although federal law requires the Corps of Engineers to consult with the tribe about its sovereign interests, permits for the project were approved and construction began without meaningful consultation. The Environmental Protection Agency, the Department of the Interior, and the National Advisory Council on Historic Preservation supported more protection of the tribe's cultural heritage, but the Corps of Engineers and Energy Transfer Partners turned a blind eye to our rights. The first draft of the company's assessment of the planned route through our treaty and ancestral lands did not even mention our tribe.

The Dakota Access Pipeline was fast-tracked from day 1 using the Nationwide

"Welcome to Standing Rock." Photograph by Nick Estes.

Permit No. 12 process, which grants exemption from environmental reviews required by the Clean Water Act and the National Environmental Policy Act by treating the pipeline as a series of small construction sites. And unlike the better-known Keystone XL project, which was finally canceled by the Obama administration last year, the Dakota Access project does not cross an international border—the condition that mandated the more rigorous federal assessment of the Keystone pipeline's economic justification and environmental impacts.

The Dakota Access route is only a few miles shorter than what was proposed for the Keystone project, yet the government's environmental assessment addressed only the portion of the pipeline route that traverses federal land. Domestic projects of this magnitude should clearly be evaluated in their totality—but without closer scrutiny, the proposal breezed through the four state processes.

Perhaps only in North Dakota, where oil tycoons wine and dine elected officials, and where the governor, Jack Dalrymple, serves as an adviser to the Trump campaign, would state and county governments act as the armed enforcement for corporate interests. In recent weeks, the state has militarized my reservation, with road blocks and license-plate checks, low-flying aircraft and racial profiling of Indians. The local sheriff and the pipeline company have both called our protest "unlawful," and Gov. Dalrymple has declared a state of emergency.

It's a familiar story in Indian Country. This is the third time that the Sioux Nation's lands and resources have been taken without regard for tribal interests. The Sioux peoples signed treaties in 1851 and 1868. The government broke them before the ink was dry.

When the Army Corps of Engineers dammed the Missouri River in 1958, it took our riverfront forests, fruit orchards, and most fertile farmland to create Lake Oahe. Now the corps is taking our clean water and sacred places by approving this river crossing. Whether it's gold from the Black Hills or hydropower from the Missouri or oil pipelines that threaten our ancestral inheritance, the tribes have always paid the price for America's prosperity.

Protecting water and our sacred places has always been at the center of our cause. The Indian encampment on the Cannonball grows daily, with nearly ninety tribes now represented. Many of us have been here before, facing the destruction of homelands and waters, as time and time again tribes were ignored when we opposed projects like the Dakota Access Pipeline.

Our hand continues to be open to cooperation, and our cause is just. This fight is not just for the interests of the Standing Rock Sioux tribe, but also for those of our neighbors on the Missouri River: The ranchers and farmers and small towns who depend on the river have shown overwhelming support for our protest.

As American citizens, we all have a responsibility to speak for a vision of the future that is safe and productive for our grandchildren. We are a peaceful people, and our tribal council is committed to nonviolence; it is our constitutional right to express our views and take this stand at the Cannonball camp. Yet the lieutenant governor of North Dakota, Drew Wrigley, has threatened to use his power to end this historic, peaceful gathering.

We are also a resilient people who have survived unspeakable hardships in the past, so we know what is at stake now. As our songs and prayers echo across the prairie, we need the public to see that in standing up for our rights, we do so on behalf of the millions of Americans who will be affected by this pipeline.

As one of our greatest leaders, Chief Sitting Bull of the Hunkpapa Lakota, once said: "Let us put our minds together and see what life we can make for our children." That appeal is as relevant today as it was more than a century ago.

II.

LIVING HISTORIES

"Flag Avenue." Photograph by Nick Estes.

6

"THEY TOOK OUR FOOTPRINT OUT OF THE GROUND"
AN INTERVIEW WITH LaDONNA BRAVEBULL ALLARD

Nick Estes

This interview was conducted on January 10, 2018.

NICK ESTES: I'm here today with LaDonna Bravebull Allard, who helped found Sacred Stone Camp in April 2016. Can you introduce yourself?

LADONNA BRAVEBULL ALLARD: My name is LaDonna Bravebull Allard. My real name is Tamakawastewin, or "Her Good Earth Woman." I'm an enrolled member of the Standing Rock Sioux Tribe. I come from the Ihanktonwan Pabaksa, Sissintonwan Dakota. On my father's side, I'm Hunkpapa, Sihasapa, and Oglala Lakota, and I'm Dakota on my mother's side.

NE: What I find inspiring about your work, LaDonna, is that you started as a historian and continue to be a historian. I knew your work through the Tribal Historic Preservation Office (THPO). Of course, that work evolved into community activism. Can you talk about how your experience at THPO informed Standing Rock's struggle against the Dakota Access Pipeline (DAPL)?

LBA: My life has been in history. I have a degree in history and historical research, and I spent about twenty-five years compiling the history of the Standing Rock Sioux Tribe and the Oceti Sakowin. In the 1990s we created the Tribal Historic Preservation Office for the Standing Rock Sioux Tribe, and I've been working with historic preservation since then. I was working as a Section 106 Coordinator of the National Environmental Policy Act for the Tribal Historic Preservation Office when the DAPL proposal came before us.

At that time, and I have to tell you the truth, I never considered myself an activist. I've always considered myself a historian and researcher. But when I realized that DAPL was outside my back door, where my family lived, and where we grew

LaDonna Bravebull Allard. Photograph by Michelle Latimer.

up, it seemed too close to me. The fact that I know every historical site, sacred site, burial site, village site, traditional cultural properties, and ceremonial sites in that area, I couldn't believe they were going to put an oil pipeline through it! The whole idea of what the land *is* has been put on the sidelines through this whole process from 2014 until the present. Nobody is talking about the Arikara village site DAPL went through, the Arikara burials, the destruction of the effigies that were laid out in rock on the hill. . . . There is so much stuff out there, and it breaks my heart that they destroyed our cultural patrimony. As I tell people, *they took our footprint out of the ground*. And who has the right to do that?

Our people and our histories have a right to live. We have a right to share that history with the next generation. Our history is amazing. Our history enhances the American history. For me, it hurts my heart that they destroyed these histories. If you don't stand up and protect what your ancestors put in the ground, what are you doing on this earth? Our grandfather Tatanka Ohitika had sun dances down on the Cannonball River with Wise Spirit. At that time, they put medicine in the ground. Everybody who came to the camps could feel that medicine. They put that medicine in the ground to pray for our water and to pray for our earth. Who has the right to take that away?

So for me, it becomes personal and spiritual. It's also about preservation, protection, and, first and foremost, the water, which is our first medicine. If we don't stand up and protect those things, we are ending the future for coming generations.

NE: There is the prophecy of Zuzeca Sapa, or the Black Snake, that became prevalent around the struggle to stop the Keystone XL Pipeline. But it's an old prophecy. Can you talk about what it means?

LBA: When we were kids, our grandmothers used to talk about this Black Snake that would be coming to destroy the earth. I remember them all sitting and talking at the table, and, you know, the kids weren't supposed be listening but we always were. *[laughs]* They were talking about whether this Black Snake in the prophecy was the interstates, because they were building all these interstates back then. The interstates were covered with black tar. "Well, maybe this was the Black Snake?" I remember them saying, "But how could that be? The interstates are covering the Indian trails and the Indian roads. How would that destroy the world?"

I remember that as a child. As you get older you don't think about things like this anymore. Then we started seeing the oil. When they have an oil spill, it destroys the water. It kills the animals. It kills all the microorganisms and the insects. It kills the grass, the plants, and everything that grows. When we saw the pipelines being built that pushed this black fluid through, then we understood: this is what is coming to kill the world. The prophecy says that when the Black Snake comes, we will stand up and stop it. We have no other choice but to stop the Black Snake to save the world. People may think that is a farfetched idea. But it is a reality because we must stop destroying what gives us life.

NE: When Sacred Stone was founded, it was named after the spherical shaped stones that were once carved at the confluence of the Missouri and Cannonball Rivers. Sacred Stone, or Inyan Wakanaganapi Oti, is the name for the area. Can you talk about the significance of this name and its history?

LBA: As a child—it hasn't been that long and most people think I'm old, but I'm not that old—the Missouri River would hit the mouth of Cannonball River causing a whirlpool action. I remember seeing the whirlpool as a child. It created these round sandstones all along the river. You could walk along the shore and see the round sandstones. They were everywhere. Some were huge. Some were small. If you live along the Missouri River, you know that Missouri has a really strong undertow. That undertow caused the sand to stir up. The Indian people called it the Place that Makes the Sacred Stones, or Inyan Wakanaganapi Oti, and the Cannonball River was called the River of the Sacred Stone. As I was going through and reading some old documents of Ella Deloria, I found the reference to the original name of my home. When they were talking about what to name this camp, I said, "Well, just call it its real name: the Place that Makes Sacred Stones." That's the way it's supposed to be.

Cannon Ball, North Dakota, where I'm from, was named after Lewis and Clark. When they came down the river and when they saw the round sandstones, the only things they could equate it to were cannonballs. Indian people didn't know what cannonballs were. So Lewis and Clark wrote in their documents, "the Cannonball River." When the community of Cannon Ball was first started, it was just called Inhanktonwan. Then it became the community of Cannon Ball after Lewis and Clark. I don't know how many people know Cannon Ball's named after Lewis and Clark. When Lewis and Clark came through, it was just as the large village—there was a Mandan village there of about two thousand people—had just suffered from a great smallpox epidemic. When you look at the confluence of the Cannonball River where the Sacred Stones are made, it was a place of passage, which means that the river was narrow. It was an easy crossing for many people. At one of the banks you had a Mandan village. On the other point you had an Arikara village. And then you had a Yanktonai village, or Inhanktonwan. If you go through the history, there were also Cheyenne and Pawnee. It was a multitribal area. I would always think when the camps had started, "How did the people know to camp here? Did they know this was a village site? Did they know this was a trade area? Did something happen that was beyond us start happening there? Was it our grandfathers who put the medicine in the ground?"

I want people to understand that this was not something a long, long, long time ago. It's not ancient. My grandfather, Tatanka Ohitika, was recorded by Frances Densmore in 1910. He died soon after that. But we can hear his voice and recordings. My grandmother was born in 1908 and grew up along the Cannonball. So it's not generations and generations ago. I grew up on the Cannonball where we got the water straight from the river and hauled it up every day. It's not ancient history we're talking about. It's our history of *now*.

We know who we are. We know our history. We know our stories. We know our way of life. We know these sites. When you know something and the outside world comes in and tries to destroy it, you have no choice but to stand up. That's how I feel. I never felt I was an activist, but I felt I was put in a position where I had no choice. They pushed me against a wall, and I couldn't go anywhere. I had to put one foot in front of the other, move forward, and say, "No!" It was not something that was planned or designed. It was something that happened.

NE: These questions of history are really important. As you pointed out in September 2016, the day DAPL private security unleashed attack dogs on unarmed Water Protectors was the exact same anniversary of the 1863 Whitestone Hill Massacre. You reminded us that it was a massacre largely forgotten to even the U.S. military. In the aftermath of the Dakota Uprising in 1862 and the Dakota expulsion from Minnesota Territory, the "Columns of Vengeance," as they were called, hunted down and killed your ancestors and my ancestors as punishment. The Whitestone Hill Massacre was payback and punishment for Dakota resistance. How do you see those convergences of history, the entanglement of past and present whether it's the U.S. military in the nineteenth century or DAPL, Morton County, and the

LBA: Unresolved to this day! I can tell you my story, which is my grandmother's story, which is my great-grandmother's story. That is what I know.

Nape Hota Winyan, Grey Hand Woman, was in Minnesota. They came and arrested her father. She and her mother took off across country—running. They were unsure of where to go. As you know, her father was one of the thirty-eight men hanged in Mankato. They came all the way to James River Valley for asylum. They came into the camp of Big Head, and he welcomed them. There were many refugees that came from Minnesota into the Inhanktonwan camp.

For a whole year, the people in this camp got ready. The spiritual leaders gathered everyone saying, "We have to prepare for a hard winter. We've got to hunt." They called all the tribes to come and hunt. Our grandfather Tatanka Ohitika was there because he could call the buffalo. The people went out and hunted, and they brought in a lot of buffalo. It was a great fair where all the tribes came together. Everybody was trading and gathering. They had ceremonies, dances, songs, and even gambling. They had fun. It was getting to the point when everyone was starting to break the large camp to start moving back to their homes for winter. It was because of this event that all the men were gone from camp. The women that were still there were getting hides ready and drying meat.

My grandmother, who was nine years old, talked about this. The reason why we know is because she was one of the few people interviewed about the Whitestone Massacre. She said, "That day the men all rode out to meet some soldiers, they said, were coming, and they never came back." She was sitting there playing. At just about dusk, all of a sudden people started screaming, and people started running. She got up and she started running. People were in the middle of chaos. People were running in all directions. She fell. Something hot hit her, and she fell down. She didn't realize at that time she was shot. They shot her in the hip. She laid there in the field just as the sun was going down. It was dark. All she could hear was people screaming.

We are talking just about her, but in the meantime all the tribal people, Big Head, his people, and Tatanka Ohitika, went out. They took a white flour sack and put it on a stick because they were told that the white people had a truce if they put up a white flag. They took this flour sack and went out and met the soldiers. As they got there, the soldiers surrounded them, took them hostage, and wouldn't let them go back to the camp. Two battalions stood on each side of this ravine. The women and children ran down the hill through the ravine. As soon as they got into the ravine, the soldiers started shooting at them. There was no escape because nobody had weapons. There was no firing back. This was out and out, pure massacre. Finally a warrior was able to break through the end to try to get women and children out of that ravine. There was a man named Little Ghost who was a child. His mother tied him to a horse, roped him on that horse, and hit that horse to make it leave. He was able to get away. The mother and daughter ran. The family was separated, and I don't think they found each other until a few years after. The young boy ended up in Spirit Lake. The mother and daughter ended up in asylum in Sisseton. The mothers put their babies on the little travois of dogs and sent the dogs out to take their babies to safety. People were making their children run. Everything was chaotic. People were screaming and hollering everywhere.

My grandmother said she laid on that field calling, "Ina! Ina!" ("Mother! Mother!"). All she could hear was screaming and gunfire. All through the night the soldiers went and killed the wounded, tracking them down, men, women, children, and babies. Then the order came out from the soldiers, "Kill every dog." The soldiers went around and killed every dog. Did I mention the dogs were carrying the babies? They killed every dog. I was listening to the military reports, and they said they shot two thousand dogs that day.

As the morning sun rose, there was death everywhere. You could see what had happened. There was, what you could call, "friendly fire." In all the chaos, the soldiers shot each other. So there were some casualties from friendly fire. I don't know why, because they randomly killed the wounded, they picked my grandmother up and threw her in the back of a buckboard. They didn't kill her like the rest of her family and everybody else. Then they marched the men who they had taken hostage and any other remnants they could find. In the meantime, the soldiers were given the order to burn everything. They took their time. They poked holes in every cooking pot. They destroyed everything so nothing could be of use again. They piled it in huge piles, all the buffalo meat, the robes, the homes, everything, and set it on fire. As the fire burned, the tallow ran like rivers down the prairie.

This was the first time that the slash-and-burn tactic was used. You would see slash-and-burn used in Indian Country from this point on at Sand Creek and many other massacres. This was the first time where they burned everything. They killed all the dogs. They threw the babies and everything into the fire and burned it. Then the soldiers were given the order to track any wounded down and kill them. In the meantime, they marched this whole group of prisoners from the James River to the Missouri River. Many were sick or wounded. When they got to the river, they loaded them on a boat. They took them down to what became known as the Crow Creek Reservation; at that time, it was a prisoner of war camp. The people were released on the banks of the river with no food, no shelter, nothing. There were many deaths, many deaths. The other group ran and continued to fight as the soldiers came after them. At Apple Creek, they were able to win a battle. You don't hear about Apple Creek much because we won. They were able to hold the soldiers back to allow the women and children to get across the river.

Everybody in Cannon Ball are descendants of these people. I did a survivors list. We had to put together families again. Grandma took in two grandchildren.

Auntie took two nephews and nieces. They formed families again. Those are the people of Cannon Ball, each and every one of them.

On that day, September 3, if Nape Hota Winyan would have died, none of us would be here. But she survived the prisoner of war camps. When she was released, she came back to Cannon Ball where she married. My grandfather on my other side, Tatanka Ohitika, married in Crow Creek. From the documents, we know that he left his wife and child when they released him. He came back to Cannon Ball and married my grandmother, Holy Generation Woman. Because these people survived, we're here. So September 3 is a time of memory for us.

On that morning in 2016, I was telling people about the history of Whitestone, about what had happened to the people of Cannon Ball. And they called me. J. R. American Horse said, "LaDonna, the bulldozers are here." I was like, "What?" "The bulldozers are here." I said, "Stop them!" I was doing an interview with Amy Goodman from *Democracy Now!* I said, "Amy, I have got to go." She said, "I'm following you." I got in my truck and got up there. Just as I got up there, I watched this guy jump out of this white truck and pepper spray a whole line of women and children. At that time, the young men came and were trying to get in front of the women and children. They pushed the fence down to try to prevent them from being pepper sprayed. Then they sicced the dogs on us. I remember I was standing there in the field. It was like I froze. There was a big black and white dog with blood dripping from its mouth and a big grey-headed pit bull on the other side. I was standing there thinking, "Where am I? How could this be happening on this day? How could they attack on this day?" It's like you go through post-traumatic stress, historic grief, all of this stuff. I was just like, "Where am I? Is this what America is?" Then I went to the road. There was a policeman standing there. I said, "Stop them!" And he said, "Ma'am, I'm only supposed to watch the road."

In that moment, everything changed. *Everything* changed for me. It was no longer just saying, "No, we didn't want something" or "Let's follow the law." It was, "Man, we got to stand up! They're going to kill us all!" It's terrible to think like that. It was shocking to me. I don't think I slept for days after that. It's still shocking to me.

Every incident that happened, with the police and the military actions, happened on an event of something that already happened in Indian Country. It was like we were repeating everything all over again. It was like our ancestors were standing with us saying, "You stand, and we stand with you. It's okay." It was really hard some days to watch people get hurt. But I saw amazing bravery. I saw who we were and who we still *are*.

NE: Many of the stories you are sharing are similar to the stories I heard about my great-great-grandmother, Melissa DuFonde. She was orphaned during the 1862 uprising and sent to Crow Creek. Since she was young at the time, we don't know much about her Dakota Tiospaye or about our connections to our relatives out east. Yet, like you said, we didn't cease to be people; we didn't just end there at genocide. Our families and our nations reconstituted themselves. That's a courageous act, too, to become a nation again in times of genocide and war. Neither of which have entirely ended.

The most compelling thing for me about the camps was all the young people, who were the leaders and the sparks for the larger movement that spread. It was a youth-led movement from the beginning. Certain names of those young people who were there in the beginning come to mind: Bobbi Jean Three Legs, Jasilyn Charger, Tokata Iron Eyes, Joseph White Eyes, Zaysha Grinnell, and there were many others. How did this all start? What is the background to this story?

LBA: This was a process. The tribe first started talking about what to do about DAPL in 2015. They started working with the youth. The first project they did was going to the schools and asked the children from first grade on up to talk about what the water and the river meant. All of these kids wrote letters. When we read through the letters, they were so touching: "My grandma said we did this at the river and we did this at the river." We decided to do some interviews and make short videos to put the stories out there—water is life. The kids did interviews. They talked about what they thought, and they were little kids. I think the youngest was three years old. Amazing! So the kids spoke. As this started going around the rez, the chairman at that time went to each one of the districts and was telling the districts, "This is coming! I want you to know this is going to happen."

Down in Wakpala, there was a group that got together. It was Bobbi Three Legs, Waniya Locke, and Honorata Defender. These three young women got together and said, "Well, what can we do? Let's have a run." They did a short run from Wakpala to Mobridge for the water. They did a run into the Army Corps meeting at Grand River. Then they did a run to Sacred Stone. These were young people who actually knew what they were doing. They put their feet and their prayers on the ground. They were standing up. It was just amazing. These young people are the beginning of the movement.

We were at the Long Soldier District, and Joye Braun, Jasilyn Charger, Joseph White Eyes, and Wiyaka Eagleman were there. They came to talk about the fight against the Keystone XL Pipeline. I remember Joye saying, "Is there anywhere to start a camp?" At the end of the meeting, I said, "Joye, I have some land. You can look at it." She agreed to come down the next day and look at it. In the meantime in Bear Soldier District, they were having meetings and organizing.

There were a lot of things happening. There were a lot of people talking about change. Today, I listen to people ask, "Who was the leader and who started it?" It was these young people. It was them who put their feet on the ground to stand up.

When they first came down and saw the grounds, Joye said, "This would be good." We asked, "When?" "April 1, we'll start the camp." That was the day we were giving testimony to the Army Corps saying, "We object." I don't even know how everything came to be other than that's the way it was. At the meeting, Oceti Sakowin came, all of the Indian nations. They had the riders come in with horses. They had the youth running in. They had the mothers and children walking in. They had the Indian motorcycle groups ride in. People from all the Dakota, Nakota, Lakota reservations drove in. I was shocked. I was amazed so many people came to help, to give testimony. From there, they rode the horses and ran down to Sacred Stone.

I remember pulling in and watching them as they were putting up the tipis. There was still snow on the ground. Everything happened as it just happened. Allen Flying By came and said, "I brought my pipe. I'm going to pray." Faith Spotted Eagle said, "I came to pray." Elizabeth Lone Eagle said, "My daughter came with water to pray for the water." Everything just happened.

We opened the camp with ceremony, with prayer, with water, with song, and with all the horse riders. Then the tipis went up. The first one to stay that night was Joye Braun. There wasn't even any wood. There was no planning and no money. So Joye spent a very cold night that first night. The next night we were able to get wood. Jasilyn Charger, Joseph White Eyes, and Wiyaka Eagleman all got together. People started bringing out food for them. By the end of the week, we moved the camp down below the hill out of the wind. The community of Cannon Ball and Standing Rock started bringing in food and to help. We had Honor the Earth come to help us. We were just living on the ground.

I remember I came down one day and walked into camp after work. There were all these people sitting around the fire. They were roasting deer meat on the grill. The women were cutting meat on the side to dry it. Kids were running and screaming. All of these people sitting around the fire were telling stories and what it was like to live on the river. Here was the catch. Nobody was speaking English. They were all speaking Dakota. I looked at them and I thought, "This is how we're supposed to live. This makes sense to me." Every day I came down to the camp and saw such blessings. I saw our culture and our way of life come alive. Nobody can take that away from me.

This lady told me, she said, "I wanted to come to the camps, so I packed up everything. But by the time I arrived at the camps, it was dark. I pulled in not knowing anything. I pulled up my car and I got out. This young man ran up to me and said, 'Grandma, you need help setting up your tent?'" She said, "Oh my! Yes." So these young men came over, set up her tent, and got her all situated. She crawled in her tent. She said, "I laid there and I could hear people singing. I could hear people praying, laughing, and joking. Then I closed my eyes. When the morning came, I could hear people singing and praying. I got out of my tent and I didn't know exactly where I was. Then a young man ran up to me and said, 'Grandma, you want some coffee?' They handed me a cup of coffee. I walked and looked around everywhere and people yelled at me, 'Hey! Come eat at my kitchen!'" She said, "I went over to a kitchen and a young man brought me a chair. I sat down. They brought me food. And, I thought, 'I have never been treated so kind.'"

The essence of what this woman was telling me is the essence of who we are, our culture and our way of life. Respect your elders. Help each other. Be communal. I saw amazing blessings there.

In one given day, the most I had to deal with was seventeen. That was my highest number of prayer ceremonies. They would take me to the river and we'd pray. Water from all over the world came to be put in the Cannonball River. I was a part of so many tribal prayer ceremonies. That is never going to change. That is the greatest honor I have ever been able to witness. Even though I did not understand many of the other cultures, I was honored to be able to pray with so many people. Every day there were people coming in: "We came to pray." So we'd go down to the river.

This is my own thing: we went and got samples of the river. We put them in glass jars. When we got the water, the water was kind of murky and had stuff floating in it. Then, on April 1, 2017, we had an anniversary gathering to remember. I got little glass vials for everyone to take some water from the Cannonball River. We went down in a prayer ceremony and filled our little glass vials. This time the water was *clear* and *clean*. I still have it sitting in my room. I think, "Is this all the prayers that came to my river from all over the world? Is this all the waters that came to help heal the river?" I'm going to stand with that—that's what I believe.

This whole movement, I sat and watched as these young people sat around the fire and came up with ideas of what to do. I remember when they were sitting there joking, "Well, let's run to Omaha!" "We don't got no money!" This one young man said, "We got prayer. Let's just do it!" So they sat around and said, "Okay, we're going to go this day." They ran to Omaha, met with the Army Corps, and delivered some petitions. The next time they were there, they joked, "We might as well run to Washington, D.C." The next thing I knew, they chose to run to Washington, D.C. As they ran across the country, they spoke about what they were doing everywhere, whether it was a rest stop alongside the road, going through towns. It was because of them that so many people came. We met the youth runners. They said, "If you need help, we're here." The youth were amazing.

But that's not the big thing about them. What I had seen was these youth coming down to camp. Some of them had never been exposed to ceremony, song, culture, history. I watched them as they stood up and learned to sing the songs. They stood up and learned their cultural languages. I had seen a pride out of these youths. I had seen them stand up for what they believe in. I had seen amazing warriors, each and every one of them.

We can live a thousand years, and people are always going to remember what happened here because we're not done yet.

NE: In Kul Wicasa Camp, when I was there, one of the elders from the Yankton Reservation was telling us that they had zero youth suicides in their community at the beginning of the winter season when the DAPL protests were going on. It was a strange thing for that time of year. The only explanation she could give is that even if young people hadn't gone to the camps, they were inspired by them. What you're describing is one of those things that can't be counted or quantified— it's absolutely immeasurable. You can't take those things away. You can't take away that experience of empowerment.

People forget, when they see the reporting in the local media, whether in South Dakota or North Dakota, that Native people at this time in particular were criminalized. There were also accusations of disorder and chaos, that Native people don't know what they want. How can they worry about a pipeline when their own communities are in dire poverty? Yet, what I saw was free clinics, free legal aid, free kitchens, and different forms of schools and education. There were no police, but there was security. There were no prisons. Everyone that I passed said "Hi." This was much in the same experience the Unci had who went to your camp. You had health care, legal aid, education, community, food, no prisons, no prisons, a sense of security. Most poor communities in the United States and in North America don't have those things. So when people ask, "What do you want?" Yes, we want to stop this pipeline. But we also have a larger vision of the future of how we should be living. And that's a threat to the order of things, not just in the Deep North on the plains. It's a threat to the entire order of things that is based on the profit motive.

While there has been a lot of focus on the camps during the protests, there is still ongoing movement on the ground. It didn't just stop. Where are we going? What's Sacred Stone doing now in carrying on that vision?

LBA: One thing I always stress to people. First, *I'm still here*. I have not quit fighting. I still live here. When I look around my community before the camps happened, we were in pretty bad shape. When the camps left, we were in a little worse shape. One reason is because we had to deal with all the racism and prejudice that came out. It was out in the open in all our surrounding areas. I was used to it. We can deal with it. Another reason is because everybody thought that Standing Rock got all this money. They lost grants and funding. People were in devastation. Then the propaganda was sent out there that some had more than everybody else, the divide-and-conquer tactic. To me, this is still my community.

When the camps were ending, we loaded up semitrucks and went to every home and gave every home food. Then we went to the Cannon Ball community. We planted 350 trees. That's one of the biggest things I heard my grandma talk about, all the trees the Army Corps took when they flooded us. Then we fed the community. We cleaned the community twice. We asked, "Well, what can we do to help?" We organized a youth festival where we taught youth how to write their own narratives, fly drones, do poetry, do music, and do photography. Then we had the Mni Wiconi Healing Gathering because what I was seeing was so many people were hurt after what happened at the camps between being shot, maced, water cannoned, then injured and traumatized. We had a Mni Wiconi Healing Gathering for one week. I called Arvol Looking Horse and asked, "What do we do?" He suggested, "Just bring everybody and pray." So that's what we did. It was a really good gathering.

We understand that the reservations are so poor that we get stuck in this economic situation of fossil fuels. I do know that our future, our sovereign future, first comes with food. We planted huge gardens. We gave out produce to the people. That's nice, but how do we become green? Right now, we have MIT out of Boston coming. We went out to Boston and talked with them, saying, "You guys have the technology. We need help." So they're here to listen. We're going to do a demonstration on a trailer that we have built. It has solar, wind, a water purification system, and Internet. We can pull this trailer into anywhere and provide energy for a whole home. And it has to be inexpensive because people don't have a lot of money. I'm trying to figure out ways to do this so it doesn't cost a lot of money, so it doesn't cost millions. We're working on developing a solar grid and taking care of all the legal issues so that we can have a pilot project in Cannon Ball to reduce the energy bills by using solar. We're putting up greenhouses to produce our own food. The first step toward sovereignty is food, always, so we can feed our own people. I tell people that in order to be green does not mean we do it tomorrow. That means we set up a twenty-year plan of installing these projects and divesting from fossil fuels to make a better life for ourselves.

On a national and global level, we started the divestment campaign asking banks to divest from fossil fuels, asking nations to divest from fossil fuels. You heard today, New York City is divesting! We are now in the billions of dollars from people divesting from fossil fuels. China has now made a resolution that they will no longer allow gas-driven cars in their country in 2020. Downtown Paris is eliminating all cars. There's these things that are happening all over the world right now as we're looking at alternatives. How do we move into the future?

We've been going around talking to everybody. Invest in your communities. Invest in gardens. Invest in local businesses in your community rather than investing in these large fossil-fuel companies. One step at a time. Now the insurance companies and the insurers of fossil-fuel companies have now pulled their insurance. So there are a lot of things happening. I was with all these Native women and I said, "Holay! They must be scared of Indian women!"

People in Washington State are standing up, people in Mexico (I'm going down to Mexico soon), people in Nicaragua, El Salvador, Chile, Bolivia, Columbia, Palestine, India, the Samis, Norway, Sweden. Everybody is standing up.

People realize culture is really important. History, spirituality, and your way of life are important. How does that help? I am moving forward to develop a village

and a camp. The village will be a green village where people can live who will be
the educators. The camp will be for the children. We've decided eight years old is
a good age because then they can be away from their mom for a longer period of
time. For seven days, we'll teach history, culture, language, tradition, and living
off the land. Then we go to the nine-year-olds. Seven days. Then the ten-year-olds
and the eleven-year-olds. The way we got it worked out, we'll be with the teen-
agers in the month of August. We also need to teach people how we live off the
land, going into the communities and helping communities. I plan in the middle
of April, it depends on the weather, to do a big river cleanup from one end of the
reservation to the other. I think it's 120 miles of cleanup. Let's clean up our river.
I figure, if we're going to talk about it, we might as well do it.

So we are doing a lot of things. Now's the time for change. We can't talk about
it anymore. We just have to go out and do it. People ask me all the time, "What
should I do now?" I say, "Pick up a garbage bag and go pick up garbage. Clean
every creek, waterway, pond, lake, river, ocean, sea, everywhere." I believe that one
simple action can change the world. Clean up our communities. If it's just picking
up cans, picking up garbage, everything helps. We've got to take a vested interest
in our world. Everybody has to.

See why I'm a problem? *[both laugh]*

7

MNISOSE

Craig Howe and Tyler Young

Mnisose (muh-nee-show-shay, the Missouri River) is a living being. It flows from the confluence of two smaller rivers, the Jefferson and the Madison, whose headwaters are in the Rocky Mountains. Her sinuous body weaves through three states and creates a border between four more before sinking her mouth into the Mississippi River, not too far north of Cahokia. Throughout her life Mnisose nurtured the adjacent fertile bottomlands by intermittently inundating them with upriver nutrients, and she served as a transportation corridor for peoples and their nonhuman relatives. Her waters and riparian areas provided sustenance to countless living beings.

In the middle of the last century, the United States proposed a massive public works project to control the seemingly unpredictable fluctuations of Mnisose. Officially titled the "Missouri River Basin Development Program," the Pick-Sloan plan was approved by Congress as part of the Flood Control Act (1944) and called for the construction of over one hundred dams within the Mnisose basin, which would ostensibly provide flood control, help regulate crop irrigation in the region, and provide the infrastructure to produce hydroelectric power. Pick-Sloan had eerily similar elements to the Dakota Access Pipeline project: the Missouri River, an enormous construction project that would create hundreds of new jobs and supplement an energy source, the U.S. Army Corps of Engineers, the states of North and South Dakota, and Lakota tribes with lands along Mnisose.

As a result of the legislation, the Army Corps of Engineers was tasked with building and operating five "main-stem" dams along the Missouri River. The resulting reservoirs disproportionately inundated tribal lands, and the Bureau of Indian Affairs—which was supposed to act as the trustee and advocate for American Indians and Indian tribes in getting a fair price for the sale of their lands—apparently appraised tribal land at pennies to the dollar (Capossela 2015). Moreover, as the water levels stabilized it became apparent that the corps had acquired from the

"Backwater Bridge." Photograph by Vanessa Bowen.

tribes much more land than was necessary for the reservoirs. In response, the Standing Rock Sioux Tribe, along with the Three Affiliated Tribes, took the lead in calling for a return of their lands that were not inundated. In 1985 the Joint Tribal Advisory Committee was established by the secretary of the interior to address these claims, and a report (U.S. Congress Senate Select Committee on Indian Affairs 1987) was issued calling for monetary damages to be awarded and excess lands returned.

The Standing Rock Sioux Tribe has a successful legacy of fighting for water rights along Mnisose, and therefore it seems appropriate that this nation is at the vanguard of advocating for its rights, the rights of its citizens, and the rights of all peoples in and along Mnisose against the Dakota Access Pipeline. Its actions are grounded in the history of this land and flow from the treaties its forefathers and their Lakota and Dakota relatives negotiated with the United States at Fort Laramie in 1851 and 1868.

In choosing the treaty process, the United States implicitly recognized that American Indian tribes were autonomous sovereign nations. That sovereignty was explicitly recognized and articulated by three U.S. Supreme Court decisions between 1823 and 1832 that are collectively known as the Marshall Trilogy. Named after John Marshall, the chief justice of the Supreme Court from 1801 until his death in 1835, those decisions established that Indian tribes were separate and distinct political entities existing within the United States as "nations within a nation," each with its own governmental system that had been established prior to the arrival of Europeans. Seen as such, Indian nations possess inherent powers that were not given to them by Congress or any other entity of the U.S. government.

Through negotiating the 1851 and 1868 treaties, Lakota representatives reserved for their people a large tract of their homelands centered in what is now western South Dakota, and including parts of Nebraska, Wyoming, Montana, and North Dakota. Lakota lands stipulated in the 1868 treaty included a reservation (Article 2), hunting grounds (Article 11), and unceded territory (Article 16). Together, these lands approximate the area of modern-day Germany. The northeastern boundary of this land base was in the unceded territory. It began in what is now North Dakota where the Heart River joins the Missouri River, then followed that river south to the forty-sixth parallel, which is about four miles north of the current boundary between North and South Dakota. At that point, the eastern boundary of the land base entered the reservation. The boundary is then described as "commencing on the east bank of the Missouri River where the forty-sixth parallel of north latitude crosses the same, thence along low-water mark down said east bank to a point opposite where the north line of the State of Nebraska strikes the river" (Kappler 1904b). At that point the eastern boundary of the land base leaves the Missouri River, enters the hunting grounds, and continues south to the "Republican Fork of the Smoky Hill River." Therefore, Mnisose—from the Heart River to the northern border of Nebraska—was stipulated as belonging to Lakotas.

When the United States, in 1877, took over thirty-two million acres from the southern, western, and northern areas of the 1868 treaty lands, the eastern boundary of the diminished land base remained the low-water mark of the east bank of Mnisose. But when the resultant Great Sioux Reservation was again reduced in area by the U.S. Congress on March 2, 1889, and divided into six separate reservations, the eastern borders of the four newly created Lakota reservations along Mnisose (Standing Rock, Cheyenne River, Lower Brule, and Rosebud) were stipulated as being located at "the center of the main channel of the Missouri River" (Kappler 1904a), not the low-water mark of the river's eastern bank. As such, the 1889 "Agreement" was the first instance of the United States alienating some of Mnisose from her Lakota relatives.

The constitutions of modern Lakota tribal governments were established in the wake of the Indian Reorganization Act of 1934. By then there were only three Lakota reservations with lands adjoining Mnisose (Standing Rock, Cheyenne River, and Lower Brule), yet their constitutions stipulate their eastern boundaries as those defined in 1889, namely "the center of the main channel of the Missouri River." However, only the constitution of the Standing Rock Sioux Tribe specifically states that the tribe has jurisdiction over all "waterways, watercourses and streams running through any part of the Reservation" (Standing Rock Sioux Tribe 2008). Perhaps this unique inclusion foreshadows the leading position that the Standing

Rock Sioux Tribe would take among its fellow Lakota governments in protecting water and water rights not only within its reservation, but all along the watersheds of these waterways, from their origins to their mouths and beyond.

In particular, it was and is citizens of the Standing Rock Sioux Tribe and their allies who have been in the vanguard of advocating for Mnisose, their relative. Under the guise of fighting for and protecting their water rights, they are being good relatives. In traditional Lakota thought, relatives include more than persons. They also include all living things like plants, animals, stars, and the earth herself. And according to Ella Deloria (1944) in *Speaking of Indians*, the "ultimate aim" of Lakota life is being "a good relative." It is one of the ways of being in this world that connects with the Lakota world before pipelines threatened to burrow under the belly of Mnisose, before the dams tried to control her, and before the boats plied above her backbone.

Standing Rock is where the people gathered in 2016 to protect their relative. Their numbers included Dakota, Nakota, and Lakota representatives, as well as many other Native and non-Native peoples. Along the banks of the Cannonball River near where it flows into Mnisose, the Water Protectors and Dakota Access Pipeline protesters set up their camps. What began as relatively small encampments, suddenly over the course of days grew to have populations larger than many small towns.

But unlike most towns that initially are planned, that are governed by established rules and procedures, and whose residents own or rent plots or lots, these new towns were different. The camps were the bases for protecting and protesting. They were not planned ahead of time to grow so rapidly, nor were they initially intended to be permanent. Nevertheless, the residents worked together to provide food, housing, health care, schooling, safety, sanitation, and many other aspects of community living under the stressful circumstances.

They named their main camp Oceti Sakowin (oh-chay-tee shaw-ko-ween), and in so doing introduced that term into discussions across the United States and beyond. There were relatively few people who had previously heard that term, and even fewer who understood how the confederacy was structured.

Therefore, the #NoDAPL (No Dakota Access Pipeline) movement presents a perfect opportunity to mount a concurrent and intertwined campaign of education about the origins and development of the Oceti Sakowin confederacy. Such an effort would raise awareness and understanding of the confederacy, both locally and globally. Moreover, protectors and protesters explicitly sought to incorporate Oceti Sakowin cultural concepts and philosophies into their decision making, particularly in governance and housing. But without solid foundational knowledge of the confederacy, these good-intended efforts to implement culturally relevant philosophies proved unattainable, at least within the brief period of time the camps existed.

Though the camps have been dismantled, the #NoDAPL movement continues. This chapter's contribution to that effort is twofold. First is a brief overview of the Oceti Sakowin confederacy's origins and development. This will provide a foundation upon which the perpetuation of the confederacy can build. The second contribution is a critical examination of the governance system of one nation of the confederacy. It provides a glimpse into the complexity of implementing aspects of traditional societies into modern contexts. The intent is that these contributions will have applications today and into the future, at Standing Rock and beyond.

The Oceti Sakowin Confederacy

A long time ago, the people had one council fire and made their winter home in the region of the pines at a place called Mde Wakan (muh-day waw-kawn), Sacred Lake, known today as Mille Lacs, Minnesota. They called themselves Mdewakantonwan (muh-day-waw-kawn-tone-wawn), Sacred Lake Council Fire, and they have been known by that name ever since. Mdewakantonwans are the original council fire of the Oceti Sakowin confederacy.

During the spring, the people would travel south to the region of the deciduous trees, then return to their winter homes in the region of the pines. At some point, some of the people stayed in the region of the deciduous trees and made their permanent homes there. They called themselves Wahpekute (wagh-pay-ku-tay), Leaf Shooter Council Fire, and allied themselves with Mdewakantonwans. Eventually another council fire, Wahpetonwan (wagh-pay-tone-wawn), Leaf Council Fire, joined the confederacy and then a fourth, Sisitonwan (See-see-tone-wawn), Fish Council Fire. These four council fires are Dakotas, and at that time they might have called themselves Oceti Topa (oh-chay-tee doh-paw), the Four Council Fires confederacy.

Sometime later, a fifth group was admitted to the confederacy. Its name is Ihanktonwan (ee-honk-tone-wawn), End Council Fire. Next, a sixth group joined, and its name is Ihanktonwanna (ee-honk-tone-wawn-naw), Little End Council Fire. These two council fires are Nakotas, and after they joined, the confederacy consisted of six council fires organized into two divisions, Dakota and Nakota.

Eventually the Titonwan (tee-tone-wan), Prairie Council Fire group, joined the confederacy and constituted its Lakota division. Upon their admission, the confederacy was called Oceti Sakowin, the Seven Council Fires. Their name has remained the same ever since. Nevertheless, the Oceti Sakowin confederacy is commonly and incorrectly referred to as "Sioux." That term, however, is inappropriate to use since it is not a word in any of the three divisions of the Oceti Sakowin confederacy.

The term "Sioux" is a contraction by French speakers of the Ojibwa term for the Oceti Sakowin people. The Ojibwa people and the Oceti Sakowin people were often, if not usually, in conflict. Therefore, when the first non-Native individuals were visiting with the Ojibwa people and asked the name of the Native people who lived to the west, the Ojibwas answered "Nadeowaseau," a word that means "Little Enemy." The French speakers abbreviated the Ojibwa word to the sound of its final syllable and pluralized it by adding an "x" when they spelled it. Since then, the Oceti Sakowin people have been called "Sioux." Oceti Sakowin persons, however, refer to themselves generally by the division to which they belong—Dakota, Nakota, or Lakota—or more specifically by their ancestral council fire.

Within the confederacy, the council fires were ranked relative to each other from first to last, oldest to youngest. Therefore, the highest ranked was Mdewakantonwan, then Wahpekute, Wahpetonwan, Sisitonwan, Ihanktonwan, Ihanktonwanna, and Titonwan. This is the original temporal order, from oldest to youngest, of the council fires. At some point in time, however, a reordering of this ranking occurred whereby the Titonwans were assigned the highest rank, even though they were the last and youngest of the council fires.

Internally, each council fire was comprised of distinct oyates (oh-yaw-tays), or nations. Regarding the Titonwans, there were seven such oyates: Hunkpapa (hoonk-paw-paw), Sihasapa (see-haw-saw-paw), Itazipco (ee-taw-zeep-cho), Oglala (oh-glaw-law), Mniconjou (muh-nee-kawn-zhew), Oohenunpa (oh-oh-hay-noon-paw), and Sicangu (see-chawn-ghu). Representatives of all seven of these nations signed the 1868 Fort Laramie Treaty. Today the descendants of these traditional nations are citizens of six federally recognized tribes in the United States and one first nation in Canada. Five of the six U.S. tribes govern lands in South Dakota. They are Standing Rock Sioux Tribe, Cheyenne River Sioux Tribe, Lower Brule Sioux Tribe, Rosebud Sioux Tribe, and Oglala Sioux Tribe. The connections between these modern tribes and their Titonwan oyates is complicated. For example, Hunkpapa is the ancestral oyate of the Standing Rock Sioux Tribe, whereas four oyates (Sihasapa, Itazipco, Mniconjou, and Oohenunpa) are ancestral to the Cheyenne River Sioux Tribe. Two tribes, Lower Brule Sioux Tribe and Rosebud Sioux Tribe, share a single ancestral oyate: Sicangu. The remaining traditional Titonwan nation, Oglala, is the ancestral oyate of the Oglala Sioux Tribe.

Prior to, during, and after the Marshall decisions, Oceti Sakowin oyates negotiated thirty-four treaties with the U.S. government. The first treaty was negotiated on September 23, 1805, at the mouth of the St. Peter River in Indiana Territory, near the present-day city of Mendota, Minnesota. The last one was negotiated at Fort Laramie in Dakota Territory on April 29, 1868, near the present-day town of Fort Laramie, Wyoming. It was ratified by Congress on February 16, 1869, and proclaimed by President Andrew Johnson eight days later on February 24, 1869. This treaty, commonly referred to as the 1868 Fort Laramie Treaty, is of central importance to all discussions of Lakota lands and history. It established what later would be called the "Great Sioux Reservation," an area that encompassed all of the land west of the Missouri River in what is now South Dakota, including what would later be established as the Standing Rock Reservation.

Representatives of Oceti Sakowin oyates employed a number of strategies when negotiating treaties with their U.S. counterparts. They understood whether or not they were transferring a portion of their land to the United States. In those treaties where this was the case, they knew their remaining lands were diminished in extent. They also understood that in exchange for giving up some of their lands, they were acquiring payment that might take the form of cash, annuities, or services. It is important that these treaty representatives not be portrayed as passive, subservient, or ignorant. They were human beings and therefore collectively exhibited all the characteristics of humans. The treaties they negotiated, like all U.S. treaties, are "the supreme law of the land" according to Article VI of the U.S. Constitution.

The Oceti Sakowin peoples have lived in the Northern Plains region for countless generations. The core of their traditional homelands extended west to east from the Big Horn Mountains to Lake Superior, and north to south from the Canadian border to the Platte River. Today their lands have been significantly diminished, and the shape of their boundaries systematically straightened. Whereas the traditional lands of the confederacy were contiguous, they now are divided into twenty-five distinct reservations and reserves.

In the United States, sixteen reservations are located in five states: one in Montana, one in North Dakota, nine in South Dakota, one in Nebraska, and four in Minnesota. The external boundaries of two of the nine reservations in South Dakota—Lake Traverse Reservation and Standing Rock Reservation—extend into North Dakota; therefore, lands of these two reservations are in both states. In addition to the sixteen U.S. reservations, there are nine reserves in Canadian provinces: five in Manitoba and four in Saskatchewan.

For each of the Oceti Sakowin reservations and reserves, there is today a tribe or first nation, respectively, that governs those lands. Therefore, there are twenty-five Oceti Sakowin tribes and first nations: sixteen tribes in the United States and nine first nations in Canada. In the United States, tribes are the fundamental units of federal Indian law. Yet there is no one definition of an Indian tribe. A tribe might be recognized as such by its members, by a local community, by other tribes, by a state government, or by the federal government. Who recognizes a tribe determines in large measure the tribe's rights and responsibilities. The one source of recognition that always assures a tribe of being recognized as a tribe in all contexts is that of the federal government. The U.S. government recognizes 573 Indian tribes, and the Canadian government recognizes 618 first nation communities. All twenty-five Oceti Sakowin tribes and first nations are federally recognized.

This brief overview of the Oceti Sakowin confederacy provides a basis to guide discussions of cultural relevancy. Learning Oceti Sakowin foundational knowledge does not merely illuminate one's understanding of the past. It can also serve to clarify what we see happening today. For someone just becoming familiar with the Oceti Sakowin confederacy through the publicized actions of Water Protectors, it can add a new layer of significance to the numerous images of tribal flags lining a road into a resistance camp. These are not simply representing nations coming together to protect a common relative but, in the case of the twenty-five modern Dakota, Nakota, and Lakota tribes, nations uniting in a manner that draws upon centuries of shared history. And to someone inside the resistance to the Dakota Access Pipeline, it can guide them to plan their activism, where possible, to educate others about traditional Oceti Sakowin principles.

Take, for example, that iconic row of flags at the Oceti Sakowin Water Protector Camp, which represented the participation of citizens from nations all across the globe. Flags are one of the most visible symbols we use to announce the presence of a united group of people. It seems natural, then, that Water Protectors could create their own flags to show the bonds that bring them together. A flag for the Oceti Sakowin Camp, with a design rooted in knowledge of the Oceti Sakowin confederacy, would have a profound effect. Not only would it symbolize a presence, but it would also be cause for newcomers to the movement to ask "what does it mean?" And this provides a perfect educational moment.

There isn't an official Oceti Sakowin flag. But it can easily be shown how one could design a meaningful, aesthetically pleasing flag for this purpose. The proposed flag pictured on the next page has an irregular pentagon-shaped field that fills the fly, or right, side. The left vertex of this field is fixed at the center of the flag and points toward the hoist, or left side. In this field are four white diamond shapes in a square pattern. The four diamonds represent the four Dakota oyates. A narrow white band separates this field from a chevron-shaped field that likewise points toward the hoist side. In it are two diamonds representing the two Nakota oyates. Another narrow white band separates this chevron from a swallow-tailed field that fills in the hoist side of the flag. This field contains one diamond that represents the single Lakota oyate. The positions of the fields and their colors (indicated in parentheses following) differentiate the respective divisions of the Oceti Sakowin confederacy. The right, or eastern (blue), field is the Dakota division. The middle field is the southern (red) Nakota division. The left, or western (yellow), field is the Lakota division. Furthermore, the size of each field corresponds to the current relative population of its division. From largest to smallest, they are Lakota, Dakota, and Nakota.

Proposing a new culturally relevant flag design is relatively simple once the foundational knowledge is understood. It could have been accomplished during the period the camps were active and flown with the many other flags. Similarly, with regard to models of traditional Lakota governance, there are analogs to the Standing Rock camps. Before exploring them, however, it is imperative to state that these models can be examined as case studies of how cultural ideals were put into action. Useful models should be descriptive as opposed to prescriptive. In other words, they should generate multiple alternatives on an ongoing basis instead of a single solution that is imputed to be the only acceptable possibility.

Traditional Lakota Governance

Traditional Lakota governance can be viewed as a fluid system of strategies for responding to stressful situations, thus the analog to the Standing Rock camps.[1] No single system was relied upon during all times of the year, nor for all social and residential groups. The basic social unit of Lakota society was a tiyospaye (tee-yo-shpaw-yay), or extended family, so when it encamped together, kinship governed its internal interactions. On the other hand, the basic residential community of Lakota society, an otonwahe (oh-tone-waw-hay), was comprised of the members of multiple tiyospayes and therefore can be examined for models of governing socially diverse communities.

An otonwahe was similar to a modern town, but whereas towns today are typically conceived of as stationary, in Lakota society otonwahes were mobile. Regardless of how often they moved or where they were located, each maintained an oceti, or council fire, to signal its independence. Otonwahes featured a certain system of governance when they were located in place, but other systems were temporarily implemented when they moved, when they coalesced into what might be called cities, or when they were established for specific communal purposes, such as buffalo hunts or ceremonies. Also, when the number of residents of an otonwahe reached a threshold, it appears additional levels of governance were put in place.

Lakota governance was complex and situational. For instance, when an otonwahe was situated at a site, it typically had four types of governing offices: omniciye (oh-munee-chee-yay), itancan (ee-tawn-chawn), wakiconza (waw-kee-kone-zaw), and akicita (aw-kee-chee-taw). Residential communities with enough residents to constitute an otonwahe would have had these four governing offices.

The Otonwahe

Day-to-day otonwahe. The decision-making authority within an otonwahe was placed in the hands of a council of respected men. Not limited by a specified number, nor inclusive of all eligible members, this group of men, the omniciye, tended to consist of older and respected men residing in the otonwahe. Admittance to the omniciye was by consent of its sitting councilmen. The omniciye convened regularly around the otonwahe's oceti, in a central meeting lodge where it deliberated on matters of public interest, determined its relations with other otonwahes, ruled on disputes between the otonwahe's residents, and decided where and when to move the otonwahe. One of its key decisions, which occurred infrequently, was to choose from among its members an itancan, or leader of the otonwahe.

The itancan occupied the catku (chaught-ku), or position of honor, in the omniciye meeting lodge, and it was the invitation by his fellow members of the omniciye to sit there that signaled his promotion to this office. He was the leader of the omniciye and therefore of the otonwahe. Once appointed, he generally held this office for life, although the omniciye reserved the power to depose him. The role was usually, but not always, assigned hereditarily, passing from father to son. A man whose accomplishments were sufficiently impressive, though, could win the endorsement of the omniciye and earn this position. The itancan was the executive of the otonwahe, working to realize the omniciye's resolutions, appointing akicitas to enforce these decisions, and leading the otonwahe's larger military campaigns.

Ideally, an otonwahe would have had four wakiconzas selected by the omniciye. Any man residing in the otonwahe, including members of the omniciye, could fill the role of wakiconza. During a wakiconza's one-year term, however, any other governing roles he may have had were suspended. During the day-to-day governance of the otonwahe, the wakiconzas mediated disputes among the residents of the otonwahe as well as between the people and the leaders, represented the decisions of the omniciye, refereed games among the people, and provided advice to the itancan. They were considered hunka, or relative, to everyone residing in the otonwahe.

The akicitas in an otonwahe were a police force of sorts. Appointed individually or as members of an okolakiciye (oh-ko-law-kee-chee-yay), or society, these public servants enforced otonwahe policies and social mores. Even the omniciye, the itancan, and the wakiconzas were not exempt from the judgment and sentences of the akicitas. Different groups of men would serve as akicitas over the course of a year and during more specific otonwahe functions. The lead akicita was the eyapaha (ay-yaw-paw-haw), or crier, in the otonwahe. He was charged with announcing policies, moves, summons before the governing bodies, general news and also with maintaining the otonwahe's oceti. While akicitas could be called into this compulsory service by governing officials for a variety of purposes, the charge of akicitas was consistent: to enforce the authority of their appointers.

These descriptions provide an outline for the day-to-day governance of a civil, stationary, Lakota otonwahe. However, different structures governed the otonwahe during special times. Two such instances were when an otonwahe was moving from one site to another and during the wanasapi (waw-naw-saw-pee), or communal buffalo chase. In both cases, authority shifted from the day-to-day consultative type to a more exclusive authoritarian type.

Moving the otonwahe. Throughout the year, for various reasons, otonwahes moved en masse. As a community, all of the residents, all together, moved their otonwahe. The decision to move an otonwahe was made deliberatively by the omniciye, but the move itself was conducted under the exclusive authority of the wakiconzas. They alone decided when the tipis should be taken down, how far to travel, when and where to rest during the day to separate the journey into four equal segments, and when and where to erect tipis again at the end of the day. They decided whether the existing akicitas would police the move, or to appoint new akicitas for this purpose. In addition to compelling compliance with the pace and direction of the move, these akicitas scouted for game to feed the otonwahe residents, and for enemies from which to protect the residents. When the move was completed, oversight of the otonwahe transferred from the wakiconzas back to the omniciye, and authority reverted from exclusive to consultative.

Hunting buffalo communally. An otonwahe, either independently or in collaboration with one or more other otonwahes, conducted a wanasapi in order to efficiently and collectively obtain meat for its residents. In many instances, a wicasa wakan (wee-chaw-shaw waw-kawn), medicine man, performed rituals to discern a probable location of a herd of buffalo. Whether by this or some other process, once a herd was located the omniciye decided when to hunt, how long to hunt, whether to invite neighboring otonwahes, and other logistical concerns. During the hunt, governing authority shifted from the omniciye to the wakiconzas, and changed from a consensual model to an exclusive model. The akicitas policed the hunters and enforced the wakiconzas' decisions. Wakiconzas advised whether the hunt was complete or was to continue for more meat, and after a successful hunt apportioned any surplus meat. Once sufficient meat had been accumulated, the authority of the wakiconzas ended and the omniciye resumed its day-to-day consultative authority.

Moving the otonwahe and hunting buffalo communally were two civil functions of the otonwahe that required a significant change in the day-to-day governing system. During these operations, the margin for error was dramatically reduced. In the first case, all of the otonwahe residents were exposed and therefore vulnerable to outside forces. In the latter case, all of the residents were depending on the hunt for meat to cure and store for times of scarcity. In both cases, authority shifted from the omniciye to the wakiconzas, and it changed from consensual to exclusive. Thus, during these critical times we see a change in who had authority as well as a change in the nature of that authority.

Otonwahe tanka. Another governmental shift occurred when many otonwahes convened, typically in the summer, for any number of purposes, including tribal deliberations, appointment to tribal offices, and preparation for public ceremonies. Even though a resulting otonwahe tanka (oh-tone-waw-hay tawn-kaw), similar to a city, coalesced for a relatively brief period of time, it nevertheless faced unique challenges, one of which was maintaining social unity among its residents—and by extension, their tiyospayes.

Integral components of Lakota social order that mitigated this potential disunity were okolakiciyes that cross-cut social units as well as residential communities. Because their memberships were drawn from across different tiyospayes and otonwahes, okolakiciyes inherently promoted integration among the residents of an otonwahe tanka. It is not surprising, therefore, that okolakiciyes assumed decision-making authority at all levels of governance in an otonwahe tanka.

A member of any of these societies was a naca (naw-chaw). Whereas each of the men in a day-to-day omniciye may have been affiliated with a different okolakiciye, the nacas governing an otonwahe tanka all belonged to the same okolakiciye. The nacas convened regularly around the otonwahe tanka's oceti in a central meeting lodge where they deliberated on matters of national interest. One of their key decisions was to appoint four wicasa yatapikas (wee-chaw-shaw yaw-taw-pee-kaws), or shirt-wearers.

During large gatherings, wicasa yatapikas assumed a position of prestige. They tended to be younger and to have distinguished themselves in battle. They were guardians of the entire oyate, or nation, both literally and figuratively. As such, they were referred to as "praiseworthy men." Their office was denoted by a shirt fringed with hair, which the people considered "owned by the tribe." As was the case with an itancan, a wicasa yatapika held the title for life, although the nacas could depose him. Unlike an itancan, though, this office was not hereditary.

Ceremonial otonwahe. The role of wicasa wakan, or holy man, was conferred by the spirits. His authority was understood to come from direct communications with Wakan Tanka, the Great Mystery. He was relied upon for intelligence on the whereabouts of buffalo and to foretell the success of a war campaign, among many other things. Similar to a naca, a wicasa wakan belonged to one of a select set of okolakiciyes. During a Sun Dance, the governing authority of the otonwahe tanka shifted from the nacas to the wicasa wakan. Then at the end of the ceremony the authority of the wicasa wakan ended.

When the purpose was fulfilled for which an otonwahe tanka coalesced, then it devolved into a number of otonwahes. Under the authority of their wakiconzas, these otonwahes set off for distant places. Upon arrival there, the governing authority of each would shift from its wakiconzas to its omniciye. The different otonwahes would thereby resume their day-to-day organizational structures once again.

Principles of Lakota Governance

This critical examination of traditional forms of Lakota governance illustrates possible avenues for extending the #NoDAPL movement. The following observations identify trends in traditional Lakota governing structures, and then abstract from these trends principles of Lakota governance.

There is a set of governing systems from which to choose. There is no fixed, unitary system of authority applicable throughout the course of a typical annual cycle. While all of the civil systems share the similarities of a council, its leader, and their enforcers, the order and nature of their authority varies. Complementary systems of governance are substituted seamlessly in predictable ways to meet the needs of specific situations.

The day-to-day system relies on deliberation, consensus, and delegation. Decisions are resolved after careful consideration and discussion. It is very rare that the decision making and the execution of decisions are done by the same office. It is similarly rare that the office carrying out a decision acts alone. Rather, it delegates to a small group of lead deputies or implementers, who in turn appoint their own enforcers to ensure the policy's implementation.

At critical times, a system of exclusive authority emerges. When a situation has a narrow margin for error, all decision making shifts to a small and select group whose authority is unimpeachable and whose decisions are unquestionable. Such times are finite in duration, and upon their conclusion decision making reverts to a deliberative and consensual model.

During large gatherings, subgroups that cross lines of difference cohere the assembly. Participants in a large assembly are also members of subgroups according to their affinities and skills. These subgroups cross-cut normal organizations and contribute to the unity of the assembly. Some of these subgroups even play governing roles over the assembly, ensuring that the interests of all those gathered are put before the interests of any single constituent.

Through all we have examined so far, a critical characteristic of traditional Lakota governance is its complexity. Therefore, to implement a governing system based on traditional concepts would not be easy or simple. That work, though, could be rewarding in that it would offer future encampments on Lakota lands an opportunity to implement a governance system that is culturally grounded in Lakota tradition. Such opportunities appear to be intermittent and short-lived.

Protest movements are by their nature ephemeral, whereas Mnisose is eternal. She has nourished us since time immemorial. As good relatives, one of our responsibilities is to reciprocate that life-sustaining kindness. That is what the protectors and protesters and their allies have done and are doing.

In some ways, the Oceti Sakowin confederacy is similar to Mnisose. It has organized its seven council fires since the mists of long ago, and hopefully will continue to do so far into the future. This is our time to educate about the confederacy, to draw upon its concepts and philosophies to inform not only our lives but, more importantly, all aspects of our societies. In order to have an ongoing presence now and in the future, it is imperative that principles of the confederacy inform what its citizens do and how they do it. Whether drawn from the past or developed anew, these principles are the foundation for tribal sovereignty.

NOTE

1. This section is an updated version of a white paper that the Center for American Indian Research and Native Studies (CAIRN) produced for Hopa Mountain in 2014, and that was revised and published as Howe and Katz 2015.

REFERENCES

Black Elk, Nicholas. 1984. *The Sixth Grandfather: Black Elk's Teachings Given to John G. Neihardt*. Edited by Raymond A. DeMallie. Lincoln: University of Nebraska Press.

Buechel, Eugene, ed. 1970. *A Dictionary of the Teton Dakota Sioux Language*. Pine Ridge, S.Dak.: Red Cloud Indian School.

Buechel, Eugene, and Paul Manhart. 1998. *Lakota Tales and Text: In Translation*. Chamberlain, S.Dak.: Tipi Press.

Capossela, Peter. 2015. *The Land along the River: The Ongoing Saga of the Sioux Nation Land Claim, 1851–2012*. Sioux Falls, S.Dak.: Mariah Press.

Deloria, Ella. 1944. *Speaking of Indians*. New York: Friendship Press.

DeMallie, Raymond A., ed. 2001. *Handbook of North American Indians*, vol. 13, pt. 2. Washington, D.C.: Smithsonian Institution Press.

Densmore, Frances. 1918. *Teton Sioux Music*. New York: De Capo Press.

Flood Control Act of 1944, Publication L. No. 78-534, 58 Stat. 887.

Hassrick, Royal B. 1964. *The Sioux: Life and Customs of a Warrior Society*. Norman: University of Oklahoma Press.

Howe, Craig, and Abe Katz. 2015. "Traditional Lakota Governance." *Rootstalk* 1 (spring 2015): 35–40.

Kappler, Charles J., ed. 1904a. "An act to divide a portion of the reservation of the Sioux Nation of Indians in Dakota into separate reservations and to secure the relinquishment of the Indian title to the remainder, and for other purposes." In *Indian Affairs: Laws and Treaties*, 1:328–39. Washington, D.C.: U.S. Government Printing Office.

Kappler, Charles J., ed. 1904b. "Treaty with the Sioux—Brulé, Oglala, Miniconjou, Yanktonai, Hunkpapa, Blackfeet, Cuthead, Two Kettle, Sans Arcs, and Santee—and

Arapaho, 1868." In *Indian Affairs: Laws and Treaties*, 2:998–1007. Washington, D.C.: U.S. Government Printing Office.

Maynard, Eileen, and Gayla Twiss. 1970. *Hechel Lena Oyate Kin Nipi Kte: That These People May Live*. Washington, D.C.: U.S. Government Printing Office.

One Feather, Vivian. 1974. *Itancan*. Pine Ridge, S.Dak.: Red Cloud Indian School.

Powers, William K. 1975. *Oglala Religion*. Lincoln: University of Nebraska Press.

Price, Katherine. 1996. *The Oglala People, 1841–1879*. Lincoln: University of Nebraska Press.

Standing Rock Sioux Tribe. 2008. *Constitution of the Standing Rock Sioux Tribe*. National Indian Law Library. https://narf.org/nill/constitutions/standingrock/index.html.

U.S. Congress Senate Select Committee on Indian Affairs. 1987. *Final Report and Recommendations of the Garrison Unit Joint Tribal Advisory Committee*. Washington, D.C.: U.S. Government Printing Office.

Walker, James R. 1917. *The Sun Dance and Other Ceremonies of the Oglala Division of the Teton Dakota*. Anthropological Papers of the American Museum of Natural History 16.2. New York: American Museum of Natural History.

Walker, James R. 1980. *Lakota Belief and Ritual*. Edited by Raymond J. DeMallie and Elaine A. Jahner. Lincoln: University of Nebraska Press.

Walker, James R. 1982. *Lakota Society*. Edited by Raymond J. DeMallie. Lincoln: University of Nebraska Press.

Wissler, Clark. 1912. *Societies and Ceremonial Associations in the Oglala Division of the Teton-Dakota*. American Museum of Natural History Anthropological Papers 11.1. New York: American Museum of Natural History.

8

MNI WICONI
WATER IS [MORE THAN] LIFE

Edward Valandra

Why Stand with Water

"MNI WICONI!" The Water Protectors' call circled the world in late 2016, and for many people, the call continues to resonate. This collective cry captures more than the human experience with water. Yes, we understand that all water-dependent life perishes without healthy water. We all have experienced thirst that only water quenches. We know almost all flora and fauna struggle and die without water; the World Wide Web alerts us immediately to drought-stricken areas. And, for the better part of history, Western-based societies have used water as a conventional utility in the service of humankind, for example, hydroelectric power.

So when both the Dakota Access Pipeline (DAPL) and Keystone XL Pipeline (KXL) invaded Oceti Sakowin Oyate homeland, endangering the water for millions, we challenged the Western assumptions behind these projects, especially the DAPL pipeline—#NoDAPL. Our initial challenge seemed orthodox enough. Prior to our Hunkpapa Titunwan relatives establishing the Sacred Stone Camp, they, through colonizer political channels such as the National Environmental Policy Act and National Historic Preservation Act, informed Energy Transfer Partners (ETP), DAPL supporters such as North Dakota, the U.S. Army Corps of Engineers, and the Interior Department of their opposition to DAPL.

Going deeper, though, our people also challenged the fundamental mindset behind the projects—the Western metaphysics driving modern development. For example, in another essay, I challenged the "positive development" ideology that DAPL's backers used to justify it and to overlook its dangers:

This $3.7 billion, 1,172-mile pipeline will transport between 470,000 to 570,000 barrels of oil per day from the Bakken/Three Forks formations in North Dakota for domestic consumption: "Its goal is to relieve transportation strains on rail for crude transportation and safely transport U.S. crude oil to U.S. markets via pipeline to further the goal of energy independence."

The stated goal, of course, appeals to mainstream thinking, U.S. nationalism, and economics: Americans will be less dependent on foreign oil, while simultaneously growing their economy. For example, a few of the windfalls that Energy Transfer Partners (ETP) attributes to DAPL include: labor income ($1.9 billion); right-of-way payment of landowners ($190 million); local use, gross receipts, and lodging taxes during construction ($10 million); and state individual income tax revenue ($28 million). These monetary figures reveal the Western assumption that development is inherently beneficial and everyone wins.[1]

When both the Sacred Stone and Spirit Camps were established; when the Oceti Sakowin Oyate reignited its ancient, sovereign fire; and when thousands of people from all over the world either descended on the Spirit Camp as Water Protectors or tracked it on social media: water-is-life surged through consciousness, not solely as an environmental cause célèbre but as Mni Oyate (Water Nation). Development's excesses (pollution, contamination, damming) show the West's blindness to who water is, and this blindness dictated the United States' response. Unable or unwilling to distinguish Water Protectors from conventional protesters, and unable or unwilling to differentiate between water as a quantifiable utility, for example, acre-foot, and water as a rights holder, that is, as possessing personhood, the United States defaulted to its standard post-9/11 policy, a militarized police reaction. Corporate-influenced governments showed zero tolerance for ways of knowing that question a Westernized lifestyle.[2]

This essay first discusses Indigenous sovereignty. Sovereignty is germane to the DAPL controversy, because the struggle is fundamentally a culture or paradigm war. Without first examining sovereignty, the uninitiated get lost in the political complexities and fail to name what North Dakota's and the United States' actions really represent: differences in world view and colonization. Second, I show how the narrowness of the Western concept of legal standing impacts nonhumans and their status as rights holders. Third, since the first two discussions are about comparative world views, I formulate how whites apply their Otherizing of nonwhites to the Natural World as well. Fourth, I discuss Mni Wiconi from our perspective and how it informs our resistance to DAPL. Finally, I dissect how colonization works hand in glove with corporate development to marginalize our voices, using Western procedures to do it. Here ETP's narrative about its decision-making process for DAPL is one-sided, hence self-serving. The corporate process favored non-Indigenous protocols, and the subsequent narratives from such protocols worked against both Indigenous communities and the Natural World. Naming this colonized process helps us understand DAPL's political strategy: to present ETP as a good neighbor when it is not. Moreover, the state's militarized police and the corporate security reaction to the Oceti Sakowin Oyate and its allies exposed ETP's good neighbor rhetoric as nothing more than a public relations lie. It is about the genocide of a people whom we call the Mni Oyate.

Indigenous Sovereignty Is All about My Relatives

Why did we, the Oceti Sakowin Oyate, take the stand we did? This question opens a discussion on a core issue rarely heard in Western circles: Indigenous sovereignty and where it originates. The Oceti Sakowin Oyate predates modern states, and our sovereignty flows directly from our origin story: how we came to be and the primary responsibility given us. By framing our existence in relationship with the Natural World, our story counters the Western assumption that the Natural World's sole purpose is to serve humankind—the tenet of today's Anthropocene era. Our oral stories remind us that such a mindset, sovereignty without the Natural World's inclusion, leads to Earthwide extinction as a wholly human-induced catastrophe.[3] In fact, today's mass extinction replays one of our oral history stories, "The Great Race." Sometime in ages past, the Oceti Sakowin Oyate did not live as good relatives with the Natural World. As a result, our right to exist lay in nonhumans' hands. The Water Protectors' actions within our homeland prove that the Oceti Sakowin Oyate learned our lesson from the race. We must follow our original instructions: *to be a good relative*. Since water is our relative, we protect all our relatives from harm. Resisting DAPL was our response to a relative's call for help; answering that call was and remains our responsibility.

Compared to Indigenous sovereignty, Western sovereignty is a construct of human thinking, unconnected to the Natural World on which humans depend, hence a fiction. Western sovereignty's ultimate expression is the modern state, the basic characteristics of which include a bounded territory, absolute jurisdiction within its exterior boundaries, a self-recognized legitimacy, and a political architecture that provides for national expression (e.g., war declaration, a national capital, chosen leaders, bureaucracy, social contract or compact). Since the mid-twentieth century, the United Nations (UN) has become the organization that embodies these sovereign characteristics. People from modern states prove their sovereignty not by practicing how they are in relationship with the Natural World but merely by belonging to this club.

The UN's self-constructed origin story aligns with Westernized ideals. One year after the UN Charter's ratification, Sumner Welles, a white male who served as a U.S. State Department diplomat, delivered a lecture in October 1946, "The English Speaking Democracies." He spoke of the promise of a UN organization:

The nations of the world are engaged in an endeavor to fashion an international order through which *humanity* can obtain peace, and men and women everywhere can achieve the assurance of security, of liberty, and of ordered progress. As governments and organized groups search for the most effective means of achieving that ideal, they must necessarily seek to utilize in the structure to be erected those elements which have already proved themselves to be worthy and which can, *because of actual human experience*, be depended upon to support the stresses to which that new structure will be subjected, especially during the years of its initial growth.[4]

Welles is, of course, referring to the Enlightenment (ordered progress) as *the* human experience and to democratic values (a social compact providing, among other things, liberty) as the requisite elements. But both are drawn from a Western perspective, which he expects the UN to universalize for all humanity.

Welles knew full well that colonization and oppression persisted at the UN's birth. Examining the UN's fifty-one Founding Member States (FMS), self-determining peoples might rethink joining. For instance, of only three FMS from the African continent, one was South Africa, a modern state notorious for apartheid. European FMS had been busily colonizing both Africa's Indigenous Peoples, as an outcome of the 1884 Berlin Conference, and Southeast Asia. Moreover, twenty Latin American FMS, themselves on a path from being colonized to becoming modern states, nonetheless condoned genocide against Indigenous Peoples. Britain opposed Irish home rule, and the United States has continued its illegal occupation of the Kingdom of Hawaii since 1898. Yet, despite these and many other FMS violations of humanitarian, democratic values, Welles invoked the infamous writ large apologia, the white man's burden, in order to explain them away: "It was in part an outgrowth of that belief on the part of many of the English-speaking peoples that they must assume what was often termed 'the white man's burden.'"[5] In other words, whites get to determine for nonwhites how much civilization they can handle. Whites thereby control nonwhite self-rule, because only nonwhites who have internalized colonization are allowed into the club. With white oversight, nonwhites will monitor themselves and not regress to their non-Western, traditional lifeways.

Welles also knew full well that the United States, an FMS, had meat-bearing skeletons in its closet. Constitutionally sanctioned separate but equal doctrine normalized white American discrimination: Black Codes, Jim Crow, Japanese-American internment camps, and the unresolved American question, Do Indigenous Peoples have the right of self-determination? To deflect UN critics by acknowledging humanity's shortcomings, adroitly, Welles mounted a critique of FMS and future non-FMS that subscribe to a master race ideology.

> In a world in which even some of the oldest democracies have become permeated with the poison engendered by the doctrines of the "master race," and where the persecution and obliteration of millions of human beings because of their race or creed have, tragically enough, become almost common place, and where tolerance in certain of our English-speaking democracies is decried as either being impossible or even undesirable. . . . For no world order can ever be created upon the corrupt and disintegrating hatred which intolerance brings about. Discrimination against

any race, or intolerance against any religion, can only lead to the eventual eruption of every one of those brutal forces which result in war, and in the suppression of all those individual freedoms in which we believe.[6]

Welles's critique served at least two purposes. First, given the UN's FMS profile, his words reflected an aspirational goal. Because the master race ideology has yet to be disavowed, Welles's words veiled the UN's shaky foundation today. Second, FMS and other club members could shield themselves from forces, such as other ways of experiencing or knowing the world, that would challenge Western hegemony and its paradigm. The right to be a distinct people who base their sovereignty on non-Western principles, like recognizing the Natural World's personhood, could be targeted as subversive or dangerous to the West.

For instance, when confronted with a non-West sovereign that recognizes Natural World standing, as the Oceti Sakowin Oyate's Sacred Stone and Spirit Camps did, the United States, a FMS, condoned militarized police and a corporate mercenary campaign. But even the United States could not justify to the world the violence it arrayed against us.[7] Indeed, whenever "NoDAPL" broke through corporate-controlled media, U.S. propaganda labeled Mni Wiconi action as an environmental protest at best and a threat to its nation (read: terrorism) at worst. To Welles I say "yes," a "world order" can exist on hatred at a high cost. The UN's inability to prevent its member states and others from resorting to violence shows a weak center, one that cannot hold.

Another indicator of U.S. hatred toward Indigenous Peoples occurred sixty-two years after the UN's founding and nine years before the Sacred Stone Camp and Spirit Camp. In September 2007, the UN General Assembly approved the Declaration on the Rights of Indigenous Peoples. However, Canada, Australia, New Zealand, and the United States (CANZUS) rejected it and were the only FMS to do so.[8] While not a perfect document, the declaration contains provisions that "protect" non-Western ways of knowing. As our NoDAPL action shows, Indigenous nations reject development's underlying assumption: that the Natural World is an object and therefore rightless.

From Standing Bear to Standing Trees: The Unthinkable

The Sierra Club's 1972 federal lawsuit to protect a natural area from commercial development showed the West's resistance to recognizing other ways of understanding the world—not even Native in this case.[9] The Sierra Club lost its lawsuit because it did not have "standing." Standing is a legal—albeit human—concept. It means a person must have suffered a direct harm or wrong or be likely to suffer one from another person to have standing in a court. The Sierra Club's lawsuit failed because the club could not show a direct injury to it or any of its members from the development project.

However, before the court ruled to deny the Sierra Club standing, Christopher

Stone penned a theory for the West: if nature is to be protected from development, it must be accorded legal standing. He contended that the Natural World, or at least its "natural objects," should be afforded personhood. The Western world view, of course, defines a person as a human being; but that definition has a checkered past. For example, the U.S. Constitution counted Indigenous Peoples who had been taken from the African continent against their will and made slaves in a pre-1865 U.S. society as three-fifths of a person. Peoples indigenous to North America, especially where the United States now illegally occupies, did not enjoy standing until 1879, when a federal judge issued a habeas corpus writ for Standing Bear, a Ponca leader, whom the U.S. military had detained. The U.S. argument against granting habeas corpus to Standing Bear centered on whether, like the Natural World, Indigenous Peoples qualify as persons.

> In response to the writ, Mr. Lamberston, the United States Attorney, argued that by the very words of the habeas statute Congress had reserved the right to file the writ to "those persons unlawfully detained." Mr. Lamberston argued that Standing Bear was not a person because he was an Indian, therefore, he had no right to sue out the writ in a court of laws.[10]

Standing Bear v. Crook was asking nineteenth-century white society to consider the unthinkable: Indigenous Peoples are persons, that is, human beings who can suffer harms, injuries, or wrongs from others. What Stone proposed a century after *Standing Bear* about valuing the "rightless" for themselves rang loud in this trial.

> Until the rightless thing receives its rights, we cannot see it as anything but a thing for the use of "us"—those who are holding rights at the time. . . . There will be resistance to giving things "rights" until it can be seen and valued for itself; yet it is hard to see it and value it for itself until we can bring ourselves to give it "rights"—which is almost inevitably going to sound inconceivable to a large group of people.[11]

Before heralding the 1879 decision as white enlightenment, we must remember that little has progressed for Indigenous Peoples in the 138 years (and counting) since *Standing Bear*. Whites still defend "Indian" sport mascots, such as the Washington Redskins, Cleveland Indians, Kansas City Chiefs, or Edmonton Eskimos. Since most sports mascots draw from the animal kingdom,[12] Indian-as-mascot sends a clear message that whites—and those who agree with them—believe Indigenous Peoples are not human beings. The popular cowboys and Indians figurines (which anyone can purchase in the states today) send the same message: Native lives do not matter, because Natives are not fully human.

The U.S. government institutionalized the message as well: the Interior Department is the site for Americans to negotiate their relationships with Indigenous Peoples. The Interior Department is responsible for the stewardship of trees, streams, lakes, "wildlife," minerals, land, and other natural wonders—the nonhuman presences to whom Stone proposed acknowledging personhood and standing. *Standing Bear* long since ruled that Indigenous Peoples are persons, hence rights holders. Why, then, is the State Department, where human relationships are primary, not the appropriate place for negotiating relations with Indigenous nations?

For Stone, Indians-as-mascots does not relegate Indigenous Peoples to rightless things, useful only for season tickets and a mass TV audience; it rather exposes whites' failure to recognize Indigenous Peoples as fully human. Whites' interest in maintaining Indigenous Peoples' rightlessness lies in maintaining their epic myth: our land was for them to freely take. The myth whitewashes their genocidal invasion. Indeed, as unconditional rights-holders, Indigenous Peoples demand to be made whole, that is, to have our pre-1492 self-determination actualized, however much colonizers breach it. In addition to compensation, both land return and decolonization are the sine qua non for restoring Indigenous Peoples' wholeness.

However, the notions that Indigenous Peoples are human beings and that Mni Oyate are persons—unconditional rights-holders and not objects for whites to use—are anathemas to Western thinking: heresies. While Stone's theory for granting standing to nonhuman things faced incredulity from white society, the Water Protectors experienced far worse. Why? Because nineteenth-century, dehumanizing, and violent white doctrines—right of discovery, plenary power, and dependent domestic nations—still control Indigenous Peoples' fate. Mainstream society finds overturning these doctrines as unthinkable today as pre-1865 white society found overturning slavery unthinkable or pre-1990 white South Africa found overturning apartheid unthinkable. The militarized police re/action at Spirit Camp and a U.S. president's subsequent 2017 executive orders to authorize DAPL and other Western development projects proved the point: Americans still find it culturally unthinkable that Indigenous Peoples—not to mention the Natural World—are rights holders.

For the West, it is equally unthinkable to stand with the Natural World—in our case, with Mni Oyate—as a person, yet doing so affirms Mni Oyate as a holder of rights. Possessing rights means the Mni Oyate could, from a denial or violation of their rights, suffer a harm, injury, or wrong. To imagine this idea is to imagine that the Mni Oyate has legal standing. Stone argues that the West's anthropocentrism—or as he termed it, "the psychic and socio-psychic aspects"—throws self-interest in the way: Why should humanity accept the Mni Oyate as a rights holder if it restricts how humans interact with water or the Natural World? In short, "What is in it for 'us'?"[13]

With this reservation as to the peculiar task of the [human self-interest] argument that follows, let me stress that the strongest case can be made from the perspective of human advantage for conferring rights on the environment. Scientists have been warning of the crises the earth and all humans on it face if we do not change our ways—radically—and these crises make the lost "recreational use" of rivers seem absolutely trivial. The earth's very atmosphere is threatened with frightening possibilities; absorption of sunlight, upon which the entire life cycle depends, may be diminished; the oceans may warm (increasing the "greenhouse effect" of the atmosphere), melting polar ice caps, and destroying our great coastal cities; the portion of the atmosphere that shields us from dangerous radiation may be destroyed.[14]

The culture shift facing the West boils down to how it defines a person, possessed of rights. Comparatively, the non-West continues stepping forward to making the shift: when human activity harms or injures specific natural objects or things, those harmed must be counted as persons with legal standing. For example:

> In India, a court recognized Himalayan glaciers as legal persons, and the Ganges and Yamuna Rivers were given the same status as a human being. "This means legal guardians can now represent the waterways in court over any violation."
> In New Zealand, the Whanganui River is now recognized as a legal person. The Maori Nation fought nearly 150 years for the river to be recognized as an ancestor.
> In 2008, Ecuador built nature's rights into its constitution, ensuring that the country's entire ecosystem has a "right to exist, persist, maintain and regenerate."[15]

Responding to endangered, if not collapsing, ecosystems, these non-West efforts prove humanity can thread the needle of legal standing for the Natural World.

Otherizing the Natural World

The West, by contrast, defends only humans' rights. Almost two decades after Stone wrote, Joel Schwartz questioned the premise of nature as a rights holder: instead of considering the natural rights of persons who have legal standing because they have been harmed, he asked whether nature has the moral agency that rights require.[16] The ethical environmentalism that Stone and others advocated extends morality beyond the human circle to include nature. Schwartz believed this approach to be wrong:

> Ethical environmentalism goes beyond Kantian morality by extending the applicability of the moral law, which no longer applies simply to relations among people, but also to relations between people and all natural objects. This expanded moral law asks people to regard as immoral the preference for human interests over those of animals, vegetables, and minerals. Anthropocentrism—the preference for our

species over others—is held to be no less immoral than the selfish and unfair preference for oneself over other people.[17]

Schwartz argued that human free agency and speech give us moral capacity, and consent is instrumental in having and exercising rights. The social contract or compact formalizes moral capacity. Human beings secure our rights, then, when we give our individual consent to form a sociopolitical body that protects our rights against the actions of others. Since the Natural World can neither "represent nor speak" for itself, Schwartz saw no moral imperative:

> Stone simply assumes that nature, like the other entities that he mentions, can be represented; and even if it can be, he wrongly ignores the question of what entitles anyone to act as nature's representative. Nature cannot consent to being represented; it gives us no sense of how its "rights" are to be secured or who (since it cannot be what) is to secure them.[18]

His words echo *Dred Scott v. Sandford*.[19] Dred Scott—though clearly a human being—had no legal standing. White law treated him as a nonperson object, denied the natural rights that his white, human owner enjoyed. It took a civil war among whites to break their hold on the idea—almost—that owning humans could be sustainable.[20]

For the West, recognizing the Natural World's personhood and rights raises the same issues that *Dred Scott* and *Standing Bear* raised: What view of reality grants a society to take from the Natural World without any thought of the harm that such taking causes? Schwartz's criticism goes to the core of how the West frames its experiences: no other reality matters, except that of humans.

Realizing Schwartz's argument cannot fully hold without qualification, Sandra Postel argues for a water ethic but within Schwartz's framework: human beings, not nature, are best suited to decide what is in nature's best interests. Her notion of human stewardship of the Natural World would involve a colonizing-like balancing act at best:

> Instead of asking how we can further control and manipulate rivers, lakes, and streams to meet our ever-growing demands, we would ask instead how we can best satisfy human needs while accommodating the ecological requirements of freshwater ecosystems. . . . Embedded in this water ethic is a fundamental question: Do rivers and the life within them have a right to water?[21]

She tries to mitigate anthropocentrism's harms without changing the human-centrism that causes them. The Oceti Sakowin Oyate's response to her question is tentative: "Yes, but." We pause because she misses the nub: "Is water a rights holder?" As a people, we addressed this unequivocally in our action against DAPL: Mni Oyate does have rights, including the right to life, because Mni Oyate has personhood.

Western societies and their cultural heirs balk at our stand, though, because of how they see their place in the natural order. When the West engages in its global colonization projects, it Otherizes non-Westernized peoples. Otherizing uses socially constructed differences to claim that nonwhites are inferior, devoid of basic human rights. Colonizers use the construct to rationalize harming others for colonizers' benefit. With whites' hegemony at stake, the West institutionalized society-wide Otherizing that persisted well into our grandparents' and parents' generation: the United States' separate but equal doctrine, South Africa's apartheid, or Europe's anti-Semitism.

Colonization's Otherizing classifies non-Western peoples as nonpersons and therefore non–rights holders. In a colonizer framework, Otherizing implies that they, too, are objects or things no different from the things in nature (recall placing Indigenous Peoples under the U.S. Interior Department's jurisdiction, not the State Department's). Stone's proposal challenged the West, as #NoDAPL did, to examine a core cultural belief. The West's inability to conceptualize the Natural World as little more than its playground has made it difficult for Western-based societies to grasp the Indigenous idea that the Natural World possesses personality. For example, a 1977 Haudenosaunee delegation to Geneva, Switzerland, told the world how Western development had altered the Natural World and that perhaps it was time for the West to rethink its core assumptions about the Natural World:

> Western culture has been horribly exploitative and destructive of the Natural World. Over 140 species of birds and animals were utterly destroyed since the European arrival in the Americas, largely because they were unusable in the eyes of the invaders. The forests were leveled, the waters polluted, the Native people[s] subjected to genocide. The vast herds of herbivores were reduced to mere handfuls, the buffalo nearly became extinct. Western technology and the people who have employed it have been the most amazingly destructive forces in all of human history. Not even the Ice Ages counted as many victims. . . .
>
> The majority of the world does not find its roots in Western culture or traditions. The majority of the world finds its roots in the Natural World, and it is the Natural World, and the traditions of the Natural World, which must prevail if we are to develop truly free and egalitarian societies.[22]

Serving development projects globally, colonizers from the West, including non-West societies who have adopted Western culture, have exploited every "object" or "thing" on Earth without a moral pang. They have targeted the Natural World for Otherizing regardless of the harms that follow. To persist in its course of mass harm and destruction, the West embraces a confounding paradox of anthropocentric thinking—that we can have it both ways. Mni Wiconi shows we cannot have Westernized water and drink it too. Coming to terms with the Natural World without having to change our behavior toward nature is folly of the deadliest kind. If we are to form sustainable relationships with/in the Natural World, then we have to live by the good relative mandate.

More Than Life

Postel observed that the much vaunted, globalized marketplace fails to value the most essential components of life.

> Better pricing and more open markets will assign water a higher value in its economic functions, and breed healthy competition that weeds out wasteful and unproductive uses. But this [marketplace] will not solve the deeper problem. What is needed is a set of guidelines and principles that stops us from chipping away at natural systems until nothing is left of their life-sustaining functions, which the marketplace fails to value adequately, if at all.[23]

Eons before Postel called for a global ethic to value the Natural World's life-sustaining functions rather than to use them for profits, the Oceti Sakowin Oyate lived—and, since our colonization, has struggled to live—by such an ethic. Phil Wambli Nunpa, Sicangu Lakota Treaty Council director, explained that "*Water is alive*: we call it mni wiconi, water is life."[24]

The Oceti Sakowin Oyate acknowledge water as a distinct peoples—Mni Oyate (Water Nation). Of course, to claim that water is alive counters the West's construction of it as an inanimate object of nature. U.S. law concerns water quality in order "to restore and maintain the chemical, physical, and biological integrity of the nation's waters" so that it is fit for human consumption.[25] Water-usage rights are construed as either riparian or by prior appropriation. Water development projects serve flood control, irrigation, or hydroelectricity. All human-centered, these uses of water do not include a view of water as being alive, let alone conceptualizing it as a person possessed of legal standing.

We, by contrast, recognize water as having personhood, independent of humans "giving" that standing or status, because of our *Otokahe Ka Gapi*: the story of First Beginnings or Creation. Through our story, fundamental values shape the Oceti Sakowin Oyate and our relationship with the Natural World.

> Inyan was in the beginning. Inyan began Creation by draining its blood to create. The first Creation was Maka, the Earth. After Maka, another need arose and Inyan drained its blood to address that need for Maka. As this [giving-of-self] process continued, Inyan grew weaker and weaker as its energy continued to flow into each Creation. . . .

Once Creation was complete, Inyan was dry and brittle and scattered all over the world. Today we use the Inyan oyate, the Stone People, in our inipi ceremony. . . . When the stones are brought in, we address them as tunkan oyate ("the oldest Creation Nation"). This [inipi ceremony] reminds us that the stones were in the beginning as Inyan.

Through this story . . . we all come from one source, Inyan. We were all created out of Inyan's blood. To address all Creation as a relative, we use the phrase mitakuye oyas'in, "all my relatives."[26]

Another term our people use to describe our shared Creation with the Natural World and universe is wakan. "Wa" is anything that is something, and that something possesses force-energy; "kan" describes a vein or channel from which something—such as force or energy—flows. Our Haudenosaunee relatives recognize a similar force-energy that they call orenda. For them, it is present in all natural presences, and these presences are fully capable of exerting it. This force-energy—wakan—and its power to flow are evident in the First Beginning when Inyan "opened all of his veins and his blood left him, and Inyan saw that his powers went from him in the blood and formed the edge of Maka."[27] From Inyan's unselfish act of giving, he became the stones or rocks, that is, the dry and brittle material we encounter in nature. Significantly, how his blood transformed into the Mni Oyate, which then flowed around Maka, is how we come to know water as our relative.

In the Oceti Sakowin Oyate's world view, "ni," a root term found throughout D/L/Nakota vocabulary, expresses aliveness. Mni (water), Wiconi (life), Wicozanni (health), Woniya (life-breath), Inipi (steam purification), and Niya (an infant's first vital breath) together convey that water manifests life in our consciousness daily. For instance, George Sword shared his insight about the Inipi ceremony, illustrating how the ceremony not only reenacts the First Beginnings—when Inyan released a force-energy that flowed, enveloping Maka and imparting life to the Water Nation—but also binds the Mni Oyate and the Oceti Sakowin Oyate as intimate relatives.

The white people call it a sweat lodge. The Lakotas do not understand it so. The Lakota think of it as a lodge to make the body strong and pure. They call it *initi*. . . . The *ni* of a Lakota is that which he breathes into his body and it goes all through it and keeps it alive.

The spirit of the water is good for the *ni* and it will make it strong. Anything hot will make the spirit of water free and it goes upward. . . . An *initi* is made close so that it will hold the spirit of the water. Then one in it [the initi] can breathe it [the Mni Oyate] into the body. It [the Mni Oyate] will then make the *ni* strong, and they will cleanse all in the body. They wash it and it comes out on the skin like *te mini* [sic]. *Te mini* [sic] is sweat. It is the water on the body. A Lakota does not *inipi* to make the water on the body. He does it to wash the inside of the body.

When a Lakota says *ni*, or *ini*, or *inipi*, or *initi*, he does not think about sweat. He thinks about making his *ni* strong so that it will purify him.[28]

Acknowledging that water has its own agency, which is personhood's attribute, causes Westernized folks to raise their eyebrows, as perhaps James Walker did when Sword explained this to him over a century ago. Yet recent water studies support Sword's claim.

Dr. Masaru Emoto's water research challenges, if not defies, Western views about the Natural World as spiritless, inanimate objects. On one level, human bodies, on average, contain between 60 and 70 percent water by weight, but 99 percent of the molecules throughout the human body have water as a primary constituent. Therefore, normal body functions have a direct relationship with water. Dehydration reminds us of this relationship. But water has other qualities that suggest a much greater relational role than the West has imagined.

Studies of mindfulness, however controversial, suggest that water responds qualitatively to intentionality. For example, an apple is about 80 percent water. Positive intentionality (good words and good thoughts) toward one half of an apple and negative intentionality (bad words and bad thoughts) toward the other half produce difference responses: the first half stays healthy, the second rots.[29]

Since the human body, like an apple, is mostly water, both Sword and Emoto experienced water's responsiveness to intentions. Sword's observations that water has a spirit came from his ceremonial experiences and from our Creation story, while Emoto used technology to test what we already knew about the Mni Oyate. In both cases, intentionality provided the conduit in water's relationship with humanity. For example, one of Emoto's experiments subjected water in various containers to either harsh or euphonious music, offensive or nurturing language (either written or verbal), and negative or positive thoughts. He then froze the water to examine its crystalline structure. Was there any difference between water that had been intentionally treated well or badly? The results showed that water responds to intentions and reflects their qualities.

All the classical music that we exposed the water to resulted in well-formed crystals with distinct characteristics. In contrast, the water exposed to violent heavy metal music resulted in fragmented and malformed crystals at best.

But our experiment didn't stop there. We next thought about what would happen if we wrote words or phrases like "Thank you" and "Fool" on pieces of paper, and wrapped the paper around the bottles of water with the words facing in. . . .

Water exposed to "Thank you" formed beautiful hexagonal crystals, but water exposed to the word "Fool" produced crystals similar to the water exposed to heavy-metal music, malformed and fragmented.[30]

Emoto's results are no surprise to the Oceti Sakowin Oyate and other Indigenous Peoples. From both Sword and Emoto, we can emotionally and intuitively begin to understand the relationship between these two peoples: humans and water. Sword described water's direct, salutary effect on us as extremely positive: water makes the Oceti Sakowin Oyate spiritually and physically strong from within, because love and gratitude are the two emotions we most often express in our lifeway through our prayers and songs. Hence, we integrate water's effect when we either breathe its vapor during an inipi ceremony or drink it. But the Mni Oyate also possesses another quality whose implication is significant: that water has memory.

In 1988, Jacques Benveniste (1935–2004), an immunologist from France, articulated a theory of water memory. Like Emoto's water studies and the Oceti Sakowin Oyate's understanding that water is alive, his theory remains controversial in the West. The theory states that water records, retains, and transmits information about its environment. Benveniste's theory explains that water molecules, through ionic attraction to one another, form closed structures—"structured memory." These structures have the capacity to record and store the electromagnetic signature, which means information about whatever object (or event) they come in contact with. Moreover, because the signature is electromagnetic, dilution does not affect the information's integrity. Hence, when we consume water in any form, water transmits to us the information it holds. With every drink or breath of water vapor, the Mni Oyate and human beings are bidirectionally communicating, however unaware we may be that this two-way communication is going on.

The West continues to struggle metaphysically with what Indigenous Peoples have embraced since time immemorial, namely, the Natural World has personality and personhood, and nature's peoples are capable of having agency in relationships, such as mirroring emotions and even hashing things out. This deeper awareness of who the peoples of the Natural World are shows why Oceti Sakowin Oyate's action against DAPL is of a different order altogether. It comes from a far deeper understanding, from how we understand reality and the world we inhabit. As I explained in "We Are Blood Relatives":

> That water is alive—and therefore possesses personality or personhood—defines our cultural response to DAPL. Our definition challenges the West's anthropocentrism, which accords person/peoplehood only to humans. Hence the Western way of life would both deny and defy water as having personhood. Yet the United States can arbitrarily recognize fictional entities like corporations as legal persons, while denying personhood to humans who become subject to the Thirteenth Amendment's slavery exception.
>
> The Mni Oyate, then, is not unlike Indigenous peoples from Africa who, for 245 years in America, were racially constructed, socially viewed, institutionally handled, and economically exploited in the service of Western development. Similarly

Western development frames water as a resource and as property: humans can own water and the [purported] right to harm water.

By contrast, our relationship with water is framed not as possessing rights over water but as protecting the rights of water. The Oceti Sakowin Oyate's original set of instructions requires us to be good relatives to the natural world. "What responsible conduct does water expect from us?" is a development question that we take seriously, however alien the question is to ETP and those behind the DAPL project.

This culture-based understanding motivates the Oceti Sakowin Oyate to challenge the DAPL. How could it not? . . . During ceremonies such as the Sun Dance, individuals release blood from their bodies—as Inyan did at Creation—so that all life may continue on Earth. By weight, the human body is at least half water, making the Oceti Sakowin Oyate a blood relative of Mni Oyate. We are members of the Water Nation.[31]

Standing with Mni Oyate

When the Oceti Sakowin Oyate met modernity at Standing Rock, both the media (mainstream and social) and the West, responding as it did with state violence (militarized police and corporate security), missed the motivating core of our action. The media labeled our challenge to DAPL as environmental justice—a label that was not altogether incorrect. After all, ETP relocated DAPL just north of the Standing Rock Reservation after whites in Bismarck had objected to the pipeline as well, since it had originally been planned to cross the Mni Sose just north of their city. Clean water is an environmental concern, and oil spills contaminate water. But when the Oceti Sakowin Oyate argued precisely as the whites did about the pipeline's dangers, a militarized reaction rather than a route change was the response. Everyone knows why. Whenever a modern state pursues development, Native Peoples are expendable: our lives and losses are valued less than those of whites.

Unpacking the militarized police reaction to the Spirit Camp is complicated. One piece is the history of U.S. violence against us. Ever since 1851, Americans have waged war against the Oceti Sakowin Oyate, requiring us to fight back in self-defense. We successfully outfought the U.S. military in our homeland during the latter half of the nineteenth century, then again at Wounded Knee in spring 1973, and most recently in the latter part of 2016 when the Mni Wiconi call gained international traction.

Another piece is our sovereignty and U.S. treaties with us. When North Dakota and ETP managed through the DAPL decision-making process to marginalize a sovereign peoples' voice, the Oceti Sakowin Oyate asserted its sovereignty. The Americans' 1851 and 1868 Fort Laramie Treaties recognize our national boundaries, which DAPL crosses. But because of Americans' colonization and illegal occupation of our homelands, Americans willfully ignore their own treaties and trample on human, if not nature's, rights to life for the sake of Western development.

ETP's narrative about its decision-making process and the "public hearings" it held on DAPL invoked a process that did not include but marginalized our voices. Again, from "We Are Blood Relatives":

> In its August 2016 progress report almost two years later, ETP stated the Dakota Access "has held 154 meetings with local elected officials and community organizations" and held "five public Open House meetings in North Dakota." To the uninitiated, Dakota Access comes across as a responsible corporate neighbor. What the progress report failed to mention, however, is that Indigenous peoples, such the Hunkpapa Titunwan (Standing Rock Sioux Tribe), were not included in these meetings. In their failure to understand that Indigenous peoples have a nation-to-nation relationship with the United States, Dakota Access and the U.S. Army Corps of Engineers put Indigenous peoples in the position of having to react to the Corps' environment assessment after the fact.
>
> While we must analyze how U.S. colonization marginalizes our voices procedurally, the marginalization we experienced with DAPL is not the reason we take the stand we do. The Oceti Sakowin Oyate's and its allies' resistance to DAPL aims to protect water from harm.[32]

Controlling the national DAPL narrative was crucial for ETP, North Dakota, and other pro-DAPL stakeholders, for example, Wells Fargo, Royal Bank of Canada, and investors. Mainstream, corporate media colluded with state and corporate security forces to intentionally mislabel the NoDAPL action as violent and to imply that individuals at the camps were violent too, even implying that in our own homeland, we are terrorists. State and corporate forces used these insinuations to rationalize their militarized violence to shut down the Mni Wiconi action. But social media exposed the state and corporate lie. Social media recordings and other alternative media outlets at the Sacred Stone and Spirit Camps presented nonviolent, prayerful Water Protectors subjected to state/corporate intimidation and violence.

By complicating the corporate narrative, social media helped globalize NoDAPL and decentered state and corporate violence. Social media showed families, groups, and individuals arriving with supplies—food, water, medical, and other humanitarian items needed—from communities and organizations; they showed welcoming ceremonies when Indigenous nations arrived and posted their national flags to signify international solidarity; they showed the outpouring of goodwill, friendship, healing, and ceremonies at the camps; and they showed Indigenous leaders engaged in nonviolent decolonizing actions, even under the threat of state violence and incarceration. The images that went out over social media and other alternative news outlets left the West's institutions bewildered.

In contrast to the state's weaponized response, Indigenous Peoples conducted daily water ceremonies for the Mni Oyate throughout the camps. Our peoples showed a watching world that contrary to state and corporate press conferences and releases that framed the Mni Wiconi action as near terrorism, the Water Protectors engaged in prayerful relationships and peaceful activities among themselves and with the Mni Oyate. They modeled human beings who value water intrinsically, rather than as another resource to exploit. Water memory theory advises us to make peace with our relative, water—to recognize water as a legal person who is alive, who has agency and memory, and who holds legal standing.

> Structural memory enables water to take an impression [or imprint] of anything that happens around it, and to connect all living systems together. And each one of us is a link in an endless chain of information transmission. But, in addition, each of us is also a source of information. Every one of our actions, a thought, an emotion, an uttered word separates from us and becomes part of the overall—and ergo—information environment.
>
> Informational dirt is poisoning the water, accumulating layer by layer in its memory. If that process were to continue endlessly, the water could lose its mind.
>
> But [water] is endowed with a self-cleansing capacity. This occurs at the moment of phase transition, when it vaporizes and then condenses and falls as rain, or when it freezes and then melts. Shaking off the informational grime, water preserves its basic structure. That is the program for life.[33]

What is the Mni Oyate remembering of the humans at Standing Rock, and what stories will Water People transmit as they flow around the planet? What memories of Standing Rock will water eventually carry through our bodies too? We can only ponder. State militarized law enforcement and hired private, corporate security personnel stood against Water Protectors across an erected barrier, such as we see in fear-based societies uncertain of their legitimacy. They even used water to harm us with their water cannons, deployed in subfreezing temperatures. Threatening or engaging in violence is how humans—the presumed beings of moral agency—respond to nonviolent action in defense of the Natural World. The contrast between modernity's violence and traditional peacemaking could not have been more stark and clear to the Mni Oyate. Perhaps the Mni Oyate witnessed humans on the cusp of an existential epiphany.

Beyond political outcomes, the NoDAPL action created a watershed moment in human consciousness—maybe water appreciates puns too. Indigenous Peoples sheared away how the West thinks about the Natural World to reveal water as living peoples. Indeed, they are our relatives and we theirs. Our Original Instructions give us the responsibility to be in a good way with each other. That good way includes aiding the Water People when they are threatened. For the Oceti Sakowin Oyate and our allies, serving as water's protectors was and remains the right course, the one that matters most. Within our bodies, being a good relative is how we want the Mni Oyate to remember us.

NOTES

1. Edward Valandra, "We Are Blood Relatives: No to the DAPL," in "Standing Rock, #NoDAPL, and Mni Wiconi," Hot Spots, *Cultural Anthropology* website, December 22, 2016, http://www.culanth.org.

2. Richard Kluger in *Simple Justice* (New York: Alfred A. Knopf, 1976) noted that "Americans more than most people tend to believe that progress must be upward linear, steadily and unbrokenly upward, or it is not progress at all" (774).

3. See Elizabeth Kolbert's *The Sixth Extinction: An Unnatural History* (New York: Picador, 2014).

4. Sumner Welles, "The English Speaking Democracies," in *Co-operation between Canada and the United States in the Search for World Peace: A Series of Lectures* (Winnipeg: J. W. Dafoe Foundation, 1946), 20–21. Emphases mine.

5 Welles, "The English Speaking Democracies," 5.

6. Welles, "The English Speaking Democracies," 22–23.

7. Alice Matthews, a Malaysian citizen, in September 2016 questioned President Obama about the Dakota Access Pipeline during a town hall youth conference in Laos. See "President Barack Obama on #NoDAPL and Dakota Access Pipeline," YouTube, September 8, 2016, https://www.youtube.com.

8. In May 2016 Canada fully supported, without qualification, the declaration. Australia, New Zealand, and the United States have officially supported the declaration with qualifications.

9. *Sierra Club v. Morton*, 405 U.S. 727 (1972).

10. Mary Kathryn Nagle, "Standing Bear v. Crook: The Case For Equality under Waaxe's Law," *Creighton Law Review* 45 (2012): 458.

11. Christopher Stone, "Should Trees Have Standing?—Toward Legal Rights for Natural Objects," *Southern California Law Review* 45, no. 450 (1972): 8–9.

12. The Indian-as-mascot apologists retort that other sports teams have human mascots (Minnesota Vikings, Tampa Bay Buccaneers, New England Patriots, etc.). However, these mascots focus on an activity and are not racially objectifying. Anyone can be a pirate, patriot, saint, etc., but not everyone can be Native. See Living Justice Press's "Convention Style Sheet for Native Subject-Matters," http://www.livingjusticepress.org/.

13. Stone, "Should Trees Have Standing?" 44.

14. Stone, "Should Trees Have Standing?" 45.

15. *Time Inc.*, "The Legal Rights of Nature," The Brief, 2017, http://time.com/4728311/the-legal-rights-of-nature/.

16. The inalienable rights outlined in the whites' 1776 Declaration of Independence did not apply to the Indigenous peoples from the African continent, who became

slaves, and North American continent, or to anyone who was not white, a male, propertied, Christian, and heterosexual.

17. Joel Schwartz, "The Rights of Nature and the Death of God," *Public Interest* 97 (1989): 5.

18. Schwartz, "The Rights of Nature and the Death of God," 6.

19. *Dred Scott v. Sandford*, 60 U.S. 393 (1856).

20. The much-heralded Thirteenth Amendment carves out an exception to involuntary servitude.

21. Sandra Postel, "The Missing Piece: A Water Ethic," *The American Prospect* 19, no. 6 (2008): A15.

22. Akewsasne Notes, *Basic Call to Consciousness*, rev. ed. (Summertown, Tenn.: Native Voices, 1981), 76–77.

23. Postel, "The Missing Piece," A14.

24. Brave Heart Society video, https://www.facebook.com/, October 13, 2016. Emphasis mine.

25. 33 U.S.C §§ 1251 et seq.

26. Albert White Hat Sr., *Reading and Writing the Lakota Language* (Salt Lake City: University of Utah Press, 1999), 27–28.

27. Tom Simms, *Otokahekagapi (First Beginnings): Sioux Creation Story* (Chamberlin, S.Dak.: Tipi Press, 1987), 11.

28. George Sword, "*Ni, Ini,* and *Initi*," in *Lakota Belief and Ritual* (Lincoln: University of Nebraska Press, 1991), 100.

29. Valandra, "We Are Blood Relatives."

30. Masaru Emoto, *The Hidden Messages in Water* (Hillsboro, Ore.: Beyond Words Publishing, 2004), xxiv–xxv.

31. Valandra, "We Are Blood Relatives."

32. Valandra, "We Are Blood Relatives."

33. "Structured Water: Future of Medicine?," part 8 of 8, YouTube, November 7, 2009, https://www.youtube.com.

9

THE GREAT SIOUX NATION AND THE RESISTANCE TO COLONIAL LAND GRABBING

Roxanne Dunbar-Ortiz

This excerpt from An Indigenous Peoples' History of the United States
*unpacks the origin of the nineteenth-century treaties and colonial land
grabbing that have repeatedly denied the Sioux the right to their land.*

The first international relationship between the Sioux Nation and the U.S. government was established in 1805 with a treaty of peace and friendship two years after the United States acquired the Louisiana Territory, which included the Sioux Nation among many other Indigenous nations.[1] Other such treaties followed in 1815 and 1825. These peace treaties had no immediate effect on Sioux political autonomy or territory. By 1834, competition in the fur trade, with the market dominated by the Rocky Mountain Fur Company, led the Oglala Sioux to move away from the upper Missouri to the upper Platte near Fort Laramie. By 1846, seven thousand Sioux had moved south. Thomas Fitzpatrick, the Indian agent in 1846, recommended that the United States purchase land to establish a fort, which became Fort Laramie. "My opinion," Fitzpatrick wrote, "is that a post at, or in the vicinity of Laramie is much wanted, it would be nearly in the center of the buffalo range, where all the formidable Indian tribes are fast approaching, and near where there will eventually be a struggle for the ascendancy [in the fur trade]."[2] Fitzpatrick believed that a garrison of at least three hundred soldiers would be necessary to keep the Indians under control.

Although the Sioux and the United States redefined their relationship in the Fort Laramie Treaty of 1851, this was followed by a decade of war between the two parties, ending with the Peace Treaty of Fort Laramie in 1868. Both of these treaties, though not reducing Sioux political sovereignty, ceded large parts of Sioux territory by establishing mutually recognized boundaries, and the Sioux granted concessions to the United States that gave legal color to the Sioux's increasing economic dependency on the United States and its economy. During the half century

"Warrior by Choice." Photograph by Michelle Latimer.

before the 1851 treaty, the Sioux had been gradually enveloped in the fur trade and had become dependent on horses and European-manufactured guns, ammunition, iron cookware, tools, textiles, and other items of trade that replaced their traditional crafts. On the plains the Sioux gradually abandoned farming and turned entirely to bison hunting for their subsistence and for trade. This increased dependency on the buffalo in turn brought deeper dependency on guns and ammunition that had to be purchased with more hides, creating the vicious circle that characterized modern colonialism. With the balance of power tipped by midcentury, U.S. traders and the military exerted pressure on the Sioux for land cessions and rights of way as the buffalo population decreased. The hardships for the Sioux caused by constant attacks on their villages, forced movement, and resultant disease and starvation took a toll on their strength to resist domination. They entered into the 1868 treaty with the United States on strong terms from a military standpoint—the Sioux remained an effective guerrilla fighting force through the 1880s, never defeated by the U.S. Army—but their dependency on buffalo and on trade allowed for escalated federal control when buffalo were purposely exterminated by the army between 1870 and 1876. After that the Sioux were fighting for survival.

Economic dependency on buffalo and trade was replaced with survival dependency on the U.S. government for rations and commodities guaranteed in the 1868 treaty. The agreement stipulated that "no treaty for the cession of any portion or part of the reservation herein described which may be held in common shall be of any validation or force against the said Indians, unless executed and signed by at least three fourths of all the adult male Indians."[3] Nevertheless, in 1876, with no such validation, and with the discovery of gold by Custer's Seventh Cavalry, the U.S.

government seized the Black Hills—Paha Sapa—a large, resource-rich portion of the treaty-guaranteed Sioux territory, the center of the Great Sioux Nation, a religious shrine and sanctuary. When the Sioux surrendered after the wars of 1876–77, they lost not only the Black Hills but also the Powder River country. The next U.S. move was to change the western boundary of the Sioux Nation, whose territory, though atrophied from its original, was a contiguous block. By 1877, after the army drove the Sioux out of Nebraska, all that was left was a block between the 103rd meridian and the Missouri, thirty-five thousand square miles of land the United States had designated as Dakota Territory (the next step toward statehood, in this case the states of North and South Dakota). The first of several waves of northern European immigrants now poured into eastern Dakota Territory, pressing against the Missouri River boundary of the Sioux. At the Anglo-American settlement of Bismarck on the Missouri, the westward-pushing Northern Pacific Railroad was blocked by the reservation. Settlers bound for Montana and the Pacific Northwest called for trails to be blazed and defended across the reservation. Promoters who wanted cheap land to sell at high prices to immigrants schemed to break up the reservation. Except for the Sioux units that continued to fight, the Sioux people were unarmed, had no horses, and were unable even to feed and clothe themselves, dependent upon government rations.

Next came allotment. Before the Dawes Act was even implemented, a government commission arrived in Sioux territory from Washington, D.C., in 1888 with a proposal to reduce the Sioux Nation to six small reservations, a scheme that would leave nine million acres open for Euro-American settlement. The commission found it impossible to obtain signatures of the required three-fourths of the nation as required under the 1868 treaty, and so returned to Washington with a recommendation that the government ignore the treaty and take the land without Sioux consent. The only means to accomplish that goal was legislation, Congress having relieved the government of the obligation to negotiate a treaty. Congress commissioned General George Crook to head a delegation to try again, this time with an offer of $1.50 per acre. In a series of manipulations and dealings with leaders whose people were now starving, the commission garnered the needed signatures. The Great Sioux Nation was broken into small islands soon surrounded on all sides by European immigrants, with much of the reservation land a checkerboard with settlers on allotments or leased land.[4] Creating these isolated reservations broke the historical relationships between clans and communities of the Sioux Nation and opened areas where Europeans settled. It also allowed the Bureau of Indian Affairs to exercise tighter control, buttressed by the bureau's boarding school system. The Sun Dance, the annual ceremony that had brought Sioux together and reinforced national unity, was outlawed, along with other religious ceremonies. Despite the Sioux people's weak position under late nineteenth-century colonial domination, they managed to begin building a modest cattle-ranching business to replace their former bison-hunting economy. In 1903, the U.S. Supreme Court ruled, in *Lone*

Wolf v. Hitchcock, that a March 3, 1871, appropriations rider was constitutional and that Congress had "plenary" power to manage Indian property. The Office of Indian Affairs could thus dispose of Indian lands and resources regardless of the terms of previous treaty provisions. Legislation followed that opened the reservations to settlement through leasing and even sale of allotments taken out of trust. Nearly all prime grazing lands came to be occupied by non-Indian ranchers by the 1920s.

By the time of the New Deal–Collier era and nullification Indian land allotment under the Indian Reorganization Act, non-Indians outnumbered Indians on the Sioux reservations three to one. However, the drought of the mid- to late 1930s drove many settler ranchers off Sioux land, and the Sioux purchased some of that land, which had been theirs. However, "tribal governments" imposed in the wake of the Indian Reorganization Act proved particularly harmful and divisive for the Sioux.[5] Concerning this measure, the late Mathew King, elder traditional historian of the Oglala Sioux (Pine Ridge), observed: "The Bureau of Indian Affairs drew up the constitution and by-laws of this organization with the Indian Reorganization Act of 1934. This was the introduction of home rule. . . . The traditional people still hang on to their Treaty, for we are a sovereign nation. We have our own government."[6] "Home rule," or neocolonialism, proved a short-lived policy, however, for in the early 1950s the United States developed its termination policy, with legislation ordering gradual eradication of every reservation and even the tribal governments.[7] At the time of termination and relocation, per capita annual income on the Sioux reservations stood at $355, while that in nearby South Dakota towns was $2,500. Despite these circumstances, in pursuing its termination policy, the Bureau of Indian Affairs advocated the reduction of services and introduced its program to relocate Indians to urban industrial centers, with a high percentage of Sioux moving to San Francisco and Denver in search of jobs.[8]

Mathew King has described the United States throughout its history as alternating between a "peace" policy and a "war" policy in its relations with Indigenous nations and communities, saying that these pendulum swings coincided with the strength and weakness of Native resistance. Between the alternatives of extermination and termination (war policies) and preservation (peace policy), King argued, were interim periods characterized by benign neglect and assimilation. With organized Indigenous resistance to war programs and policies, concessions are granted. When pressure lightens, new schemes are developed to separate Indians from their land, resources, and cultures. Scholars, politicians, policymakers, and the media rarely term U.S. policy toward Indigenous peoples as colonialism. King, however, believed that his people's country had been a colony of the United States since 1890.

The logical progression of modern colonialism begins with economic penetration and graduates to a sphere of influence, then to protectorate status or indirect control, military occupation, and finally annexation. This corresponds to the process experienced by the Sioux people in relation to the United States. The economic penetration of fur traders brought the Sioux within the U.S. sphere of influence. The transformation of Fort Laramie from a trading post, the center of Sioux trade, to a U.S. Army outpost in the mid-nineteenth century indicates the integral relationship between trade and colonial control. Growing protectorate status established through treaties culminated in the 1868 Sioux treaty, followed by military occupation achieved by extreme exemplary violence, such as at Wounded Knee in 1890, and finally dependency. Annexation by the United States is marked symbolically by the imposition of U.S. citizenship on the Sioux (and most other Indians) in 1924. Mathew King and other traditional Sioux saw the siege of Wounded Knee in 1973 as a turning point, although the violent backlash that followed was harsh.

Two decades of collective Indigenous resistance culminating at Wounded Knee in 1973 defeated the 1950s federal termination policy. Yet proponents of the disappearance of Indigenous nations seem never to tire of trying. Another move toward termination developed in 1977 with dozens of congressional bills to abrogate all Indian treaties and terminate all Indian governments and trust territories. Indigenous resistance defeated those initiatives as well, with another caravan across the country. Like colonized peoples elsewhere in the world, the Sioux have been involved in decolonization efforts since the mid-twentieth century. Wounded Knee in 1973 was part of this struggle, as was their involvement in UN committees and international forums.[9] However, in the early twenty-first century, free-market fundamentalist economists and politicians identified the communally owned Indigenous reservation lands as an asset to be exploited and, under the guise of helping to end Indigenous poverty on those reservations, call for doing away with them—a new extermination and termination initiative.

NOTES

1. Miguel Alfonso Martínez, *Human Rights of Indigenous Peoples: Study on Treaties, Agreements and Other Constructive Arrangements between States and Indigenous Populations. Final Report*, UN Document E/CN.4/Sub.2/1999/20, June 22, 1999. See also Erica-Irene A. Daes, *Human Rights of Indigenous Peoples: Report of the Working Group on Indigenous Populations on Its Seventeenth Session (Geneva, 26–30 July 1999)*, UN Document E/CN.4/Sub.2/1999/19, August 12, 1999.

2. Robert A. Trennert, *Alternative to Extinction: Federal Indian Policy and the Beginnings of the Reservation System, 1846–51* (Philadelphia: Temple University Press, 1975), 166.

3. Article XII, 1868 Ft. Laramie Treaty, in Roxanne Dunbar-Ortiz, *The Great Sioux Nation: Sitting in Judgment on America* (1977; repr. Lincoln: University of Nebraska Press, 2013), 99.

4. Testimony of Pat McLaughlin, then chairman of the Standing Rock Sioux government, Fort Yates, North Dakota (May 8, 1976), at hearings of the American Indian Policy Review Commission, established by Congress in the act of January 3, 1975.

5. See Kenneth R. Philip, *John Collier's Crusade for Indian Reform, 1920–1954* (Tucson: University of Arizona Press, 1977).

6. Matthew King quoted in Dunbar-Ortiz, *The Great Sioux Nation*, 156.

7. For a lucid discussion of neocolonialism in relation to American Indians and the reservation system, see Joseph Jorgensen, *Sun Dance Religion: Power for the Powerless* (Chicago: University of Chicago Press, 1977), 89–146.

8. There is continuous migration from reservations to cities and border towns and back to the reservations, so that half the Indian population at any time is away from the reservation. Generally, however, relocation is not permanent and resembles migratory labor more than permanent relocation. This conclusion is based on my personal observations and on unpublished studies of the Indigenous populations in the San Francisco Bay area and Los Angeles.

9. The American Indian Movement convened a meeting in June 1974 that founded the International Indian Treaty Council (IITC), receiving consultative status in the UN Economic and Social Council (ECOSOC) in February 1977. The IITC participated in the UN Conference on Desertification in Buenos Aires, March 1977, and made presentations to the UN Human Rights Commission in August 1977 and in February and August 1978. It also led the organizing for the Non-Governmental Organizations (NGOs) Conference on Indigenous Peoples of the Americas, held at UN headquarters in Geneva, Switzerland, in September 1977; participated in the World Conference on Racism in Basel, Switzerland, in May 1978; and participated in establishing the UN Working Group on Indigenous Populations, the UN Permanent Forum on Indigenous Issues, and the 2007 UN Declaration on the Rights of Indigenous Peoples. See Walter R. Echo-Hawk, *In the Light of Justice: The Rise of Human Rights in Native America and the UN Declaration on the Rights of Indigenous Peoples* (Golden, Colo.: Fulcrum, 2013); Vine Deloria Jr., *Behind the Trail of Broken Treaties: An Indian Declaration of Independence* (1974; repr. Austin: University of Texas Press, 1985); Roxanne Dunbar-Ortiz, Dalee Sambo Dorough, Gudmundur Alfredsson, Lee Swepston, and Peter Wille, eds., *Indigenous Peoples' Rights in International Law: Emergence and Application* (Kautokeino, Norway: Gáldu; Copenhagen: IWGIA, 2015).

10

THE SUPREME LAW OF THE LAND
STANDING ROCK AND THE DAKOTA ACCESS PIPELINE

Jeffrey Ostler and Nick Estes

This revised essay was originally published in Indian
Country Today Media Network *on January 16, 2017.*

On December 4, 2016, opponents of the Dakota Access Pipeline (DAPL) won a
major victory when the Army Corps of Engineers announced it would not grant
an easement for the pipeline to be built under Lake Oahe on the Missouri River.
The Water Protectors who heroically resisted the pipeline for months celebrated
the decision, but realized that the corps' decision did not mean the Black Snake was
dead. The corps stated that it would pursue further review and analysis through
an Environmental Impact Statement, and it could still grant an easement at some
future date.

Donald Trump's election only enhanced the sense that the fight is not won.
Not only has Trump held financial interest in the pipeline (and likely still does),
he is a friend of the fossil-fuel industry and has never shown respect for American Indian nations.

Pipeline advocates have challenged the Standing Rock Sioux Tribe's contention that the pipeline is being constructed across lands recognized by the United
States as Sioux territory in the 1851 Fort Laramie Treaty. Just days after the corps'
decision not to grant an easement, outgoing North Dakota governor Jack Dalrymple wrote an op-ed piece stating that "the pipeline's permitted route never crosses
tribal land. Those opponents who cite the 1851 Treaty of Ft. Laramie to dispute
who owns the lands conveniently ignore the later treaty of 1868."[1] It is worth examining these claims in detail.

A close look at the record shows that Standing Rock and the Sioux Nation did
not cede the 1851 treaty lands. Furthermore, Standing Rock retains water rights
from the 1851 treaty and subsequent treaties. These water rights give the tribe
jurisdiction over the Missouri River at the point of DAPL's proposed crossing.

"Stolen Land." Photograph by Nick Estes.

There is no question about the accuracy of Standing Rock's contention that the pipeline is being constructed across lands recognized as Sioux territory under the 1851 treaty. That treaty stated that the northern boundary for Sioux territory was at the Heart River, north of the DAPL route. At first glance, it may seem as though the Sioux ceded these lands under the 1868 treaty. Article 2 of the 1868 treaty established a "permanent reservation" for the Sioux with a northern boundary at the current border between the states of North and South Dakota, in other words, south of the DAPL route.[2] In 1978, however, the Indian Claims Commission (ICC) reviewed the 1868 treaty negotiations and concluded that "the Indians cannot have regarded the 1868 Treaty as a treaty of cession. No-where in the history leading up to the treaty negotiations themselves is there any indication that the United States was seeking a land cession or that the Sioux were willing to consent to one."[3] The famous Jesuit missionary Father Pierre-Jean De Smet, acting as an unofficial liaison for the commissioners, assured Lakotas and Dakotas at the time that the treaty provided them with many benefits "without the least remuneration or cession of lands on their part."[4] Without this assurance, they would not have signed.

As of this date, the majority of the Sioux tribes, including the Standing Rock Sioux, have rejected the ICC's decision to award monetary compensation for lands north of the permanent reservation established under the 1868 treaty. The Sioux tribes have also rejected monetary compensation for the theft of their sacred Black Hills. After a military expedition commanded by George Armstrong Custer discovered gold in the Black Hills in 1874, the United States coerced a minority of Sioux chiefs and headmen into signing an agreement in 1876 that ceded the Black Hills along with unceded lands outside the 1868 treaty's permanent reservation. But the 1876 agreement violated a provision in the 1868 treaty that any future land cession must "be signed by at least three-fourths of all the adult male" tribal members. After decades of litigation, the ICC ruled in 1974 that the 1876 agreement was an unconstitutional seizure under the Fifth Amendment. In 1980, the U.S. Supreme Court upheld the ICC's decision, observing: "a more ripe and rank case of dishonorable dealing will never, in all probability, be found in our history."[5] Although the Supreme Court's decision focused on the illegal taking of the Black Hills, it reinforced a growing legal recognition that the United States had unjustly taken Sioux lands.

Under U.S. law, the federal government does not have authority to return lands illegally taken, and so the courts remedied the taking of lands outside the 1868 treaty's permanent reservation and the Black Hills by awarding monetary compensation. The Sioux Nation, however, has consistently rejected monetary compensation for the stolen lands and has instead argued for the return of the majority of Black Hills lands that are under federal ownership. (Private property would remain in private hands.) Although Standing Rock would have a legitimate moral claim to lands south of the Heart River—across which DAPL is being constructed—the tribe is not arguing for the return of those lands. Nonetheless, the tribe's position that the pipeline is being built across 1851 treaty lands and that these lands have never been legitimately ceded is historically accurate and legally sound.

Standing Rock has strongly opposed the pipeline's current route since 2014, arguing that DAPL crossing the Missouri River would negatively impact the tribe's water supply and violate its water rights. Once again, the tribe's position is supported by treaties now codified within Sioux Nation tribal constitutions. The 1851 treaty described Sioux territory as extending as far east as the Missouri River, a boundary designated by Article 2 of the 1868 treaty as the "low-water mark" on the river's east bank. The Standing Rock constitution, however, delineates reservation boundaries and jurisdiction according to the 1889 Sioux Agreement. Section 3 of the agreement puts Standing Rock's eastern frontier as "beginning at a point in the center of the main channel of the Missouri River, opposite the mouth of the Cannon Ball River," a location just south of the larger antipipeline encampment.[6] Both the encampment and the DAPL Missouri River crossing site are technically outside reservation limits, but they are still on unceded treaty lands.

The Standing Rock constitution was drafted with incredible foresight in order to protect tribal water; it reserves jurisdiction over "all rights-of-way, waterways, watercourses[,] and streams running through any part of the Reservation."[7] In spite of this, just months after the constitution's adoption in 1959, the corps completed construction of the Oahe Dam. As a result, fifty-six thousand acres of Standing Rock river lands were flooded and destroyed, hundreds of families dislocated, and the corps assumed primary jurisdiction over the Missouri River and its shoreline without Standing Rock's consent. Congress authorized Oahe Dam under the 1944 Flood Control Act (alternatively known as the Pick-Sloan Plan), which also authorized the construction of five more dams on the Missouri's main stem, all disproportionately flooding Native lands. Pick-Sloan dams set into motion what the late Standing Rock Sioux scholar Vine Deloria Jr. characterized as "the single most destructive act ever perpetrated on any tribe by the United States."[8] In total, 550 square miles of Native lands (half the size of Rhode Island) were destroyed, and more than nine hundred Native families were dislocated. The Sioux were deracinated—violently uprooted—from their river.

Did the corps overstep its authority? Certainly, it did. The Flood Control Act only authorized the corps to construct dams—*not* to expunge tribal jurisdiction. Its less-than-precise language in Section 4 opened the river for "public use" and "recreational purposes." It did not strip any tribe of its authority or jurisdiction over the Missouri River. Still, the corps condemned lands under "eminent domain," and Congress awarded compensation in the 1958 Standing Rock Sioux Tribe Act. Yet neither the Flood Control Act that took the land nor the Standing Rock Sioux Tribe Act that awarded compensation for taking the land explicitly extinguished tribal jurisdiction; and neither authorized or provided any compensation for the corps taking the river itself from the tribes.

The Sioux Nation has since contended that the Missouri River and its shoreline were never legally ceded, and they are right. The corps altering the flow of the river contravenes a 1908 Supreme Court decision known as the Winters Doctrine. The doctrine holds that however diminished current reservation boundaries may be, tribes retain senior, reserved rights to water flowing through the originally defined boundaries established by treaty, statute, or executive order. Whether by dam or by ruptured oil pipeline, altering the flow of the Missouri River or any river within Sioux treaty territory violates the spirit of the Winters Doctrine. But the Sioux Nation has yet to legally invoke the doctrine because of rightful fear that any quantification of water rights, as history has shown, would likely result in endless constraints and the diminishment of tribal sovereignty. Nevertheless, Standing Rock and the Sioux Nation maintain a legitimate moral claim to the river.

As we await the Environmental Impact Statement as to whether or not the corps should grant DAPL an easement to cross the Missouri River, Standing Rock's argument for treaty rights alone is compelling. This does not diminish other grievances, such as the pipeline company's brazen defilement of tribal burial and cultural sites, or North Dakota's copious use of violence against unarmed Water Protectors. For those who argue that Native treaties are archaic documents that are no longer valid, a certain document older than the treaties, the U.S. Constitution, regards them as "the supreme law of the land." Are we to blame Standing Rock for asking the United States to obey its own Constitution?

NOTES

1. Jack Dalrymple, "Dakota Access Pipeline: Mob Rule Triumphed over Law and Common Sense," *Star Tribune*, December 15, 2017, http://www.startribune.com.

2. "Treaty with the Sioux—Brulé, Oglala, Miniconjou, Yanktonai, Hunkpapa, Blackfeet, Cuthead, Two Kettle, Sans Arcs, and Santee—and Arapaho, 1868," in *Indian Affairs: Laws and Treaties*, ed. Charles J. Kappler, vol. 2: *Treaties* (Washington, D.C.: Government Printing Office, 1904), 998–1007.

3. *Sioux Tribe et al. v. United States*, 42 Ind. Cl. Comm. 1978 (1978) at 225.

4. Hiram Martin Chittenden and Alfred Talbot Richardson, eds., *Life, Letters, and Travels of Father Pierre-Jean De Smet, S.J., 1804–1873*, 4 vols. (New York: Francis P. Harper, 1905), 3:915.

5. *United States v. Sioux Nation of Indians, et al.*, 448 U.S. 371 (1980) at 388.

6. "Treaty of Fort Laramie with the Sioux etc., September 17, 1851," in Kappler, *Indian Affairs*, 2:594; "Treaty with the Sioux . . . and Arapaho, 1868," 998; "An Act to Divide a Portion of the Reservation of the Sioux Nation of Indians in Dakota . . . ," *U.S. Statutes at Large* 25 (1889): 889.

7. Constitution of the Standing Rock Sioux Tribe, art. 1.

8. Vine Deloria Jr., introduction to Michael L. Lawson, *Dammed Indians Revisited: The Continuing History of the Pick-Sloan Plan and the Missouri River Sioux* (Pierre: South Dakota State Historical Society Press, 2009), xv.

III.

LEGAL AND SOCIOPOLITICAL LANDSCAPES
AND STATE VIOLENCE

"Money Protectors." Photograph by Nick Estes.

11

STRIKING AT THE HEART OF CAPITAL
INTERNATIONAL FINANCIAL INSTITUTIONS AND INDIGENOUS PEOPLES' HUMAN RIGHTS

Michelle L. Cook

From the Pequot War, to Wounded Knee, to Sand Creek the Indian wars in the United States of America continue.[1] The near yearlong occupation and continued struggle by Indigenous[2] peoples and their allies against the Dakota Access Pipeline (DAPL) and its lead company Energy Transfer Partners (ETP)[3] highlighted for Americans, and the world community, the twenty-first-century power of Indigenous-led movements. The world also witnessed the reprehensible state violence and repression they face when exercising their basic human rights to self-determination over their traditional lands in the United States.[4] While perhaps shocking for some, sadly, the tragedy is that the violence that occurred at Standing Rock is not a rare, unique, or exceptional case. It is a microcosmic reoccurrence of the same patterns of dishonorable history, colonization, and oppression presently reconstituted, recycled, and repeated in the lives of Indian peoples and Indigenous peoples throughout the world.[5] The stand against DAPL was one of the largest intertribal gatherings providing mutual aid and defense in over a century,[6] also consisting of thousands of non-Indigenous allies throughout the United States and the rest of the world. Yet, Indigenous peoples and allies experienced extreme human-rights violations at Standing Rock. Human-rights violations relating to the criminalization of dissent and suppression of the DAPL protest are detailed in a report to the UN Special Rapporteur on the Rights of Indigenous Peoples, Victoria Tauli-Corpuz. The report highlights:

> On September 3, 2016, about 200 water protectors were gathered in a peaceful march and pipe ceremony when they encountered workers bulldozing an ancestral burial site identified in court filings the previous evening as an area of historical, archaeological, spiritual, and cultural significance. Security guards employed by Frost Kennels LLC and 10-Code Security arrived with attack dogs that bit a number of indigenous water protectors.

"Sister Water Protectors." Photograph by Nick Estes.

On October 27, 2016, hundreds of law enforcement in Humvees and helicopters discharged a Long Range Acoustic Device sound weapon, explosive teargas grenades, chemical agents, Tasers, rubber bullets, batons and a Directed Energy weapon on water protectors. 142 people were arrested, some in the midst of prayer ceremonies. The most violent attacks occurred on November 20 on the Backwater Bridge after a few individuals tried to remove abandoned vehicles that law enforcement used to barricade Highway 1806. Law enforcement immediately began shooting Specialty Impact Munitions (SIM) and chemical agents at the individuals as a crowd began to gather. More law enforcement agencies arrived in armored vehicles and used high pressure fire hoses to spray water protectors, and shot SIM, chemical agent canisters, explosive teargas and "stinger" grenades indiscriminately into the crowd over a period of about ten hours, without any warning. Over 200 people were injured, including a 31-year-old Navajo woman permanently disabled after she was shot in the eye with a tear gas canister launched by an officer.[7]

Today, Indigenous peoples throughout the world continue to face physical or cultural extinction when their rights are violated for natural resource extraction by companies and third parties.[8] Indigenous rights violations in the United States, such as those occurring as DAPL was constructed, are not isolated events but part and parcel of a historic legacy of violent dispossession of Indian peoples from their territories for mineral resources and fossil fuels, such as oil and gas, often by private, local, state, and federal actors.[9] Indian legal scholar Robert A. Williams Jr. writes:

> Colonization of one race of peoples by another race then, indelibly inscribes a legal system of racial discrimination based on cultural differences, denying rights of self-determination to the colonized race which has been displaced from the territory desired by the colonizer race.[10]

In other words, occurrences like DAPL are part of a larger structure, not simply an event.

The coordinated response to the encampment by police and private security actors demonstrates the layers of thoughtful repression employed to violently subjugate Indian people, so as to thwart assertions of treaty rights and sovereignty, allowing natural resource extraction and transportation for oil.[11] The criminalization of Water Protectors at DAPL continues to be assessed and documented where some eight hundred people faced charges,[12] many of whom being mischarged, falsely charged, and overcharged demonstrating a general climate of law enforcement repression against Indigenous peoples and their allies for a private pipeline.[13]

The encounter made visible and laid bare for the world to witness the stark, shocking, and terrorizing abuse of Indian people by a network of corporate actors, private security actors, state police, and federal authorities.[14] Violations of human rights at Standing Rock were facilitated by international banks and financial institutions through project finance to DAPL/Bakken pipeline and through corporate finance to the shippers and joint owners of the DAPL/Bakken pipeline.[15] This chapter documents discrete aspects of the collective DAPL divestment movement focusing on the role of Indigenous peoples, specifically Indigenous women, in shaping legal change in banks and financial institutions and advancing Indigenous human rights globally.[16] This chapter also highlights the critical Indigenous legal methodology of the Indigenous women's divestment delegations to archive their engagements with banks and financial institutions in Norway, Germany, and Switzerland. The chapter finishes looking forward toward the economies of the future.

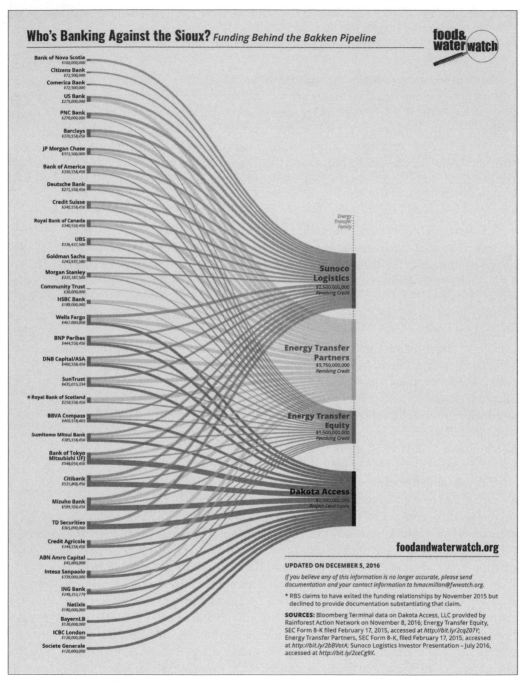

Sources of funding for the Bakken Pipeline. Copyright Food & Water Watch / foodandwaterwatch.org.
Reprinted with permission.

The Bakken Pipeline, Dakota Access/Bayou Bridge Pipeline Corporate Ownership

The Dakota Access Pipeline is the northern section of the larger Bakken pipeline system. DAPL is a 1,168-mile-long pipeline transporting over five hundred thousand barrels of crude oil per day from the Bakken region of North Dakota across four states to southern Illinois.[17] The pipeline continues south from Patoka, Illinois (the south terminal of DAPL) to Nederland, Texas.[18] In Nederland, the Bakken connects with the Bayou Bridge pipeline.[19] Louisiana has been operational since 2016; phase two of the project, to St. James, Louisiana, was expected to be completed by the second half of 2018 but is now expected to be completed in the first quarter of 2019.[20]

Both the DAPL/Bakken Pipeline and the Bayou Bridge Pipeline are joint ventures between Energy Transfer and Phillips 66, forming a single system for shipping Bakken oil to the Gulf of Mexico market,[21] including for export. ETP and Phillips 66 have both been building out export capacity at facilities where DAPL oil is sent.[22] DAPL is now owned collectively, as a joint venture, by four U.S. corporations: Energy Transfer, Phillips 66, Enbridge, and Marathon.[23]

Starving the Black Snake: DAPL and Divestment

Solidarity with Standing Rock sparked direct actions and an international Indigenous-led movement for bank divestment aimed at the companies that own the Dakota Access Pipeline.[24] In August, the Public Accountability Initiative published corporate-level financing information for two Energy Transfer entities that have since merged.[25] On September 6, 2016, Food and Water Watch published an iconic Sankey graph with additional information suggesting the flow of the international bank financing of DAPL, both at the project level and at the corporate level with general purpose funds.[26]

Less than a month later under the direction of Women of All Red Nations cofounder Phyllis Young, the Standing Rock Sioux Tribal Council passed Resolution 591-16, committing to divest from, and sever any ties with, "any and all banks, mutual funds, securities companies, or other financial entities that invest in, or otherwise financially support any aspect of the Dakota Access Pipeline Project."[27] The tribe defined the call and scope of divestment in this historic tribal resolution and set a model for larger divestment movements.

The graph that informed this commitment to divest revealed a web of finance directed at the DAPL/Bakken Pipeline and at the Energy Transfer family of companies. The exposed web of finance did not include the financial institutions lending to the other DAPL owners and/or shippers Enbridge, Marathon, and Phillip 66. European banks such as Norway's Den Norske Bank (DNB), Switzerland's Credit Suisse and Union Bank of Switzerland (UBS), and Germany's Deutsche Bank and

BayernLB were among banking entities identified providing project and/or corporate financing to DAPL and its corporate owners.[28]

In the context of DAPL, the divestment movement means that the financial institutions and banks insuring and providing loans and credit to ETP for DAPL have found themselves "in a higher-risk situation than they bargained for, which many regretted after factoring in harm to their reputations, as well as loss of over $81 million in individual accounts and $4.3 billion from cities."[29] One case study estimates that costs to ETP and other firms with ownership in DAPL incurred no less than $7.5 billion due to DAPL as well as $4.4 billion in account closure costs to banks financing DAPL.[30]

In addition to banks, investor and pension funds have also divested from DAPL and its corporate owners. Pension funds such as the California Public Employees' Retirement System (CalPERS) announced that it joined more than one hundred fellow investors in asking major U.S. and international banks backing DAPL to address the concerns of the Standing Rock Sioux Tribe.[31] Norway's KLP, an employee pension fund, also divested and removed its investments from the companies behind DAPL.[32] In 2019 Norway's Sovereign Wealth Fund announced it is pulling investments from oil and gas production companies.[33]

Indigenous peoples, especially Indigenous women, are on the forefront of the movement requesting financial institutions and banks to immediately withdraw current, and prohibit future, lending commitments to companies funding fossil fuels and involved with Indigenous human rights violations. Indigenous leadership has integrated that divestment focus with similar campaigns against Enbridge, Kinder Morgan, and TransCanada,[34] the three companies behind three tar sands pipeline projects: Line 3, Trans Mountain, and Keystone XL respectively.[35] The commonality is that, as with DAPL, these pipelines are being pursued without the free, prior, and informed consent (FPIC) of Indigenous peoples.[36]

Within the campaigns for divestment from DAPL,[37] Indigenous peoples, specifically Indian women, have taken international platforms and are creating opportunities to voice their concerns on the impact of oil spills directly with individual bank representatives.[38] LaDonna Bravebull Allard, Lakota historian, member of the Standing Rock Sioux Tribe, and founder of Sacred Stone Camp, states, "We are Native women of the land and water standing up to protect our future and the future for all humankind. We are asking bank and insurance companies to divest from fossil fuels and invest in your communities. Mni Wiconi, Water is Life."[39]

Emergence of the Women's Divestment Delegation

The women's divestment delegation to Europe emerged in part from an inability to secure safe and civil dialogue with bank representatives in North Dakota regarding human-rights violations relating to Energy Transfer's conduct and the use of excessive force by law enforcement during the construction of the pipeline.

In January 2017 a group of Indigenous women from the Standing Rock encampments secured a meeting with the Bank of North Dakota and requested the bank to decline accepting loans to fund the militarization of Morton County Police. In a letter, signed by the "First Nations Grandmothers, Mothers, Daughters, Sisters, and Wives," the women pleaded:

> We are determined to hold a prayerful space. However, you should know that although we are unarmed, we have been shot with pepper spray, bean bags, rubber bullets, and kinetic impact projectiles, resulting in permanent bodily injury, including loss of hearing, permanent loss of eyesight from being shot in the head, and the maiming of limbs. . . . The unnecessary, non-professional, and unethical use of so-called "non-lethal" weapons and use of force are currently being investigated by the Department of Justice and the United Nations, and have been condemned by members of the United States Congress. Our fear is that the police will escalate to unwarranted lethal force and the murder of one or many of us Natives and US citizens. . . . Please stop the eight million dollar loan. . . . Stop the funding of unnecessary police violence. Stop the genocide of indigenous people on treaty land and home fronts.[40]

The bank refused to meet with the women and forbade them from entering its building, attending their scheduled meeting, or standing upon its property. Instead, the bank locked its doors and called the police. Law enforcement was dispatched into the area to surveil and surround the Indigenous women and their supporters. The women were told that charges of kidnapping could be filed against them, as the bank had locked individuals and workers inside the building. The police and the bank denied them the opportunity to have civil dialogue regarding their concerns over the funding of militarized law enforcement and Indigenous human-rights violations at the DAPL encampments.

The political landscape of North Dakota comingled with oil and gas interests also compromised attempts for accountability and justice. In October 2016 Trump had $500,000 to $1 million in investments in ETP;[41] by December 2016 during his presidential run he sold those shares. Kelsey Warren, ETP owner and its principal beneficiary, contributed $100,000 to Trump's presidential campaign. In January 2016, as one of his first executive actions, Trump reversed the Obama administration's halt on DAPL, permitting the pipeline to cross under the Missouri River.[42] ETP later contributed $15 million to North Dakota to offset the $38 million cost of DAPL policing.[43]

Hence, the delegation to European banks emerged from an essential need to create spaces for fair and civil engagement regarding the financing of Indigenous human-rights violations, in spaces that were less hostile toward Indigenous peoples than what was experienced in North Dakota and more broadly in North American. Autumn Chacon, Diné artist, activist, and Water Protector, explained, "In

North Dakota, when we attempt to sit down and have meetings with the bank, or the executives of the project affecting us, the doors will be locked before we even get to the building. The police will be called, we are threatened with arrest. What options are we then left with?"[44]

Indigenous Bank Engagements

The Indigenous Women's Divestment Delegations to Europe created a platform to bring Indigenous women who have witnessed and were harmed by human-rights abuses at Standing Rock to meet directly with bank representatives, insurance companies, and parliament members across Europe to urge them to divest from DAPL and exclude short-sighted extractive-industry companies in the United States and Canada from their investment portfolios.[45] The delegations, organized and led by Indian women, met face-to-face with the representatives of the financial institutions and decision makers whose choices directly impact their bodies, lives, rights, and futures as Indian women and Indian people.

Monique Verdin, council woman of the United Houma Nation whose ancestral territory is impacted by the Bayou Bridge Pipeline, stated:

> I come from a place just south of "Cancer Alley," just north of the "Dead Zone." This is in Louisiana and it used to be known as Balbancha in our language. My Houma ancestors have inhabited the Yakne Chitto (Big Country) for thousands of years. We are surrounded by a web of fossil fuel pipelines, a culprit responsible for contributing to some of the most rapid land loss in the world, in an area with a unique and high level of biodiversity. Yet, the risks and vulnerabilities have not deterred Energy Transfer Partners or Phillips 66 in their ultimate pursuits to push dirty crude through precious territories. It is with a heavy heart, but also hope, that I am journeying with the delegation across the sea to remind and re-warn the European banks funding and facilitating the pipelines about the devastating damage, bad practices and false promises of these companies. They are gambling with the sacred waters and life source for the Houma Nation, indigenous communities, and everyone tied to the Mississippi River Watershed, from North Dakota to the Gulf of Mexico, and they must be held accountable.[46]

With actions from the Trump administration that disregard basic rights of consultation by terminating an Obama-era anticipated environmental impact statement for DAPL,[47] it is critically important to focus strategic efforts within the international arena to convince other nations, as well as banks overseas and in North America, to stop funding businesses in fossil energy growth projects that are involved in and connected to Indigenous human rights violations. Despite the Trump administration's termination of an environmental impact statement, Indigenous women remain undeterred in their quest for truth, justice, and healing regarding the violation of Indigenous peoples' and Indigenous women's rights related to the construction of DAPL and similarly situated projects and companies.

Indigenous peoples are determined to continue education and advocacy efforts related to economic human rights and bank divestment from companies causing and/or contributing to Indigenous human-rights violations in the United States and globally. Direct engagement between Indigenous peoples and financial decision-makers is an opportunity to evaluate the efficacy of human-rights policies at banks from an Indigenous perspective. Direct Indigenous engagement also serves to educate investors, shareholders, decision makers, and the public on the shortfall between the normative human-rights standards of FPIC and its negative counterpart: a coercive Indigenous consultation model typically forced on Indigenous peoples by state and nonstate actors for natural resource extraction. Indigenous peoples empower divestment movements to push for decolonization of capital and its financial structures. Indigenous women and peoples should be supported and amplified as it is Indigenous peoples' practices and visions that have the knowledge to create, nurture, and bring forth the future economies and structures that will reevaluate wealth and equilibrate economic inequality.

Indigenous Women's Leadership and Moral Clarity

Within their matrilineal societies Indigenous women are integral to their tribal economics and have always held power.[48] They continue to seek financial accountability and justice for their people. Elouise Cobell of the Blackfoot Nation, for example, challenged the fraudulent accounting of Indian trust lands and won the largest settlement against the federal government in U.S. history for the mismanagement of Indian monies. When she first questioned the Bureau of Indian Affairs regarding their accounting of her trust account, she was told to "go home and learn how to read a financial statement." She was told, "she wasn't 'capable' of understanding it."[49] She proved them all wrong. Cherokee economist Rebecca Adamson also blazed trails for financial independence and economic human rights in Indian Country by creating "one of the first microfinance loan funds in the US with the Oglala Sioux in South Dakota: the Lakota Fund."[50] The tradition continues with recent actions from Ethel Branch, attorney general of the Navajo Nation, who filed a complaint against Wells Fargo for their "widespread system of unfair deceptive, fraudulent, and illegal practices." The complaint alleges that

> since at least 2009 and continuing through 2016, Wells Fargo employees at branches on the Navajo Nation routinely opened unauthorized savings and credit accounts, misled customers into opening unnecessary accounts, obtained debit cards without customers' consent, and enrolled customers in online banking without proper consent.[51]

Indigenous women are still maintaining and forming critical interrogations for more just and self-determined economies, including the creation of Indigenous economic institutions and public banks that can provide alternative large-scale financial services to cities divesting from Wall Street.[52] Jaqueline Fielder, Mnicoujou Lakota and Mandan-Hidatsa, founding member of Indigenous-led Mazaska Talks (Money Talks), and co-founder of SF Public Banks, regards public banking as a spectrum of social ills facing not only Indigenous peoples but the global community, stating:

> Such a bank would invest in community development, and all interest gained for a public bank counts as income for the state which—rather than providing profits and bonuses for private shareholders—can be reinvested into the city or reduce the tax burden. Whether from a moral or a financial perspective, public banking just makes sense.[53]

Supporting and centering Indigenous women leading North American fossil energy divestment campaigns is a powerful tool in creating legal change and accountability within the financial arena.

Wašté Win Yellowlodge Young, Ihunktowanna/Hunkpapa of the Standing Rock Sioux Tribe and former tribal historic preservation officer, explains:

> Our Delegation's presence puts a face to the indigenous communities and lives who have been displaced, abused, and adversely affected by extractive industries throughout the world. We are here to call for accountability for the destruction of our way of life and rights violations that occurred with the Dakota Access Pipeline and other ongoing pipeline projects funded by European financial institutions such as Credit Suisse and Deutsche Bank.[54]

As protectors and guardians of their territories' lands and waters, Indigenous women are the foundation, backbone, and future of their tribal nations, perpetuating the survival and cultural well-being of all Indigenous people.

Divestment and Intersectional Commitment

Indigenous women in the United States experience unique human-rights violations and adverse impacts when extractive industries and fossil-fuel infrastructure such as DAPL enter their traditional lands and territories. One of the adverse impacts of extractive industries is increased crime and sexual violence from influxes of hundreds of oil workers forming "Man Camps" in or near Indigenous people's territories. For example:

> In North Dakota, the man camps created during the Bakken oil boom drastically increased the levels of violent crime perpetrated against women and girls—and

particularly native women and girls. Studies conducted during the peak of the oil boom—from 2010 to 2013—showed that the number of reported domestic violence incidents and sexual assaults increased by hundreds, flooding and overwhelming service providers. Victim advocates from the Mandan, Hidatsa, and Arikara Nation—a native nation that became ground zero for the increase in violent crimes that accompanied the boom—have reported a doubling, and in some instances a tripling, in the number of calls that victim-service providers receive for domestic violence, sexual assault, and sex trafficking.[55]

Lack of legal remedy and accountability for sexual crimes committed exasperates the violence and "often allows perpetrators to evade justice" due to complexities of jurisdiction.[56] For Indigenous women, non-Indian perpetrators predominate the statistics: "Over 84% of Native women experience domestic or sexual violence. And over 97% of them are victimized by non-Indians."[57] For non-Indian oil workers who commit sexual violence against Indian women on Indian reservations, jurisdictional gaps created by the Supreme Court between tribal, state, and federal jurisdiction law enforcement effectively means no recourse for Indigenous women.[58] In the context of the U.S. legal system, there is a good chance perpetrators won't be prosecuted.[59] Indigenous women are already targeted, facing murder rates more than ten times the national average.[60] Not only are Indian women disproportionately murdered, but many Indigenous women remain "missing." A recent report "identified 506 unique cases of missing and murdered American Indian and Alaska Native women and girls across the 71 selected cities—128 (25%) were missing persons cases, 280 (56%) were murder cases, and 98 (19%) had an unknown status."[61] The predatory economy coupled with the chilling statistics that "1 in 3 Native women will be raped in her life time" and that "86% of reported rapes are perpetrated by non-Native men" means Indigenous women living on or near man camps are uniquely targeted and face extreme danger as a result of oil extraction, infrastructure, and transport through their lands and territories.[62]

When carrying out risk-based human-rights due diligence regarding their business partners and investment, banks and financial institutions that operate and invest in projects or companies operating within the ancestral lands of Indigenous peoples within the United States should interact and seek meaningful and effective participation and consent from Indigenous women. Indigenous peoples and specifically women deserve forums where they can provide banks and financial institutions information regarding the impacts of extractive industries on their lands, lives, bodies, and human rights. Indigenous divestment efforts focus on accountability for the victims and demand remedies for these harms within banking institutions and the financial industry, an industry that provides the liquidity that corporations such as ETP require to expand and grow. The survivors of DAPL, and broadly Indigenous peoples who stood in solidarity with Water Protectors at Standing Rock, are determined to continue action, education, and advocacy efforts to further discipline banks for facilitating companies that are causing and/or contributing to Indigenous human-rights abuses in the United States.[63]

Indigenous women will continue a long legacy of protecting Indigenous economic rights. They will also establish the expectation among financial institutions that investing in projects or companies that negatively impact Indigenous peoples' rights will lead to meetings with Indigenous women, in person, who seek accountability and request divestment.

Methodology of the Delegation

The centering of Indigenous women and the power of their personal narratives to redirect and create legal change is supported by theories of critical race and critical legal studies.[64] Critical divestment examines the origin stories of the banks and frames them as fundamental pillars and extensions of historic and present-day colonization of Indigenous peoples' lands to fight against racism that is institutionalized by law and finance. Critical intersectional Indigenous divestment strategies in the U.S. context anticipate and prepare for delayed and often ultimately unjust outcomes in domestic legal proceedings, particularly from the U.S. Supreme Court.[65] From 1988 to 2008, "the Court has ruled against tribal interests about 75 percent of the time."[66] In a political environment where state authorities routinely violate Indigenous peoples' treaty rights, rights of assembly and free speech, and criminalize the Indigenous human-rights defenders who exercise these rights,[67] Indigenous women by necessity are creating, developing, and pursuing diverse international theaters of engagement and resistance for the protection of their lands and people.

The divestment strategy is intersectional and transnational, reflecting the frontline impacts financed by a global banking system. The methodology of the delegations taps into long practiced traditions of Indigenous international diplomacy, what Indian scholars like Robert A. Williams Jr. call "Indian legal diplomacy" and Nick Estes has called "indigenous internationalism."[68]

Indigenous tribal lands are ground zero for extreme energy development and extraction for natural resources and fossil-fuel development.[69] It is estimated that right now, "there are 5,000 distinct indigenous societies on earth. . . . Yet all now face this latest iteration of an historic colonial advance—the highly accelerated drive by global corporations seeking access to land and resources."[70] According to former UN special rapporteur Erica-Irene A. Daes:

> The legacy of colonialism is probably most acute in the area of expropriation of indigenous lands, territories and resources for national economic and development interests. In every sector of the globe, indigenous peoples are being impeded in every conceivable way from proceeding with their own forms of development, consistent with their own values, perspective and interests.

Much large-scale economic and industrial development has taken place without recognition of and respect for indigenous peoples' rights to lands, territories and resources. Economic development had been largely imposed from outside, with complete disregard for the right of indigenous peoples to participate and control implementation and benefits of development.[71]

Additionally, "a high percentage of these last resources are found today on land where native peoples thrive, as they have for millennia. And so we have the roots of serious conflict: invasions, double dealing and forced removal, cultural and political assaults, and very often, extreme violence."[72] Oil, gas, and mineral resources are also found in the lands of Indigenous peoples in the United States. For example, "Native American reservations cover just 2 percent of the United States, but they may contain about a fifth of the nation's oil and gas, along with vast coal reserves."[73] In 2011, researchers found:

> American Indian lands are estimated to include nearly 30 percent of the nation's coal reserves west of the Mississippi, as much as 50 percent of potential uranium reserves, and up to 20 percent of known natural gas and oil reserves. These lands also may contain rare earth minerals, increasingly sought after for use in manufacturing.[74]

Violent dispossession of Indigenous peoples' land for resource extraction by companies continues, with brutality, as exemplified in the case of DAPL. Standing Rock made visible the legacy of a colonial legal framework in the United States, which consistently fails to protect and continues to deny basic fundamental freedoms and humans rights to Indigenous peoples including but not limited to free, prior, and informed consent.

Banks and financial institutions are not gender or race neutral; nor is the implementation of their human-rights policies. These institutions continue to be cornerstones in ongoing human-rights abuses and violence against Indigenous peoples, and the obscurity of that role must be illuminated and raised up within public consciousness to change regulatory frameworks and business behavior that fail to protect Indigenous peoples. These economic institutions are structures that limit access to justice and accountability for Indigenous peoples, who without support, assistance, and resources can neither directly nor effectively participate and engage with financial decision-makers. Indigenous peoples must have opportunities in setting the tone, the discourse, and the narrative of how bankers and financiers should respect and interact with Indigenous peoples around the world. Engagement with banks through direct contacts and public media relating to divestment is an innovative approach to creating racial justice and economic democracy, by directing demands straight at the heart of capital's most powerful players. The delegation's methodology, beyond divestment, includes advocating for respect of tribal sovereignty and Indigenous rights, investment in women, climate justice, and transparent, just, and accountable banking institutions and economic systems. Another key element is drawing public attention to the lack of meaningful regulations and legal mechanisms available to Indigenous people for holding banks and corporate actors accountable for human-rights violations.

The methodology also encourages Indigenous peoples and communities to envision, imagine, nurture the economies of the future; economies that include and value Indigenous peoples. It is in the time of financial crises, when cash becomes worthless or unstable due to international forces, that visions and practices of local liberated economic structures are most important. For Venezuelans when the banks crashed and hyperinflation of bank notes soared, it was a return to barter economies that helped the poorest, most rural people survive.[75] The poor, those without access to banking services, are the ones who have to survive economic calamity and carry the economic hardship. In this country, while oil was abundant, accessible, and cheap, the cost of food and medicine, items necessary for life, skyrocketed. It is for these reasons that Indigenous peoples must create, foster, and nurture economic independence to protect their people and future generations from international economic instability that impacts their livelihoods. It is when dollars and banknotes become worthless that the dangers of total dependency on capital and international financers becomes most visible, and the practices and visions of alternative economic structures become most critical.

Financing DAPL and Divestment

Divestment is a powerful strategy in the world of social justice movements in response to legal and moral failures of governance. From divestment campaigns relating to South African racial apartheid to boycott, divest, and sanction movements,[76] it has been a tool used by communities seeking justice and visibility. As for Indigenous peoples, First Nations have engaged with financial institutions, banks, and international credit rating agencies to challenge tar sands oil extraction and advocate for rights to economic self-determination.[77] Native American peoples have also engaged with the financial industry in defense of their rights and well-being.[78] Divestment is a tool of resistance to extractivist economies undermining Indigenous peoples' human rights and putting at risk their cultural and physical survival.[79] Divestment has provided an opportunity for mass mobilization and education about critical issues that have a serious impact upon people, including a banking industry that remains unaccountable to Indigenous peoples, citizens, and victims of human-rights abuses. Indigenous peoples are skillfully deploying this tactic to stop the flows of capital at the source, sources of finance that sustain oil companies and other similarly situated extractivist corporations, negatively impacting their land and futures.

Critical and intersectional divestment calls for robust human-rights frameworks beyond securing Indigenous peoples' consent. Banks and financial institutions must comply with international human-rights standards, with regard to oil and gas investments, as well as all other investments that impact Indigenous peoples whether they are in palm oil, megadams, or private prisons,[80] including immigrant detention facilities.[81] Divestment lends itself to an intersectional community of shared political concerns including tribal sovereignty, water, climate, justice, and corporate accountability; hence it is much more than just reducing carbon emissions.

Divestment provides a space to systematize and map the financial and economic topography and the streams of capital that flow into companies that sustain projects like DAPL within Indigenous territories. Targeting the capital, banks, and financial institutions that create the economic infrastructure housing and directing the flows of credit and capital supporting corporations like ETP and their harmful actions against Indigenous peoples and other populations is necessary. Revealing the obscured economic architecture and actors required to sustain harmful resource extraction and development in Indigenous ancestral lands and territories is necessary but difficult.[82] Mapping the financial infrastructure allows the public and Indigenous peoples to identify points of pressure and intervention to intercept and stop the flows of capital that facilitate and insure projects and companies that abuse Indigenous peoples' human rights. The Indigenous-centered and Indigenous-focused methodology of the delegation can be replicated and developed so that more Indigenous peoples can directly participate and engage with the banks and financial institutions that impact their human rights, their lands, and peoples.

Banks and Financing Colonialism

Banks have always financed colonialism. European banks are at the genesis of contemporary colonization of Indigenous peoples' lands and territories.[83] The origin stories and formations of modern banks and corporations begin in the east from Europe. Italy, for example, is birthplace to some of the world's oldest financial institutions and financial instruments. Italian merchant banking houses such as Florence's Medici Bank (1397), Genoa's Banco di San Giorgio (1406), and Banca Monte dei Paschi (1472) are some of the oldest banks in the world. Bonds and other financial security instruments and markets were developed in European places of trade, including Venice. Terms like "risk" and "bank" derive from Italian words "rischio" and "banco."[84] Insurance was developed in Italy to cover the liability of imperial and mercantile voyages, which amounted to "large capital outlays that literally sailed out of sight."[85] The Venetians devised "marine insurance" and "underwriting" as means of hedging the risk of trading voyages.[86]

The English and Dutch East India Company also shaped "the foundation for the modern economy."[87] The Virginia Company that colonized America's mid-Atlantic coast, the still thriving Hudson Bay Company, and the East India Company were all chartered by Queen Elizabeth in 1600 for exploration and overseas trade.[88] In 1602, the Estates-General of the Dutch Republic chartered the Dutch East India

Company, Vereenigde Oost-Indische Compagnie (VOC).[89] The VOC, said to be one of the first corporations, was an innovative corporate/state hybrid with the quasi-sovereign authority to wage war overseas, negotiate treaties, create coin, and establish colonies.[90] Jan Pieterzoon Coen, the seventeenth-century governor-general of the Dutch East India Company, wrote to his managing directors:

> You gentlemen should well know from experience in Asia that trade must be driven and maintained under the protection and favour of your own weapons, and the weapons must be wielded from the profits gained by trade; so that trade cannot be maintained without war, nor war without trade.[91]

Wars for resources, capital, and trade continue to be maintained through violence, often to the detriment of Indigenous peoples who occupy lands where raw materials for natural resource extraction are sourced. European banks were fundamental to the historic and contemporary colonization of Indigenous people's lands and territories, playing a fundamental role in financing "Manifest Destiny" and the colonization of the "New World."[92] Colonization is therefore embedded in the deep structure of modern financial systems. The enduring original colonizing mission of facilitating resource extraction by merchants is now reinscribed and continued in the twenty-first-century financing of modern extractive industries. Similar to Antony Anghie's assertion that colonialism shapes international law, colonialism also shapes international finance. Violence and colonialism remain deeply entrenched within the bones and DNA of banks and are continuing salient features of the extraction economy.[93] Today, European financial institutions and their forms of economic exchange continue to play a central role in the colonization of Indigenous peoples, as they continue to invest and do business with corporations that violate Indigenous peoples' territorial and human rights. There must be a true accounting of what international finance is from Indigenous peoples' perspectives, even if this means uncovering a "dark history of bankers and empire."[94] In order to understand the current dilemma and inequality within the business and human-rights framework, one must go back to the historic formations of states, banks, and corporations. Deconstructing through a critical lens the creation stories and histories of banks and corporations demonstrates how the financialization of colonialism through trading companies set the stage and custom for modern corporate behavior and banks that fund Indigenous human-rights violations.

Norway

Norway Human-Rights Record

Norwegian financial institutions are a critical site for the Indigenous divestment movement for various reasons including their human-rights record. Norway signed and ratified numerous international treaties including the International Covenant on Civil and Political Rights (ICCPR), International Covenant on Economic, Social and Cultural Rights (ICESCR), International Convention on the Elimination of All Forms of Racial Discrimination (ICERD), and Indigenous and Tribal Peoples in Independent Countries Convention, 1989 (No. 169).[95] Under the Human Rights Act of 1999, ICESCR, ICCPR, and the Convention on the Elimination of All Forms of Discrimination against Women have been incorporated into Norwegian law, and ICERD "has been incorporated through Section 5 of the Ethnicity Anti-Discrimination Act."[96] Article 112 of the Norwegian Constitution also sets aside a unique provision relating to the management and protection of natural resources:

> Every person has the right to an environment that is conducive to health and to a natural environment whose productivity and diversity are maintained. Natural resources shall be managed on the basis of comprehensive long-term considerations which will safeguard this right for future generations as well. The authorities of the state shall take measures for the implementation of these principles.[97]

Implementation of human-rights obligations falls on the ministries of Norway, who are "responsible for following up the recommendations of various treaty bodies within their sectors."[98] The Norwegian Supreme Court has also created extensive case law based on the conventions and the cases of the European Court of Human Rights.[99] Norway also supports a UN mandate for human-rights defenders.[100] State Secretary Bård Glad Pedersen of the Ministry of Foreign Affairs noted that many countries are endeavoring to limit human-rights defenders' activities, which puts them "in need of protection due to their work to uncover the abuse of power on the part of national authorities and other actors."[101] Norway has ratified all international agreements on human rights and has specifically incorporated the Convention on the Elimination of All Forms of Discrimination against Women into its Human Rights Act.

Norway, with a commitment to women's rights and human rights,[102] is a country positioned to be sympathetic toward Indian women's requests to divest their banks and state pension funds from pipeline companies responsible for egregious human-rights violations against Indian women and others.[103] Norway, and its financial sector, has an obligation and role in implementing and enforcing lawful business, human-rights, and Indigenous-rights obligations and standards.

U.S. citizens, furthermore, have previously challenged the Norwegian state's investment in oil and gas development within the territorial boundaries of the United States. In 2011 Norway's state oil company Statoil was receiving "harsh criticism" for its activities in questionable projects in Alberta, Canada, and the Marcellus Formation, which extends under the Appalachian Mountains in West Virginia, Pennsylvania, and parts of Ohio and New York.[104]

Norway's Den Norske Bank (DNB)

Beginning in October 2016, Sámi advocates from Norway along with Indigenous people and their organizations worked together with U.S. Indigenous peoples to convince Norway's Den Norske Bank, the largest financial services group in Norway, to divest from DAPL.[105] In October lawyers from the Water Protector Legal Collective (WPLC) provided the Sámi representatives with a report detailing arrests and violence,[106] urging DNB to immediately consider "the consequences and ramifications of continuing to support the 'wrong team' in . . . one of the most profound violations of Native American sovereignty to occur in the United States," and to protect its reputation by adhering to international and national laws in accordance with human rights.[107] The report to DNB reminded its executives of the considerable size of its lending commitments to DAPL and the Energy Transfer companies, totaling about $460 million. WPLC wrote that this lending "implicates DNB in the ongoing violations of human rights occurring in North Dakota."[108] On October 9, 2016, the president of the Norwegian Sámi Association personally delivered the human-rights report to DNB representatives and the Norwegian Council on Ethics for the Government Pension Fund.[109]

On November 6, 2016, Harald Serck-Hanssen, DNB's executive vice president and head of Large Corporates and Internationals, commented on the situation in North Dakota by announcing that as a result of concerns about the project's compliance with the bank's own guidelines and values,

> our policy is clear that we only finance projects that meet DNB's requirements with respect to environmental and social conditions. We have intensified the dialogue with our customers and emphasized that respect for the indigenous people's rights is an important value for us as a bank. We also urge that the dialogue be continued with the indigenous people to find solutions to the conflict. We expect the companies and the responsible authorities to take a serious view of the situation, contribute to reducing the level of conflict and continue to seek acceptable solutions.[110]

DNB would initiate a new objective and fact-based evaluation of how the Indigenous peoples' rights were being treated in the process, using its relationship with the project to encourage a more constructive effort to resolve the conflicts involved. Failing this, the bank planned to reevaluate its role in helping to finance it.[111] On November 17, 2016, DNB sold off its holding of shares in ETP, worth $3 million, or less than 1 percent of the $460 million in liquidity DNB was continuing to provide to DAPL and the Energy Transfer companies. Some headlines failed to make this distinction, and DNB was credited with divesting from DAPL in error a first time.[112] On November 30, 2016, DNB announced that it was engaging the law firm of Foley Hoag LLP to investigate the allegations of DAPL's human-rights abuses and the project's adherence to International Finance Corporation's standards, and then to provide advice.[113] DNB then stated in January 2017 that the new Trump administration giving the project a carte blanche would have no effect on DNB's commitments or its "ongoing investigation in regard to how Indigenous rights are safeguarded in the process."[114]

Despite off-loading $3 million of ETP shares, DNB maintained the lines of credit to DAPL.[115] Indigenous peoples were determined "to keep working together to keep the pressure on DNB and other Nordic banks that are investing in the pipeline and to force them to pull their lines of credit as well."[116] Indigenous women began organizing a Norwegian delegation as a means to sustain pressure on DNB to pull their remaining lines of credit. The women planned on-the-ground meetings where they would share firsthand with Norwegian parliamentarians and the DNB representatives how DAPL is disregarding Indigenous rights and why they needed to cancel its lines of credit immediately.[117] The delegations aimed to educate the bank and the Norwegian people about how the project violated Indigenous rights to consultation and consent and how it has induced the local authorities to abuse the human rights of those defenders they have detained. In addition to providing information regarding DAPL's use of private security actors and the use of attack dogs on Indigenous people exercising their rights of assembly, speech, and free exercise of religion, the intent of the meetings with DNB representatives and other banks was to request that these institutions divest from DAPL and the companies behind it. Further, they requested that the banks review overall fossil-fuel investments in the United States, particularly those contested by Indigenous peoples.

The Indigenous women's divestment delegation arranged to arrive in Oslo, Norway, to meet with DNB in late March. On March 24, 2017, DNB quietly dropped out of its lending agreement with Energy Transfer Equity (ETE, the parent company of ETP).[118] On March 26, 2017—three days before scheduled meetings with the delegation—DNB sold its $120 million loan funding the Dakota Access Pipeline.[119] Senior DNB executive Harald Serck-Hanssen stated, "By selling our stake, we wish to signal how important it is that the affected Indigenous population is involved and that their opinions are heard in these types of projects."[120]

Collective strategic public pressure from many sources, as well as direct actions held at banks,[121] had tipped the scales for DNB to divest from DAPL.[122] This was a divestment victory, one far larger than the $3 million in ETP shares DNB had sold months before. In July, DNB exited its agreement with Marathon.[123] DNB remained as a lender on ETP, Sunoco Logistics, Phillips 66, and Enbridge credit facility agreements.[124]

In October 2017, the Women's Earth and Climate Action Network arranged a second delegation to Europe. The next month, in November, state news in Norway reported on the public misconception that DNB had fully divested from DAPL.[125]

In December 2017, Energy Transfer remade its credit facility agreement, and DNB ended its relationship with the company. However, DNB does remain a financier of Enbridge and Phillips 66 according to public records.[126]

Norwegian Government Pension Fund Global (GPFG) and the Council on Ethics

Norway maintains the lion's share of the world's oil and gas investments. The Norwegian Government Pension Fund Global, formerly the Petroleum Fund of Norway, is the largest in the world.[127] The fund tops out at $1 trillion, followed by Abu Dhabi Investment Authority at $825 billion, and China Investment Corporation at $814 billon.[128] To put that in perspective, it equates to the entire economy of Mexico and provides $190,000 for each of their 5.2 million citizens.[129] The fund, moreover, owns "$667 billion of shares in more than 9,000 companies around the world including Apple, Nestle and Microsoft,"[130] owning on average 1.3 percent of every publicly traded company in the world.[131] The purpose of the fund "is to facilitate the government savings needed to meet the expected rise in public pension expenditures in the coming years, and to support long-term management of petroleum revenues."[132]

In early 2017 the Norwegian GPFG had $11.6 billion invested in DAPL companies despite the growing evidence against its legality.[133] Even the entity created to carry out the project, Dakota Access LLC, continued to be in the GPFG's investment portfolio and not excluded.[134]

The delegation met with the GPFG Council on Ethics twice in 2017 and requested the GPFG to end its relationship to companies involved in DAPL.[135] The women argued that maintaining these banking relationships violated the fund's ethical guidelines with respect to human rights and international law, specifically section 3 of those guidelines, "criteria for conduct-based observation and exclusion of companies," which warns against

> unacceptable risk that a company contributes to or is responsible for . . . (a) serious or systematic human rights violations as murder, torture, deprivation of liberty, forced labor, and the worst forms of child labor; (b) serious violations of the rights of individuals in situations of war or conflict; (c) severe environmental damage; (d) acts or omissions that on an aggregate company level lead to unacceptable greenhouse gas emissions; (e) gross corruption; or (f) other particularly serious violations of fundamental ethical norms.[136]

By the sheer size of their holdings, Norway's international financial institutions have a deep and reverberating impact on the rights and survival of Indigenous peoples in the United States and throughout the world. Norway has been called the "guardian" of human rights and has adopted the UN Declaration on the Rights of

Indigenous Peoples;[137] yet the GPFG has not "excluded," or even put under "observation," investments in DAPL owners and shippers. The delegation continues to request that the GPFG's Council on Ethics exclude DAPL companies from its investment universe.[138] The delegations during the meetings requested that Norway's members of Parliament and other relevant actors and stakeholders create a sound and robust Indigenous rights policy within the GPFG's ethical guidelines to enunciate the Council on Ethics's obligations, legal evaluations, and determinations in regarding violations of Indigenous peoples' rights when assessing companies for their investment portfolio.[139]

Indigenous women created an international platform to bring attention to the human-rights abuses at Standing Rock by confronting and educating representatives of DNB and the GPFG, as well as public officials. They made clear, in person, how oil and gas investments and decisions made five thousand miles away directly impact Indigenous human rights in North America, elevating the imperative that banks and other financial institutions in Norway divest from DAPL and its corporate owners.[140] At the time the Norwegian Sovereign Wealth Fund began investigating allegations of human-rights violations by ETP they also announced considerations for more divestment from fossil fuels.[141] In March 2019, Norway's Sovereign Wealth Fund announced it is pulling investments from oil and gas production companies.[142] While the exclusion did not include all of the DAPL owners, it is nonetheless a significant move representing the shifting attitudes regarding oil and gas investments.

Switzerland

Credit Suisse

Credit Suisse is one of the world's largest banks and one of Europe's leading funders of fossil fuels and climate change.[143] Founded in 1856, Credit Suisse, based in Zurich, currently operates in about fifty countries.[144] As DAPL was being constructed, Credit Suisse had lending commitments of $60 million to ETE (the parent company),[145] over $163 million to ETP,[146] and $100 million to Sunoco Logistics,[147] all at the corporate level. According to the Society for Threatened Peoples, a nongovernmental organization, the interactions between Credit Suisse and Energy Transfer intensified its relationship with the Energy Transfer family of companies by

> participating in a new loan issue for Sunoco Logistic Partners on December 16, 2016;
>
> acting as joint-lead manager of books, as of January 11, 2017, for two new long-term senior notes for ETP worth $1.5 billion, with maturities as distant as 2027 and 2047;

> lending a $2.2 billion senior secured-term loan to ETE on February 3, 2017;[148] and
>
> increasing its managed shares of ETP sevenfold and quadrupling the ones on ETE between October 1 and December 31, 2016, despite escalations of the protests on the ground at that time.[149]

In regard to ETP, Credit Suisse maintains that its "transactions include the provision of loans, the issuing of securities (notes), and advisory mandates."[150] Despite documented violations of human and Indigenous peoples' rights at Standing Rock during DAPL construction,[151] Credit Suisse has maintained its banking relationship with ETP.[152]

In April 2017 the Indigenous Women's Delegation met with Credit Suisse's director of public policy involving sustainability affairs, its chief risk officer, the global head of sustainability and head of public policy of Swiss Universal Bank, and the managing director of investment banking in its oil and gas group regarding the ongoing violations of human, and specifically Indigenous, rights resulting from DAPL in Standing Rock. In a two-hour meeting, the delegation provided information about some of the human-rights violations, including the use of attack dogs by unlicensed private security actors on September 3, 2016. Credit Suisse was also provided with general information on the use of excessive force against nonviolent Indigenous peoples, as well as the surveillance and targeting of movement leaders by state and private security actors, and given copies of pending legal filings on excessive force, *Vanessa Dundon, et al. v. Kyle Kirchmeier, et al.* (8th Cir.), Case No. 17-1306.[153]

While Credit Suisse has claimed that the meeting with the Indigenous Women's Delegation "was an open, transparent exchange and the discussion took place in a constructive atmosphere,"[154] the women were preemptively told not to bring "weapons." The representatives declined to give business cards bearing their names when asked for them. The bank sent five male representatives, some of whom interrupted the women while they were giving their testimony to them.

When the women provided historic analysis of genocide and forced removal of Indian peoples from their traditional lands and territories, and its continued legacy on the realization and contemporary enjoyment of Indigenous human rights in the United States, a Credit Suisse representative became visibly uncomfortable and interrupted the women stating, "We here in Europe, we take the word 'genocide' very seriously." Similar dismissive and disrespectful behavior was also documented by other Indigenous peoples engaging with Credit Suisse on matters relating to racism and the legal history of Indigenous peoples' rights in the United States.[155]

The second meeting was, unfortunately, similar with the use of offensive racial stereotyping by bank representatives. When the women mentioned that the request for no weapons in the previous meeting was unnecessary and insensitive, bank representatives responded, "I apologize. We wanted to make sure you didn't bring any tomahawks or spears." The delegates assured the bank representatives that they usually do not check tomahawks and spears in their briefcases or checked bags for professional meetings, and they did not require a spear to get their points across.

While not a direct financer of DAPL at the project level, Credit Suisse is nonetheless a key player in the financial apparatus behind violations against Indigenous people in North Dakota. Loans give aid to companies that harm Indigenous peoples by threatening their physical and cultural survival and through severe oil contamination in their only source of water for its private benefit. The Department of Interior recognized those impacts stating,

> The Standing Rock and Cheyenne River Sioux Reservations are the permanent and irreplaceable homelands for the Tribes. . . . Their core identity and livelihood depend upon their relationship to the land and environment—unlike a resident of Bismarck, who could simply relocate if the pipeline fouled the municipal water supply, Tribal members do not have the luxury of moving away from an environmental disaster without also leaving their ancestral territory. This underscores the far-reaching effects of a DAPL spill's potential environmental impacts on the Tribes' historic, cultural, social, and economic interests.[156]

Despite the exchange of information regarding business conduct and Indigenous human-rights violations, Credit Suisse continues to fund DAPL owners, keeping them as business partners. Credit Suisse maintains the position that

> an in-depth analysis of the participation in transactions with Energy Transfer Equity was carried out using the RRRP [Reputational Risk Review Process] and direct talks were held with representatives of the company. The DAPL was one of the issues addressed in this context; pipeline security, accident responses, the protection of biodiversity and habitats, and the consultation with local communities, including the indigenous population, were discussed in detail. The regulatory permitting process that applies to a project like the DAPL at the level of individual states and at a national level in the US was also discussed. Based on the satisfactory assessment of these aspects, approval was granted for a business relationship with the company.[157]

In April 2018 Indigenous women set up an art installation, a symbolic camp, a tipi, on the steps of Credit Suisse corporate headquarters in Zurich. Later they confronted Credit Suisse CEOs and their shareholders at their annual general shareholders' meeting demanding accountability for oil and gas projects and extractive companies financed by Credit Suisse in their ancestral territories.[158] Their intervention was featured and televised on Swiss TV. On this occasion Credit Suisse CEOs ordered and sipped espresso while the women appealed to their shareholders regarding Indigenous human rights.

The dismissive attitude and use of racially charged stereotypes sidelines good faith dialogue, nor does it provide hope that engagement with banks will result in preventing violence and conflict in impacted territories of Indigenous peoples. The Credit Suisse bankers' unfamiliarity with Indigenous peoples' sovereignty and the denial of historic acts of genocide and its lingering impacts on the lives of American Indian women is consistent with the bank's disregard for their human rights today.

Bank representatives, whether in the United States or abroad, must be educated about the unique legal status and juridical personality of Indigenous peoples in the United States, and be respectful of Indigenous peoples' historic experiences when engaging with them, affording tribal sovereigns the utmost respect. Credit Suisse, moreover, should show consideration for the unique and serious human-rights violations experienced by Indigenous women and pay these women respect for their courage to vocalize that experience to protect their lands, people, water, and climate.[159] The bank's continued financing of DAPL owners and operators, and its failure to effectively implement its human-rights policy in relationship to DAPL, feeds into the adverse impacts described in the personal narratives, observations, and lived experiences of Indigenous women. Regardless of the form of finance Credit Suisse provides companies, project or corporate, it is wrong to deny and violate human rights and Indigenous peoples' free, prior, and informed consent. It is repugnant to remain neutral and violently push through Indigenous peoples' territories with militarized police and corporate actors for oil, and the profit of few.

Union Bank of Switzerland (UBS)

The Union Bank of Switzerland, headquartered in Zurich and formed by a merger between UBS and Swiss Bank Corporation in 1998, is Europe's second largest bank and one of its major fossil-fuel investors.[160] In 2016 UBS had approximately $336,437,500 committed to ETP.[161] Its business partnership with ETP made it accountable for links and contributions to violations of human rights occurring in Standing Rock. UBS has participated in many revolving credit facilities and term loans to ETP subsidiaries working on DAPL rather than direct financing.[162]

The women met with several of UBS's representatives including the executive director of Environmental and Social Risk, the director of Corporate Responsibility Management, the managing director of Environmental and Social Risk, the head of Responsibility Management, and the corporate historian and head of the Historical Archives.[163]

UBS's Environmental and Social Risk Policy Framework specifies in regard to controversial activities that it "will not knowingly provide financial or advisory services to corporate clients whose primary business activity, or where the proposed transaction, is associated with severe environmental or social damage," specifically those involving "(h) Indigenous peoples' rights in accordance with IFC Performance Standard 7."[164]

When delegates asked, "How much more credible evidence of violence against Indigenous peoples do you need to drop this bad actor ETP?" a UBS representative replied, "We really appreciate the report of the UN Special Rapporteur." The delegation responded that many UN special rapporteurs have reported abuses since September 2016, along with multiple reports by Amnesty International and other independent third parties. The delegation also provided domestic court filings and the Standing Rock Sioux Tribe's request for precautionary measures to the Inter-American Commission as well as their own eyewitness accounts.

As of December 2017, UBS has not renewed their loan commitments to ETP on either a project level or corporate level. Indigenous women continue to request that UBS formally exclude all DAPL-related companies including Phillips 66 and Enbridge.

Project and Corporate Finance

When the Indigenous women divestment delegation met with banks, the bank representatives commonly made distinctions between project-level and corporate-level finance relating to DAPL. The Indigenous women, however, recognized the pattern of distinctions without differences being used to avoid accountability for Indigenous human-rights violations stemming from business relationships and investments. While the project-level loan was $2.5 billion to complete the DAPL/Bakken Pipeline, the total coast was $4.8 billion. Moreover, since running up credit line balances, DAPL entities have rolled those balances over into longer term debt, in the form of bonds.[165]

Many were thrilled to hear of U.S. Bank's environmental policy change to "not provide project financing for the construction of oil or natural gas pipelines."[166] Similar enthusiasm was shown for DNB's announcement to sell shares from DAPL.[167] However, these banks, while ending project-level financing, are still providing corporate-level financing to the DAPL owners despite the human-rights violations and conduct.[168] As for U.S. Bank:

> During DAPL's construction, U.S. Bank provided Energy Transfer Partners with a $175 million line of credit. Just six weeks ago, U.S. Bank recommitted to Energy Transfer on that deal, but the new agreement no longer discloses how much each bank has committed. Now they say they will stop "project financing"? U.S. Bank knows that the average consumer would not pay attention to the complicated bigger picture, so it was a very clever public relations move—and many green groups bought it.[169]

Banks are using the distinction between project-level and corporate finance to divest in one area of a company while continuing to finance the company in another. Indigenous peoples, however, are requesting full divestment from the projects and all companies responsible for Indigenous human-rights violations: "If U.S. Bank is going to stop financing pipelines, it has to stop lending at the corporate level, too."[170]

John Ruggie, the UN secretary-general's special representative for Business and Human Rights, further elaborates on the UN Guiding Principles on Business and Human Rights (UNGPs) and how banks can be involved in human-rights abuses though the provision of products and services, noting:

> For example, providing a general corporate loan to a private prison company that is alleged to engage in severe human rights abuses ought to require a very deep dive by the bank, coupled with the imposition of strict conditions if it decides to go ahead with the loan. If the bank does neither and yet proceeds, then it is squarely in "contribution" territory for any adverse impacts, even though the loan is not asset or project specific. Where the real challenge to banks lies is in their need to obtain sufficient information in the case of a company that is not as obviously high-risk from a human rights perspective as in this example. That may well call for more effort to be dedicated to human rights due diligence in some instances. But the concern cannot simply be excluded based on the type of financing involved.[171]

According to Ruggie, banks can contribute to human-rights abuses regardless of the type of financing involved or whether the loan was asset or project specific.

Indigenous peoples are goaded into spending precious time and resources arguing that violations occurred, violations that are only denied by the banks who continue to finance DAPL and its owners. The debate on project and corporate finance is not the only conversation we should have. The conversation we should have is the financing of racial gaps, between those who benefit from resource extraction and those who are harmed by extraction, environmental racism. The conversation we should have is how the planet's survival is tied to and dependent on the protection and restoration of Indigenous human rights. Only by squarely facing the deficiencies in domestic and international systems that fail to effectively regulate and hold these actors accountable will there be potential for business and human rights to exist together. As NGOs, banks, and states argue the semantics of project and corporate finance, the planet burns, the waters spoil, and Indigenous human-rights defenders remain in urgent danger, disappeared, murdered, and assassinated for protecting their lands and resources from extraction financed by international banks far away from the violence. There were 321 human-rights defenders killed in 2018; 77 percent of those killed worked on land, Indigenous, and environmental rights.[172] Indigenous peoples are protecting land and life and cannot be expected to follow the pace set by the banks, academics, or organizations. Indigenous peoples and those most targeted and most in need of protection should create, define, and lead the mechanism of grievance and remediation to set the tone, in a fast stride toward justice and accountability.

Credit Rating Agencies and Insurance

Indigenous women have also met with the credit-rating agency Morgan Stanley Capital International (MSCI)[173] and global insurers like Swiss Re and Allianz,[174] some of the world's largest insurers and reinsurers.[175] Indigenous women are demanding that Indigenous women's human rights and climate risks be integrated and accurately measured, evaluated, and reflected in the rating systems of actors like MSCI. Indigenous women are also demanding the inclusion of accurate assessments of Indigenous human-rights risks in the evaluations by insurance agencies underwriting companies and projects like DAPL.

Large-scale extractive industries require insurance for their projects; often this insurance is provided despite documented human-rights and environmental risks of oil spills and harm to human health. Often the insurance policies fail to sufficiently cover damages relating to spills, contamination, climate catastrophes,[176] and harm to human and environmental health. Insurance and credit-rating agencies have a role and responsibility toward human rights and climate justice. Indigenous engagements with insurance and credit-rating agencies are vital sites for advancing Indigenous peoples' rights and climate justice within the financial arena.[177]

Looking Forward: A New International Economy

While 2017 saw Norway's largest bank DNB, Germany's BayernLB, BNP Paribas, and the Netherlands-based bank ING sell assets, loans, and credit due to the DAPL controversy and lack of full consultation, none of the banks have excluded or ceased corporate financing to all the companies behind DAPL.[178] As of April 2017, Netherlands ABN Amro, DNB, ING, and Italian Intesa Sanpaolo banks that were previously on ETE's revolving credit did not support ETE's credit renewal.[179] Intesa Sanpaolo has since not renewed their loans to ETE—parent of the family of companies behind the pipeline.[180] Intesa has, however, committed to lend $50 million to Phillips 66,[181] founding owners of DAPL and the Bayou Bridge Pipeline crossing Louisiana.[182]

Banks such as U.S. Bank and Parisian BNP Paribas made statements exiting tar sands projects.[183] BNP Paribas, for example, states that they no longer would do business with producers, distributors, marketers, or traders focused on oil and gas from shale or tar sands. BNP Paribas also said it will not finance projects mainly involved in the transport and export of oil and gas from shale or oil sands and will quit financing oil and gas exploration and production in the Arctic.[184] However, BNP Paribas remains invested in other sectors rife with human-rights violations such as private prisons.[185]

In the process of engaging with banks, Indigenous women are observing how global capital impacts Indigenous peoples specifically through the financing of projects or the provisions of loans to companies tied to and responsible for human-rights violations or violence against Indigenous peoples. Indigenous movements for divestment and financial accountability are challenging the erroneous interpretations of banking and human rights between project and corporate finance used by banks.[186] However, their ability to fully engage hinges on financial data transparency and accessibility.[187] Moreover the available mechanisms of accountability, remedy, and justice within banks are tragically ineffective, inaccessible, or altogether absent in protecting and/or adequately responding to the violations of Indigenous peoples' human rights.

Indigenous women and peoples are challenging global financial systems by engaging with divestment, as well as realizing their own personal and collective power in shaping change in that discrete area of the fossil-fuel and extractive and infrastructure industries. To question like similar thinkers, "how do we create and proliferate a compelling vision of economies and ecologies that center humans and the natural world over accumulation of material?"[188]

Indigenous women are mastering the language and lexicon of banking and finance and in doing so are raising questions, for example, about what options Indigenous peoples have in developing sovereign, self-determined, sui generis economic systems that are not premised on fossil fuels, global bank involvement, or colonial economic modalities and mediums of exchange. As the late Arthur Manuel stated, "we must always keep in mind that taking care of Mother Earth is the most contribution we can make. This is how we can support a new international economy that is not based on the outdated and environmentally unsound laissez-faire concepts of economics."[189] The result may be more "disciplining" of the banks financing violations of Indigenous rights, fossil fuels, private prisons, and more.[190]

Conclusion

As the four-hundred-year anniversary of the *Mayflower* landing on the shores of what would become America approaches, the world should ask how far the rights of Indigenous peoples have advanced in the United States, the hemisphere, the world. Has the displacement and dispossession of Indigenous peoples from their lands in order to extract natural resources for corporate profit abated or ceased? Indigenous peoples do not seem safer when corporations and banks can abuse their rights. Human rights and its institutions do not seem to effectively work when these companies lay waste to Indigenous lands. Indigenous peoples do not seem safer when the rule of law deteriorates with each corporate lobby's political campaign contribution. Indigenous peoples are not safer when states fail to protect them and in fact allow ancestral lands and waters of Indian Nations to be compromised for the wealth of European banks.

Financial injustice and economic inequality remain constant features in the everyday lives of Indigenous peoples and the world.[191] Whether it is estimates that eight men own the same wealth as half of the world, or Credit Suisse's role in the

2008 housing crisis in selling subprime loans and mortgages, or the release of the Paradise Paper's findings on off-shore investments, banks and financial institutions continue to wield incredibly complete yet silent and hidden power over the global economy and daily life.[192] Banks, mutual funds, pension funds, and insurance companies, for example, are the most common specific type of individual or organization that controlled the shareholdings in very large corporations,[193] with the richest 1 percent owning more than half the world's wealth.[194]

Banks and international financial institutions deeply affect the rights and the very survival of Indigenous peoples in the United States. European states are frequently at or near the head of international civil liberties and political rights rankings and have adopted the UN Declaration on the Rights of Indigenous Peoples. Now is the time to realize those human-rights commitments by taking action and excluding companies contributing to climate insecurity and Indigenous human-rights violations from banking investments. In order to prevent these horrific abuses from reoccurring in the future, there must be effective changes in regulatory systems, law, policy, and bank compliance procedures in alignment with human rights and Indigenous self-determination.

Standing Rock and the violations that occurred there are reflections on the international community's commitments to enforce and implement their human-rights obligations and standards. DAPL is responsible for one of the greatest human-rights abuses against the Indian Nations and Native peoples to occur in the United States in the twenty-first century. Banks and financial institutions must not remain complicit or neutral when companies in extractive industries that they financially advise, enable, invest in, and facilitate put Indigenous peoples' very existence and survival at risk. Many banks and financial institutions continue to maintain business relationships with DAPL owners, which continues to violate internationally recognized human rights, and specifically Indigenous rights. Banks maintain these relationships despite the evidence of these violations and Indigenous peoples' sincere and desperate cries for visibility and justice.

Yet the need to implement Indigenous human rights is critical for the global community's ability to protect and preserve what is left of the planet's biodiversity, waters, and forests. Empirical data illustrate that Indigenous rights to land and resources halts deforestation, mitigates climate change, and improves conservation of the world's biodiversity.[195] A recent study found that when Indigenous peoples' land rights are secured deforestation has either ceased or has been drastically reduced. The study found that the capacity of Indigenous peoples to restore damaged lands and forests is better than states, and that securing Indigenous land rights is critical to halting deforestation and mitigating climate change.[196] Protection and fulfillment of, as well as respect for, Indigenous peoples' communal property rights are critical for the protection of the planet's biodiversity.[197] Climate justice cannot occur without decolonization and the restoration of Indigenous peoples' rights over their lands, forest, and ancestral territories.

Securing Indigenous peoples' ability to deny or withhold their consent to development projects in their traditional territories is critical to ensuring their human rights, physical existence, and cultural survival. Indigenous peoples are the protectors of the world's last regions on biodiversity; therefore implementing their right to FPIC over their homelands, and supporting their right to say "No" to harmful development projects occurring within those territories, protects not just Indigenous peoples, but the world's remaining natural resources. Without land rights and right to consent, Indigenous peoples will continue to disproportionately experience environmental exploitation, conflict, and violence when it comes to invasive energy development by multinational corporations.

Indigenous peoples are more than "risks." Indigenous peoples are "peoples" with the right of self-determination.[198] However, for Indigenous peoples, "the overarching issue . . . is their ability to make this sovereign decision independently and in accordance with tribal priorities."[199] The inability of tribal sovereigns' decisions like FPIC to be respected by state and corporate actors remains in too many cases ignored and unfulfilled in the United States.

Indigenous women and peoples in the divestment movement are seeking to change those unjust norms, to bring justice and accountability. They are trying to create a consequence, a repercussion, for the horrific treatment of Indigenous people and the abuse of their rights as a result of DAPL. Without a consequence to businesses involved in the violations of rights and dignities in Standing Rock, it sets a dangerous precedent, and sends a dangerous message to oil companies operating in Indian Country and the rest of the world, that Indigenous lives and futures do not matter and will be collateral damage in an insatiable lust for fossil fuel financed by international banks like Credit Suisse. With no consequence other companies will assume a social license to conduct themselves in the same indignant Indigenous-rights-abusing manner. Creating consequences for human rights for companies like banks and financial markets is therefore important beyond the reservation boundaries of Standing Rock; it is necessary for the planet.[200]

Standing Rock, hopefully, will mark a much-needed and long sought-after turning point in the discourse of Indigenous peoples' human rights in America in favor of one that supports Indigenous self-determination and treaty rights and demands accountability and remedy from state and nonstate actors that undermine and compromise the enjoyment of those rights and fundamental freedoms. Standing Rock was a place of hope, and the fire for justice still burns bright in the hearts of all who supported the call of the Oceti Sakowin. Standing Rock, like Selma, represents and marks a moment of societal shift that will continue to emerge and hopefully inspire the creation and development of more just and liberated economic institutions including but not limited to public banks and tribally owned banking systems.[201]

Standing Rock has empowered a generation to demand justice and accountability. The torch and spirit of this historic movement for water, life, and human rights broke through the doorways of banks and financial institutions seeking a reckoning, truth, and accountability from the economic powers behind destructive projects like DAPL.

Indigenous peoples will continue to demand that financial institutions that fund these companies mitigate, divest, and exclude actors linked and contributing to Indigenous human-rights violations and unethical business practices.[202] The wheel of justice regarding this historic and ongoing situation is still in spin, and there remain opportunities for civil society to divest and stand for Indigenous peoples' survival by requiring their banks and financial institutions to do what is right and step away from companies that violate the climate and Indigenous peoples' human rights.[203]

Indian women are challenging the world's largest oil and gas funders. In doing so they are lifting the veil that obscures the indispensable historic and contemporary role banks and financial institutions continue to play in creating the international global economic apparatus that sustains and perpetuates the companies responsible for the colonization and exploitation of Indigenous peoples' lands and resources. Dr. Sara Jumping Eagle, Oglala Lakota and Mdewakantonwan Dakota living and working on the Pine Ridge Reservation and divestment delegate, explains: "The connections between who we are as Lakota Oyate—our health, our lands and water, our spirituality, our self-empowerment and self-esteem—are deeply rooted; the actions we take to protect our land and water, our future, and our children's water can only help us all. We all have the power—*wowasake*—within us to make a difference in this world."[204]

The experience of Standing Rock has displayed the interdependence between banks, states, and corporations. Visibility of the financial streams and flow highlighted the key role of banks in sustaining and perpetuating the companies responsible for the violations of Indigenous peoples' rights. Understanding and challenging, whether in the streets, courts, or board rooms, the deleterious role these banks play and how they operate with near impunity are imperative for the enjoyment of human rights not only for Indian Country, but also for the United States and global civil society.[205]

Notes

1. "Power is war, a war continued by other means. This reversal of Clausewitz's assertion that war is politics continued by other means . . . implies that the relations of power that function in a society such as ours essentially rest upon a definite relation of forces that is established at a determinate, historically specifiable moment, in war and by war. . . . The role of political power, on this hypothesis, is perpetually to reinscribe this relation through a form of unspoken warfare; to reinscribe it in social institutions, in economic inequality, in language, in the bodies themselves of each and every one of us": Michel Foucault, *Power/Knowledge: Selected Interviews*

and Other Writings, 1972–1977, ed. and trans. Colin Gordon (New York: Harvester, 1980), 90; Patrick Wolfe, *Traces of History: Elementary Structures of Race* (London: Verso, 2016): "Invasion is a structure, not an event. . . . Race is colonialism speaking, in idioms whose diversity reflects the variety of unequal relationships into which Europeans have co-opted conquered populations. . . . The incompleteness of racial domination is the trace and achievement of resistance, a space of hope."

2. United Nations Subcommision on Prevention of Discrimination and Protection of Minorities, *Study of the Problem of Discrimination against Indigenous Peoples*, UN Document E/CN.4/Sub.2/1986/7/Add. 4, 1986, para. 379: "Indigenous communities, people and nations are those which, having a historical continuity with pre-invasion and pre-colonial societies that developed on their territories, consider themselves distinct from other sectors of the societies now prevailing in those territories, or parts of them. They form at present non-dominant sectors of society and are determined to preserve, develop and transmit to future generations their ancestral territories, and their ethnic identity, as the bases of their continued existence as peoples, in accordance with their own cultural patterns, social institutions, and legal systems."

3. "Bakken," Energy Transfer LP, March 23, 2019, http://www.energytransfer.com/ops _bakken.aspx: "The Dakota Access Pipeline ('Dakota Access') and the Energy Transfer Crude Oil Pipeline ('ETCO'), collectively the 'Bakken Pipeline' went into service on June 1, 2017. The Bakken Pipeline is a 1,915-mile, mostly 30-inch pipeline system that transports domestically produced crude oil from the Bakken/ Three Forks productions areas in North Dakota to a storage and terminalling hub outside Patoka, Illinois, and/or down to additional terminals in Nederland, Texas. The Bakken Pipeline is a joint venture between Energy Transfer Partners with a 38.25 percent interest, MarEn Bakken Company LLC ('MarEn') with a 36.75 percent interest, and Phillips 66 Partners with a 25 percent interest. MarEn is an entity owned by MPLX LP and Enbridge Energy Partners L.P. . . . Dakota Access consists of approximately 1,172 miles of 30-inch diameter pipeline traversing North Dakota, South Dakota, Iowa and Illinois. Crude oil transported on Dakota Access originates at six terminal locations in the North Dakota counties of Mountrail, Williams and McKenzie. The pipeline delivers the crude oil to a hub outside of Patoka, Illinois where it can be delivered to the ETCO pipeline for delivery to the Gulf Coast, or can be transported via other pipelines to refining markets throughout the Midwest."

4. "Water Protectors File Arguments in the 8th Circuit on Militarized Policing," Water Protector Legal Collective, May 25, 2017, https://waterprotectorlegal.org; "This matter challenges the indiscriminate, undifferentiated use of dangerous weapons that cause severe injuries against people engaged in First Amendment activity" (opening brief *Dundon et al. v. Kirchmeier et al.*). *Dundon et al. v. Kirchmeier et al.*, First Amended Civil Rights Class Action Complaint for Damages and Injunctive and Declaratory Relief, January 29, 2018, No. 1:16-cv-406 DLH-CSM, http://www .sfbla.com/wp-content/uploads/2017/07/1st-Amd-Complaint.pdf. Standing Rock, Cheyenne River, and Yankton Sioux Tribes, "Request for Precautionary Measures

Pursuant to Article 25 of the [Inter-American Commission on Human Rights] Rules of Procedure Concerning Serious and Urgent Risks of Irreparable Harm Arising Out of Construction of the Dakota Access Pipeline," December 2, 2016, https://www.scribd.com.

5. "Human Rights Defenders under Threat – A Shrinking Space for Civil Society," Amnesty International, May 16, 2017, https://www.amnestyusa.org; "207 Environmental Defenders Have Been Killed in 2017," *The Guardian*, June 6, 2018, https://www.theguardian.com: "What's driving this violence? The short answer is: industry. The most deadly industries to go up against were agribusiness and mining. Poaching, hydroelectric dams and logging were also key drivers of violence, Global Witness found. Many of the killings recorded occurred in remote villages deep within mountain ranges and rainforests, with indigenous communities hardest hit."

6. Jack Healy, "From 280 Tribes, a Protest on the Plains," *New York Times*, September 11, 2016, https://www.nytimes.com.

7. University of Arizona School of Law, Indigenous Peoples Law and Policy Program, *Indigenous Resistance to the Dakota Access Pipeline: Criminalization of Dissent and Suppression of Protest*, March 16, 2018, https://law.arizona.edu/sites/default/files/Indigenous%20Resistance%20to%20the%20Dakota%20Access%20Pipeline%20Criminalization%20of%20Dissent%20and%20Suppression%20of%20Protest.pdf.

8. Jeremy Kryt, "Guns, Farms, and Oil: How Colombian Tribes Are Being Driven to Extinction," *Earth Island Journal*, January 16, 2015, http://www.earthisland.org/journal/index.php/: "'We don't want to be wiped out, and we don't want to lose who we are,' says Governor Santos Sauna, who is also a *Mama*. 'We don't want tourists coming here either—too much tourism damages the psychology of the tribe. The only thing we want,' he says, 'is to be left alone'"; Bianca Jagger, "Stop the Murder of Environmental Defenders in Latin America," *Huffington Post*, May 10, 2017, https://www.huffingtonpost.com; Solicitor Hilary C. Tompkins, "Tribal Treaty and Environmental Statutory Implications of the Dakota Access Pipeline," M-37038 (withdrawn memo), United States Department of Interior, December 4, 2016, https://shadowproof.com/wp-content/uploads/2017/02/document_ew_05.pdf: "The Standing Rock and Cheyenne River Sioux Reservations are the permanent and irreplaceable homelands for the Tribes. Their core identity and livelihood depend upon their relationship to the land and environment—unlike a resident of Bismarck, who could simply relocate if the [Dakota Access] pipeline fouled the municipal water supply, Tribal members do not have the luxury of moving away from an environmental disaster without also leaving their ancestral territory."

9. "Equator Principle Disaster Projects," BankTrack, 2017, https://www.equatorbanksact.org/disaster_projects.

10. Robert A. Williams Jr., "The Rehnquist Court's Perpetuation of European Cultural Racism against American Indian Tribes," in Cases and Materials on Federal Indian Law, ed. David H. Getches, Charles F. Wilkinson, and Robert A. Williams Jr., 5th ed. (St. Paul: West Group, 2005), 36.

11. Alleen Brown, Will Parrish, and Alice Speri, "Leaked Documents Reveal Counterterrorism Tactics Used at Standing Rock to 'Defeat Pipeline Insurgencies,'" *The Intercept*, May 27, 2017, https://theintercept.com.

12. "Request for Human Rights Hearing on Suppression of Indigenous Resistance: 60 Organizations File Request to Inter-American Commission on Human Rights," Water Protector Legal Collective, March 6, 2019, https://waterprotectorlegal.org.

13. Dahar Jamail, "Settler State Repression: Standing Rock Battles Continue in the Courts," Truthout, May 3, 2017, http://www.truthout.org; University of Arizona School of Law, *Indigenous Resistance to the Dakota Access Pipeline* : "As of the writing of this report [March 2018], there are seven federal cases, three of which are plea deals with the prosecution recommending 36 months of prison time. Out of an initial total of 832 North Dakota state criminal cases: approximately 300 remain open and unresolved; 174 are proceeding to trial; 102 are inactive or in warrant status; 316 were dismissed; 20 were acquitted at trial; 13 were convicted at trial; 82 were resolved with pre-trial diversion; 120 took plea agreements; and 4 are on appeal."

14. Victoria Tauli-Corpuz, "Report of the Special Rapporteur on the Rights of Indigenous Peoples on Her Mission to the United States of America," UN Document A/HRC/36/46/Add.1, August 9, 2017, paras. 63–74, http://ap.ohchr.org/documents/dpage_e.aspx?si=A/HRC/36/46/Add.1.

15. M. Cook and H. R. MacMillan, "Money Talks, Banks Are Talking: Dakota Access Pipeline Finance Lessons," *Mouvements* (forthcoming); Jo Miles and Hugh MacMillan, "Who's Banking on the Dakota Access Pipeline?" Food & Water Watch, September 6, 2016, https://www.foodandwaterwatch.org; see MazaskaTalks.org/banks for an expanded web. Some $2.5 billion of the $4.8 billion Bakken Pipeline project was financed through a project specific loan. The remaining $2.3 billion was financed at the corporate level by ETP. After the Bakken Pipeline was completed, MarEn provided $2 billion, and ETP paid off the balance it had accumulated on its $3.75 billion credit facility. See links and argument at August 17–18, 2016 ("ETP Presents at 'CITI One-on-One MLP/Midstream Infrastructure Conference'"), "Money Talks. Who's Talking?": https://cdn.knightlab.com/libs/timeline3/latest/embed/index.html?source=1mMZlb7_fcpLgLPG21ihHARJj7oqkSfVJmju86Xr-fi-M&font=Default&lang=en&initial_zoom=2&height=650.

16. Adrienne Maree Brown, *Emergent Strategy: Shaping Change, Changing Worlds* (Chico, Calif.: AK Press, 2017), 19: "We must imagine new worlds that transition ideologies and norms, so that no one sees Black people as murderers, or Brown people as terrorists and aliens, but all of us as potential cultural and economic innovators. This is a time-travel exercise for the heart. This is collaborative ideation— what are the ideas that will liberate us all?" For more generalized information, see Cook and MacMillan, "Money Talks, Banks Are Talking."

17. "Bakken," Energy Transfer LP, March 23, 2019, http://www.energytransfer.com/ops_bakken.aspx

18. "2016 Citi One-On-One MLP/Midstream Infrastructure Conference" (presentation), Energy Transfer, Investor Relations, August 2016, slides 8 and 15, https://ir.energytransfer.com.

19. Sunoco Logistic Partners L.P., Form 8-K (annual report), U.S. Securities and Exchange Commission, August 2, 2016, https://www.sec.gov/Archives/edgar/data/1161154/000119312516675095/d215460d8k.htm. The Bayou Bridge Pipeline ("BBP"), an extension of DAPL, runs from Nederland, Texas, to Lake Charles.

20. "Bayou Bridge Pipeline: Fact Sheet," Bayou Bridge Facts, March 2018, https://bayoubridge.com/docs/Bayou-Bridge-fact-sheet-3-12-18.pdf: "The Bayou Bridge Pipeline currently delivers multiple grades of crude oil from terminal hub facilities in Nederland, Texas, to terminal facilities and refineries in Lake Charles, Louisiana. The approximately $750 million expansion currently underway will allow the Bayou Bridge Pipeline to connect to an existing market hub in St. James, Louisiana. The new segment of the Bayou Bridge Pipeline will consist of approximately 163 miles of buried 24-inch pipe and will run from Lake Charles, Louisiana, to St. James, Louisiana. Crude from the St. James terminaling facilities will then be redistributed to refineries located throughout the Louisiana gulf coast region."

21. "2016 Citi One-On-One MLP/Midstream Infrastructure Conference," Energy Transfer.

22. Phillips 66 ups export capacity at Beaumont terminal at end of 2017: "Phillips 66 Reports Fourth-Quarter Earnings of $3.2 Billion or $6.25 per Share" (press release), Phillips 66, February 2, 2018, https://investor.phillips66.com; ETP touts ~400,000 barrels of oil per day capacity at Nederland terminal: "2018 MLP & Energy Infrastructure Conference" (presentation), Energy Transfer, Investor Relations, May 23, 2018, slide 8, https://ir.energytransfer.com.

23. For an illustration of the DAPL/Bakken/Bayou Bridge expansion project, see "J.P. Morgan 2018 Energy Conference" (presentation), Energy Transfer, Investor Relations, June 19, 2018, slide 16, http://ir.energytransfer.com; "Credit Suisse Conference" (presentation), Phillips 66, Investors, February 13, 2018, slide 7, http://investor.phillips66.com; Energy Transfer Partners, Form 10-K (annual report), U.S. Securities and Exchange Commission, February 23, 2018, at 15, https://www.sec.gov/Archives/edgar/data/1161154/000116115418000018/etp12-31x201710k.htm.

24. Ari Paul, "7 Things the Defund DAPL Campaign Has Achieved So Far (Including $28 Million in Personal Accounts Moved)," *Yes! Magazine*, December 22, 2016, http://www.yesmagazine.org.

25. Hugh MacMillan, "Who's Banking on the Dakota Access Pipeline?" LittleSis, August 17, 2016, https://littlesis.org/maps/1634-who-s-banking-on-the-dakota-access-pipeline.

26. Miles and MacMillan, "Who's Banking on the Dakota Access Pipeline?"; Cook and MacMillan, "Money Talks, Banks Are Talking," http://www.mouvements.info/defund-dapl.

27. Standing Rock Sioux Tribal Council, Resolution 591-16, October 4, 2016, published

in Matt Remle, "Standing Rock Sioux Tribe Ends Relationships with Financial Institutions that Support Dakota Access Pipeline," Last Real Indians, http://lastrealindians.com.

28. Miles and MacMillan, "Who's Banking on the Dakota Access Pipeline?"

29. Kelly Trout, "Banking on Climate Change: Fossil Fuel Report Card 2017," Oil Change International, June 21, 2017, http://priceofoil.org (internal citations omitted); Lynda V. Mapes, "Seattle Returns to Wells Fargo Because No Other Bank Wants City's Business," *Seattle Times*, May 14, 2018, https://www.seattletimes.com: "In the end, the city renewed its contract with Wells Fargo last week, and council members held a public briefing on the signing of the contract in a public work session Monday. The contract ties the city of Seattle and Wells Fargo together for three more years beginning Jan. 1 with two optional one year extensions after that. The city finance office began briefing the mayor and council about the situation last February as it became clear the city would have no takers no matter how it sliced up the business. The main piece of city business—handling depository services—could only be done by a large bank, and there were no takers in that limited class. The city cycles about $3 billion a year through Wells Fargo—all the revenue the city receives, even from parking meters. The city's average daily balance in the bank has been about $10 million, according to Wells Fargo."

30. Carla F. Fredrick, Mark Meany, Nicolas Pelosi, and Kate R. Finn, *Social Cost and Material Loss: The Dakota Access Pipeline*, First Peoples Investment Engagement Program, November 2018, https://www.colorado.edu/project/fpiep: "This case study estimates that the costs incurred by ETP and other firms with ownership stake in DAPL for the entire project are not less than $7.5 billion, but could be higher depending on the terms of confidential contracts. The banks that financed DAPL incurred an additional $4.4 billion in costs in the form of account closures, not including costs related to reputational damage. Further, at least $38 million was also incurred by taxpayers and other local stakeholders. All of these figures are estimated based on publicly reported data to demonstrate the magnitude of financial losses caused by poor social risk management."

31. "CalPERS Joins Investors Calling on Banks to Address Concerns Surrounding Dakota Access Pipeline," CalPERS, February 17, 2017, https://www.calpers.ca.gov; "Investor Statement to Banks Financing the Dakota Access Pipeline," CalPERS, February 16, 2017, https://www.calpers.ca.gov.

32. Camila Domonoske, "Norwegian Pension Fund Divests from Companies Behind DAPL," National Public Radio, March 17, 2017, http://www.npr.org.

33. Richard Milne, "Norway's $1tn Wealth Fund Set to Cut Oil and Gas Stocks," Financial Times, March 8, 2019.

34. Water Protector Legal Collective, letter to Credit Suisse Bank, May 31, 2017, https://waterprotectorlegal.org; Jessica Chin, "Indigenous Activists Are Building Tiny Houses to Protest B.C. Trans Mountain Pipeline," *Huffington Post*, September 8, 2017, http://www.huffingtonpost.com: "Their investment is only going to become

more risky and uncertain as the direct action and legal challenges escalate"; "Indigenous Groups Lead Movement to Call on Banks to Drop Enbridge's Controversial Line 3 Pipeline," Rainforest Action Network, September 25, 2017, https://www.ran.org; the letter, dated September 21, 2017, is available at https://d3n8a8pro7vhmx.cloudfront.net/honorearth/pages/2406/attachments/original/1506371831/Line_3_Bank_Letter_-_FINAL.pdf?1506371831: "We urge your institutions not to arrange or renew business relationships, including corporate level finance and revolving credit, with Enbridge Inc. and its subsidiaries, until it ceases expanding tar sands operations."

35. See MazaskaTalks.org/banks.

36. United Nations Declaration on the Rights of Indigenous Peoples, G.A. Res. 61/295, UN Document A/RES/61/295, September 13, 2007, http://www.un.org/esa/socdev/unpfii/documents/DRIPS_en.pdf, Article 18: "Indigenous peoples have the right to participate in decision-making in matters which would affect their rights, through representatives chosen by themselves in accordance with their own procedures, as well as to maintain and develop their own indigenous decision-making institutions"; Article 19: "States shall consult and cooperate in good faith with the indigenous peoples concerned through their own representative institutions in order to obtain their free, prior and informed consent before adopting and implementing legislative or administrative measures that may affect them"; Article 32(2): "States shall consult and cooperate in good faith with the indigenous peoples concerned through their own representative institutions in order to obtain their free and informed consent prior to the approval of any project affecting their lands or territories and other resources, particularly in connection with the development, utilization or exploitation of mineral, water or other resources"; United Nations Human Rights Office of the High Commissioner, "Free, Prior and Informed Consent of Indigenous Peoples," September 2013, https://www.ohchr.org: "*Free* implies that there is no coercion, intimidation or manipulation. *Prior* implies that consent is to be sought sufficiently in advance of any authorization or commencement of activities and respect is shown to time requirements of indigenous consultation/consensus processes. *Informed* implies that information is provided that covers a range of aspects, including the nature, size, pace, reversibility and scope of any proposed project or activity; the purpose of the project as well as its duration; locality and areas affected; a preliminary assessment of the likely economic, social, cultural and environmental impact, including potential risks; personnel likely to be involved in the execution of the project; and procedures the project may entail. This process may include the option of withholding consent. Consultation and participation are crucial components of a *consent* process."

37. "Tour of Standing Rock Native Defenders in Europe," Pressenza, May 18, 2017, https://www.pressenza.com: Rachel Heaton, Wašté Win Young, Naát'áaníí Nez Means, and Rafael "Tufawon" Gonzalez; Jackie Fielder, "Indigenous Divestment Delegation Goes to Europe," Last Real Indians, May 21, 2017, http://lastrealindians

.com: "The action is part of a month-long European tour called 'Stand Up with Standing Rock,' which aims to call on European banks to divest from pipeline projects being planned without the Free, Prior, and Informed Consent of Indigenous People. Among these pipelines are the Dakota Access, Keystone XL, Trans Mountain, Line 3, Energy East, LNG, and many more."

38. "Impacts of an Oil Spill from the Dakota Access Pipeline on the Standing Rock Sioux Tribe," Standing Rock Sioux Tribe, February 21, 2018, https://www.standingrock.org/sites/default/files/uploads/srst_impacts_of_an_oil_spill_2.21.2018.pdf: "In 2017, the Standing Rock Sioux Tribe Department of Game and Fish has prepared a report entitled Missouri River High Consequence Area Assessment: Establishing Baseline Ecological Information and Impacts to Hunting and Fishing from the Proposed DAPL Pipeline in the Event of an Oil Spill in the Missouri River in North Dakota Adjacent to the Standing Rock Reservation. This report documents the significant impacts of an oil spill on sensitive wetland habitat, macroinvertebrates, shellfish, fish, birds and waterfowl, as well as on mammals and big game on the Standing Rock Reservation. The report finds that subsistence hunting and fishing by Tribal members shall be adversely affected by an oil spill from DAPL."

39. "Indigenous Women's Delegation Pursues Fossil Fuel Divestment across Europe, amidst Growing Global Movement" (press release), Women's Earth & Climate Action Network (WECAN), October 17, 2017, http://wecaninternational.org.

40. Brenda Norrell, "Indigenous Women to Bank of North Dakota: Stop Loan to Militarize Police at Standing Rock," Censored News, January 30, 2017, https://bsnorrell.blogspot.com.

41. Todd Davis, "Financial Interest between Donald Trump and Dakota Access Pipeline Goes Both Ways," *Dallas News*, October 2016, https://www.dallasnews.com: "ETP's chief executive Kelcy Warren has donated $103,000 to the Trump for president campaign and $66,800 to the Republican National Committee since Trump secured its nomination, according to the report. . . . The media outlet reports that through the Republican presidential candidate's financial disclosure form for the Federal Election Committee, Trump has between $500,000 and $1 million invested in Energy Transfer Partners."

42. "President Trump Takes Action to Expedite Priority Energy and Infrastructure Projects" (press release), White House, January 24, 2017, https://www.whitehouse.gov.

43. Associated Press, "North Dakota to Sue Feds over Pipeline Protest Police Cost," *MPR News*, February 12, 2019, https://www.mprnews.org: "North Dakota will sue the federal government to try to recoup the $38 million. . . . President Trump last year denied a state-requested disaster declaration to cover the state's costs. The Justice Department eventually did give the state a $10 million grant for policing-related bills. Texas-based pipeline developer Energy Transfer Partners chipped in $15 million."

44. "Indigenous Women of Standing Rock and Allies to Speak Out during Divestment Delegation to Norway" (press release), WECAN, March 24, 2017, http://wecaninter national.org/news.

45. "Indigenous Women's Delegation Pursues Fossil Fuel Divestment across Europe," WECAN.

46. "Indigenous Women's Delegation to Europe Continues Push for Fossil Fuel Divestment by Major Banks" (press release), WECAN, April 18, 2018, http://wecaninter national.org.

47. Army Department, "Notice of Intent to Prepare an Environmental Impact Statement in Connection with Dakota Access, LLC's Request for an Easement to Cross Lake Oahe, North Dakota," *Federal Register*, January 18, 2017, 82 FR 5543, 5543–45, https://www.federalregister.gov; President Donald J. Trump to the Secretary of the Army, "Memorandum on Construction of the Dakota Access Pipeline," January 24, 2017, https://www.gpo.gov.

48. Mary J. Rivers, "Navajo Women and Abuse: The Context for Their Troubled Relationships," *Journal of Family Violence* 20, no. 2 (April 2005), 85: "The Navajo tribe is historically matrilineal; property is owned by and passed on to women." This article is available from the website of the Navajo Department of Health (http://www .nec.navajo-nsn.gov) in the section on Psychosocial Research.

49. Bethany R. Berger, "Elouise Cobell," Cobell Scholarship, 2015, http://cobellscholar .org/wp-content/uploads/2015/11/cobell_chapter.pdf: "Cobell starting asking the BIA for an accounting of her trust monies when she was just 18."

50. Morgan Simon, "We're Not Done with DAPL: How Investors Can Still Support Indigenous Rights," *Forbes*, November 1, 2018, https://www.forbes.com: "Research being led at the Wharton School of Business by Deloitte and Touche Professor Witold Jerzy Henisz found that 'investors proximate to indigenous land claims experience 60–160% increases in material credit events such as lawsuits, regulatory inquiries, and actions as well as labor-related actions. Yet, creditors don't seem to take the higher incidence of these events into account in assessing and pricing risk nor in structuring the terms of covenants. Typically, when a risk is shown to be material, creditors develop the capability to assess and monitor that risk. That should be happening here.' So while the recognition of Social and the corresponding social risks were at the core of the conflict over DAPL, the real consequences of poor social behavior won't be adequately exposed and addressed until ESG investors have adequate social metrics and access to optimal data for assessing social risk."

51. "Navajo Nation Sues Well Fargo for Alleged Predatory Tactics," *AP News*, December 12, 2017, https://www.apnews.com/22f0762b2a4f468494dd2b4ad7bea6ed.

52. Deona Anderson, "Standing Rock's Surprising Legacy: A Push for Public Banks," *Yes! Magazine*, January 2, 2019, https://www.yesmagazine.org: "'When we were organizing around getting [Seattle] to divest, the question all along was what to do with the city's money,' [Matt] Remle said. 'And our philosophy was it's not going to

be a victory to close accounts with Wells Fargo and go to Bank of America.' Organizers saw public banks as the solution. A public bank is an institution owned by a governmental body, funded with taxpayer money, and mandated to serve the public interest. In summer 2017, Remle and other Seattleites started advocating for the city to establish a public bank, a process that could take years"; Kurtis Wu, "Divestment and Public Banking: How the Divest DAPL Movement Is Driving Financial Change," OpenInvest blog, March 14, 2018, https://www.openinvest.co/blog: "A year ago today the SF Defund Dakota Access Pipeline (DAPL) Coalition pushed the San Francisco Board of Supervisors (equivalent to a city council) to pass a resolution that would divest San Francisco from the financial institutions funding the Dakota Access Pipeline (DAPL). But the victory was short lived when the City discovered that it couldn't divest because there was no alternative institution that could manage the huge investments of a major US city. Unfortunately, most of the big banks invest in the DAPL, and credit unions, a good alternative for regular folks, simply do not have the capacity or infrastructure to handle billions of dollar in cash flows of major cities. Other major cities that originally celebrated divestment were running into the same issue: where do we put the money? The answer: a public bank"; Jackie Fielder "Questions Remain as Treasurer's Public Bank Task Force Comes to a Close," *San Francisco Examiner*, September 23, 2018, http://www.sfexaminer.com.

53. Jackie Fielder, "Divestment Activists Focus on Moving the Money," Last Real Indians, August 2017, http://lastrealindians.com.

54. "Indigenous Women's Delegation to Europe Continues Push for Fossil Fuel Divestment," WECAN.

55. Mary Kathryn Nagle and Gloria Steinem, "Sexual Assault on the Pipeline," *Boston Globe*, September 29, 2016, https://www.bostonglobe.com.

56. "Maze of Injustice: The Failure to Protect Indigenous Women from Sexual Violence in the USA," Amnesty International, 2007, http://www.amnestyusa.org.

57. Nomination of Senator Jeff Sessions to be Attorney General of the United States, January 16, 2017, Questions from Sen. Al Franken, question 15, https://www.judiciary.senate.gov/imo/media/doc/Sessions%20Responses%20to%20Franken%20QFRs.pdf.

58. Sierra Crane-Murdoch, "On Indian Land, Criminals Can Get Away with Almost Anything," *The Atlantic*, February 22, 2013, https://www.theatlantic.com: "In 1978, the Supreme Court case *Oliphant v. Suquamish* stripped tribes of the right to arrest and prosecute non-Indians who commit crimes on Indian land. If both victim and perpetrator are non-Indian, a county or state officer must make the arrest. If the perpetrator is non-Indian and the victim an enrolled member, only a federally certified agent has that right. If the opposite is true, a tribal officer can make the arrest, but the case still goes to federal court.

"Even if both parties are tribal members, a U.S. attorney often assumes the case, since tribal courts lack the authority to sentence defendants to more than three years in prison. The harshest enforcement tool a tribal officer can legally wield over a non-Indian is a traffic ticket. The result has been a jurisdictional tangle that often makes prosecuting crimes committed in Indian Country prohibitively difficult. In 2011, the U.S. Justice Department did not prosecute 65 percent of rape cases reported on reservations. According to department records, one in three Native American women are raped during their lifetimes—two-and-a-half times the likelihood for an average American woman—and in 86 percent of these cases, the assailant is non-Indian." See also "Maze of Injustice," Amnesty International; Nomination of Senator Jeff Sessions to be Attorney General of the United States, Franken question 15.

59. "Maze of Injustice," Amnesty International; Nomination of Senator Jeff Sessions to be Attorney General of the United States, Franken question 15.

60. "Missing and Murdered Native Women – Public Awareness Efforts," National Indigenous Women's Resource Center, November 30, 2016, http://www.niwrc.org: "the U.S. Department of Justice has found that in some tribal communities, American Indian women face murder rates that are more than 10 times the national average. Since 2005, there has been increased awareness of the pattern of the disappearance of Native women and the failure of the criminal justice system to adequately respond to the crisis."

61. Annita Lucchesi and Abigail Echo-Hawk, "Missing and Murdered Indigenous Women & Girls: A Snapshot of Data from 71 Urban Cities in the United States," Urban Indian Health Institute (a Division of the Seattle Indian Health Board), November 2018, http://www.uihi.org.

62. "Maze of Injustice," Amnesty International.

63. Mikael Homanen, "Depositors Disciplining Banks: The Impact of Scandals," ProMarket, May 9, 2018, https://promarket.org.

64. Derrick A. Bell, "Who's Afraid of Critical Race Theory," *University of Illinois Law Review* 893 (1995), https://sph.umd.edu/sites/default/files/files/Bell_Whos%20Afraid%20of%20CRT_1995UIllLRev893.pdf (internal citations omitted): "As to the what is, critical race theory is a body of legal scholarship, now about a decade old, a majority of whose members are both existentially people of color and ideologically committed to the struggle against racism, particularly as institutionalized in and by law. Those critical race theorists who are white are usually cognizant of and committed to the overthrow of their own racial privilege." Mari Matsuda, "Looking to the Bottom: Critical Legal Studies and Reparations," *Harvard Civil Rights-Civil Liberties Law Review* 22, no. 2 (1987): 323; see also Mari J. Matsuda, "Public Response to Racist Speech: Considering the Victim's Story," *Michigan Law Review* 87, no. 8 (August 1989): 2323, http://fs2.american.edu/dfagel/www/Class%20Readings/Matsuda/Response%20To%20Racist%20Speech.pdf (internal citations omitted): "There is an outsider's jurisprudence growing and thriving alongside mainstream jurisprudence in American law schools. The new feminist jurisprudence is a lively example of this. A related, and less-celebrated, outsider jurisprudence is that belonging to people of color."

65. Daiva K. Stasiulis, "Relational Positionality of Nationalism, Racism, and Feminism,"

in *Between Woman and Nation*, ed. Caren Kaplan, Norma Alarcon, and Minoo Moallem (Durham, N.C.: Duke University Press, 1999), 194: "'Relationality,' 'positionality,' and 'relational positionality' are concepts developed by antiracist and postcolonial feminists to explain the fluidity of individual and group identities at the crossroads of different systems of power and domination. They refer to the multiple relations of power that intersect in complex ways to position individuals and collectives in shifting and often contradictory locations within geopolitical spaces, historical narratives, and movement politics."

66. Matthew L. M. Fletcher, "The Supreme Court and the Rule of Law: Case Studies in Indian Law," *The Federal Lawyer*, March/April 2008, http://www.fedbar.org/Publi cations/The-Federal-Lawyer.aspx.

67. "Eight States Have Proposed Bills in 2019 Hyper-Criminalizing Pipeline Protest," The Real News Network, March 8, 2019, https://therealnews.com: "Eight states are considering bills that would hypercriminalize protests on property owned by the fossil fuel industry. The Real News traced these bills to two industry-funded organizations: the American Legislative Exchange Council and the Council of State Governments. They're funded by companies like Koch Industries, Chevron, ExxonMobil, and Energy Transfer Partners."

68. Robert A. Williams Jr., *Linking Arms Together: American Indian Treaty Visions of Law and Peace, 1600–1800* (Oxford: Oxford University Press, 1997). Nick Estes, "Indigenous Peoples Day, Challenging Colonialism in Albuquerque and Beyond," Indian Country Today, October 9, 2015, https://indiancountrymedianetwork.com/ history/events/indigenous-peoples-day-challenging-colonialism-in-albuquerque -and-beyond/ (no longer available).

69. "What Is Extreme Energy?" Extreme Energy Initiative, Human Rights Consortium, 2017, https://extremeenergy.org.

70. Jerry Mander, "Introduction: Globalization and the Assault on Indigenous Resources," in *Paradigm Wars; Indigenous People's Resistance to Globalization*, ed. Jerry Mander and Victoria Tauli Corpuz (San Francisco: Sierra Club Books, 2006), 4.

71. Erica-Irene A. Daes, *Indigenous Peoples and Their Relationship to Land. Final Working Paper*, UN Document E/CN.4/Sub.2/2001/21, June 11, 2001, paras. 49–50.

72. Mander, "Introduction," 4.

73. Reuters, "Trump Advisors Aim to Privatize Oil-Rich American Indian Reservations," *CNBC*, December 5, 2016, https://www.cnbc.com.

74. Maura Grogan with Rebecca Morse and April Youpee-Roll, *Native American Lands and Natural Resource Development*, Revenue Watch Institute 3 (2011), Natural Resource Governance Institute, https://resourcegovernance.org.

75. Andreina Aponte, "Fish for Flour? Bartering Is the New Currency in Collapsing Venezuela," Reuters, June 13, 2018, https://www.reuters.com: "The rise of barter exchange, amid hyperinflation and a dearth of cash, is a reflection of how the once-prosperous country is reverting to the most rudimentary of mechanisms of commercial exchange."

76. Paul Lansing, "The Divestment of United States Companies in South Africa and Apartheid," *Nebraska Law Review* 60 (1981), http://digitalcommons.unl.edu/nlr. "What Is BDS?" BDS Movement, 2017, https://bdsmovement.net.

77. Crystal Lameman, "Life above the Alberta Tar Sands—Why We're Taking the Government to Court, *The Guardian*, April 8, 2015, https://www.theguardian.com: "Will divestment from these companies change everything? No, but combined with such things as indigenous rights practices we will make a difference. Will it define solidarity between frontline impacted communities, the climate change movement and responsible investors? Yes." Arthur Manuel and Grand Chief Ronald M. Derrickson, *Unsettling Canada: A National Wake-Up Call* (Toronto: Between the Lines, 2015), 155.

78. Reed Montague and Steven Heim, "Indigenous Peoples and Engagement Timeline for Sustainable and Responsible Investing (1971–2005)," Green Money, July 2015, https://greenmoney.com/timeline1.

79. Tracey Osborne, "Native American Fighting Fossil Fuels," Scientific American, Voices (blog), April 19, 2018, https://blogs.scientificamerican.com/voices/native-americans-fighting-fossil-fuels/.

80. Hiroko Tabuchi, "How Big Banks Are Putting Rain Forests in Peril," *New York Times*, December 3, 2016, https://www.nytimes.com; "Equator Principles Disaster Projects," BankTrack; "Report: The Banks That Finance Private Prison Companies," In the Public Interest, November 17, 2016, https://www.inthepublicinterest.org: "*The Banks That Finance Private Prison Companies* shows that six banks have played large roles in bankrolling CoreCivic and GEO Group: Wells Fargo, Bank of America, JPMorgan Chase, BNP Paribas, SunTrust, and U.S. Bancorp. The report also reveals how these banks profit from providing credit, bonds, and loans to private prison companies. The report concludes with a call for banks to stop financing the private prison industry."

81. Max Abelson, "Ocasio-Cortez Wants Hearing on Banks Funding Immigrant Prisons," Bloomberg, February 25, 2019, https://www.bloomberg.com/news/articles/2019-02-25/ocasio-cortez-wants-hearing-on-banks-funding-immigrant-prisons: "JPMorgan Chase & Co. and Bank of America Corp., the two biggest U.S. banks, are among lenders to GEO Group Inc. and CoreCivic Inc., which run facilities that have held immigrant families."

82. For a start, BanksTalking.org has a chronicle of public information from the U.S. Securities & Exchange Commission on financing commitments.

83. William N. Goetzmann, *Money Changes Everything: How Finance Made Civilization Possible* (Princeton, N.J.: Princeton University Press, 2016); Peter James Hudson, *Bankers and Empire: How Wall Street Colonized the Caribbean* (Chicago: University of Chicago Press, 2017): "From the end of the nineteenth century until the onset of the Great Depression, Wall Street embarked on a stunning, unprecedented, and often bloody period of international expansion in the Caribbean. A host of financial entities sought to control banking, trade, and finance in the region. In the process, they not only trampled local sovereignty, grappled with domestic

banking regulation, and backed US imperialism—but they also set the model for bad behavior by banks, visible still today."

84. Sylvia Poggioli, "In Italy, Art as a Window into Modern Banking," National Public Radio, January 31, 2012, https://www.npr.org.

85. Diego Puga and Daniel Trefler, *International Trade and Institutional Change: Medieval Venice's Response to Globalization*, NBER Working Paper 18288, August 2012, http://www.nber.org.

86. Roger Moody, *The Risks We Run: Mining, Communities and Political Risk Insurance* (Utrecht, The Netherlands: International Books, 2005), 50.

87. Goetzmann, *Money Changes Everything*.

88. Goetzmann, *Money Changes Everything*.

89. Goetzmann, *Money Changes Everything*.

90. Goetzmann, *Money Changes Everything*.

91. William J. Bernstein, *A Splendid Exchange: How Trade Shaped the World* (New York: Grove Press, 2008), 218.

92. Goetzmann, *Money Changes Everything*; Hudson, *Bankers and Empire*: "From the end of the nineteenth century until the onset of the Great Depression, Wall Street embarked on a stunning, unprecedented, and often bloody period of international expansion in the Caribbean. A host of financial entities sought to control banking, trade, and finance in the region. In the process, they not only trampled local sovereignty, grappled with domestic banking regulation, and backed US imperialism—but they also set the model for bad behavior by banks, visible still today."

93. Anthony Anghie, *Imperialism, Sovereignty and the Making of International Law* (Cambridge: Cambridge University Press, 2004), 3, https://kingdomofhawaii.files.wordpress.com/2011/04/anghie-imperialism-sovereignity-and-the-making-of-international-law.pdf.

94. Hudson, *Bankers and Empire*.

95. United Nations Human Rights Office of the High Commissioner, "Common Core Document Forming Part of the Reports of States Parties: Norway," UN Document HRI/CORE/NOR/2017, October 13, 2017, paras. 88–94, https://undocs.org/en/HRI/CORE/NOR/2017.

96. United Nations Human Rights Office of the High Commissioner, "Common Core Document Forming Part of the Reports of States Parties: Norway," paras. 103 and 105.

97. Norwegian Constitution, art. 112, https://www.stortinget.no/en/In-English.

98. United Nations Human Rights Office of the High Commissioner, "Common Core Document Forming Part of the Reports of States Parties: Norway," para. 112.

99. Arnfinn Bårdsen and Petter Wille, "Guardians of Human Rights in Norway: Challenging Mandates in a New Era," May 11, 2016, https://www.domstol.no/globalassets/upload/hret/artikler-og-foredrag/guardians-of-human-rights---11052016.pdf.

100. Ministry of Foreign Affairs, "Extended Mandate for Human Rights Defenders," Government.no, March 31, 2014, https://www.regjeringen.no/en.

101. Ministry of Foreign Affairs, "Extended Mandate for Human Rights Defenders."

102. Ministry of Foreign Affairs, "Norway Intensifies Efforts to Promote Human Rights," Government.no, December 12, 2014, https://www.regjeringen.no/en; "Human Rights," Gender in Norway: Information and Resources on Gender Equality and Gender Research in Norway, June 1, 2015, http://www.gender.no.

103. Victoria Tauli-Corpuz, "Report of the Special Rapporteur on the Rights of Indigenous Peoples," reported, "militarized, at times violent, escalation of force by local law enforcement and private security forces . . . the aggressive manner in which peaceful demonstrations were met by local, state, private and national guards . . . testimonies of war-like conditions and cases of blunt force trauma and hypothermia as a result of battery with batons, attack dogs and water cannons blasting individuals at freezing temperatures . . . protestors being strip searched and placed in kennels as temporary holding cells during various and frequent mass raids by local, state and federal enforcement officials, sometimes in the middle of a spiritual and cultural energy cleansing ritual" and information that "over 700 indigenous and non-indigenous people were arrested during the protests, some of whom remain in custody."

104. Nina Berglund, "Shale Gas Protests Spoil Statoil's Party," News in English, June 21, 2011, http://www.newsinenglish.no.

105. Alexis Bonogofsky, "How Indigenous Activists in Norway Got the First Bank to Pull Out of the Dakota Access Pipeline," Truthout, November 28, 2016, http://www.truthout.org.

106. Beaska Niillas and Michelle Cook, "Divest Now! Sami People and Standing Rock Camp Attorneys Work Together to Get Norway DNB to Divest from DAPL," Censored News, November 10, 2016, https://bsnorrell.blogspot.com.

107. Water Protector Legal Collective (formerly Red Owl Legal Collective), letter to DNB, November 8, 2016, 14, http://martinezlaw.net/wp-content/uploads/2016/11/20161108-DNB-Bank-Divestment-Letter-ROLC.pdf.

108. Water Protector Legal Collective, letter to DNB, 14.

109. Niillas and Cook, "Divest Now!": "Norwegian Sámi Association – NSR stand with Standing Rock and works together with Standing Rock Camp Attorneys and Red Owl Legal Collective to make DNB and Norway divest from Dakota Access pipeline. The Camp Attorneys have provided information of all the violations of indigenous peoples and human rights. This information was provided DNB and the Norwegian Council on Ethics for the Government Pension Fund Global by NSR on Wednesday October 9th. . . . The Norwegian Sámi Association, The Sámi Parliament of Norway, and Norwegian environmental organizations have joined together to show their support for the Standing Rock Sioux Tribe in protecting clean water and fighting against the Dakota Access Pipeline project; they have strongly urged DNB and Norway to divest from DAPL."

110. Eirik Landsend Henriksen, "DNBs kommentar til situasjonen i North Dakota" [DNB Comment on the Situation in North Dakota], DNB Nyheter, updated January 27, 2017, https://dnbnyheter.no.

111. Henriksen, "DNBs kommentar til situasjonen i North Dakota."

112. Tracy Loeffelholz Dunn, "Norway's Largest Bank Divests from Dakota Access, Launches Own Investigation," *Yes! Magazine*, November 7, 2016, http://www.yes magazine.org.

113. Henriksen, "DNBs kommentar til situasjonen i North Dakota."

114. Henriksen, "DNBs kommentar til siuasjonen i North Dakota."

115. Bonogofsky, "How Indigenous Activists in Norway Got the First Bank to Pull Out of the Dakota Access Pipeline."

116. Bonogofsky, "How Indigenous Activists in Norway Got the First Bank to Pull Out of the Dakota Access Pipeline."

117. "Indigenous Women's Divestment Delegation to Norway," WECAN, March 2017, http://wecaninternational.org/uploads/cke_images/SPOKESWOMEN---Indige nous-Women-s-Divestment-Delegation-to-Norway-4-24.pdf.

118. U.S. Securities and Exchange Commission, "Energy Transfer Equity, L.P.," https://www.sec.gov/Archives/edgar/data/1276187/000127618717000034/0001276187 -17-000034-index.htm.

119. Reuters, "Norwegian Bank DNB Sells Its Share of Dakota Pipeline Funding," *Fortune*, March 26, 2017, http://fortune.com.

120. "Standing Rock Sioux Hails Norway DNB Bank Dumping Dakota Access," teleSUR, March 27, 2017, http://www.telesurenglish.net/news/Standing-Rock-Sioux-Hails -Norway-DNB-Bank-Dumping-Dakota-Access-20170327-0034.html.

121. Nika Knight, "Activists around the World Take #NODAPL Fight to Banks," *Common Dreams*, December 1, 2016, https://www.commondreams.org; Indigenous Youth Council, "DNB out of DAPL," YouTube, November 27, 2016, https://www .youtube.com: "DNB Bank is a Norwegian Bank funding 10% of DAPL via loans to Energy Transfer Partners. Due to public pressure, DNB pulled their assets out of DAPL last week and now it's time they withdraw their loans as well!"

122. Dunn, "Norway's Largest Bank Divests from Dakota Access."

123. U.S. Securities and Exchange Commission, Marathon old agreement, https://www.sec .gov/Archives/edgar/data/1510295/000151029516000111/0001510295-16-000111 -index.htm; U.S. Securities and Exchange Commission, Marathon most recent agreement, https://www.sec.gov/Archives/edgar/data/1510295/000151029517000078 /0001510295-17-000078-index.htm.

124. Carl-Gøran Larsson, "DNB sa de solgte seg ut av 'The Black Snake' – har fremdeles 7 milliarder i lån til oljerør-firmaene" [DNB said they sold out of "The Black Snake"— still have 7 billion in loans for oil pipeline companies], NRK Sápmi, November 7, 2017, https://www.nrk.no.

125. Larsson, "DNB sa de solgte seg ut av 'The Black Snake.'"

126. Enbridge: U.S. Securities and Exchange Commission, https://www.sec.gov /Archives/edgar/data/895728/000119312516718317/0001193125-16-718317-index .htm, and then two deals (same filing link): https://www.sec.gov/Archives/edgar /data/895728/000119312516718317/d407725dex104.htm and https://www.sec .gov/Archives/edgar/data/895728/000119312516718317/d407725dex1010.htm;

Phillips 66 Partners (current holder of DAPL ownership stake): U.S. Securities and Exchange Commission, https://www.sec.gov/Archives/edgar/data/1572910 /000157291016000146/0001572910-16-000146-index.htm and https://www.sec .gov/Archives/edgar/data/1534701/000153470115000038/0001534701-15-000038-index.htm.

127. "Norway Government Pension Fund Global," Sovereign Wealth Funds Institute, https://www.swfinstitute.org/swfs/norway-government-pension-fund-global/. "Factbox: Norway's $960 Billion Sovereign Wealth Fund," Reuters, June 2, 2017, https://www.reuters.com.

128. Niall McCarthy, "Norway's Sovereign Wealth Fund Hits $1 Trillion," *Forbes*, September 22, 2017, https://www.forbes.com.

129. McCarthy, "Norway's Sovereign Wealth Fund Hits $1 Trillion."

130. McCarthy, "Norway's Sovereign Wealth Fund Hits $1 Trillion."

131. Richard Milne, "Norway's $905bn Oil Fund Flexes Its Shareholder Muscles," *Financial Times*, March 7, 2017, https://www.ft.com.

132. United Nations Human Rights Office of the High Commissioner, "Common Core Document Forming Part of the Reports of States Parties: Norway," para. 27.

133. Dan Robert Larsen and Magne Ove Varsi, "FN-rapportør vil ha oljefondet ut av omstridt oljerørprosjekt i USA" [UN Rapporteur wants the oil fund out of controversial oil pipeline projects in the United States], NRK Sápmi, April 28, 2017, https://www.nrk.no.

134. "Observation and Exclusion of Companies," Norges Bank Investment Management, June 29, 2017, https://www.nbim.no/en/the-fund/responsible-investment/ exclusion-of-companies/.

135. Gwladys Fouche, "Native Americans to Meet Norway's Wealth Fund Watchdog over Pipeline," Reuters, March 27, 2017, http://www.reuters.com; Gwladys Fouche, "Norway Wealth Fund Watchdog Reviewing Investment in U.S. Pipeline Firm," Reuters, October 23, 2017, https://www.reuters.com: "The ethics watchdog for Norway's $1 trillion sovereign wealth fund is reviewing allegations that U.S. pipeline operator Energy Transfer Partners may breach the fund's investment guidelines."

136. "Guidelines for Observation and Exclusion of Companies from the Government Pension Fund Global," Council on Ethics for the Government Pension Fund Global, http://etikkradet.no/files/2017/04/Etikkraadet_Guidelines-_eng_2017_web.pdf.

137. Bårdsen and Wille, "Guardians of Human Rights in Norway."

138. Dakota Access, LLC ("Dakota Access") is a Delaware limited liability company authorized to do business in North Dakota and engaged in the business of constructing the 1,154-mile-long crude Dakota Access Pipeline (the "Pipeline").

139. "Guidelines for Observation and Exclusion of Companies from the Government Pension Fund Global," Council on Ethics for the Government Pension Fund Global.

140. "10 Banks Financing Dakota Access Pipeline Decline Meeting with Tribal Leaders," BankTrack, January 13, 2017, http://www.banktrack.org/show/article/10_banks_ financing_dakota_access_pipeline_decline_meeting_with_tribal_leaders: "Backed

by hundreds of thousands of online signatures and commitments to #Defund-DAPL, organizers from more than 25 grassroots groups have vowed that the campaign will continue and intensify in the coming weeks, building up to a planned 'global week of action' unless all 17 of the banks act. The ask for the banks is to discontinue loan disbursements in consultation with Native leaders until outstanding issues are resolved, and Free, Prior, and Informed Consent from Indigenous peoples is upheld."

141. Fouche, "Norway Wealth Fund Watchdog Reviewing Investment"; Adam Vaughan, "World's Biggest Sovereign Wealth Fund Proposes Ditching Oil and Gas Holdings," *The Guardian*, November 16, 2017, https://www.theguardian.com; "Norwegian Oil Fund Recommends Divesting $37 Billion from Oil and Gas Industry after Meeting Standing Rock Activists in Ongoing Global Divestment Push" (press release), WECAN, November 20, 2017, http://wecaninternational.org/news/1839/press-release_-norwegian-oil-fund-recommends-divesting-$37-billion-from-oil-and-gas-industry-after-meeting-standing-rock-activists-in-ongoing-global-divestment-push: "'Last year we saw the largest gathering of Indigenous nations ever in opposition to the Dakota Access Pipeline; last month Indigenous people led the largest ever protest of bank investments in fossil fuels; and this month Indigenous people have pushed one of the most powerful investors in the world to recommend ditching oil and gas. All of these historical events prove that Indigenous people and other frontline communities move mountains when given a platform. We are still here, fighting for the sustainability of our communities and yours.'—Jackie Fielder, Mnicoujou Lakota (Cheyenne River), Mandan, and Hidatsa (Three Affiliated Tribes), Organizer with Mazaska Talks."

142. Milne, "Norway's $1tn Wealth Fund Set to Cut Oil and Gas Stocks."

143. Greenpeace and BankTrack, "Swiss Banks in the End of Fossil Fuel Age," https://www.greenpeace.ch: "As this report demonstrates, in Switzerland, two of the country's biggest banks—Credit Suisse and UBS—provide more finance for extreme fossil fuels on a per capita basis than their peers in any other European nation"; Intergovernmental Panel on Climate Change (IPCC), "Global Warming of 1.5°C," October 8, 2018, https://www.ipcc.ch/sr15/: "An IPCC Special Report on the impacts of global warming of 1.5°C above pre-industrial levels and related global greenhouse gas emission pathways, in the context of strengthening the global response to the threat of climate change, sustainable development, and efforts to eradicate poverty."

144. "Our Company," Credit Suisse, 2017, https://www.credit-suisse.com/us/en.html.

145. Energy Transfer Equity, Amendment and Incremental Commitment Agreement No. 3, U.S. Securities and Exchange Commission, February 17, 2015, https://www.sec.gov/Archives/edgar/data/1276187/000127618715000007/ete101commitmentagreement.htm.

146. Energy Transfer Partners, Form 8-K (annual report), February 10, 2015, https://www.sec.gov/Archives/edgar/data/1012569/000101256915000015/etp217158-k.htm.

147. Sunoco Logistics Partners, Form 8-K (annual report), U.S. Securities and

Exchange Commission, March 20, 2015, https://www.sec.gov/Archives/edgar/data/1161154/000116115415000024/a25billionamendedandrestat.htm.

148. "BRIEF–Energy Transfer Equity Says Entered into Senior Secured Term Loan Agreement with Credit Suisse," Reuters, February 3, 2017, http://www.reuters.com.

149. *Society for Threatened Peoples vs. Credit Suisse*, OECD Watch, April 24, 2017, https://complaints.oecdwatch.org/cases/Case_475; Greenpeace, "Credit Suisse's Ongoing Banking Relationship with DAPL Related Companies" (letter), February 16, 2017, https://www.greenpeace.ch: "We also strongly feel that Credit Suisse Sustainability team has seriously downplayed the role of the bank. The fact that your team members said that Credit Suisse's role in financing DAPL related companies is insignificant is simply not true. Greenpeace Switzerland has further investigated into the amounts of finance provided by Credit Suisse and compared it to the other banks' role. What we have found is that Credit Suisse has provided/participated in loan issues 7 times since 2011 (not including bond issues) and the total amounts to USD 1.38 billion, which is more than any other bank has provided (including allocations to DAPL project, and based on the information publicly available)"; Greenpeace, "Credit Suisse Ongoing Financing of Controversial Pipeline Companies" (letter), June 6, 2018, https://www.greenpeace.ch.

150. "Dakota Access Pipeline," Credit Suisse, 2017; "Credit Suisse Meeting with Standing Rock Sioux Delegation," Credit Suisse, Corporate Communications, April 4, 2017, https://www.credit-suisse.com/us/en.html: "Credit Suisse is not involved in the project financing of the Dakota Access Pipeline (DAPL). Allegations that Credit Suisse is the biggest lender to DAPL are false and are firmly rejected by the bank. Credit Suisse has business relationships with companies undertaking the construction and operation of the pipeline."

151. Standing Rock, Cheyenne River, and Yankton Sioux Tribes, "Request for Precautionary Measures"; Tauli-Corpuz, "Report of the Special Rapporteur on the Rights of Indigenous Peoples"; Tompkins, "Tribal Treaty and Environmental Statutory Implications"; "Bakken," Energy Transfer LP: "Dakota Access, LLC ('Dakota Access') is developing a new pipeline to provide crude oil transportation service from point(s) of origin in the Bakken/Three Forks play in North Dakota to Patoka, Illinois"; Dakota Access, LLC is a Delaware limited liability company authorized to do business in North Dakota and engaged in the business of constructing the 1,154-mile-long crude Dakota Access Pipeline.

152. "Credit Suisse Agents $2.2B Energy Transfer Partners Facility," *abf Journal*, February 6, 2017, http://www.abfjournal.com.

153. "Water Protectors File Arguments in the 8th Circuit on Militarized Policing," Water Protector Legal Collective.

154. "Credit Suisse Meeting with Standing Rock Sioux Delegation," Credit Suisse, Corporate Communications.

155. Lisa Schlein, "Standing Rock Tribe's Fight against Pipelines Goes Global," VOA, June 8, 2017, https://www.voanews.com.

156. Tompkins, "Tribal Treaty and Environmental Statutory Implications," 30.

157. "Dakota Access Pipeline," Credit Suisse.
158. "Indigenous Women's Delegation to Europe Continues Push for Fossil Fuel Divestment," WECAN; WECAN, "Indigenous Women's Divestment Delegation Confronts Credit Suisse at Shareholder Meeting," YouTube, May 22, 2018, https://www.youtube.com.
159. See Roxanne Dunbar-Ortiz, *An Indigenous Peoples' History of the United States* (Boston: Beacon, 2014).
160. "UBS Switzerland," BankTrack, August 8, 2017, https://www.banktrack.org.
161. Alexandra Jacobo, "Meet the Bank Financing the Dakota Access Pipeline," Nation of Change, September 7, 2016, http://www.nationofchange.org.
162. Greenpeace, "UBS: Quit Fossil Fuels!," BankTrack, May 2017, https://waterkeeper.org/app/uploads/2017/05/170502-UBS-digital_FINAL-1.pdf.
163. "Divest, Invest, Protect," WECAN.
164. "Environmental and Social Risk (ESR) Policy Framework," UBS, https://www.ubs.com/global/en/ubs-society/our-documents.html.
165. Cook and MacMillan, "Money Talks, Banks Are Talking."
166. "2017 Environmental Responsibility Policy," U.S. Bank, https://www.usbank.com: "The company does not provide project financing for the construction of oil or natural gas pipelines."
167. "DNB Has Sold Its Part of Dakota Access Pipeline Loan," DNB, March 26, 2017, http://feed.ne.cision.com/wpyfs/00/00/00/00/00/3D/38/06/release.html; Reuters, "Norwegian Bank DNB Sells Its Share of Dakota Access Pipeline Funding."
168. Mazaska Talks, "But Wait, U.S. Bank Has Not Stopped Funding Pipelines," *Yes! Magazine*, May 16, 2017, http://www.yesmagazine.org (internal citations removed): "Despite this new policy, U.S. Bank continues to provide hundreds of millions of dollars of corporate financing to pipeline companies for general use, *including pipeline construction.* U.S. Bank is behind many oil giants, including Enbridge, Energy Transfer Partners, Phillips 66, and Marathon. All four of these companies own major stakes in the Dakota Access pipeline, and Phillips 66 and Marathon are the primary shippers of oil through DAPL. U.S. Bank also finances Cabot Oil & Gas, DTE Energy, EQT, National Fuel Gas, Plains, Range Resources and Williams."
169. Mazaska Talks, "But Wait, U.S. Bank Has Not Stopped Funding Pipelines."
170. Mazaska Talks, "But Wait, U.S. Bank Has Not Stopped Funding Pipelines."
171. John G. Ruggie, "Comments on Thun Group of Banks: Discussion Paper on the Implications of UN Guiding Principles 13 & 17 in a Corporate and Investment Banking Context," Institute for Human Rights and Business, February 21, 2017, https://www.ihrb.org: "The UNGPs stipulate three categories of business involvement in human rights harm. The critical distinction that banks (and other businesses) should be making is not only between 'their own activities' versus harms in which they may otherwise be involved. Perhaps even more important in practice, especially for banks, is the distinction between harm they may 'contribute to' and harm that may be committed by a third party to which they are 'directly

linked' through their business relationships even without their having caused or contributed to the harm. This distinction is important because the two situations have very different implications for what banks, or any other businesses, should do about that actual or potential harm (see bullets 2 and 3 above), including in relation to remedy."

172. "Front Line Defenders Global Analysis 2018," 2019, 4, https://www.frontlinedefen ders.org.

173. "Indigenous Women's Delegation Takes Fossil Fuel Divestment Demands to New York City and Washington D.C." (press release), WECAN, October 9, 2018, https:// wecaninternational.org.

174. "About Us, Facts and Figures," Swiss Re Group, 2017, https://www.swissre.com: "The Swiss Re Group is a leading wholesale provider of reinsurance, insurance and other insurance-based forms of risk transfer. Dealing direct and working through brokers, our global client base consists of insurance companies, mid-to-large-sized corporations and public sector clients. From standard products to tailor-made coverage across all lines of business, we deploy our capital strength, expertise and innovation power to enable the risk-taking upon which enterprise and progress in society depend"; "Fact Sheet," Allianz, At a Glance, March 8, 2019, https://www .allianz.com/en: "The Allianz Group is a global financial services provider with services predominantly in the insurance and asset management business. 92 million retail and corporate clients in more than 70 countries rely on our knowledge, global presence, financial strength and solidity. In fiscal year 2018 over 142,000 employees worldwide achieved total revenues of 130.6 billion euros and an operating pro t of 11.5 billion euros. Allianz SE, the parent company, is headquartered in Munich, Germany."

175. "The World's Largest Public Companies," *Forbes*, 2018, https://www.forbes.com/ global2000/list/#tab:overall; Corinne Jurney, "The World's Largest Public Companies 2017," *Forbes*, May 24, 2017, https://www.forbes.com.

176. Arthur Nelsen, "Climate Change Could Make Insurance Too Expensive for Most People – Report," *The Guardian*, March 21, 2019, https://www.theguardian.com: "Nicolas Jeanmart, the head of personal insurance, general insurance and macroeconomics at Insurance Europe, which speaks for 34 national insurance associations, said the knock-on effects from rising premiums could pose a threat to social order. 'The sector is concerned that continuing global increases in temperature could make it increasingly difficult to offer the affordable financial protection that people deserve, and that modern society requires to function properly,' he said."

177. Rebecca Marston, "What Is a Rating Agency?" *BBC News*, October 20, 2014, http:// www.bbc.com.

178. "DNB Has Sold Its Part of Dakota Access Pipeline Loan," DNB: "'During the process, we have met several interest groups and listened to their suggestions. We have met, among others, representatives from the Standing Rock Sioux Tribe. We have also engaged in an ongoing dialogue with the company building the pipeline. Many

of our customers have contacted us and expressed what they expect from us as a Norwegian bank. In our evaluations, we have taken account of all the input we have received," says Serck-Hanssen. Following the sale of the loan, DNB no longer has any direct financial exposure to the Dakota Access Pipeline." Terje Solsvik, "Norwegian Bank DNB Sells Its Share of Dakota Pipeline Funding," Reuters, March 26, 2017, http://www.reuters.com. "BayernLB Withdraws from Follow-on Financing for Dakota Access Pipeline (DAPL)," BayernLB, February 22, 2017, https://www.bayernlb.com. BNP Paribas Securities Corp., "BNP Paribas Exits Dakota Access Pipeline," Global News Wire, April 5, 2017, https://globenewswire.com. "ING and the Dakota Access Pipeline," ING, updated March 21, 2017, https://www.ing.com; Julia Carrie Wong, "Dakota Access Pipeline: ING Sells Stake in Major Victory for Divestment Push," *The Guardian*, March 21, 2017, https://www.theguardian.com.

179. Alison Kirsch, "Energy Transfer: Which Banks Continue to Support the Company Behind DAPL?" Rainforest Action Network, April 6, 2017, https://www.ran.org/energy_transfer_refinance.

180. Kirsch, "Energy Transfer."

181. U.S. Securities and Exchange Commission, "Third Amendment to [Phillips 66's] Credit Agreement," October 3, 2016, https://www.sec.gov/Archives/edgar/data/1534701/000153470117000051/psx-20161231_ex104.htm; U.S. Securities and Exchange Commission, February 20, 2015, https://www.sec.gov/Archives/edgar/data/1534701/000153470115000038/0001534701–15–000038-index.htm (prior amendment).

182. "Bayou Bridge," Energy Transfer LP, November 2017, http://www.energytransfer.com/ops_bayou_bridge.aspx: "The Bayou Bridge Pipeline is a joint venture between ETP and Phillips 66 Partners, LP, in which Energy Transfer has a 60% ownership interest and serves as the operator of the pipeline."

183. "US Bank Is No Longer Financing Enbridge," MN 350, November 2, 2017, http://www.mn350.org/us-bank-is-no-longer-financing-enbridge/. "BNP Paribas Takes Further Measures to Accelerate Its Support of the Energy Transition" (press release), BNP Paribas, CSR, October 11, 2017, http://www.bnpparibas.de/en.

184. "BNP Paribas Takes Further Measures to Accelerate Its Support of the Energy Transition," BNP Paribas.

185. "The Banks That Finance Private Prison Companies," In the Public Interest.

186. Thun Group of Banks, "UN Guiding Principles on Business and Human Rights: Discussion Paper for Banks on Implications of Principles 16–21," Business & Human Rights Resource Center, October 2, 2013, https://business-humanrights.org/en; Thun Group of Banks, "Discussion Paper on the Implications of UN Guiding Principles 13 &17 in a Corporate and Investment Banking Context," Business & Human Rights Resource Center, 2017, https://business-humanrights.org/sites/default/files/documents/2017_01_Thun%20Group%20discussion%20paper.pdf. David Kinley, "Artful Dodgers: Banks and Their Human Rights Responsibilities," Sydney Law School Research Paper No. 17/17, March 1, 2017, https://www.ssrn.com: "At the root of this thinking lie the intertwined notions of 'proximity' and

'directness.' That is specifically; the proximity of a bank to a human rights impact will be determined by the directness of its actions in effecting that impact. It is, according to the Thun Group, only when the bank's actions are sufficiently direct that any responsibility or liability will be borne by the bank."

187. Zachary M. Seward, "This Is How Much a Bloomberg Terminal Costs," *Quartz*, May 15, 2013, https://qz.com: "Bloomberg is currently charging single-terminal subscribers $2,000 a month for two-year contracts."

188. Brown, *Emergent Strategy*, 18.

189. Manuel and Derrickson, *Unsettling Canada*, 11.

190. Mikael Homanen, "Depositors Disciplining Banks: The Impact of Scandals," Pro-Market, May 9, 2018, https://promarket.org.

191. Navajo Nation Division of Economic Development, "Navajo Nation Comprehensive Economic Development Strategy," April 2018, 18, https://advancedbusinessmatch .com/wp-content/uploads/2018/07/NNDED_CEDS_FINAL_041618-LOW-RES .pdf: "Considering a federal tax withholding due on income, less than $.35 of every dollar is spent on the Nation"; Navajo Nation Human Rights Commission, "Assessing Abuse of Navajo Customers When Purchasing Vehicles in Border Towns," March 7, 2014, http://www.nnhrc.navajo-nsn.gov/docs/NewsRptResolution/Public HearingReports/NNHRC_AutoReport.pdf: "Overall, the Commission heard numerous accounts of unscrupulous and unconscionable auto deals that raised more questions about not only the legitimacy of these deals but about consumer rights and the protections afforded to the Navajo consumer."

192. "An Economy for the 99%," Oxfam, January 2017, https://www.oxfam.org/sites/ www.oxfam.org/files/file_attachments/bp-economy-for-99-percent-160117-en .pdf. "Credit Suisse Agrees to Pay $5.28 Billion in Connection with Its Sale of Residential Mortgage-Backed Securities," U.S. Department of Justice Office of Public Affairs, January 18, 2017, https://www.justice.gov. Michael Forsythe, "Paradise Papers Shine Light on Where the Elite Keep Their Money," *New York Times*, November 5, 2017, https://www.nytimes.com; "Paradise Papers: Secrets of the Global Elite," International Consortium of Investigative Journalists, 2017, https://www.icij.org/ investigations/paradise-papers/.

193. David Peetz and Georgina Murray, "Who Owns the World? Tracing Half the Corporate Giants' Shares to 30 Owners," The Conversation, April 11, 2017, http://the conversation.com/us; David Peetz and Georgina Murray, "The Financialization of Global Corporate Ownership," in *Financial Elites and Transnational Business: Who Rules the World?* ed. Georgina Murray and John Scott (Cheltenham, U.K.: Edward Elgar, 2012), 26–53.

194. David Meyer, "The Richest 1% Now Own More than 50% of the World's Wealth," *Fortune*, November 14, 2017, http://fortune.com: "The Swiss bank released its latest Global Wealth Report on Tuesday, together with a statement that contained the immortal phrase, 'The outlook for the millionaire segment is more optimistic than for the bottom of the wealth pyramid.'"

195. David Kaimowitz, "What Do Forest Rights Have to Do with Climate Change?" Ford Foundation, July 24, 2014, https://www.fordfoundation.org: "Because of the fundamental link between climate and vegetation—globally, a fifth of carbon emissions come from the conversion of forests and peat lands for development or other uses—the world needs traditional communities to help stave off global warming by protecting their lands and managing them sustainably. For that to be possible, the communities need support to defend their territories, cultures and livelihoods from those who seek to profit from the land, and destroy it in the process."

196. Caleb Stevens, Robert Winterbottom, Katie Reytar, and Jenny Springer, "Securing Rights, Combating Climate Change: How Strengthening Community Forest Rights Mitigates Climate Change," World Resources Institute, July 2014, https://www.wri.org.

197. Indian Law Resource Center, *Conservation and Indigenous Peoples in Mesoamerica: A Guide*, January 2015, 41, http://www.indianlaw.org.

198. United Nations Declaration on the Rights of Indigenous Peoples, Article 3: "Indigenous peoples have the right to self-determination. By virtue of that right they freely determine their political status and freely pursue their economic, social and cultural development."

199. Grogan, Morse, and Youpee-Roll, *Native American Lands and Natural Resource Development*.

200. "Indian Country" is defined by federal statute codified at 18 U.S.C. §, which includes tribal trust lands/reservation, dependent Indian communities, and Indian allotments held in trust status.

201. Joshua Sabatini, "San Francisco Advances toward Launching a Public Bank," *San Francisco Examiner*, December 3, 2017, http://www.sfexaminer.com. Fielder, "Divestment Activists Focus on Moving the Money." Mark Fogarty, "Divesting in DAPL in Favor of American Indian-Owned Banks," Indian Country Today, February 21, 2017, https://newsmaven.io/indiancountrytoday: "The Federal Deposit Insurance Corp. has designated 18 commercial banks as American Indian-owned banks. As a group they have $2.7 billion in assets and all have their deposits insured by the FDIC. The group tends to be community banks, some quite small, others with more than a quarter billion dollars of assets. A majority of them are based in Oklahoma, but there are also institutions in North Carolina, Colorado, Missouri, Iowa, Minnesota, Wisconsin, Montana and North Dakota"; "Minority Banking Timeline: Blackfeet National Bank," Partnership for Progress, https://www.fedpartnership.gov/minority-banking-timeline/blackfeet.

202. Jenny Denton, "Banks Turn a Blind Eye to Human Rights Abuses in Borneo," *Crikey*, May 12, 2017, https://www.crikey.com.au/2017/05/12/banks-implicated-in-borneo-human-rights-disaster/.

203. Tauli-Corpuz, "Report of the Special Rapporteur on the Rights of Indigenous Peoples."

204. "Indigenous Women of Standing Rock and Allies to Speak Out," WECAN.

205. "Supreme Court Rules that World Bank Group Can Be Sued in U.S. Courts," Center for International Environmental Law, February 27, 2019, https://www.ciel.org: "In a historic decision, today the United States Supreme Court decided 7–1 to overturn the International Finance Corporation (IFC)'s claim to absolute immunity from lawsuits. Under the *Jam v. IFC* decision, international organizations like the IFC and the World Bank can now be sued in US courts, including in relation to their commercial activities."

12

BEYOND ENVIRONMENTALISM
#NoDAPL AS ASSERTION OF TRIBAL SOVEREIGNTY

Andrew Curley

In 2016, the people of the Standing Rock Sioux Tribe mobilized to prevent a large, crude oil pipeline from crossing through their unceded territories and threatening the Missouri River alongside the tribe's eastern boundary. This became the #NoDAPL movement that galvanized hundreds of thousands of Water Protectors at its peak and helped popularize the phrase "mni wiconi," or "water is life." The national media that descended into the remote, rolling grasslands of the Standing Rock Sioux reservation interpreted what they saw through frameworks dominant in mainstream U.S. culture. Building on the trope of "the ecological Indian," for many watching from their television screens or over the Internet, "water is life" was the only message coming out of this struggle. But for tribal people and members of the Standing Rock Sioux Tribe, #NoDAPL was also a struggle over ancestral lands wrongly stolen through violence and guile.

The oil pipeline disrupts the territorial integrity of the Great Sioux Nation, a larger nation that comprises all Lakota, Nakota, and Dakota peoples. The Standing Rock Sioux Tribe's challenge to DAPL was about the nation's right to their lands, land that was part of a larger territory guaranteed in the Treaty of Fort Laramie in 1868 (Dunbar-Ortiz 2013; Estes 2016). It was a recognition of a common struggle for land that brought other Indigenous nations from across the continent to Standing Rock to lend political support and material assistance to the nation as it attempted to halt the construction of a pipeline that was also a land grab. Indigenous nations that maintain complicated relationships with extractive industries, such as the Navajo Nation, supported the #NoDAPL movement. This would seem like a contradiction if we look at the struggle as simply an environmental issue. Too often we think of Indigenous peoples as natural environmentalists. We are not. We happily engage in the worst forms of extractive industries, yet maintain our rights to the lands that we've relied upon for thousands of years. Reducing Indigenous nations to natural environmentalists leads to the misguided assumption that environmental justice will resolve legacies of colonialism. We need to recognize that Indigenous movements, mobilizations, and resistances, when examined, often speak to the original displacement, dispossession, and attempted genocide of Indigenous peoples on the continent.

Sovereignty and the Ecological Indian

In popular media, Indigenous peoples are understood as victims of progress. It was ideas of modernization and development that prevented Indigenous nations from maintaining Indigenous lifeways. Popular in both public understanding and in the social sciences, "modernization" became a self-serving logic and set of practices that continued to the larger project of settler-colonialism. Non-Natives saw tribes as backward and unproductive on their lands. But with colonialism came industrialization, exploited and enslaved labor, and class stratification. Such social processes eventually led to the inequality of environmental risk on the poor and the racially marginalized. Some of the earliest environmental laws had less to do with our ideas of "nature" and more with the lived, working environment. These were labor laws that ensured workers did not work under dangerous conditions (Gottlieb 2005).

It was not until the 1960s and 1970s when non-Native activists and organizers challenged the industry's right to pollute and pillage the environment. This was the beginning of the modern environmental movement. At the time non-Native environmental organizers and activists quickly associated naturalism and environmentalism with the ethos of Native American culture and spirituality. Not only was this stereotyping racist, but it muted the political claims of Indigenous actors and activists who rooted their work in understandings of tribal "sovereignty" and "self-determination" that sought to restore national land bases. These were claims for liberation from colonialism and capitalism and were not limited to threats against the environment (Smith and Warrior 1996).

Today, Indigenous peoples, including those in tribal government, understand sovereignty, self-determination, and struggles for the land as projects for national liberation and decolonization. Understanding Indigenous resistance against extractive industries as a struggle for the land and not simply for notions of the "environment" is difficult for academics, journalists, and others not connected with Indigenous communities. These political claims with deep history and decades of injustice fail to enter into the mainstream's public portrayal of Indigenous struggles. Instead, tribes are depicted as naturalist and inherently environmentalist (Lewis 1995, 439). Native communities are complicated and impacted by a range of issues. Many have grown dependent on extractive industries for jobs and revenues (Hosmer, O'Neill, and Fixico 2004). In the Navajo Nation, coal workers identify with their work and industry (O'Neill 2005; Powell 2017). They see themselves as working-class miners whose participation in extractive industries helps them to stay on their land and maintain connection with their culture and families (Curley 2016).

Upstream from Standing Rock on the Missouri River, the government of the "Mandan, Hidathsa, and Arikara Nation" in Fort Berthold benefits from the oil boom in North Dakota that led to the development of DAPL in the first place (Parker 2014). But this government supported Standing Rock's efforts to stop and move the pipeline.[1] If we were to rely on the framework of the ecological Indian, we would find the actions of these tribal governments contradictory (Nadasdy 2005). However, if we understand tribal support for Standing Rock as a challenge to continued colonialism and the appropriation of Native lands for projects that put Native communities at the highest risk of environmental damage, we can understand the actions of tribal governments who simultaneously support Standing Rock's claim and the industries that caused the problem in the first place.

To understand what happened at Standing Rock we need to amplify the critique that is muted in popular media and mainstream considerations, the critique of DAPL as a continuation of colonialism through its dispossession of Indigenous lands. This is a form of struggle all Indigenous nations within the United States can understand. The entire legal-political apparatus of tribal sovereignty is based on a premise of White supremacy that allows for U.S. unilateral extinguishment of tribal treaty rights (Wilkins and Lomawaima 2001; Williams 2005). For the Standing Rock Sioux Tribe (and other tribes along the Missouri River), tribal members felt the full force of this colonial relationship in the 1940s when the U.S. Army Corps of Engineers flooded thousands of acres of their most productive ancestral lands—ostensibly protected in treaty—in order to dam the Missouri River for the benefit of downstream White communities (Olson 1990; Lawson 1994). The selection for dam sites along the Missouri River disproportionately impacted tribes and was done for "political" reasons with the interest of White "urban centers" (Schneiders 1997, 245). Most tribes along the Missouri River eventually agreed to dam construction, flooding, and even federal "termination" in order to stave off even worse and possibly more violent removal and dispossession (Estes 2013). This colonial inequality resurfaced again in 2016 in the construction of DAPL, which snaked through burial sites and spots of spiritual importance. All of these lands were guaranteed to the Sioux people in treaty agreements made in 1854 and again in 1868. Included in these lands were the Black Hills and much of the land near the Missouri River. It is ironic that the most fervent defenders of the water stored in these colonial dams are the Indigenous nations displaced by their construction. Most Indigenous peoples recognize colonial dispossession and displacement when we see it. This is how we resonate with the struggle in Palestine and other sites of colonial encroachment throughout the world. Indigenous nations recognized Standing Rock as a resistance to colonization, regardless of our differing relations with extractive industries or other problematic industries in our communities.

White Supremacy in Federal Indian Law

There is a lot of confusion about the rights of Indigenous nations within colonial law. This is because Indigenous nations simultaneously maintain notions of aboriginal rights and lesser rights defined in colonial laws. In the United States, the federal government claims total rights over all Indigenous nations and their lands. With violence, the United States maintains its dictatorial powers over Indigenous nations. In the course of daily administration, federal and state officials invented mechanisms of legal chicanery they would later deploy again and again to undermine the rights of nations within its prejudiced legal system (Wilkins and Lomawaima 2001).

Although colonialism began in 1492, the United States did not legally define the status of Indigenous nations within its federal system until the 1820s. After its war against Great Britain, the United States held tremendous war debts that it repaid through the selling of Indigenous lands under the feet of people who didn't realize they were part of an abstract calculus of empire. For legal consistency, U.S. governing officials had to nullify aboriginal title to acquire tribal lands for free (Kades 2000). Indigenous peoples, as nations or as individuals, responding to colonial pressures sold lands to encroaching settlers on their own accord. But competing claims over the same plots of land made titling confusing. Indigenous peoples sold lands to settlers that the U.S. government unilaterally alienated and sold to other settlers. Aboriginal title was an existential threat to the United States. Its treasury was dependent on legalized theft. To resolve this problem, the U.S. Supreme Court's first chief justice, John Marshall, reduced the title of Indigenous nations to that of "tribes" that could not own their lands. The right of domination went to the original colonists, Great Britain; in fact the right of tribes to speak on their own behalf was extinguished by virtue of them not being Christians (Miller 2010). In a series of decisions between 1823 and 1832, Marshall defined the status and rights of Indigenous nations within the United States as "tribes," uncivilized peoples dependent on the United States and subject to its complete and sometimes arbitrary authority. Most of these rulings concerned the Cherokee Nation fighting the state of Georgia, who wanted to open up Indian lands for large-scale and intensified plantation slavery (Baptist 2016). Marshall successfully limited the rights of tribes but placed final authority over tribes in the federal government.

The Cherokee, Chickasaw, Choctaw, Creek, Seminole, and other nations of the Southeast and Ohio Valley were removed to "Indian territory," modern Oklahoma, based on characterizations of Indigenous nations that are not too different from today's mainstream depictions of Indigenous nations as inherent environmentalists. It is from these racist understandings where legal concepts such as "domestic dependent" and "plenary power" originate. This was how the U.S. Supreme Court systematically extinguished tribal rights to land and justified the continued colonization of Indigenous lands (Deloria and Lytle 1983). For more than a hundred years following the Marshall decisions, the explicit goal of U.S. federal policy was to kill, remove, or assimilate Indigenous peoples whose lives stood in the way of territorial expansion and wealth accumulation. The United States created reservations in the 1840s and explicitly worked to "civilize" tribal peoples until notions of "development" replaced it.

The supposed nadir of Indigenous political and cultural life was at the beginning of the twentieth century when our numbers appeared at our lowest (Thornton 1987; Maddox 2006). This was the period of "the vanishing Indian," long predicted by colonialists and popularized in the U.S. media through dime novels, exotic photography, and salvage anthropology meant to document these cultures before they disappeared. These White documentarians came into Indigenous communities looking for cultural difference and practices that were assumed to be premodern. It was an approach blinded by its own presumptions. Missing from these accounts were Indigenous political claims—rights defined against the colonial state. Instead, tribes were seen as defying progress with preindustrial ideas of nature. It is this trope that recycled into media accounts and activist literatures of #NoDAPL, which deny the territorial claims of the Standing Rock Tribe and the larger Great Sioux Nation.

In the 1930s the Roosevelt administration created legal-political apparatuses through which tribes could exercise limited notions of "sovereignty" and self-determination for modernization and development. The ushering in of tribal governments with rights and powers not practiced in most Indigenous communities had profound implications on social, cultural, and political life for tribes. Tribal governments were created through the Indian Reorganization Act of 1934. These governments were comprised of "councils," that is, legislative bodies, whom the United States recognized as the "governing authority" over the rest of the tribe.

Since the advent of colonization, Europeans looked toward concentrated power with which to negotiate. Often Indigenous nations did not maintain political systems of absolutism and inherited monarchical powers. The few nations who did practice tyranny are the most celebrated in Western histories as the civilized tribes of the continent, including Inca, Aztec, and slave-owning nations in the southeast. For most nations, political power was not concentrated or hereditary. Consequently, concessions from one group might not have had any legal bearing for the rest of "the tribe" within that nation's jurisprudence. Of course this should have been obvious, but it was not to most colonial administrators and treaty makers. They sought "governing authorities" and made the creation of male leadership and tribal councils a central focus of their treaty negotiation (Deloria and Wilkins 2010). Not only did this engender patriarchy into societies that maintained strong matrilineal institutions, it also proved ineffective for land concessions (Goeman and Denetdale 2009). The Indian Reorganization Act helped to resolve some of these issues. At the same time, Congress passed legislation, such as the Indian

Mineral Leasing Act of 1938, that allowed these newly minted governing authorities to sign on to mining and leasing contracts (Allison 2015).

Despite the paternalistic tone of these arrangements, they did provide Indigenous nations with a new source of legal authority over their territories. The crucial advantage of the Indian Reorganization Act is that it created contiguous lands where possible. However, some reservations were factionalized beyond repair, alienated from years of allotment. For tribes such as the Navajo Nation, our reservation expanded. The process was not uniform. It varied in place and context. For the Standing Rock Sioux Tribe, and other Sioux nations, much of their best lands were lost in colonial allotments. Despite treaties, the Great Sioux Nation was splintered into five smaller reservations (Pine Ridge, Rosebud, Lower Brule, Cheyenne River, and Standing Rock), and each was further reduced in size through allotment. Then in the 1940s, the Army Corps of Engineers flooded the Missouri River Valley. These were the remaining lands of Indigenous nations, whose last remaining pristine lands were lost in the flooding.

Since the 1820s, federal policy has oscillated between outright "elimination" and genocide (Wolfe 2011) and assimilation, legibility, and "forced federalism" (Corntassel and Witmer 2008). Today there remains ambiguity about the rights of tribes under colonial law. As nations who ought to be independent of the United States, Indigenous jurisdictions are a blight on the national consciousness. Tribal rights, lands, and traditional economies stand in the way of the expansion of resource capitalism across the continent. Processes of "recognition" and corporate practices of sovereignty help facilitate this process (Coulthard 2007). Yet tribes have advanced their claims through a discourse of "sovereignty" despite its inherent limitations and basis on notions of White supremacy. Indigenous activism in the 1960s and 1970s persuaded Congress to pass the Indian Self-Determination and Educational Assistance Act of 1975. Perhaps this legislative reform was done to undermine revolutionary organizing among Indigenous peoples at the time. But it also ushered in the discourse of "tribal sovereignty" or the process of reworking tribal governments toward a stronger sense of local control while keeping in place key elements of colonial authority. These legislative reforms allowed for tribes to take over and run colonizing institutions but have done nothing to give them powers on par with international states.

Today "sovereignty" is understood as a problematic concept. Some argue this is because of the European origin of the term, while I would suggest the main problem is that tribal governments have not been given enough power to be called "sovereign." But it is also necessary for continued resistance against colonialism (Barker 2005). In the case of DAPL, the Standing Rock Sioux Tribe, a product of this process of attempted elimination and assimilation, used its status as a tribal entity with government-to-government relations with institutions of the executive branch to protest DAPL's proposed route. In the end a more militant form of resistance was needed, a form of civil disobedience along the route of the pipeline to draw national attention to the injustice of land theft. It was through this direct action that Standing Rock witnessed more of its grievances addressed.

Land as Site of Struggle

Land is much more than a site for cultural and spiritual practice, it is also space for social reproduction. Without land, life is not possible. For the Standing Rock Sioux Tribe, and all tribes, they understood their struggle was one for their rights to life and survival (Estes 2016). And in many ways this is the broader definition of tribal sovereignty. In Indigenous scholarship we have debated its narrower legal-political meaning or whether or not it is an "appropriate" concept (Alfred 2006). But this is looking at the issue backward. Rather than fixating on the word *sovereignty* and why it is an "inappropriate" concept for tribes because of the Western origin of the word, we should understand how everyday tribal actors understand it. For tribal peoples it both has legal-political meaning *and* also evokes a right to land and self-determination. These are the terms of the issues for most tribal actors. We understand and relate based on the similarity of our struggles: it is to preserve a land base and our rights that we oppose DAPL and other colonial encroachments from the Pacific Ocean to Palestine, even when we maintain contradictory relationships with extractive industries.

Indigenous activism increased in the United States during the 1960s and 1970s when tribal peoples created organizations and institutions to unite tribes across the United States and articulate grievances against the settler-colonial state. It was usually young people and women who led these movements. In 1969, urban Natives from the Bay Area occupied the then abandoned Alcatraz Island and declared it Indigenous land. Others led a walk across Indigenous communities throughout the United States to Washington, D.C., called the Trail of Broken Treaties. Many of these activists eventually occupied the Bureau of Indian Affairs building in Washington, D.C. The resistance at Wounded Knee in 1973 was the culmination of years of struggle to create national movements across Indigenous lands and territories (Smith and Warrior 1996).

When we look at Indigenous support from across the country for the rights of Standing Rock people to their land, we recognize that it was through an understanding of sovereignty and self-determination that Indigenous peoples were able to connect with the struggle. Despite centuries of settler-colonialism, Indigenous peoples in North America successfully fought back against colonialists and the legal structures of land theft. Since the Marshall Trilogy defined us as "wards" or "domestic dependent" nations in the 1820s, we have resisted exile and elimination. We resist successfully through action, even when we lose in the courts of the colonial government. And through land occupation and a refusal to move, we eventually gain jurisdiction over our national land base, still unceded.

In 2016 the Standing Rock Sioux Tribe sued the Army Corps of Engineers for violating its own laws and neglecting consultation with the tribe over the proposed route of the pipeline. These laws require government-to-government consultation between the tribe and entities of the federal government, including the corps. From the perspective of the Standing Rock Sioux Tribe, the Army Corps of Engineers decided what it was going to do anyway and simply notified the tribe of its decision. The tribe produced maps, surveys, and arguments in court and to the corps as to why the route infringed on tribal jurisdiction. They documented sites of spiritual significance and known grave sites. All of this was disregarded in the interest of oil, development, and colonization. The tribe challenged this wanton disregard in colonial courts that predictably ruled against the claims of the nation.

It was women and everyday community members who initiated the physical challenge to the route of DAPL, putting themselves at risk to the violence of construction firms. Their bravery in the face of obvious injustice inspired people from all across the country to join. The tribal government was quick to support it and found ways to use the tribe's resources to tell the Indigenous side of the story. This form of direct resistance was riskier for those involved. A non-Native resister nearly lost her arm when police used water cannons on people on a frigid night of demonstration. It was the only way to force the U.S. government to uphold its own weak environmental laws and promises to respect tribal sovereignty.

Indigenous organizers and activists regularly refer to treaty rights when challenging institutions of colonization. This is done to challenge the legacy of the Marshall Trilogy and White supremacy inherent in colonial law. It was on the same Standing Rock reservation in 1974 when Indigenous peoples from across the country came together to form the International Indian Treaty Council to petition for the rights of tribes within international law. Their years of work eventually led to the passage of the Declaration on the Rights of Indigenous Peoples in 2007 within the United Nations that serves in some ways as a future basis for claims against colonial countries like the United States. Through continued struggle against the racist assumptions of colonial law, Indigenous peoples work to preserve their unceded territories and national rights to self-determination. Although these struggles are clearly linked to campaigns for environmental justice, they are better understood as struggles for territorial independence.

Conclusion

Today we are working to understand the deeper meanings and implications of the NoDAPL movement at Standing Rock. For many non-Native participants and witnesses, the movement was about the tribe's fight to protect water and the environment. This was a popular framing simply because it spoke to larger politics of climate change and the fossil-fuel industry—the antagonists in the story. It was a framing that social movements and organizations leveraged to gain support for the struggle. But it had the negative effect of characterizing Indigenous peoples as inherent environmentalists, which builds on an older, uglier stereotype of Indigenous peoples that was used to dispossess Indigenous peoples of the right of nationhood and that serves as the justifying basis for colonial laws.

This caused confusion for even frontline participants who needed to know what the struggle was about. Because there were thousands of people who fought against the construction of DAPL from across the country, there were literally thousands of competing claims to the core meaning of NoDAPL. It is important to prioritize Indigenous claims, especially those of the people from the communities most impacted by the route of the pipeline. I am not writing from such a perspective. I am writing as a member of the Navajo Nation who worked in solidarity with NoDAPL from the "triangle region" of North Carolina. I joined with Indigenous students in the region to partner with environmental groups who rallied in support for the Standing Rock Sioux Tribe. We raised money and called for boycotts on some of the institutions like Wells Fargo that funded the construction of the pipeline. NoDAPL, like Idle No More and other recent movements, was not just about stopping the pipeline; it was a way for Indigenous peoples from across the continent to critique centuries of colonialism and displacement.

This brings us to the framework and framing that limited tribal grievance to environmental claims. Because of the nature of the Standing Rock Sioux Tribe's challenge of the project as one in violation of federal environment and government-to-government relations, many media interpreted the struggle as one that was only about the environment and water. This framework was reinforced through the efforts of environmental groups who established near the DAPL construction as Water Protectors. Although there are clearly environmental concerns with DAPL, it is also important to remember the longer history of colonial dispossession. Rooting the resistance in Indigenous histories and struggles for the land gives us a fuller sense of what happened and how we can better support Indigenous nations to defeat the empire.

NOTE

1. "The Mandan, Hidatsa, and Arickara Nation's Support for the Standing Rock Nation" (letter to Dave Archambault II), Mandan, Hidatsa & Arickara Nation, August 22, 2016, http://www.mhanation.com/main2/Home_News/Home_News_2016/News_08_2016_August/The%20Mandan%20Hidatsa%20Arikara%20Nations%20Support%20for%20the%20Standing%20Rock%20Nation.pdf (no longer available).

REFERENCES

Adams, D. W. 1995. *Education for Extinction: American Indians and the Boarding School Experience, 1875–1928*. Lawrence: University Press of Kansas.

Alfred, G. T. 2006. "Sovereignty—An Inappropriate Concept." *The Indigenous Experience:*

Global Perspectives, edited by Roger C. A. Maaka and Chris Andersen, 322–36. Toronto: Canadian Scholars' Press.

Allison, J. R. 2015. *Sovereignty for Survival: American Energy Development and Indian Self-Determination*. New Haven: Yale University Press.

Baptist, E. E. 2016. *The Half Has Never Been Told: Slavery and the Making of American Capitalism*. London: Hachette UK.

Barker, J., ed. 2005. *Sovereignty Matters: Locations of Contestation and Possibility in Indigenous Struggles for Self-Determination*. Lincoln: University of Nebraska Press.

Corntassel, J., and R. C. Witmer. 2008. *Forced Federalism: Contemporary Challenges to Indigenous Nationhood*. Norman: University of Oklahoma Press.

Coulthard, G. S. 2007. "Subjects of Empire: Indigenous Peoples and the 'Politics of Recognition' in Canada." *Contemporary Political Theory* 6:437–60.

Curley, A. 2016. "Taa' hwo' aji' t'eego: Sovereignty, Livelihood, and Challenging Coal in the Navajo Nation." PhD dissertation, Cornell University.

Deloria, V. 1985. *American Indian Policy in the Twentieth Century*. Norman: University of Oklahoma Press.

Deloria, V., Jr., and C. M. Lytle. 1983. *American Indians, American Justice*. Austin: University of Texas Press.

Deloria, V., Jr., and D. E. Wilkins. 2010. *Tribes, Treaties, and Constitutional Tribulations*. Austin: University of Texas Press.

Dunbar-Ortiz, R. 2013. *The Great Sioux Nation: Sitting in Judgment on America*. Lincoln: University of Nebraska Press.

———. 2014. *An Indigenous Peoples' History of the United States*. Boston: Beacon.

Estes, N. 2016. "Fighting for Our Lives: #NoDAPL in Historical Context." The Red Nation, September 18. https://therednation.org/.

Estes, N. W. 2013. "A History of Loss: The Lower Brule and Fort Randall Dam." PhD dissertation, University of South Dakota.

Fried, M. H. 1975. *The Notion of Tribe*. Menlo Park, Calif.: Benjamin-Cummings Publishing.

Goeman, M. R., and J. N. Denetdale. 2009. "Native Feminisms: Legacies, Interventions, and Indigenous Sovereignties." *Wicazo Sa Review* 24:9–13.

Gottlieb, R. 2005. *Forcing the Spring: The Transformation of the American Environmental Movement*. Washington, D.C.: Island Press.

Hosmer, B. C., C. M. O'Neill, and D. L. Fixico. 2004. *Native Pathways: American Indian Culture and Economic Development in the Twentieth Century*. Boulder: University Press of Colorado.

Kades, E. 2000. "The Dark Side of Efficiency: Johnson v. M'Intosh and the Expropriation of American Indian Lands." *University of Pennsylvania Law Review* 148:1065–1190.

Lawson, M. L. 1994. *Dammed Indians: The Pick-Sloan Plan and the Missouri River Sioux, 1944–1980*. Norman: University of Oklahoma Press.

Lewis, D. R. 1995. "Native Americans and the Environment: A Survey of Twentieth-Century Issues." *American Indian Quarterly* 19:423–50.

Maddox, L. 2006. *Citizen Indians: Native American Intellectuals, Race, and Reform.* Ithaca: Cornell University Press.

Miller, R. J. 2010. *Discovering Indigenous Lands: The Doctrine of Discovery in the English Colonies.* Oxford: Oxford University Press.

Nadasdy, P. 2005. "Transcending the Debate over the Ecologically Noble Indian: Indigenous Peoples and Environmentalism." *Ethnohistory* 52:291–331.

Olson, P. A. 1990. *The Struggle for the Land: Indigenous Insight and Industrial Empire in the Semiarid World.* Lincoln: University of Nebraska Press.

O'Neill, C. 2005. *Working the Navajo Way: Labor and Culture in the Twentieth Century.* Lawrence: University Press of Kansas.

Parker, A. 2014. "Sovereignty by the Barrel: Indigenous Oil Politics in the Bakken." Paper delivered at the Native American Indigenous Studies Association Annual Meeting, Austin, Texas, May.

Powell, D. E. 2017. *Landscapes of Power: Politics of Energy in the Navajo Nation.* Durham, N.C.: Duke University Press.

Reisner, M. 1993. *Cadillac Desert: The American West and Its Disappearing Water.* New York: Penguin.

Schneiders, R. K. 1997. "Flooding the Missouri Valley: The Politics of Dam Site Selection and Design." *Great Plains Quarterly* 17:237–49.

Smith, P. C., and R. A. Warrior. 1996. *Like a Hurricane: The Indian Movement from Alcatraz to Wounded Knee.* New York: New Press.

Starn, O. 2011. "Here Come the Anthros (Again): The Strange Marriage of Anthropology and Native America." *Cultural Anthropology* 26:179–204.

Thornton, R. 1987. *American Indian Holocaust and Survival: A Population History since 1492.* Norman: University of Oklahoma Press.

Trafzer, C. E., J. A. Keller, and L. Sisquoc. 2006. *Boarding School Blues: Revisiting American Indian Educational Experiences.* Lincoln: University of Nebraska Press.

Wilkins, D. E. 2011. *American Indian Politics and the American Political System.* Lanham, Md.: Rowman & Littlefield.

Wilkins, D. E., and K. T. Lomawaima. 2001. *Uneven Ground: American Indian Sovereignty and Federal Law.* Norman: University of Oklahoma Press.

Wilkinson, C. F. 2005. *Blood Struggle: The Rise of Modern Indian Nations.* London: W. W. Norton.

Williams, R. A., Jr. 2005. *Like a Loaded Weapon: The Rehnquist Court, Indian Rights, and the Legal History of Racism in America.* Minneapolis: University of Minnesota Press.

Wolfe, P. 2011. "After the Frontier: Separation and Absorption in US Indian Policy." *Settler Colonial Studies* 1:13–51.

13

RESOLUTIONS

Layli Long Soldier

This poem was originally published as "Resolution 6" in WHEREAS, a poetry collection by Layli Long Soldier. The text at left is from a social media post by Mark K. Tilsen, Pine Ridge, South Dakota, on September 20, 2016; the text at right is from a personal interview with Waniya Locke in Standing Rock, South Dakota, on September 19, 2016.

(6) *I too urge the President to acknowledge the wrongs of the United States against Indian tribes in the history of the United States in order to bring healing to this land although healing this land is not dependent never has been upon this President meaning tribal nations and the people themselves are healing this land its waters with or without Presidential acknowledgment they act upon this right without apology:*

these Direct Action Principles

have been painstakingly drafted

at behest of the local leadership

from Standing Rock

and are the guidelines

for the Očhéthi Šakówiŋ camp

I acknowledge a plurality of ways

to resist oppression

To speak to law enforcement

be really clear always ask

who what when where why

e.g. Officer, my name is _____

please explain

the probable cause for stopping me

you may ask

does that seem reasonable to you

we are Protectors

we are peaceful & prayerful

"isms" have no place

here we all stand together

we are non-violent

we are proud to stand

no masks

respect locals

no weapons

or what could be construed as weapons

property damage does not get us closer

to our goal

all campers must get an orientation

Direct Action Training

is required

for everyone taking action

no children

in potentially dangerous situations

we keep each accountable

don't give any further info

•

People ask why do you bring up

so many other issues it's because

these issues have been ongoing

for 200 years they're inter-dependent

we teach the distinction

btwn civil rights & civil liberties

btwn what's legal & what isn't legal

the camp is 100% volunteer

it's a choice to be a Protector

liberty is freedom

of speech it's a right

to privacy a fair trial

you're free

from unreasonable search

free from seizure of person or home

& civil disobedience: the camp is

an act of civil disobedience

now the law protects the corporation

so the camp is illegal

you must have a buddy system

to these principles

this is a ceremony

act accordingly

someone must know when you're leaving

& when you're coming back

"Riders." Photograph by Michelle Latimer.

14

CENTERING SOVEREIGNTY
HOW STANDING ROCK CHANGED THE CONVERSATION

Elizabeth Ellis

Yes, there is oil in the Dakota Access Pipeline, and yes, there is little legal recourse left to the Standing Rock Sioux Tribe.[1] But there is also a fire burning in the heart of Indigenous America, and it has ignited a generation of activists and forged broad solidarity unlike any we have ever seen.

In the spring of 2016, the Standing Rock Sioux Tribe captured the attention of the world as they took on a global oil corporation and the federal government on the American Great Plains. In 2015 Energy Transfer Partners (ETP), the company behind the Dakota Access Pipeline (DAPL), announced plans to run an oil pipeline through the Standing Rock Sioux treaty lands. This pipeline would cross over sacred sites, gouge through burial grounds, and pass under Lake Oahe, the reservoir that provides this reservation's primary source of drinking water. More importantly, this pipeline would be built against the wishes of the Standing Rock Sioux tribal government and in violation of treaties that the Sioux signed with the federal government. In early spring 2016 this conflict escalated as ETP began the physical construction of the pipeline. Looking for help, LaDonna Bravebull Allard, a tribal historian of the Standing Rock Sioux, invited supporters to camp on her lands along the Cannonball River and to stand with her and the Standing Rock Sioux as they placed their bodies and prayers in the path of the pipeline. Incredibly, tens of thousands of people answered her call and traveled to Standing Rock Sioux territory.

By late summer more than ten thousand people had journeyed to Standing Rock to support the fight against the pipeline, and thousands more came to the camps over the course of the fall. Donations poured in from around the globe. In New York, Los Angeles, Philadelphia, Denver, and cities across the United States, local organizers staged solidarity actions to raise awareness, garner public support, and collect funds and supplies to send to Water Protectors on the front lines. Many more Americans called the U.S. Army Corps of Engineers (ACOE), wrote to

President Barack Obama, and engaged in a massive public debate about the rights of Native Americans to water and environmental resources.

This pressure on the ground at Standing Rock and from the public at large stymied the construction of the Dakota Access Pipeline. By the time that President Obama left office in January 2017, this popular resistance had convinced his administration to order a halt of construction and a federal environmental review of the project. When the Obama administration announced that the Army Corps of Engineers would not grant final permit to ETP in December 2017, Indigenous Americans celebrated, albeit tentatively, their massive victory in forcing the federal government to take their environmental concerns seriously.[2] Incredibly, this coalition of Native and non-Native allies had compelled the federal government to take action to protect the rights of an Indigenous nation.

However, when President Donald Trump took office, he promptly reversed the Obama administration's decisions. Trump's January 2017 executive order expediting the pipeline negated the Obama administration's mandate for a complete environmental impact assessment and stifled the period of public comment. As with so many of the flurry of orders the president has signed, the administration did not follow customary procedure, and it waived the typical fourteen-day waiting period after congressional notification. This enabled construction crews to promptly return to drilling under Lake Oahe and facilitated the forced removal of the final Water Protectors who remained at camps along the pipeline route.[3]

With Trump's support the ACOE ultimately granted ETP the final permit they needed to build this pipeline, and the state and federal government supplied the military force necessary to physically remove Water Protectors from this route.[4] Thus despite the objection of the Standing Rock Sioux Tribe and the opposition of hundreds of other Native nations within the United States, the federal government facilitated the completion of this pipeline. The devastating conclusion of this conflict has left many Americans asking, did all of this effort make any difference? And in light of our current political moment, does the fight at Standing Rock still matter?

Yes, and more than most of us could have possibly imagined in 2016. Certainly, this fight matters because it is the most recent chapter in a centuries' old saga of American colonial violence against Native people. It is also significant because it illuminated the willingness of the federal government to bend and sidestep regulations designed to protect the environment and all Americans to support corporate profit.

However, it is also tremendously important because of the ways that Standing Rock opened up a national discussion about treaty rights and Native sovereignty in the twenty-first century. In 2016, while most of the American public was fixated on the Olympics in Rio de Janeiro and the U.S. presidential election, the Standing Rock Sioux Tribe forged the largest pan-Indigenous alliance in North American history. Into this frenetic cultural conversation, Standing Rock Water Protectors managed to capture the nation's attention and garner support from an American public that had previously been largely oblivious to the ongoing struggles of Native people to defend their lands and communities. Over the course of 2016, the #NoDAPL movement built a massive, intersectional alliance by drawing on popular perceptions of Native peoples and linking the struggle of the Standing Rock Sioux Tribe to other contemporary fights for social justice. By first setting up digital platforms where Native people's voices could be heard, and then using these spaces to generate popular support, Water Protectors educated the public about the historical relationships between the United States and the Great Sioux Nation and thereby forced a national focus on Native sovereignty in the modern era.

The combination of this broad support for the Standing Rock Sioux Tribe and the reconceptualization of the fights for justice for Native Americans not as issues of minority rights within the United States, but as fights against a colonial government for self-determination has had powerful implications. For the many Americans who, prior to Standing Rock, would have insisted that the United States' exploitation of Native Americans was a nineteenth-century crime and that Native people are simply a descendent minority within our modern nation, the coverage of Standing Rock destroyed these comforting national narratives. This fight forced non-Indigenous Americans to acknowledge not just the existence of real, modern, Native Americans but also that unresolved treaty claims and U.S. colonization of Indigenous peoples and lands are very current problems.

Furthermore the conversations about water rights, self-determination, police violence, and racism that the #NoDAPL movement fostered have also forged a new intersectional platform that applies Indigenous perspectives of settler-colonial nationalism to critique oppression across the United States. Through the networks and spaces that Water Protectors carved into the national media and public discourse, Indigenous activists have obtained new platforms to reach the public at large and are providing critical voices to challenge xenophobic and exploitive federal policies. In effect then, Standing Rock not only changed the conversation about Indigenous-specific issues, but also forged a broad alliance that is poised to have tremendous impact on a wide spectrum of contemporary fights for social justice in the Americas.

Building Intersectional Support

Between May and December 2016 more than 360 Native nations from around the world joined the fight against DAPL and offered support to the Standing Rock Sioux Tribe. These allies included Indigenous peoples from South and Central America, Australia, the Pacific Islands, and the Arctic North. For decades, Navajo people have struggled to obtain access to safe, clean drinking water as mining plants have spilled millions of gallons of toxic waste into the rivers that supplied the nation's water for drinking, bathing, and farming.[5] For the last two years Apache people have fought to prevent the federal government from providing permits to copper mining companies to carve up Oak Flat, which is a space they consider sacred.[6] Apaches, Navajos, and so many other Native Americans perceive the threat of DAPL not just as a danger for the Standing Rock Sioux, but as a critical threat to Indigenous sovereignty and resources.

Moreover the exploitation of Indigenous resources frequently enables violence against Indigenous women, and so the threat of colonial resource extraction resonates with communities who have suffered gender-based violence. For example, in 2016 in Honduras, Lenca environmental activist Berta Cáceres was murdered after she led the opposition against an Agua Zarca hydroelectric dam.[7] During the oil boom in 2010–13 in North Dakota, the rates of violence and sexual assault against Arikara, Mandan, and Hidatsa women skyrocketed due to the increase of man camps in the region.[8] On the Fort Berthold reservation, for example, between 2011 and 2012 the rates of violence against women tripled as the result of the influx of oil workers in the region.[9] In sum, Indigenous people worldwide empathized with the people of Standing Rock, and they recognized that the implications of this fight could have repercussions that impact all Native nation's abilities to control their resources in the twenty-first century.

Yet the immense breadth of solidarity of the Standing Rock movement is wholly unprecedented in American history. I teach early American history to university students, and in my courses I frequently cover multinational Native resistance movements. Pontiac's War, for example, is commonly described as the largest pan-Indian movement in American history. In 1763, at the end of the Seven Years War, British forced-moved into the Ohio River Valley and Great Lakes to claim the forts and territories of the French as their spoils of war. Under the guidance of Delaware spiritual leader Neolin and the Odawa political leader Pontiac, Shawnee, Delaware, Odawa, Potawatomi, Miami, Wyandot, and other Native nations joined forces to oppose British expansion into their homelands. This movement led to a powerful spiritual revival and dealt a profound blow to the British Empire before this Indigenous alliance crumbled in 1764. For years my students have asked why more nations did not join Pontiac, or other resistance movements like the Yamasee War against South Carolinians, or the Pueblos in their war against the Spanish. Or they have asked why all Native peoples did not just band together to confront British, French, Spanish, or American colonizers. For years I have emphasized that while Native people certainly made alliances and took collective actions, the many Native polities of North America had different priorities, political strategies, and long histories of antagonistic relationships with their neighbors and disparate cultural values. I explained that pan-Indigenous resistance was just not a viable option. I was wrong. Native nations who have fought, disagreed, and who have little in common culturally or politically came together to support Standing Rock and to build what is unquestionably the largest international Indigenous movement in American history.

This solidarity is even more remarkable because the supporting groups included individuals and representatives from Native nations whose economies are directly tied to energy extraction. These groups include the Crow Nation, which depends on coal extraction, and the Osage Nation, which garnered substantial profit from oil extraction in the early twentieth century. My own nation, the Peoria Tribe of Indians of Oklahoma, sent a statement of support to the Standing Rock Sioux, and this is quite surprising considering that many of our citizens have personal ties and economic investments in the Oklahoma and Texas oil industries.[10] So the support of these nations came not just from Native peoples' sense of obligation to honor and protect all of our relations (including animals, rivers, and lands), but also from a sense of the critical importance of supporting Native peoples' rights to determine what can be done with their territories and resources. In effect, this solidarity is drawing on something even deeper than an Indigenous environmentalism and sense of obligation to our sacred and ancestral places.

If this immense coalition of Native people is unprecedented, perhaps even more so was the broad support from non-Indigenous allies. Jewish, Quaker, Lutheran, Muslim, and many other religious groups sent members to Standing Rock, staged demonstrations, and lobbied U.S. representatives.[11] Members of the Black Lives Matter network traveled to Stranding Rock and voiced their support for the Sioux as a fight against environmental racism and police violence, and as connected to their efforts to provide clean water to Flint, Michigan.[12] Perhaps more surprisingly, support from a couple thousand American veterans provided critical leverage for the Standing Rock Sioux Tribe. In late November as the violence escalated, the ACOE demanded that the Water Protectors move from their camps along the Cannonball River by early December. Roughly two thousand veterans journeyed to Standing Rock in the midst of the heavy snow and whipping winds, and they offered to put their bodies physically between the Water Protectors and the government forces. Merely days after their arrival, Obama cancelled the forced removal deadline and signed an order that mandated an environmental review and denied ETP the final construction permit. While the Trump administration overturned this order, this was nonetheless a striking demonstration of the power of solidarity.[13] Altogether, estimates suggest that more than ten thousand people journeyed to Standing Rock to physically defend the lands, and tens of thousands more took to the streets in cities across the country and pressured their representatives to take action to halt this pipeline and the ongoing violence against Native people.[14]

In 2016, I was working at the University of Pennsylvania and living in Philadelphia as the DAPL conflict escalated. According to the estimates of the U.S. Census Bureau, in 2016 the population of Philadelphia was 44 percent African American, 45 percent white, 14 percent Latin American, and 7 percent Asian. Less than 1 percent of the population identifies as Indigenous or Native American, and the state of Pennsylvania has no federally recognized Native nations within its borders.[15] Although Philadelphia prides itself on having a strong connection to early American history, and celebrates its role in the American Revolution, there is little public representation or celebration of the Lenape people who called this region home. In effect this meant that there is limited cultural memory of Indigenous people within the city as well as limited discussions of Indigenous peoples or issues in Philadelphia schools, museums, or plazas.

Despite having minimal visibility of Native people, a strong solidarity movement to support Standing Rock emerged in Philadelphia. In fact, the organizers of Philly with Standing Rock were primarily non-Native Americans. They were Euro-American settlers who had long been committed to environmental activism, or black community advocates who were working on issues of environmental justice, or people of Indigenous descent who traced their cultural identities to Central American, South American, or Caribbean communities. Most of the folks in this group had no experience working with Native American nations or communities and were deeply unfamiliar with Indian law or history in the U.S. context. But it didn't matter, and they worked tirelessly to advocate for the Standing Rock Sioux Tribe and to engage the public on this issue. Between September and December Philly with Standing Rock organized numerous demonstrations to raise awareness, rallies to show solidarity, actions to deliver petitions to the office of the ACOE, and protests outside of financial institutions such as Wells Fargo, TD Bank, and Sunoco.

All of these events demonstrated the solidarity of this diverse group of supporters. At an action organized by a local temple outside of the Wells Fargo on Market Street, on November 2, 2016, I remember seeing a young woman holding a sign that read "another Jew against genocide" with images of concentration camps pasted alongside what appeared to be photos of the Wounded Knee Massacre. The power plants that supply energy to Philadelphia residents are located in the southwest quadrant of the city, and their emissions emanate into the surrounding community. Three quarters of the residents who live within one mile of these power plants are black, and a 2012 NAACP report found that African Americans suffer from asthma at three times the rate of their white counterparts in the city. Thus some of the African American organizers who led Philly with Standing Rock saw this struggle as connected to their own.[16] At one of the first rallies in the city a demonstrator who walked at the front of the crowd carried a sign that read simply "Fix Flint." In Philadelphia the calls from the national Standing Rock movement to defund Wells Fargo and TD Bank also overlapped with community initiatives to stop Wells Fargo from charging millions of dollars in fees from the city's public school funds.[17] Thus even in a city with a minimal Indigenous population, in Philadelphia there were already strong grassroots movements for social and economic justice and movements against environmental and systemic racism, and the NoDAPL movement was able to build on these networks.

My experience organizing with Philly with Standing Rock led me to ask, what was it about Standing Rock that mobilized cities like Philadelphia on a national scale? How was it that this movement gained so much traction and managed to enfold all of these community activists and ordinary Americans with little or no prior background in Native rights issues? Effectively, what was different about Standing Rock than the Navajo and Apache fights for clean water, or the battle of the Indigenous community of Isle Jean Charles in Louisiana against climate change?[18]

First and foremost this movement was built on the passion and tireless commitment of Native women, men, and youth who poured their hearts into organizing. Within the Standing Rock Sioux Tribe LaDonna Bravebull Allard put out the call for national support, Bobbi Jean Three Legs organized a youth relay run from Standing Rock to D.C. to call attention to the pipeline, and Tribal Chairman David Archambault II repeatedly broadcast requests for support to the nation. On the ground Lakota and Dakota youth and grandmothers stood their ground on the front lines and locked themselves to machinery. The world watched as peaceful demonstrators from all backgrounds were shot with rubber bullets and beanbags, tear gas, and long range acoustic devices. While Native people and their allies put their bodies on the line, Native-led environmental organizations like Honor the Earth and the Indigenous Environmental Network spread the stories from Standing Rock. There is no doubt that Lakotas and Dakotas and the citizens of the Standing Rock Sioux Tribe carried this movement and that those on the front lines gave the most to support this fight.

Second, we should not forget that the Standing Rock Sioux are the descendants of Crazy Horse, of Red Cloud, of Sitting Bull, and of the men and women who took on the federal government at Wounded Knee in 1973. In 1876 combined Lakota, Dakota, and Cheyenne forces led by these warriors famously defeated U.S. Army forces at the Battle of Greasy Grass, or as it is more commonly known, the Battle of Little Bighorn. The images of this fight and of this victory resonated across the nation and captured Americans' attention as much now as they did then. Nearly a century later, Lakota and Dakota people were again forced to take up arms against the federal government in an effort to defend their communities. More than a hundred years of genocidal policy—including corralling Native people on reservations, excising them of economic autonomy, forcing cultural assimilation through boarding schools and mission programs, and stripping juridical powers from tribal governments—has taken a tremendous toll on Lakota and Dakota people. Today their reservations in North Dakota are among some of the poorest locations in the country. Thus in the 1970s the promises of the American Indian Movement (AIM) to restore treaty rights, remedy tribal corruption, and demand real sovereignty for Native peoples had tremendous appeal to the Lakotas and Dakotas. In 1973 Oglala Lakota activists and members of AIM from many tribes seized the town of Wounded Knee—a site where the federal government massacred 150 Lakotas in 1890. Together this coalition of activists held Wounded Knee for seventy-one days as they withstood FBI bullets and blockades and protested the abusive leadership of tribal president Richard Wilson and the intervention of the federal government in Lakota politics.[19] So the conflict at Standing Rock is not a fundamentally new fight, but it is perhaps better understood as the most recent conflict in the United States' ongoing assault on the Sioux Nation and its descendants.

Leveraging Public Perception

Neither passion, nor legacy, nor crossover issues alone can explain the success of the NoDAPL movement in garnering public support for Standing Rock. Nor does it explain why so many more non-Indigenous Americans traveled to Sioux territory to participate in this fight in 2016 than did in 1973. At its height, the 1973 encampment at Wounded Knee involved two hundred people, whereas there were more than ten thousand at Standing Rock. Instead we should recognize that the resonance of this movement is the result of the expertly crafted and disseminated messaging of the #NoDAPL movement.

Most Americans are not familiar with the contours of Indian law, and unless they live in a state like Oklahoma or Montana with a high Native population, they may have minimal interaction with Native people in their daily lives. Even as late as 2015, there was rarely coverage of Indigenous issues in the mainstream U.S. media beyond the occasional exposé on drug use or domestic violence on reservations. In the United States, Native and Indigenous people are only about 2 percent of the population, and unlike our northern neighbors in Canada, we do not have dedicated Indigenous TV channels or a truth and reconciliation initiative, and in the United States there has been only minimal public discussion of Native policy in the federal government.[20]

We do, on the other hand, have lots and lots of Westerns. So in the United States, when Americans envision Native people they frequently think of Native people on horseback and in war bonnets, they probably are familiar with the Battle of Little Bighorn, and they may have images of Native peoples from Disney's *Pocahontas* singing to raccoons and painting with every color of the wind. Effectively when Americans imagine Indians, they picture Plains nations, and buckskin, eagle feathers, sage, and stoic riders with long braids sitting tall on horseback.[21]

What Standing Rock did, so expertly, was to draw on these images and stereotypes to mobilize sympathy. If we think about the rhetoric of the early movement we remember the rally cries of "water is life," "water is sacred," "honor the earth," "you can't drink oil, keep it in the soil," and "honor the sacred." The demonstrations and encampments were presented as rights to pray, as rights to defend the graves of Lakota peoples' ancestors, and as Native peoples' commitment to the land and water.[22]

I do not mean to suggest that this was not sincere, or that Standing Rock did not launch a cultural and religious revitalization of Indian country on a level that we have not seen in more than a century; it certainly did.[23] But this was also a move of tactical brilliance because this messaging drew on assumptions and stereotypes that Americans were already familiar with and couched the conflict on grounds of environment and religious justice in ways that were comprehensible to all Americans.[24]

To disseminate this message, Standing Rock activists drew on networks and strategies of Black Lives Matter, Idle No More, and the anti–Keystone XL campaign. Unlike in 1973 when Lakota and Dakota people struggled to obtain the attention of mass media and could not control the portrayal of their movement, in 2016 Native people controlled both the means and content of the messaging. The advent of social media and the subsequent democratization of information networks meant that Native peoples could tell their own stories. Via Facebook Live, Twitter, Instagram, Snapchat, and other media platforms, Native peoples and Standing Rock activists communicated directly with the American public and brought the nation to the front lines with them.

What these social media broadcasts also meant was that Native peoples could present themselves to the world as modern folks and as young men and women wearing T-shirts and jeans and shower slides or snow boots, and it provided Americans with a glimpse of the tremendous diversity of Indigenous people. On these live feeds and through Native-curated interviews, Americans saw Native Americans of all skin colors, black-presenting, white-presenting, with all kinds of hair, tattoos, and accents. This may sound trivial, but this was really the first time in the United States that there was mass and sustained coverage of Native people and of quotidian Indigenous life, and so it exposed Americans to new concepts of Native American identities in the twenty-first century.[25]

One of the challenges of framing this conflict for massive non-Indigenous audiences was that much of the early coverage of the movement was sympathetic, but also rather problematic. If the early news stories ran tragic reports of the bulldozing on Lakota gravesites and ETP's private security setting attack dogs on unarmed Native people, they also focused overwhelmingly on tropes of "ecological Indians" and defense of a "traditional" way of life. One of the first national stories run by the *New York Times* covering the movement explained that this fight was a "major environmental and cultural threat."[26] While certainly both cultural and environmental factors were central tenets of this fight, this coverage also missed a crucial component of the issue, Native sovereignty.[27]

Centering Sovereignty

When we consider the media coverage of Standing Rock from fall of 2016, we can begin to see a transition from late summer reports that centered on discussions of environmental and spiritual concerns to examinations of Native sovereignty by November. This transition was in part a switch fueled by the dialogue of Native peoples on the front lines, but also by an effort on the part of Standing Rock Water Protectors who forced these issues into public discourse. In late October, Water

Protectors set up camps in the path of DAPL along the border that the Great Sioux Nation had negotiated with the federal government in the Fort Laramie Treaty of 1851. These women and men argued that this land is their rightful land, and Water Protectors refused to move from highways and to let construction crews pass.[28]

This action helped center the public discussion on the issues of treaty rights and sovereignty. Non-Native Americans struggled with the implications of some of this sovereignty-centered advocacy, and we can see from the news coverage that non-Indigenous Americans were less comfortable with this rationale. For example, in early November the *New York Post* ran an article arguing that Native people ought to be couching their fight for their rights to prayer and to clean water in their rights as American citizens, rather than as the rights of Indian nations or people. As author Naomi Schafer Riley claimed, "tribes aren't sovereign nations, and the United States decided this one hundred years ago."[29] Native people would beg to differ on this point, and the treaties certainly do not reflect Riley's claims, but this argument nonetheless presents a critical representation of how Americans struggled to understand this fight over DAPL as a fight for Native sovereignty rather than a fight for the environment or spiritual rights.[30] As Audra Simpson has argued, it has been easier for the non-Indigenous U.S. public to embrace popular national narratives of our nation as a pluralistic society where Native people are recognized and celebrated for their culture, but where their sovereignty and the challenges that this Native sovereignty poses to the settler-colonial nation are ignored or rejected, than it is to ask Americans to grapple with the implications of Native polities that have claims to territories, resources, and jurisdictional control that antecede the sovereignty of the United States.[31]

Again, this is where the ability of Native people to control the narrative via social media became so essential. As this dialogue grew, activists like Lakota attorney Chase Iron Eyes took to Facebook to explain treaty rights. The New York Stands with Standing Rock Collective put together an online syllabus of academic resources and primary source content to help explain colonialism, treaty law, and Sioux history. Winona LaDuke traveled the country and took to Skype to explain the environmental regulations behind pipeline construction and why the use of Nationwide 12 permits was so problematic in the DAPL project. Journalists presented deep historical context on DAPL and introduced their readers to the history of the Dakota and Lakota people. Thereby the American public was exposed to unfamiliar conversations about Indigenous sovereignty, history, and law.[32]

Essentially, we can conceptualize of the NoDAPL fight as a contest of the rights of Indigenous people within the United States to clean drinking water, to the protection of the graves of their ancestors, and to pray, or we can conceptualize this as a fight between nations over territory and the struggle to force the more powerful United States to honor its international accord with the Sioux Nation.[33]

Lakota and Dakota peoples have some of the clearest land claims of all Native nations within the borders of the United States. Unlike so many Native polities, the Great Sioux Nation was not relocated across the country. While Lakota and Dakota peoples lost many thousands of acres to the federal government, the fact that they maintained a land base within their original homelands means that the modern Sioux reservations look a lot like the neat, bordered, nation-states that we frequently imagine when we think of sovereign states and nations in the European context. Thus unlike so many other nations, to understand Lakota and Dakota peoples' rights to control their territory and their communities, we do not have to move through theoretical and sometimes problematic justifications of how Native peoples' sovereignty stems from relationships among kin, through blood, through land grants from the federal government, or through spiritual relationships and obligations to lands and nonhuman relations.[34] Rather, to explain the rights of the Lakota and Dakota people to control their lands on the Great Plains, and their rights to stop a pipeline from running through their homelands, we simply needed to point to the inherent, territorial sovereignty of this Native nation that has historically controlled these lands by presence and by treaties, the latter of which deed specific provisions to protect the land in question.

This is why the efforts to reclaim the 1851 treaty lands are so critical to the national dialogue about DAPL. The 1851 Fort Laramie Treaty was the first treaty the Great Sioux Nation signed with the federal government. In 1848 prospectors discovered gold in California. It did not take long before Americans streamed west through the territory of the Plains Indian nations, using Indian resources and attacking Native communities as they traveled to California. Not surprisingly, Lakota, Dakota, Mandan, Crow, and other plains groups attacked these Anglo-American trespassers and attempted to chase them off of their territories. This violence compelled the U.S. government to intercede, and in 1851 U.S. representatives met with these groups to negotiate a peace. The United States promised the Arapaho, Arikara, Assiniboine, Cheyenne, Crow, Hidatsa, Mandan, and Sioux Nations that they would recognize their territories, provide annuities, and facilitate trade with these polities, in exchange for a cession of hostilities and the guarantee that Anglo-American settlers could pass safely through their lands. Once in agreement, all parties signed this international accord.[35]

The United States largely failed to uphold its end of the bargain, and by the 1860s Lakota and Dakota communities were again engaged in conflict with trespassing Anglo-American settlers. In 1865 Americans discovered gold in Montana and once more crossed through Sioux territory in droves. Using the Bozeman trail, settlers traversed the Powder River buffalo country where they killed buffalo and harassed Lakota and Dakota communities. Oglala Lakota leader Red Cloud led attacks against these settlers during 1866 and 1867 and yet again forced the U.S. government to enter into diplomatic negotiations in order to end this conflict. In 1868 the Sioux negotiated a second Fort Laramie Treaty with the federal government. This treaty created the Great Sioux Reservation with boundary lines that stretched north to the present-day border between North and South Dakota, south to Nebraska, east to the Missouri River, and west to present-day Wyoming. Critically though, Article 16 of this treaty contained a provision that specified that lands north of the Great Sioux Reservation, as far north as the Heart River, would be maintained as "unceded Indian territory," which is the same northern boundary as the 1851 treaty. It is through this "unceded" territory that the Dakota Access Pipeline runs today.[36]

Since the Sioux retained explicit use rights and never formally ceded this land, this construction, which occurred without their consent, should unquestionably be illegal, as it violates this international treaty. The subsequent 1877 agreement is illegal as it was signed under duress by 10 percent of Sioux headmen who relinquished their hunting rights in these unceded territories in exchange for annuities to avoid starvation. The 1868 treaty clearly stated that that international treaty could only be altered with the consent of 75 percent of adult males.[37] Nonetheless, the federal government used this treaty to lay claim to more Sioux territory, and in 1877 Congress passed an act annexing the Black Hills, which many Lakota and Dakota people consider to be the sacred "heart" of their territory and people. The federal government never paid the Sioux for the Black Hills.[38]

Twentieth-century U.S. Supreme Court cases upheld and clarified the Standing Rock Sioux's claims to have the rights to deny permission to the Dakota Access Pipeline to pass through their treaty lands. In 1923 the Sioux began to pursue legal claims against the federal government in U.S. court over the theft of the Black Hills. By 1974, more than half a century after the Sioux started pressing for legal resolution, the Indian Claims Commission ruled that the 1887 agreement and the federal government's acquisition of the Black Hills was in fact illegal, and the U.S. Supreme Court upheld this ruling in 1980. The federal government has since offered the Sioux $1.3 billion as compensation for this land, but to date the Sioux have refused these funds, meaning this land should rightfully continue to be "unceded Indian territory."[39] In addition to the findings of the Supreme Court and Indian Claims Commission regarding the 1868 treaty and the Black Hills territory, in 1908 the U.S. Supreme Court also ruled that Native nations retain water rights on their territories.[40]

So, in effect, it is rare in the United States that Native American treaty rights are as clear as this, but the Sioux Nation unquestionably has rights to this territory. At its core, the DAPL fight is largely about Native sovereignty and international treaties.

Critical Implications

Beyond the impact for the Standing Rock Sioux and the pipeline, the response to DAPL is significant for its implications to Native sovereignty at large, and this national conversation about sovereignty has opened up another conversation within Indigenous America about autonomy and self-determination in the wake of this conflict. As Joanne Barker and others argue, part of the process of U.S. colonization is the racialization and ethnicizing of Native people. By attempting to present and discuss Native people as cultural or ethnic rather than political groups, the settler-colonial government is able to undermine Indigenous claims to territory and political rights. Standing Rock then took these cultural and ethnic perceptions and used them to transition national attention back to a focus on sovereignty, treaty rights, and natural resources. However, the other critical implication of this saga is more troubling; if the Sioux had some of the clearest legal land claims and treaty rights, and still the United States failed to uphold its obligations to honor these agreements, what does this mean for Native nations going forward?[41]

For more than a century Native people have been attempting to compel the United States to honor their treaties and to respect the rights of tribal self-determination. Native nations have relied on treaties as evidence of the U.S. government's mandate to recognize Indian polities as sovereigns and to uphold their international agreements. Native people have primarily not articulated their struggles for land, water, and political rights as their individual rights as U.S. citizens, but rather as their collective rights as the people of a specific autonomous Native nation. It is worth noting that U.S. treaties with Native nations were made prior to the jurisdictional incorporations of these nations into the United States and that Native Americans did not receive citizenship from the federal government until 1924.[42] We should also not forget that some Native people completely rejected U.S. citizenship and insisted that they could not simply be forced into the United States without their consent. As Akwesane Mohawk Charles Benedict argued in 1941, when he explained the rejection of U.S. citizenship by Mohawk nationals, the assumption that the United States could incorporate Native peoples simply by passing laws or claiming to have jurisdiction over their territory was absurd. Citizenship, he argued "cannot possibly apply to Indians [Iroquois] since they are independent Nations. Congress may as well pass a law making Mexicans citizens."[43]

Does this mean we need a fundamental change in our conceptions of Native nations' relationships with the federal government, or a foundational shift in how Native peoples articulate their rights and claims to the United States? The United States decided it would not make any new treaties with Indian nations after 1871, and this has created challenges for contemporary Native communities, as they are unable to forge new treaties with provisions that could address the critical concerns of the modern era, like rights to groundwater, fishing, mining, or other implied rights.

Meanwhile, Native Americans, historians, anthropologists, legal scholars, and other advocates of Indigenous peoples have been working to figure out how to best conceptualize, embody, articulate, and fight for Native peoples' rights to use and control land and resources, to support, identify, and govern their communities, as well as how to live in ways that align with their values and world views. Many of these discussions about Native communities' rights to "self-determination" for their peoples are framed in terms of sovereignty and nation-to-nation relationships. As Joanne Barker and David Nichols argued, sovereignty as we conceptualize it today within the American context can be traced to Westphalian theories of the rights and obligations of nation-states, including the concept of treaties and legal agreements as instruments that structure international relationships. Treaties, therefore, constitute the backbone of U.S. Indian law today.[44]

However, as many scholars claim, there is a fundamental conflict between recognizing the rights of Indigenous nations to control and rule their territories and people, and acknowledging the rights of colonial empires to override these claims and exert jurisdiction and dominion over Native communities and resources. As legal scholar Bruce Duthu explains, the U.S. government has had to come up with justifications to supplant Indigenous claims because "admitting that Indians had equal claims to lands, governance structures and an enduing way of life was simply incompatible with this worldview."[45] Duthu, Barker, and many other scholars have demonstrated that by constructing narratives and national perceptions of Native Americans as primitive, landless, and lawless people, settler-colonial governments sought to undermine Indigenous territoriality and nationhood. Furthermore, by emphasizing that Native peoples were dying out and losing their essential cultural Indigeneity, they constructed Native nations and territories as things of the past rather than realities of the present. Brian Klopotek, Jean Dennison, and Audra Simpson have critiqued the very process by which the United States formally agrees to recognize Native peoples and governments within the colonial system. Again pointing to the inherent structure between these overlapping or as Simpson calls them "nesting" sovereignties, Klopotek posits that federal recognition is problematic because it "affirms the status of a tribe as an Indigenous nation with inherent rights to self-government in its homeland, but simultaneously validates the colony authority of the United States over the nation."[46] Moreover, Kevin Bruyneel, Jeff Corntassel, Richard Witmer, Russel Barsh, and James Henderson all maintain that the legal categorization of Native polities as "domestic dependent nations" has trapped Native Americans within a jurisdictional morass and in a subservient structure that fundamentally poses challenges to Native peoples' autonomy.[47]

These theorizations and interrogations of Native sovereignty are all relevant because if the Standing Rock Sioux, with their near perfect legal claims, peaceful resistance, and cultural legibility as "authentic" Indians, failed to stop the Dakota Access Pipeline, it forces us to consider whether it is time to shift away from cries to "honor the treaties" and to move beyond federal frameworks to advocate for Indigenous state autonomy. As legal scholar David Wilkins suggests, even within the contemporary era of "self-determination" policies for Native Americans, the federal government only sees Native polities as "semi-sovereign" entities, and the focus is on self-governance rather than land-based territorial sovereignty.[48] As Robert Williams reasons, throughout the nineteenth and twentieth centuries, the U.S. Supreme Court's rulings on Indian rights and laws were deeply grounded in anti-Indian racism and the justices' perceptions of Native Americans as savage and primitive people who did not possess the same rights to self-govern. Therefore, Williams calls for a shift to using international law precedents, rather than these domestic Supreme Court decisions, to ground contemporary arguments for tribal rights.[49] Alternatively, we might consider engaging in what Audra Simpson calls the politics of refusal and simply stop agreeing to be bound by the legal and territorial restrictions of the United States. Must we ground the next decades of fighting for Native rights in the United Nation's Declaration on the Rights of Indigenous Peoples? Or must we press beyond the language of Indigenous rights, which only frames Native peoples in contrast to colonial states and only provides for self-governance and cultural and territorial protections rather than full autonomy? Or perhaps we should return to the practice of negotiating with multiple empires and attempting to construct relationships directly with world powers like Spain, France, Britain, Peru, or Mexico and/or use these foreign nations to mediate negotiations among the United States and Indigenous nations.

It is perhaps too soon to assess the full impact of the NoDAPL movement on the conversation about sovereignty both among Indigenous communities and across North America at large, but what is clear is that this experience has posed challenging questions for Native peoples within the borders of the United States and that it has opened a new platform for dialogue about Native sovereignty writ large with non-Indigenous Americans.

Building on the #NoDAPL Platforms

If the battle over DAPL raises challenges to the theoretical underpinnings and structure of our modern legal system, it also has profound practical implications in the immediate future for the fight for social justice both within and beyond Indigenous America. We can see the impact of Standing Rock and the dialogue about Native sovereignty in recent movements for social justice across the nation. This discussion of sovereignty is so critical because it is the scaffolding that has supported the growth of the NoDAPL movement, which received broad support from the American public, into a movement that facilitates the critique of American racism and oppression using Indigenous sovereignty.[50]

The impact of this is perhaps most profound in U.S. debates about immigration and migration across North America. In late January 2017, U.S. president Donald Trump unveiled an executive order banning immigrants and refugees from seven majority Muslim countries.[51] In response to this policy, Indigenous organizers led by Lakota scholar and activist Nick Estes and Diné (Navajo) activist and scholar Melanie K. Yazzie organized demonstrations in solidarity with immigrant and Muslim communities within the United States and rallied around the slogan #NoBanOnStolenLand.[52] This slogan beautifully and succinctly critiques the legality and moral grounding of the Trump administration's efforts to deny entry to immigrants based on religious affiliation or national origins. Effectively, by reminding Americans that this land was not always America's and that the United States' very claims to this territory are illegal, Native activists weaponized the historical legacy of colonization and the contemporary sovereignty of Native American nations to challenge modern xenophobia.

Native nations have long fought state attempts to exert control over immigration on their territories.[53] For example, in early 2017 as Trump promised to build his border wall, the vice chairman of the Tohono O'odham Nation again challenged federal attempts to enforce this colonial border. The Tohono O'odham have territory, community, and families that stretch across the U.S.–Mexico border, and they have controlled and lived on these lands long before the United States created a border across them. Therefore Vice Chairman Verlon Jose lashed back at this proposition and announced that "only over my dead body will a wall be built" through Tohono O'odham lands.[54] Jose's statement was picked up by national media and celebrated by immigrants and American-born citizens alike. This critique of federal policy using Indigenous sovereignty again demonstrates the power of these narratives in challenging the normalization of imperial borders and exclusionary settler-colonial policies.

In the late summer and early fall of 2017, Native peoples again gained public attention as they weighed in on the national conversation about public monuments and memory. Although the debate over whether cities should remove public monuments to the confederacy has gone on for years, in summer 2017 the tenor of this argument escalated, as white supremacists held a rally in downtown Charlottesville, Virginia, where they terrorized students and local residents and killed one demonstrator. Indigenous activists drew on this conversation to raise awareness about the Trump administration's lobby to downsize several national monuments that are sacred to Native Americans, including Bears Ears National Monument. Following on the heels of the Standing Rock fight, in the spring of 2017 President Trump called for the review of national monuments that are greater than one hundred thousand acres in size and that were designated monuments after 1995. This order targeted protected wildernesses and the ancestral and sacred sites of Hopi, Navajo, Ute, Mountain Ute, Zuni, and other Native nations. This order sought to strip these areas of federal protections and expose their natural resources (including coal and timber) to corporate and private development. As critics of the efforts to keep confederate statues in public spaces argued, by choosing to protect monuments to confederate secessionists who fought to preserve slavery, while rallying for the removal of monuments that are sacred to Native people, local and national government officials illustrate that their fight over these monuments is about supporting white supremacy and settler colonialism, rather than a pure commitment to preserving the heritage of all Americans.[55]

Similarly, activists have used Indigenous histories to critique commemorations and celebrations of the colonization of North America. In August 2017, Indigenous activists in Santa Fe organized a demonstration at the annual festival celebrating the Spanish Entrada into New Mexico. They argued that the festivities celebrated the genocide of Pueblo people and demanded that the city "abolish the entrada."[56] Likewise, in New York in September 2017, the grassroots organization Decolonize This Place organized their second mass demonstration at the American Museum of Natural History on Indigenous Peoples' Day (Columbus Day) in New York City. The Decolonize This Place collective has asked that the museum take down the statue of Theodore Roosevelt that sits outside the museum and portrays President Roosevelt riding on horseback while flanked by a standing African man and a Native American man in a headdress. These activists have also demanded that the city end the celebration of Christopher Columbus and that the museum alter its exhibits of African and Indigenous peoples, which present these cultures as primitive and portray Native Americans as existing solely in the historical past.[57] Much like the movement in Philadelphia to defund Wells Fargo, the Tohono O'odham opposition to the border wall, and the #NoBanOnStolenLand demonstrations, the Columbus/Indigenous Peoples' Day demonstrations at the American Museum of Natural History demonstrate how intersectional this movement has become and highlight the ways that Indigenous sovereignty and Indigenous visibility enable forceful critiques of contemporary policy and national mythmaking.[58]

A Beginning

The closest historical event we can use to draw conclusions about the potential outcomes of the DAPL fight is the fallout of AIM's stand-off at Wounded Knee in 1973. When AIM took over Wounded Knee, its goals included the removal of tribal president Dick Wilson and of the Bureau of Indian Affairs' (BIA) influence in tribal politics, a full investigation into the murder of Wesley Bad Heart Bull (this killing prompted AIM to come to Pine Ridge Reservation) and into the ongoing violence against Lakota people both on and off reservation, the honoring of the 1868 Fort Laramie Treaty by the federal government, and a meeting with the leaders of AIM to discuss the United States' treaty obligations.[59]

Although AIM held Wounded Knee for seventy-one days and captured the attention of the nation, it largely failed to achieve these goals. Violence between the supporters of the BIA who supported the Wilson government and his opponents continued on Pine Ridge Reservation; furthermore the FBI led a brutal campaign to dismantle AIM and imprison its leaders, including Leonard Peltier, who sits in prison to this day. AIM's demands were followed by a resolution from the Lakota Treaty Council of Pine Ridge that demanded a return to the 1868 treaty and a clear rejection of the Indian Reorganization Act, Indian Citizenship Act, and all other legislation passed by Congress since 1868, yet Congress remained unmoved to take action on these treaty obligations.[60]

Historians have frequently focused on the failure of Wounded Knee to achieve

immediate change. Beyond the tragic conclusion of the Wounded Knee occupation, over the next two decades AIM's actions had massive impacts for Native
Americans at large. In 1975 Dick Wilson was replaced as a tribal president and,
in the same year, Congress passed the Indian Self-Determination and Educational
Assistance Act that gave tribes the right to administer federal assistance programs
rather than the federal government and increased the autonomy of tribal governments. In 1976 Congress passed the Indian Health Care Improvement Act, which
gave tribes the right to manage Indian Health Service programs. In 1978 the Indian
Child Welfare Act and the American Indian Religious Freedom Act acknowledged
the rights of Native people to keep adopted children within Native communities
and observe their spiritual beliefs. Equally as important, the 1970s marked the
end of the termination era of Indian policy, which sought to extinguish Native
nations' status as sovereign polities and facilitate political and cultural assimilation of Native peoples in the United States.[61]

AIM's occupation of Wounded Knee marked a turning point. It forced the federal government to take action to reform some of the laws that governed Native
people and to acknowledge that Native nations refused to be terminated, ignored,
or subjected to racial violence. Furthermore, it brought modern Native people into
the homes of non-Indigenous Americans via television reports, radio broadcasts,
and newspaper columns and garnered international visibility. We are in a corollary
moment now, but with the advantage of a much larger, more diverse movement
comprised of 360 allied Indigenous nations and hundreds of thousands of non-
Native allies, and a social media platform that reaches across continents.

The possibility then exists that this intersectional movement, guided by these
flourishing conversations about Native sovereignty, and with national attention via
social media, will catalyze a forthcoming era of policy reform and/or grassroots
networks that will be able to better protect Native communities and territories in
ways that the U.S. legal system has thus far failed to do. As we consider the legacy
and outcomes of the NoDAPL movement, it is perhaps better to conceive of this
movement not as at its conclusion but as at its beginning.

NOTES

1. "Bloomberg: Oil to Begin Flowing through Dakota Access Pipeline on May 14,"
   Democracy Now!, May 10, 2017, https://www.democracynow.org.
2. Army Department, "Notice of Intent to Prepare an Environmental Impact
   Statement in Connection with Dakota Access, LLC's Request for an Easement
   to Cross Lake Oahe, North Dakota," *Federal Register*, January 18, 2017, 82 FR
   5543, 5543–44, https://www.federalregister.gov; Hilary Beaumont, "Pipeline Halted," *Vice News*, December 4, 2016, https://news.vice.com/story/obama
   -administration-stops-dakota-access-pipeline-in-historic-decision.
3. Executive Office of the President, "Construction of the Dakota Access Pipeline"

(presidential memorandum), *Federal Register*, February 17, 2017, 82 FR 11129, 11129–30, https://www.federalregister.gov.

4. Julian Brave NoiseCat, "Surveillance at Standing Rock Exposes Heavy-Handed Policing of Native Lands," *The Guardian*, June 28, 2017, https://www.theguardian.com.

5. Brad Plumer, "How the EPA Managed to Spill 3 Million Gallons of Mining Waste into a Colorado River," *Vox*, August 10, 2015, https://www.vox.com/2015/8/10/9126853/epa-mine-spill-animas; Christina Laughlin, "Flint Is Not the Only Water Crisis America Ignored," *Huffington Post*, February 23, 2016, http://www.huffingtonpost.com.

6. Tony Dokoupil, "A Battle over Land Sacred for Apache and Lucrative for a Mining Company," MSNBC, July 31, 2015, http://www.msnbc.com/msnbc/battle-over-land-sacred-apache-and-lucrative-mining-company.

7. Nina Lakhani, "Berta Cáceres Murder: International Lawyers Launch New Investigation," *The Guardian*, November 15, 2016, https://www.theguardian.com.

8. Mary Kathryn Nagle and Gloria Steinem, "Sexual Assault on the Pipeline," *Boston Globe*, September 29, 2016, https://www.bostonglobe.com.

9. Cedar Wilkie Gillette, "Pipeline Expansion Means Increased Violence against Tribal Women," *Huffington Post*, October 20, 2016, http://www.huffingtonpost.com.

10. Julie Turkewitz, "Tribes That Live Off Coal Hold Tight to Trump's Promises," *New York Times*, April 1, 2017, https://www.nytimes.com; "Largely Forgotten Osage Murders Reveal a Conspiracy against Wealthy Native Americans," on *Fresh Air*, National Public Radio, April 17, 2017, http://www.npr.org; James Robert Allison III, *Sovereignty for Survival: American Energy Development and Indian Self-Determination* (New Haven: Yale University Press, 2015), 98–124.

11. "A Call to Prayer and Support for Standing Rock," New England Yearly Meeting of Friends (Quakers), November 3, 2016, https://neym.org; Naomi Dann, "Nine Philly Rabbis & Jewish Community Members Arrested Protesting Dakota Access Pipeline at TD Bank," *Jewish Voice for Peace*, November 2, 2016, https://jewishvoiceforpeace.org; Carole Kuruvilla, "Muslims Stand in Solidarity with Indigenous People Fighting for Sacred Land," *Huffington Post*, October 6, 2016, https://www.huffingtonpost.com; Imam Khalid Fattah Griggs, "We Are Standing Rock," Islamic Circle of North America, November 25, 2016, http://www.icna.org; Brian Roewe, "Larger Faith Community Comes to Standing Rock in Solidarity," *National Catholic Reporter*, November 7, 2016, https://www.ncronline.org; Elizabeth A. Eaton, "ELCA Presiding Bishop Issues Statement on Standing Rock," Evangelical Lutheran Church in America, November 14, 2016, https://www.elca.org/News-and-Events/7865; Verna Colliver, "CONAM Members Join Philly's Standing Rock Protest," Eastern Pennsylvania Conference, United Methodist Church, September 23, 2016, https://www.epaumc.org.

12. M. Shadee Malaklou, "DAPL and the Matter/ing of Black Life," *Feminist Wire*,

November 30, 2016, http://www.thefeministwire.com; Ashoka Jegroo, "Why Black Lives Matter Is Fighting alongside Dakota Access Pipeline Protestors," *Splinter*, September 13, 2016, https://splinternews.com.

13. Tom DiChristopher, "US Veterans Group Says Dakota Access Pipeline 'will not get completed. Not on our watch,'" CNBC, February 2, 2017, https://www.cnbc .com; James Cook, "Standing Rock: US Veterans Join North Dakota Protests," *BBC News*, December 2, 2016, http://www.bbc.com; Michael Edison Hayden, Catherine Thorbecke, and Evan Simon, "At Least 2,000 Veterans Arrive at Standing Rock to Protest Dakota Pipeline," *ABC News*, December 4, 2016, http://abcnews.go.com; Mahita Gajanan, "U.S. Army Denies Permit for Dakota Access Pipeline Construction," *Time*, December 4, 2016, http://time.com; Army Department, "Notice of Intent to Prepare an Environmental Impact Statement"; Christopher Mele, "Veterans to Serve as 'Human Shields' for Dakota Pipeline Protesters," *New York Times*, November 29, 2016, https://www.nytimes.com.

14. Charlie Northcott, "Standing Rock: What Next for Protests?" *BBC News*, December 5, 2016, http://www.bbc.com.

15. "Quick Facts: Philadelphia County, Pennsylvania," United States Census Bureau, 2010–2016, https://www.census.gov/quickfacts/fact/table/philadelphia countypennsylvania/HSG030210.

16. "NAACP Report Condemns Environmental Racism," *Philadelphia Tribune*, December 25, 2012, http://www.phillytrib.com; Janet Golden, "The Air Pollution Racial Gap: Pa. and N.J. among the Worst," *Philadelphia Inquirer*, April 25, 2014, http:// www.philly.com; "Air Pollution," *350 Philadelphia*, 2017, https://350philadelphia.org /septa/air-pollution/.

17. Dustin Slaughter, "In Photos: Protest Targets Wells Fargo over Pipeline, Philly Schools, and Trump Ties," *The Declaration*, January 20, 2017, https://phillydeclara tion.org.

18. Carolyn Van Houten, "The First Official Climate Refugees in the U.S. Race against Time," May 25, 2016, *National Geographic*, http://news.nationalgeographic.com.

19. Peter Matthiessen, *In the Spirit of Crazy Horse* (New York: Penguin Books, 1992), 58–82.

20. Anita Elash, "Native Americans Don't Have Their Own TV Channel. A Canadian Network Wants to Change That," *Public Radio International*, May 13, 2017, https:// www.pri.org.

21. Paul Chaat Smith, *Everything You Know about Indians Is Wrong* (Minneapolis: University of Minnesota Press, 2009), 18–20; Jeff Berglund, "Pocahontas," in *Seeing Red: Hollywood's Pixeled Skins*, ed. LeAnne Howe, Harvey Markowitz, and Denise K. Cummings (East Lansing: Michigan State University Press, 2013), 53; James Riding In, "Dances with Wolves," in Howe, Markowitz, and Cummings, *Seeing Red*, 91–94; Susan Tavernetti, "Writing Indian Stereotypes: The Role of the Screenplay in American Westerns," in *American Indians and Popular Culture*, ed. Elizabeth

DeLaney Hoffman (Santa Barbara: Praeger, 2012), 1:33–51; Vine Deloria Jr., *Custer Died for Your Sins: An Indian Manifesto* (Norman: University of Oklahoma Press, 1988), 2–3.

22. Jessica Ravitz, "The Sacred Land at the Center of the Dakota Pipeline Dispute," CNN, November 1, 2016, http://www.cnn.com; Barnini Chakraborty, "Obama Administration under Fire for Intervening in North Dakota Pipeline Case," *Fox News*, September 15, 2016, http://www.foxnews.com; Robet Barid, "Cries with Indians: 'Going Indian' with the Ecological Indian from Rousseau to Avatar," in Hoffman, *American Indians and Popular Culture*, 1:70–83; Amy Goodman and Denis Moynihan, "Ensuring Catastrophe: The Price of Climate Denial," *Democracy Now!*, September 14, 2017, https://www.democracynow.org; Associated Press, "No Native American Artifacts Found at North Dakota Pipeline Site, Officials Say," *Fox News*, September 28, 2016, http://www.foxnews.com; Amy Goodman, Winona LaDuke, Ajamu Baraka, and Joye Braun, "Stopping the Snake: Indigenous Protesters Shut Down Construction of Dakota Access Pipeline," *Democracy Now!*, August 18, 2016, https://www.democracynow.org.

23. Anne Spice, "A History and Future of Resistance," *Jacobin*, September 8, 2016, https://www.jacobinmag.com; Henry Gass, "Behind Dakota Pipeline Protest: Native American Religious Revival," *Christian Science Monitor*, November 1, 2016, https://www.csmonitor.com; Heather Rae, Ben Dupris, and Cody Lucich, "A Message from Native Filmmakers Fighting the Dakota Pipeline at Standing Rock," Sundance Institute, September 12, 2016, http://www.sundance.org.

24. Jack Jenkins, "How Religious Conservatives Unwittingly Laid the Groundwork to Help Native Americans Save Their Land," *Think Progress*, December 8, 2016, https://thinkprogress.org; Jenni Monet, "For Native 'Water Protectors,' Standing Rock Protest Has Become Fight for Religious Freedom, Human Rights," *PBS NewsHour*, November 3, 2016, http://www.pbs.org/newshour/rundown/military-force-criticized-dakota-access-pipeline-protests/.

25. Annabelle Marcovici, "Opposing a Pipeline Near Sacred Sioux Sites: Slideshow," *New York Times*, October 6, 2016, https://www.nytimes.com; "North Dakota Pipeline Protests: Photos," *CNN*, February 9, 2017, http://www.cnn.com/2016/09/09/us/gallery/north-dakota-oil-pipeline/index.html; Rebecca Bengal, "Standing Rock Rising: Inside the Movement to Stop the Dakota Access Pipeline," *Vogue*, November 22, 2016, https://www.vogue.com/projects/13505511/standing-rock-movement-dakota-access-pipeline/.

26. Jack Healy, "North Dakota Oil Pipeline Battle: Who's Fighting and Why?" *New York Times*, August 26, 2016, https://www.nytimes.com.

27. Editorial Board, "Time to Move the Standing Rock Pipeline," *New York Times*, November 3, 2016, https://www.nytimes.com; Dell Cameron, "Anger and Disbelief: Letters to N.D. Governor Slam Treatment of American Indians at Pipeline Protest," *Daily Dot*, September 21, 2016, https://www.dailydot.com; readers' comments on

"The Standing Rock Pipeline Protesters and Their Pyrrhic Victory," *The Economist*, December 8, 2016, http://www.economist.com.

28. Treaty of Fort Laramie with the Sioux etc., September 17, 1851, in *Indian Affairs: Laws and Treaties*, ed. Charles J. Kappler (Washington, D.C.: Government Printing Office, 1904), 4:1072, http://digital.library.okstate.edu/kappler/vol2/treaties/sio0594.htm; Kirk Johnson, "Old Treaties and New Alliances Empower Native Americans," *New York Times*, November 15, 2016, https://www.nytimes.com; Holly Yan, "Dakota Access Pipeline: What's at Stake?" CNN, October 28, 2016, http://www.cnn.com/2016/09/07/us/dakota-access-pipeline-visual-guide/index.html; Monte Mills, "How Will Native Tribes Fight the Dakota Access Pipeline in Court?" *PBS NewsHour*, February 15, 2017, http://www.pbs.org/newshour/rundown/will-native-tribes-fight-dakota-access-pipeline-court/; Paul VanDevelder, "Reckoning at Standing Rock," *High Country News*, October 28, 2016, http://www.hcn.org; Jenny Schlecht, "1851 Treaty Resonates in DAPL Discussion," *Bismarck Tribune*, November 10, 2016, http://bismarcktribune.com; Evan Simon, "Broken Promises: Standing Rock Sioux Tribe Cites History of Government Betrayal in Pipeline Fight," *ABC News*, November 22, 2016, http://abcnews.go.com; Michelle Perez, "Whose Land Is It Anyway? Why the Dakota Access Pipeline Protests Aren't Really about Oil," *Inter-American Law Review*, October 24, 2016, https://inter-american-law-review.law.miami.edu.

29. Naomi Schaefer Riley, "Protestors Should Be Fighting for Indians' Rights as Citizens, Not the Tribe," *New York Post*, November 5, 2016, http://nypost.com; Sarah Pulliam Bailey, "The Dakota Access Pipeline Isn't Just about the Environment. It's about Religion," *Washington Post*, December 5, 2016, https://www.washingtonpost.com; Stephen Pevar, "Oil and Water Don't Mix: Why the ACLU Is Standing Up for the Standing Rock Sioux Tribe," American Civil Liberties Union, February 24, 2017, https://www.aclu.org; Francine Roston, "Why I Stand with the Standing Rock Sioux," *Flathead Beacon*, November 17, 2016, http://flatheadbeacon.com; Terry L. Anderson and Shawn Regan, "No Wonder the Standing Rock Sioux Opposed the Pipeline," *National Review*, December 12, 2016, http://www.nationalreview.com.

30. Vine Deloria Jr., "We Are Here as Independent Nations," in *Say We Are Nations: Documents of Politics and Protest in Indigenous America Since 1887* (Chapel Hill: University of North Carolina Press, 2015), 133–38; International Indian Treaty Council, "Declaration of Continuing Independence (1974)," in *Say We Are Nations*, 167–71; Russel Barsh and James Henderson, *The Road: Indian Tribes and Political Liberty* (Berkeley: University of California Press, 1980), 120.

31. Audra Simpson, *Mohawk Interruptus: Political Life across the Borders of Settler States* (Durham, N.C.: Duke University Press, 2014), 2–28.

32. Jeffrey Ostler and Nick Estes, "'The Supreme Law of the Land': Standing Rock and the Dakota Access Pipeline," *Indian Country Today*, January 16, 2017, https://newsmaven.io/indiancountrytoday/archive/the-supreme-law-of-the-land-standing

-rock-and-the-dakota-access-pipeline-25phRkIJB0GmipEDLvPLPw/; Yessenia Funes, "One Treaty Could Change the Fight to Stop the Dakota Access Pipeline," *Colorlines*, November 7, 2016, https://www.colorlines.com; Kristen A. Carpenter and Angela R. Riley, "Standing Tall," *Slate*, September 23, 2016, http://www.slate .com; Associated Press, "UN Body Says Sioux Must Have Say in Pipeline Project," *Fox News*, August 31, 2016, http://www.foxnews.com; "#StandingRockSyllabus," NYC Stands with Standing Rock Collective, 2016, https://nycstandswithstandingrock .wordpress.com; Winona LaDuke, "Endangered Native Languages, Lands, and Natural Resources," keynote address at the American Philosophical Society's "Translating across Time and Space: Endangered Languages, Cultural Revitalization, and the Work of History" conference, delivered at the University of Pennsylvania, October 13, 2016; Maya Fitzpatrick and Rebecca Hersher, "'He Needs to Listen to Us': Protesters Call on Trump to Respect Native Sovereignty," National Public Radio, May 10, 2017, http://www.npr.org; Julian Brave NoiseCat, "When the Indians Defeat the Cowboys," *Jacobin*, January 15, 2017, https://www.jacobinmag.com; Honor the Earth, Indigenous Environmental Network, and Sierra Club, letter to the U.S. Army Corps of Engineers, October 10, 2016, https://d3n8a8pro7vhmx.cloudfront. net/honorearth/pages/2295/attachments/original/1477095838/DAPL_Letter_to_ Corps_10.10.16_SC_HTE_IEN.pdf?1477095838.

33. David A. Nichols, "Treaties and Sovereign Performances, from Westphalia to Standing Rock," *Origins* 10, no. 5 (2017), http://origins.osu.edu.

34. For more on alternative conceptions of Indigenous power and relationships beyond the framing of "sovereignty," see Taiaiakae Alfred, "Sovereignty," in *Sovereignty Matters: Locations of Contestation and Possibility in Indigenous Struggles for Self-Determination*, ed. Joanne Barker (Lincoln: University of Nebraska Press, 2005), 33–49.

35. Loretta Fowler, *The Columbia Guide to American Indians of the Great Plains* (New York: Columbia University Press, 2003), 63–67, 73–75; Colin C. Calloway, *First Peoples: A Documentary Survey of American Indian History*, 4th ed. (Boston: Bedford St. Martins, 2012), 369–76.

36. Ostler and Estes, "'The Supreme Law of the Land'"; "Treaty of Fort Laramie (1868)," National Archives, https://www.ourdocuments.gov/doc.php?flash=false&doc=42; Robert M. Utley, *The Last Days of the Sioux Nation*, 2nd ed. (New Haven: Yale University Press, 2004), 40–44; Kiana Herold, "Terra Nullius and the History of Broken Treaties at Standing Rock," Truthout, November 21, 2016, http://www.truthout.org; Calloway, *First Peoples*, 344–45; Jeffrey Ostler, "'The Last Buffalo Hunt' and Beyond: Plains Sioux Economic Strategies in the Early Reservation Period," *Great Plains Quarterly* 21, no. 2 (2001): 116–18; Edward Lazarus, *Black Hills/White Justice: The Sioux Nation versus the United States, 1775 to the Present* (New York: Harper Collins, 2006), 246–47.

37. North Dakota Studies Project, "Tribal Historical Overview—Establishment of the

Great Sioux Reservation—The Taking of the Black Hills," State Historical Society of North Dakota, http://www.ndstudies.org/resources/IndianStudies/standingrock/historical_blackhills.html.

38. Calloway, *First Peoples*, 346–49, 369.

39. Francine Uenuma and Mike Fritz, "Why the Sioux Are Refusing $1.3 Billion," *PBS NewsHour*, August 24, 2011, http://www.pbs.org/newshour/updates/north_america-july-dec11-blackhills_08-23/; *UNITED STATES, Petitioner, v. SIOUX NATION OF INDIANS et al.*, 448 U.S. 371, https://www.law.cornell.edu/supremecourt/text/448/371.

40. N. Bruce Duthu, *American Indians and the Law* (New York: Penguin, 2008), 105; *Winters v. United States*, 207 U.S. 564 (1908), https://supreme.justia.com/cases/federal/us/207/564/.

41. Robinson Meyer, "The Standing Rock Sioux Claim 'Victory and Vindication' in Court," *The Atlantic*, June 14, 2017, https://www.theatlantic.com; James Hill, "Trump Administration Withdraws Legal Memo That Found 'Ample Legal Justification' to Halt Dakota Access Pipeline," *ABC News*, February 23, 2017, http://abcnews.go.com; Joanne Barker, "For Whom Sovereignty Matters," in Barker, *Sovereignty Matters*, 15–17.

42. Treaty of Fort Laramie with the Sioux etc., September 17, 1851.

43. Laurence M. Hauptman, *The Iroquois and the New Deal* (Syracuse: Syracuse University Press, 1981), 6.

44. Nichols, "Treaties and Sovereign Performances"; Barker, "For Whom Sovereignty Matters," 1–8.

45. Duthu, *American Indians and the Law*, 173–79.

46. Brian Klopotek, *Recognition Odysseys: Indigeneity, Race, and the Federal Tribal Recognition Policy in Three Louisiana Indian Communities* (Durham, N.C.: Duke University Press, 2011), 2–3; Circe Sturm, "States of Sovereignty: Race Shifting, Recognition, and Rights in Cherokee Country," in *Beyond Red Power: American Indian Politics and Activism since 1900*, ed. Daniel Cobb and Loretta Fowler (Santa Fe: School for Advanced Research, 2007), 228–39.

47. Jean Dennison, "The Logic of Recognition: Debating Osage Nation Citizenship in the Twenty-First Century," *American Indian Quarterly* 38, no. 1 (2014): 3–5, 14–20; K. Tsianina Lomawaima, "The Mutuality of *Citizenship* and *Sovereignty*: The Society of American Indians and the Battle to Inherit America," *Studies in American Indian Literatures* 25, no. 2 (2013), 338–39, 344–45; Barsh and Henderson, *The Road*, 53–61; Jeff Corntassel and Richard Witmer, *Forced Federalism: Contemporary Challenges to Indigenous Nationhood* (Norman: University of Oklahoma Press, 2008), 4–9.

48. David E. Wilkins, "The Reinvigoration of the Doctrine of 'Implied Repeals': A Requiem for Indigenous Treaty Rights," *American Journal of Legal History* 43, no. 1 (1999): 5.

49. Robert A. Williams, *Like A Loaded Weapon: The Rehnquist Court, Indian Rights, and the Legal History of Racism in America* (Minneapolis: University of Minnesota Press, 2005), 159–67.

50. Erin Mundahl, "Standing Rock Protests Reborn at the Native Nations March with Shift in Focus," InsideSources, March 10, 2017, http://www.insidesources.com; Lauren Gambino, "Native Americans Take Dakota Access Pipeline Protest to Washington," *The Guardian*, March 10, 2017, https://www.theguardian.com; David Treuer, "An Indian Protest for Everyone," *New York Times*, November 26, 2016, https://www.nytimes.com.

51. "Trump's Executive Order: Who Does Travel Ban Affect?" *BBC News*, February 10, 2017, http://www.bbc.com.

52. Lenard Monkman, "'No ban on stolen land,' say Indigenous Activists in U.S.," *CBC News*, February 5, 2017, http://www.cbc.ca.

53. Evan Wyloge, "Native American Tribes Say They Won't Enforce Immigration Law," *Arizona Capitol Times*, June 14, 2010, http://azcapitoltimes.com/news/2010/06/14/indian-tribes-oppose-new-immigration-law/.

54. Dianna M. Náñez, "Tribal Leader Warns of Protest if Trump Insists on Border Wall: 'There is no word for wall in our language,'" *AZ Central*, April 25, 2017, http://www.azcentral.com/story/news/politics/border-issues/2017/04/25/tohono-odham-leader-border-wall-protests-donald-trump-physical-barrier/100726164/; Laurel Morales, "Border Wall Would Cut across Land Sacred to Native Tribe," National Public Radio, February 23, 2017, http://www.npr.org.

55. Robinson Meyer, "What Kind of Monuments Does President Trump Value?" *The Atlantic*, August 17, 2017, https://www.theatlantic.com; Susan Matthews, "The Monuments Trump Doesn't Support," *Slate*, August 18, 2017, http://www.slate.com; Conversation between David Greene and Interior Secretary Sally Jewell, "Trump Administration's Plan to Reduce Protected Land Size Criticized," National Public Radio, August 25, 2017, http://www.npr.org; Julian Brave NoiseCat, "Bears Ears Is Sacred to Native Americans. But Heritage Isn't All Equal for Trump," *The Guardian*, September 19, 2017, https://www.theguardian.com; Lena Fenton, "Will Trump Change the Way Presidents Approach National Monuments?" *The Atlantic*, September 24, 2017, https://www.theatlantic.com; Gregory Korte, "Trump Executive Order Could Rescind National Monuments," *USA Today*, April 26, 2017, https://www.usatoday.com/story/news/politics/2017/04/26/trump-executive-order-could-rescind-national-monuments/100914086/; Alfred Lomahquahu, "Op-ed: Tribes Worked Patiently for Bears Ears Monument, and It Should Endure," *Salt Lake Tribune*, February 11, 2017, http://archive.sltrib.com; Lisa Riley Roche, "Hatch Tells State Lawmakers Trump Looking at Bears Ears, Grand Staircase," *Deseret News*, February 22, 2017, https://www.deseretnews.com.

56. T. S. Last and Megan Bennett, "Protestors Crash Entrada Pageant," *Albuquerque Journal*, September 8, 2017, https://www.abqjournal.com.

57. Elena Goukassian, "Anti-Columbus Day Tour Attended by Hundreds at the American Museum of Natural History," *Hyperallergic*, October 10, 2017, https://hyperallergic.com; Dale W. Eisinger and Graham Rayman, "Protesters Call for an End to Columbus Day, Removal of NYC's Controversial Statue," *New York Daily News*, October 9, 2017, http://www.nydailynews.com.

58. Jean M. O'Brien, *Firsting and Lasting: Writing Indians Out of Existence in New England* (Minneapolis: University of Minnesota Press, 2010), xii–xv, 55–75.

59. Calloway, *First Peoples*, 549–50; Matthiessen, *In the Spirit of Crazy Horse*, 59–70; Lazarus, *Black Hills/White Justice*, 302–10.

60. Matthiessen, *In the Spirit of Crazy Horse*, 144–45; Statement of the Position of the Oglala Lakota Band of the Great Teton Nation, Mobridge, South Dakota, June 1974, Box 5, folder "Pine Ridge—Lakota Views" of the Bradley H. Patterson Files at the Gerald R. Ford Presidential Library, Ann Arbor, Mich.; Arthur S. Fleming to Edward Levi, May 10, 1976, Box 5, folder "Pine Ridge—Lakota Views," Ford Presidential Library; Traditional Chiefs and Headmen to Gerald Ford, July 24, 1975, Box 5, folder "Pine Ridge—Lakota Views," Ford Presidential Library; Zia Akhtar, "Pine Ridge Deaths, Mistrials, and FBI Counter plo Operations," *Criminal Justice Studies* 24, no. 1 (2011): 61–62, 69–73; Dean J. Kotlowski, "Alcatraz, Wounded Knee, and Beyond: The Nixon and Ford Administrations Respond to Native American Protest," *Pacific Historical Review* 72, no. 2 (2003), 204–17.

61. Francis Paul Prucha, *The Great Father: The United States Government and the American Indians*, abr. ed. (Lincoln: University of Nebraska Press, 1986), 266–367; Calloway, *First Peoples*, 553–60; Larry Nesper, "Tribal Court and Tribal State in the Era of Self-Determination: An Ojibwe Case Study," in Cobb and Fowler, *Beyond Red Power*, 244–46.

15

COUNTERTERRORISM TACTICS AT STANDING ROCK

Alleen Brown, Will Parrish, and Alice Speri

This report was originally published in The Intercept *on May 27, 2017.*

A shadowy international mercenary and security firm known as TigerSwan targeted the movement opposed to the Dakota Access Pipeline (DAPL) with military-style counterterrorism measures, collaborating closely with police in at least five states, according to internal documents obtained by *The Intercept*. The documents provide the first detailed picture of how TigerSwan, which originated as a U.S. military and State Department contractor helping to execute the global war on terror, worked at the behest of its client Energy Transfer Partners, the company building DAPL, to respond to the Indigenous-led movement that sought to stop the project.

Internal TigerSwan communications describe the movement as "an ideologically driven insurgency with a strong religious component" and compare the anti-pipeline Water Protectors to jihadist fighters. One report, dated February 27, 2017, states that since the movement "generally followed the jihadist insurgency model while active, we can expect the individuals who fought for and supported it to follow a post-insurgency model after its collapse." Drawing comparisons with post-Soviet Afghanistan, the report warns, "While we can expect to see the continued spread of the anti-DAPL diaspora . . . aggressive intelligence preparation of the battlefield and active coordination between intelligence and security elements are now a proven method of defeating pipeline insurgencies."

More than one hundred internal documents leaked to *The Intercept* by a TigerSwan contractor, as well as a set of more than one thousand documents obtained via public records requests, reveal that TigerSwan spearheaded a multifaceted private security operation characterized by sweeping and invasive surveillance of protesters.

As policing continues to be militarized and state legislatures around the country pass laws criminalizing protest, the fact that a private security firm retained by a Fortune 500 oil and gas company coordinated its efforts with local, state, and federal law enforcement to undermine the protest movement has profoundly antidemocratic implications. The leaked materials not only highlight TigerSwan's militaristic approach to protecting its client's interests but also the company's profit-driven imperative to portray the nonviolent Water Protector movement as unpredictable and menacing enough to justify the continued need for extraordinary security measures. Energy Transfer Partners has continued to retain Tiger-Swan long after most of the antipipeline campers left North Dakota, and the most recent TigerSwan reports emphasize the threat of growing activism around other pipeline projects across the country.

The leaked documents include situation reports prepared by TigerSwan operatives in North Dakota, South Dakota, Iowa, Illinois, and Texas between September 2016 and May 2017, and delivered to Energy Transfer Partners. They offer a daily snapshot of the security firm's activities, including detailed summaries of the previous day's surveillance targeting pipeline opponents, intelligence on upcoming protests, and information harvested from social media. The documents also provide extensive evidence of aerial surveillance and radio eavesdropping, as well as infiltration of camps and activist circles.

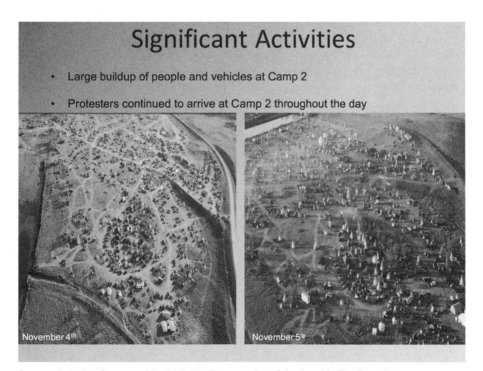

A screenshot taken from one of the "daily intelligence updates" developed by TigerSwan that were shared with members of law enforcement. Photograph of PowerPoint screen grab.

TigerSwan did not respond to a request for comment. Energy Transfer Partners declined to comment, telling *The Intercept* in an email that it does not "discuss details of our security efforts."

Additional documents, obtained via public records requests, consist of communications among agents from the FBI, the Department of Homeland Security, the U.S. Justice Department, the U.S. Marshals Service, and the Bureau of Indian Affairs (BIA), as well as state and local police. The "Intel Group," as its members refer to it, closely monitored anti–Dakota Access protests in real time, scooped up information on the Water Protectors from social media, and shared intelligence.

Included among the documents obtained via public records requests were "daily intelligence updates" developed by TigerSwan that were shared with law enforcement officers, thus contributing to a broad public–private intelligence dragnet. In the internal situation reports, TigerSwan operatives comment frequently about their routine coordination and intelligence sharing with law enforcement. The intel group went so far as to use a live video feed from a private Dakota Access security helicopter to monitor protesters' movements. In one report, Tiger-Swan discusses meeting with investigators from North Dakota's Attorney General's Office.

North Dakota's Attorney General's Office declined to comment.

TigerSwan's internal reports and the intelligence briefings shared with law enforcement name dozens of DAPL opponents. Some of those named are well-known activists, while others have minimal public affiliation with the Water Protector movement. The reports' authors often comment on camp dynamics, including protester morale and infighting, and speculate about violent or illegal actions specific individuals might take and weapons they might carry. The documents reveal the existence of a "persons of interest" list as well as other databases that included identifying information such as photographs and license plate numbers.

The situation reports also suggest that TigerSwan attempted a counterinformation campaign by creating and distributing content critical of the protests on social media.

The Intercept is publishing a first set of TigerSwan's situation reports from September 2016, which describe the company's initial operations. We are also publishing two additional situation reports dated October 16 and November 5, along with PowerPoint presentations shared with law enforcement that correspond to the same dates. The names of private individuals whose actions are not already in the public record, or whose authorization we did not obtain, have been redacted to protect their privacy. *The Intercept* will publish the remaining situation reports in the coming weeks.

In addition, *The Intercept* is publishing a selection of communications, obtained by public records requests, detailing coordination between a wide range of local, state, and federal agencies, which confirm that the FBI participated in core Dakota Access–related law enforcement operations starting soon after protests began last summer. Finally, we are publishing two additional documents, also in the public record, that detail TigerSwan's role spearheading Energy Transfer Partner's multipronged security operation.

The FBI did not respond to a request for comment.

A Public–Private Partnership

Beginning in April of 2016, Indigenous activists calling themselves Water Protectors and their allies spent months attempting to block construction of the 1,172-mile Dakota Access Pipeline, which runs near the Standing Rock Sioux Reservation in North Dakota and traverses three other states. DAPL opponents were met with a heavily militarized police apparatus including local and out-of-state police and sheriff's deputies, as well as BIA police and National Guard troops. The police became notorious for their use of so-called less-than-lethal weapons against demonstrators, including rubber bullets, bean bag pellets, long range acoustic devices (LRADs), and water cannons.

But it was the brutality of private security officers that first provoked widespread outrage concerning the pipeline project. On Labor Day weekend of 2016, *Democracy Now!* captured footage of pipeline security guards attacking peaceful protesters with dogs.

In the aftermath of that incident, Energy Transfer Partners turned to Tiger-Swan—a company with a deep background in counterterrorism operations—to oversee the work of the other security companies contracted to protect the pipeline. Other security firms working along the pipeline included Silverton, Russell Group of Texas, 10 Code LLC, Per Mar, SRC, OnPoint, and Leighton, documents show.

Based in Apex, North Carolina, TigerSwan was created by retired Army Col. James Reese during the height of the war in Iraq. Reese, a former commander in the elite army special operations unit known as Delta, entered into the exploding private security and intelligence industry hoping to compete with Blackwater, then the most successful of the private military companies supporting U.S. war efforts in the Middle East and Afghanistan. TigerSwan has an estimated 350 employees and maintains offices in Iraq, Afghanistan, Saudi Arabia, Jordan, India, Latin America, and Japan.

Records from the North Dakota Private Investigation and Security Board show that TigerSwan has operated without a license in North Dakota for the entirety of the pipeline security operation, claiming in a communication with the board, "We are doing management and IT consulting for our client and doing no security work." In September, the licensing board learned about the company's position as a Dakota Access contractor and wrote a letter to its North Carolina headquarters requesting that it submit a license application.

TigerSwan then did so, but the board denied the application on December 19. After James Reese wrote a letter objecting to the decision, the security board's executive director responded on January 10 that "one reason for the denial concerns your failure to respond to the Board's request for information as to Tiger-Swan's and James Reese's activities within the State of North Dakota." Neither TigerSwan nor the board responded to questions regarding the current status of the company's license.

The leaked situation reports indicate that during the company's first weeks working on the pipeline, TigerSwan operatives met with law enforcement in Iowa and North Dakota, including Sheriff Dean Danzeisen of Mercer County, North Dakota, who "agreed to sharing of information." (In the report, TigerSwan misspells the sheriff's name as "Denzinger.") By September 13, the documents indicate, TigerSwan had placed a liaison inside the law enforcement "joint operation command" in North Dakota. The fusion of public and private intelligence operations targeting Water Protectors was underway.

One of TigerSwan's lines of communication with law enforcement was via intelligence briefings that echo the company's internal situation reports. The briefings obtained by *The Intercept* were sent by TigerSwan's deputy security director Al Ornoski to a variety of recipients, including the Gmail account of Sheriff Danzeisen. Morton County Sheriff Kyle Kirchmeier, who was regularly involved in policing the protests, also received at least one of the TigerSwan briefings.

Danzeisen did not respond to a request for comment. A spokesperson for the Morton County Sheriff's Department wrote in an email to *The Intercept* that the department "did maintain communication with TigerSwan security in order to understand when and where DAPL construction activities were taking place. This gave law enforcement situational awareness in order to monitor and respond to illegal protest activity."

TigerSwan also aided prosecutors in building cases against pipeline opponents. According to an October 16 document obtained via a records request, the security team's responsibilities included collecting "information of an evidentiary level" that would ultimately "aid in prosecution" of protesters.

A leaked report dated September 14, 2016, indicates that TigerSwan met with the North Dakota Bureau of Criminal Investigation "regarding video and still photo evidence collected for prosecution." The same document describes plans to "continue building Person of Interest (POI) folders and coordination with [law enforcement] intelligence." TigerSwan's situation reports also describe conversations between the company's operatives and FBI agents on at least four occasions.

Activists on the ground were tracked by a Dakota Access helicopter that provided live video coverage to their observers in police agencies, according to an October 12 email thread that included officers from the FBI, DHS, BIA, state, and local police. In one email, National Security Intelligence Specialist Terry Van Horn of the U.S. Attorney's Office acknowledged his direct access to the helicopter video feed, which was tracking protesters' movements during a demonstration.

"Watching a live feed from DAPL Helicopter, pending arrival at site(s)," he wrote. Cecily Fong, a spokesperson for law enforcement throughout the protests, acknowledged that an operations center in Bismarck had access to the feed, stating in an email to *The Intercept* that "the video was provided as a courtesy so we had eyes on the situation."

Asked about the intel group, Fong replied, "The Intelligence Group was formed from virtually the beginning. It involved personnel from our [State and Local Intelligence Center], the BIA, FBI, and Justice" consisting of "around 7 people who monitored social media in particular, in this case, because that was the medium most if not all of the protestors were using."

"I'm honored that they felt that we were a big enough threat to go to this level of intervention," Ed Fallon, an activist mentioned several times in the TigerSwan documents, told *The Intercept*.

As the Water Protector movement expanded from North Dakota to other states, so did the surveillance. A report dated March 29, for instance, points to a meeting between TigerSwan and "the Des Moines Field Office of the FBI, with the Omaha and Sioux Falls offices joining by conference call. Also in attendance were representatives of the Joint Terrorism Task Force, Department of Homeland Security, Iowa Department of Emergency Services, Iowa Department of Homeland Security and Iowa Department of Wildlife. Topics covered included the current threat assessment of the pipeline, the layout of current security assets and persons of interest. The FBI seemed were [*sic*] very receptive to the information presented to them, and follow-up meetings with individuals will be scheduled soon."

TigerSwan's relationship with public police agencies was not always harmonious. The situation reports describe TigerSwan's frustration with the amount of leeway some law enforcement gave protesters in Iowa and the company's efforts to convince officers to use more punitive tactics.

In a situation report dated October 16, TigerSwan applauds a recent increase in bail in Lee County, Iowa, calling it "significant because this may impede protestors from risking arrest due to the high cost to be released from bail." The document contrasts that county's tactics to those used by others. "Calhoun, Boone and Webster county law enforcement are not supportive of DAPL Security's mission," the report says, noting those agencies' "reluctance to arrest or cite trespassing individuals."

"We need to work closer with Calhoun, Boone, and Webster county [law enforcement] to ensure future protestors will at least be fined, if not arrested," the analyst notes. "Alternatively, we could request Lee County LE speak to other counties about tactics that are working."

Contacted for comment, recently elected Lee County Sheriff Stacy Weber said he hadn't discussed TigerSwan with the previous sheriff. "As far as I knew, the protest stuff was over with, and we haven't had any protests since," he said. In fact,

An image on the homepage of the TigerSwan website headlined "Security & Safety: Vulnerability Management." Photograph from TigerSwan.com.

Weber hadn't heard of the company until earlier that week, when a TigerSwan program manager named Don Felt stopped by the office. "He dropped his card off and said he wanted to say hello," Weber said.

Find, Fix, Eliminate

TigerSwan's internal files describe its utilization of aerial surveillance, including use of helicopters and drones to photograph and monitor the pipeline opponents. The September 12 situation report notes that an operation by construction workers was "over-watched by a predator on loan to the JEJOC from Oklahoma." The TigerSwan contractor who provided *The Intercept* with the situation reports said he did not believe the company ever operated a predator drone, but metadata in images he shared pointed to a camera used by a commercially available Phantom 4 drone. One of the daily intelligence updates notes plans to obtain night-vision goggles, LRADs, body armor, and FLIR (forward looking infrared) cameras.

The reports also reveal a widespread and sustained campaign of infiltration of protest camps and activist circles. Throughout the leaked documents, TigerSwan makes reference to its intelligence-gathering teams, which infiltrated protest camps and activist groups in various states. TigerSwan agents using false names and identities regularly sought to obtain the trust of protesters, which they used to gather information they reported back to their employer, according to the TigerSwan contractor.

The September documents make numerous references to Silverton personnel, who were overseen by TigerSwan, attending protests in Iowa. Silverton did not respond to a request for comment.

Covert operations are implicit in many of the other situation reports, which are filled with details that only individuals with close and consistent access to the protesters' communities could have gathered. On a few occasions, however, the reports make that presence more explicit, for instance by referring to "sources in the camp."

For example, the November 5 situation report describes the "exploitation of documents found at Camp 1." Apparently, they didn't contain much revealing material. "Of most concern," the situation report says, "were the 'Earth First' magazines found on the camp. These magazines promote and provide TTP's [tactics, techniques, and procedures] for violent activity."

In an October 3 report, TigerSwan discusses how to use its knowledge of internal camp dynamics: "Exploitation of ongoing native versus non-native rifts, and tribal rifts between peaceful and violent elements is critical in our effort to delegitimize the anti-DAPL movement." On February 19, TigerSwan makes explicit its plans to infiltrate a Chicago protest group. "TigerSwan collections team will make contact with event organizers to embed within the structure of the demonstration to develop a trusted agent status to be cultivated for future collection efforts," the report notes, later repeating its intent to "covertly make contact with event organizers."

"At every action I went to, they had their own people walking around with a video camera getting in people's faces," Ian Souter, a protester who was described as a "person of interest" in a TigerSwan report, told *The Intercept*.

Perhaps one of the most striking revelations of the documents is the level of hostility displayed by TigerSwan toward the Water Protectors. TigerSwan consistently describes the peaceful demonstrators using military and tactical language more appropriate for counterterrorism operations in an armed conflict zone. At times, the military language verges on parody, as when agents write of protesters "stockpiling signs" or when they discuss the "caliber" of paintball pellets. More often, however, the way TigerSwan discusses protesters as "terrorists," their direct actions as "attacks," and the camps as a "battlefield" reveals how the protesters' dissent was not only criminalized but treated as a national security threat. A March 1 report states that protesters' "operational weakness allows TS elements to further develop and dictate the battlespace."

In one internal report dated May 4, a TigerSwan operative describes an effort to amass digital and ground intelligence that would allow the company to "find, fix, and eliminate" threats to the pipeline—an eerie echo of "find, fix, finish," a military term used by special forces in the U.S. government's assassination campaign against terrorist targets.

TigerSwan pays particular attention to protesters of Middle Eastern descent.

A September 22 situation report argues that "the presence of additional Palestinians in the camp, and the movement's involvement with Islamic individuals is a dynamic that requires further examination." The report acknowledges that "currently there is no information to suggest terrorist type tactics or operations," but nonetheless warns that "with the current limitation on information flow out of the camp, it cannot be ruled out."

Haithem El-Zabri, a Palestinian-American activist singled out in the reports, was shocked to hear his name mentioned in that context. "As indigenous people, Palestinians stand in solidarity with other indigenous people and their right to land, water, and sovereignty," he told *The Intercept*. "To insinuate that our assumed faith is a red flag for terrorist tactics is another example of willful ignorance and the establishment's continued attempts to criminalize nonviolent protest and justify violence against it."

Such ethnic and religious profiling of protesters was not unusual. An October 12 email thread shared among members of the intel group provides a striking example of how TigerSwan was able to cast suspicion on specific individuals and communicate it to law enforcement officials. Cass County Sheriff's Deputy Tonya Jahner emailed several other officers, including two FBI agents, with an overview of information provided by "company intel." The information pertained to a woman whom Jahner labeled as a "strong Shia Islamic" with a "strong female Shia following." The woman had "made several trips overseas," Jahner wrote.

TigerSwan agents also regularly tracked individuals' movements across state lines.

On November 4, according to one of TigerSwan's internal documents, a white SUV pulled up to a pipeline valve site in South Dakota. Approached by a security guard, the driver introduced himself as Gary Tomlin and informed the official that he was a freelance reporter covering the pipeline. In an interview, sixty-three-year-old Tomlin, who covers the local school board for the Galesburg, Illinois, *Register-Mail*, said he had set out to travel the length of the pipeline and write a story about it as a freelancer. "I had time and the ability to do it, and I thought, well, I'll go look at that sucker," he said.

A situation report from that day notes, "This is the same individual identified in the SITREP a few days ago in Illinois and Iowa." The security company, OnPoint, quickly contacted TigerSwan Intel "for an assessment of Gary Tomlin" and notified the guard in the next "sector" that Tomlin was on his way. "Movement of Spread Team 6 was conducted so as to intercept and/or observe Gary Tomlin's movement throughout the South Dakota Sector," the document states. "It is my belief," the analyst adds, "that Gary Tomlin is hiding his true intentions and that he has a plethora of information to provide to the protesters. It is estimated that he will arrive in North Dakota on the evening of the 4th or morning of the 5th."

Tomlin laughed at the notion that he was working with protesters. When he arrived at the camps in North Dakota, few people would talk openly with him.

"They were highly aware of infiltrators," he said. "I fit the profile of those security people—I'm a white old man."

Cody Hall, a prominent native activist whose movements are tracked closely in the TigerSwan reports, told *The Intercept* he knew he was being followed whenever he left the camp.

"It was obvious, they were driving in trucks, SUVs, they would be right behind me, right next to me . . . it was like, damn, man, it's like you're getting an escort," he said. "That was always the scary thing: How did they know that I was coming?"

Robert Rice hosted a series of videos critical of the pipeline protest movement without disclosing that he was working for TigerSwan. The videos, which were posted on two Facebook pages, were taken down after *The Intercept* reached out to the firm for comment.

Social Engagement Plan

A document dated October 16, obtained via a public records request, lays out the mission of the TigerSwan-led security team working in North Dakota. In addition to protecting the pipeline workers, machinery, and construction material, the company was also expected to "protect the reputation of DAPL." The public relations mission quickly became a priority for the firm, documents show. As a leaked situation report from early September puts it, success would require "strategic messaging from the client that drives the message that we are the good guys, tell the real story and address the negative messaging with good counter messaging."

On numerous occasions, TigerSwan agents stressed the need to change the public narrative established by protestors and to swing public support in favor of the pipeline. As accounts of protest repression garnered nationwide support for the NoDAPL movement, the firm's agents painstakingly collected and analyzed media coverage, warning their client about how certain incidents might be received by the public.

"This article is only in the Huffington post, but the expansion of the tribe's narrative outside of the Native American community media outlets is of concern," an October 3 report notes. TigerSwan agents regularly describe protesters' accounts of events as "propaganda."

But TigerSwan personnel did not limit themselves to monitoring the narrative— they also tried to change it.

In a report dated September 7, TigerSwan agents discuss the need for a "Social Engagement Plan." On September 22, they discuss the development of an information operations campaign run by the company's North Carolina–based intel team and Robert Rice, who without disclosing his TigerSwan affiliation posed as "Allen Rice" in a series of amateurish videos in which he provided commentary critical of the protests. The videos, posted on the Facebook pages "Defend Iowa" and "Netizens for Progress and Justice," were removed after *The Intercept* contacted TigerSwan, Rice, and the pages' administrators for comment. None responded.

With the Dakota Access Pipeline construction nearing completion, TigerSwan might have found itself out of a lucrative contract. But in the months leading up to the first oil delivery through the pipeline, the company made sure to stress the continued need for security.

"Everyone must be concerned of the lone wolf," a TigerSwan operative wrote in a March 7 report. "Should we slip from that conscience, we may all be amiss. I cannot afford this in my duties, nor will We/I allow or accept this. I cannot thank everyone enough for their support during this entire process, However, the movement continues, and We/I will not stop. That's not in my vocabulary. We will always over-watch as the protectors what is in the best interest for ETP, as we are the guardians."

In recent weeks, the company's role has expanded to include the surveillance of activist networks marginally related to the pipeline, with TigerSwan agents monitoring "anti-Trump" protests from Chicago to Washington, D.C., as well as warning its client of growing dissent around other pipelines across the country.

In a March 24 report discussing the likely revival of protests as summer approaches, TigerSwan writes, "Much like Afghanistan and Iraq, the 'Fighting Season' will soon be here with the coming warming temperatures."

IV.

ENVIRONMENTAL COLONIZATION

"We Are Watching." Photograph by Michelle Latimer.

16

HEAL THE PEOPLE, HEAL THE LAND
AN INTERVIEW WITH FREDA HUSON

Anne Spice

There are front lines everywhere. Standing Rock wasn't the first Indigenous stand against pipelines, and it won't be the last. As popular attention focused on the fight of the Oceti Sakowin to protect their territory from the threats posed by the Dakota Access Pipeline, across the colonial border to the north the Unist'ot'en clan continued to assert a quiet presence on their unceded Wet'suwet'en territory. The Unist'ot'en encampment was established seven years ago, when Freda Huson moved onto her people's land full time and began to build a permanent home. Since then, the Unist'ot'en clan and supporters from across the world have prevented the construction of numerous potential and proposed oil and gas pipelines. All visitors must go through a free, prior, and informed consent protocol before entering the territory, in accordance with the U.N. Declaration on the Rights of Indigenous Peoples and Wet'suwet'en Indigenous law. With this protocol, the Unist'ot'en people insist on their rights to their territory and refuse the incursions of the petroleum industry and the settler state. As supporters are frequently told: "This is not Canada, it is not British Columbia, it is unceded Wet'suwet'en territory." In this interview, Freda Huson outlines the history of the Unist'ot'en resistance to pipeline construction and settler-state violence and the encampment's role in promoting Indigenous resurgence through land-based cultural practice and intergenerational healing. She explains the connections between Unist'ot'en camp and the #NoDAPL movement, placing Standing Rock in a broader context of Indigenous resurgence and frontline land defense.

ANNE SPICE: So I wanted to start, since we're sitting here in the cabin that you built on your people's territory, asking you to introduce yourself, and then just tell me a little bit about your people's relation to this territory, as far back in history as you want to go.

"We Are Unarmed." Photograph by Michelle Latimer.

FREDA HUSON: I'm Freda Huson, Unist'ot'en[1] spokesperson, appointed by my clan chiefs, specifically Unist'ot'en chiefs, and the territory we are on is connected to the name *Noostel*,[2] which is one of the chief names of the Unist'ot'en and my current chief Kneadebeas used to hold that name Noostel but he is now Kneadebeas. Noostel is just sitting in waiting for the next person to come up and hold up that name.

AS: How and why did you decide to return to live on the yintah [territory]? What was the process that brought you back here?

FH: In 2009 an exploration company was trying to explore our other territory for minerals because they wanted to mine it. They'd already been one week in there, and they'd cleared the road and it was in spring when it should've been snowed in. We were going to check on our cabin and came upon a road that was plowed, so when we drove all the way in we blocked the road, because I knew that whoever was in there had to come out. It was late at night by the time we got there, so we parked the truck on the road and walked into our cabin and, sure enough, eight o' clock in the morning there was a honk on the road so I went out and met the worker there, and they were from one of the exploration companies in Smithers [B.C.]. I asked what they were doing there, [and told them] that they didn't have consent or permission to be there, and I said whoever employed you, you need to go back and tell them that the territory holders were here and said you don't have permission to be here. So he said he was going to pass the message on; we let them go back out and he said, "oh, but there's people already setting up camp back there," and I said, "ok, you go ahead, we'll go see them ourselves." We went in further to check up on what they were doing and they already had about six wall tents set up, and they had a washer and dryer, like a laundry room, shower room already set up, and the guy was clearing the land, they were making a road and it was all mucky and gross. We walked in there and stopped them and then had a chat, reiterated the same message to them: "you don't have our consent, you don't have any permission to be here." So at that point I told the workers that were there, "you have Friday till twelve noon to get everything that you have up here off our territory. If you don't have it off of here, everything that's here, according to our law, belongs to us."

I was planning on spending a weekend out there, and I ended up going straight back to my home community and sent a message to my chiefs that there was an exploration company and they were trying to do exploration, and so the chiefs all loaded up and said, "we're going out there to check, ourselves." And so my whole family went out there and they reinforced the message I gave, and they looked at everything and said, "oh I like this big tent, this one's going to be mine if you don't get it out of here." They were saying stuff like that, and then they explained to them that they don't have consent. Then the chiefs said the same thing: that you have till twelve noon to get all this off of here or this is going to belong to us. I had to go back to work, so we came back out Thursday night and spent the night out here. Smogelgem[3] and Hank and Hanky Boy, the three of them stayed out here for that whole week after we kicked them out to make sure they didn't come back in, and they lit a fire and camped out at the end of the road, and they felled down a bunch of trees all the way down the 42 [logging] road coming into Poplar Lake, and then they felled more trees on the way. They'd camped out on the road there to make sure nobody came, and when we came we removed the trees so that they could come out. And sure enough by twelve noon they were coming out.

So then we pulled away from [the office of the Wet'suwet'en] and started going independent and started dealing with industry and government on our own.[4] And that's when we found out that there were four proposed pipelines that were proposed for this territory. We found out that the GPS route was right where this cabin sits now, so that is why we chose to put this cabin right here. That happened in 2010, I believe. We started the construction of this [cabin] and what had happened was Smogelgem had secured a big grant in order to build five clan cabins when he was working at the office of the Wet'suwet'en so, this is one of the clan cabins and my uncle chose this location, so we put it right in the way of the GPS route of the pipeline's proposed route. And some supporters actually slept on the floor here, and there were twelve people crowded in here, and they said, "wow this place looks too small." That's where the bunkhouse came into being, they raised fifty grand and that following spring we had about fifty people show up here and put up that building in three weeks.

AS: And your chiefs asked you to stay on the territory?

FH: Actually, no, the reason that pushed me to move out here is, while we were burying my brother, the pipeline company came in with drill equipment to do test drilling. They already flew all the equipment to on the Shay road, about thirty kilometers up the road [from the camp]. So they already had flew in that equipment and one of the drill workers phoned one of our other Wet'suwet'en chiefs because he didn't like the way that drill company was talking about the Indigenous people—they were making fun of us and calling us down. He was upset about how they were talking about us so he phoned one of the chiefs and said that they got a call five times that said that "you need to go in now, you need to go in now." We were at my brother's wake, when we got that call. Because my brother passed away from cancer and they knew we were busy, they had some inside help telling them that we were busy. We got that call and then he showed up at the wake to talk to my chief and told him about that. I was at the wake too, so they called me over and told me what was going on. I told him "you want me to call Smogelgem down?" He said "yeah," so I phoned Smogelgem at my place and told him that the drill company's trying to go in, so my chiefs that are here told you to come down. Smogelgem offered to come out here and said, "even though Gordie's my good buddy, I'll miss the funeral and go out there. And I'll just find somebody to come with me."

So that was about ten o'clock at night, and by midnight he convinced Hank to come with him and my cousin Hanky Boy. Same three again that were at Poplar, that were the key people that blocked the road. They did the same over here, they parked on the bridge and waited there and sure enough, at five in the morning they showed up. Well they [Smogelgem, Hank, and Hanky Boy] had to drive from our home community, which is two hours, they got here two in the morning; they just sat in the truck and while they were waiting, loggers were telling them, "they're coming at this many kilometers, there's equipment already way up here at this many kilometers," so the loggers were actually helping us. That's why we don't try to block out the loggers, because they were in support of us blocking out the pipelines. And they helped us find out where everything was at. So Smogelgem told them the exact same thing I did at the other territory, said, "you have until twelve noon to get out all that equipment." But when they showed up they said "oh, but we already flew all the equipment in." [Smogelgem] says, "it's not our problem! You don't have consent, you have to have that all out of here by twelve noon or it's going to stay here." So by twelve noon they came in and trucked it all out. That's when we decided that we can't protect the territory from the reserve, it's two hours away, and if nobody's here they're going to keep trying to come in so we made the choice to *[pause]* first Smogelgem wasn't working so he moved out here and I commuted back and forth until I left my job. So that's the reason why we're out, because they're shady. Crooked dealings in what they do.

AS: I've heard you talk about the way that pipeline companies especially have tried to pitch their projects as critical infrastructure.[5] And there was that RCMP report that was talking about critical infrastructure and the "violent aboriginal extremists" that are out on the land.[6] And you've talked about how you have your own critical infrastructures on the territory. So I'm wondering how you think the way that industry approaches the land and the water and animals is different than the way that you view those same things.

FH: So industry and government always talk about critical infrastructure, and their critical infrastructure is making money, and using destructive projects to make that money, and they go by any means necessary to make that happen. So they created Bill C-51, which labels Indigenous peoples as terrorists. And we're not even terrorists, they're the ones that are terrorist because they use terrorist acts to . . . well you see what happened at Standing Rock where they used a lot of violence toward people who were peacefully protesting and trying to get them to listen to them because they're protecting their water, they're protecting their way of life. And they [the police] used all means necessary, they were militarized, and they were bringing a lot of harm to peaceful people that were trying to protect their water. So for us, our critical infrastructure is the clean drinking water, and the very water that the salmon spawn in, and they go back downstream and four years, come back. That salmon is our food source, it's our main staple food. That's one of our critical infrastructures. And there's berries that are our critical infrastructure, because the berries not only feed us, they also feed the bears, and the salmon also don't just feed us, they feed the bears. And each and every one of those are all connected, and without each other, we wouldn't survive on this planet. So, to them, they massively clear cut land, which the animals depend on, and if we don't have the animals there . . . for example, the bears will eat the berries and they'll drop it, and the waste that comes out of the bear, it's got seeds in it, so that germinates and we get more berries. We need the bears in order to keep producing our berries, and same with the salmon. The bears eat the salmon as well, because once the salmon spawn, they end up dying anyways, and that becomes food for the bears, so it's not being wasted. All of that is part of the system that our people depend on, and that whole cycle and system is our critical infrastructure, and that's what we're trying to protect, an infrastructure that we depend on. And industry and government are pushing these projects that would destroy that critical infrastructure, most important to our people.

AS: The one that actually sustains life.

FH: It's actually sustainable, and we help take care of it to ensure that the cycle is complete. For example, our people, we do not fish certain species because the numbers are low. But we're doing our part protecting it, but then we have industry which is commercial fishermen, fish all those salmon so they can't come back. So they're ruining that critical infrastructure. But we know how to manage and take care of it.

AS: Because you've been here . . .

FH: Yes, we've been here for thousands of years. And our people would actually even starve themselves in order to have salmon for the next generation. But what they consider critical infrastructure is not sustainable. You look at every industry that's ever come and gone—the fishing industry, they overexploited and over-fished, so that industry collapsed. And you look at the logging industry, right now they're overexploiting, that's going to collapse. Every industry that the so-called government and people that are part of planning their industry, they're doing it with unsustainable methods. For example, they say our people used to log. But our people did everything by hand. They didn't use massive feller-bunchers that chew up the ground and destroy all the vegetation underneath it. They did hand-falling. Smaller skidders that pulled the trees out without destroying the ground, so that when you did plant you had healthy trees. But now they destroy everything and they pretty much, I call it monocultured. It's pretty much just tree farming. And it's not been a healthy method, because they spray pesticides to help these trees grow quicker so they can recut them and mill them again. And they actually spray pesticides and stuff to kill off the [trees they don't use]. So they'll kill off all the willow, and that's the moose food, and you wonder why our moose numbers are down. Because they don't need willows for milling. So they just only put back the species like balsam, pine, spruce, and cedar. But everything else is destroyed, and they were a part of the critical infrastructure that is needed to keep the population of the moose. And even overhunting—they allow too much hunting and they don't even know how to count numbers properly, they count twenty-five moose and they times that by eight and say "yeah, there's this many moose in zone 6," so they allow hunters to overhunt the numbers. And there are not really that many moose.

AS: Maybe because they deal with each thing separately, as opposed to thinking about how they're all connected.

FH: Because this territory here, when we first moved out here, the hunters, the non-Indigenous hunters came out and took ten moose just in this small area. So it took four years for us to see a moose. We didn't even hunt this area ourselves, we closed it off to the hunters. And four years before we saw moose again. So even now we take maybe two or three. That's our limit. We give ourselves a quota, we don't go in and just shoot all the moose. And they don't just stay here, so we're protecting it for all the hunters. It's not just us, because eventually it'll be overcrowded here and the moose will travel out, they know how to swim across the river and go to the other territories, so we do our own self-sustaining.

AS: Tell me about the protocol that supporters have to go through when they enter your territory.

FH: The FPIC—free, prior, and informed consent—protocol that we use is: who are you, where are you from, how long do you plan to stay if we let you in, do you work for industry or government that's destroying our lands, how will your visit benefit Unist'ot'en, and what kind of skills do you bring. These are the basic questions we ask. And we also have a separate protocol for media people. So we ask them similar questions, asking them who are they, where are they from, who their audience is, how will that benefit Unist'ot'en.

AS: Part of that protocol is connected to this being territory that's governed by Wet'suwet'en people and not by Canada or not by British Columbia. So what's the importance of Indigenous sovereignty and asserting that sovereignty by making sure that those protocols are in place and making sure that people know when they're here that it's Indigenous law that they're meant to follow?

FH: The reason why we do the free, prior, and informed consent is to show that this is our territory, we govern it, we protect it, and we have the final say on what can or cannot happen here and people have to respect that and abide by our laws here because it's not Canada and it's not B.C. It's Wet'suwet'en land, and it's unceded. Unceded means that we've never given it up, we've never surrendered it to anybody. The province likes to call it crown land because the queen owns it, but the queen does not own it. She does not have a bill of sale or any papers that say she owns it. She has to prove to us how she thinks she owns these lands, we've never ever given it over to her. So this is still Wet'suwet'en land, and we have the final say on what happens here. Our ancestors had protected these lands for thousands of years before, that's why we still exist. And now it's our job to protect it for the next generation to ensure that everything is still intact for them. For the next seven generations.

AS: Do you think that changes the way that people act when they come to this territory?

FH: Yeah, most people are very respectful, they accept the fact that they're visiting our territory and abide by our rules. And we don't allow drugs or alcohol or firearms are not allowed in here, because it's a peaceful stand. And we have our own firearms for hunting purposes and for protection, because this is grizzly country back here and you have to be respectful of the animals. They were here, they have every right, more so than us to be here. We share that space for them and are very respectful and we never ever talk disrespectful about the animals that are here. And the grizzly is more powerful than we are, so if they're in a patch of land, we know it's theirs, we just stay outta there.

AS: You've recently built a healing center on the territory. Tell me about the vision for this space as a healing space, and where you see that going.

FH: Well over the years, our family had identified that a lot of us had gone through our own healing. Pretty much all my family has gone through sexual abuse, and physical, all kinds of abuses, and growing up in alcoholic homes. So we've seen that we have healed ourselves, and it's probably why I'm doing what I'm doing, because if I hadn't done what I'm doing I'd probably still be stuck in substance abuse like the rest of my community members. So we identified that a lot of our people have experienced trauma, whether it be physical, mental, sexually abused. Their system that's set up, the Indian Act system, the reserve system, is all an attempt to oppress our people, and they've succeeded in oppressing our people. The system is set up deliberately to make our people submissive and stay oppressed. So we realized, "How come we can't get our people out here? How come it's just non-Indigenous supporters coming here?" and we came to the realization—if we heal our people, then we'll heal our land. A lot of our people are hurting. My niece has been going to school for the last seven years to get her PhD in clinical psychology. She focused her studies on helping youth, so that was her long-term vision to develop a youth center, a healing facility to heal our youth because we keep saying our youth are going to be our leaders, so if we make healthy youth, then we'll have a healthy nation.

So we have that structure up and we actually have a pamphlet that has stories of people that have come here and that have told their story—how they've received healing—because the river is healing. People experience body healing from just going in dips in the river, and mental healing—people have said they're suicidal and have come here and they felt so accepted and it's just so peaceful here and such a different environment from the city.[7] People have been sharing their stories about receiving healing here, and we actually have people saying that they were here for three weeks for work camp and lost all their weight, because they're eating healthier and are physically active for that full three weeks. One guy said he lost twenty pounds and has never been that size and that physically fit since he was in high school. So we have various people telling their stories and how they've received healing here, so we're saying that that healing facility, just from people being here without any counseling programs running, we know it's going to work if we bring our people here to reconnect to the land and actually receive mental healing.

AS: One of the similarities I see between Standing Rock and what you've done here is that a lot of attention got focused on those areas when there was a pipeline proposed to go through. And Standing Rock and the area around it and Oceti Sakowin people have been struggling against the government and the people building dams that have flooded out their territory—they've faced a number of different struggles since America has tried to exist on that territory. And here, you got a lot of visibility when the Northern Gateway Pipeline [an Enbridge project] was proposed through. That pipeline's dead. What would you say to people who think that the struggle is all about pipelines, or that since that pipeline's not going through that the fight is over here?

FH: Well even though the Northern Gateway—which was the oil and bitumen pipeline—they think it's dead, but it's not totally dead. We're still battling Coastal Gaslink and Pacific Trails Pipeline, which is fracked gas. They want to put gas through the pipes through here to Kitimat from the Fort Nelson area. They're trying to bring fracked gas and it's going to increase fracking. So our battle is not finished yet because we're still getting mail from the oil and gas commission saying that they're going to issue out permits for Coastal Gaslink. And I believe Pacific Trails already has their permits, Pacific Trails is the one that Chevron is proposing to put through. So we're still getting mail, so that indicates to us that if they're still issuing out permits to the gas companies that our fight is not over yet.

AS: That seems to be a connection to other territories as well, that there would be fracking happening on other people's territories that's destroying that water, and then the fracked gas gets transported through here.

FH: Pretty much. They said that if any of these projects went through, the production would triple. So that's triple destruction on another Indigenous community's territories.

AS: So it's a stand of solidarity as well.

FH: Yep. And with those projects they say they're just going to dissipate if they break. But they won't dissipate if they break because it's gas. If it breaks it's probably going to be an explosion, and with the pine beetle and all the forest fires that happened in the lower mainland in British Columbia, this could be a big threat to our people if they put these pipelines through. If there's one little fire it's going to spread fast and destroy all of our twenty-two thousand square kilometers, and we can't take that risk.

AS: Exactly. So when I went to Standing Rock I went mostly to connect with people I had met here at Unist'ot'en camp. I think that this place has been a connecting point and an inspiration for a lot of different Indigenous struggles, and there have been other camps that have started up using this place as an inspiration. And there's this network of people that have been going to different front lines to help support. I'm wondering if you have other things that you think connect what happened at Standing Rock to what happened here. Where are the overlaps in the movement and the similar struggles that you face?

FH: Well with what we've been doing here we've been here seven to eight years, and we just finished our eighth annual action camp. So we've had anywhere from sixty to two hundred people at a time coming here, and those camps have been to train people. And from my understanding, a lot of the people that came here through action camp training were the people that went down to Standing Rock to help. So we basically in the last seven years trained up little pockets of people that are from all over this planet and many were from the United States too, so we've trained a lot of people to be able to stand up for this fight. For this time that is here now.

Our Facebook page was actually used to give updates on everything that was happening at Standing Rock, so we made it very public; the media was very quiet about it, but because we have such a following we were promoting Standing Rock the whole time that battle was going down, even though we weren't there, we were using our resources to make people aware, so we believe because of using our Facebook page, a lot of the high numbers that showed up there was because of our media sourcing and because of our being able to put things up and share it.

AS: What would your advice be to other Indigenous land defense movements? Especially ones that are just getting started again, or are just coming back to their own territories?

FH: Just reoccupy your lands. Do everything like your ancestors. The ancestors are here helping us. Learn everything about your history and start reconnecting back with your lands and don't be afraid to garner other supports from other people. Because we didn't know the first thing about doing protesting, or standing up. There were numerous hands that contributed and helped with what happened here. There's experienced people out there, don't be afraid to garner those supports. Because we can't claim all the credit for everything that happened here, there were so many hands that took part who had fundraising experience and put a lot of these structures up. And then we have people that know how to do nonviolent direct action; they came up and provided training so we have all kinds of skilled people. Have nonviolent direct action training, and hold many of them so they have a lot of skilled people that can do things safely and keep themselves safe. We have that action training every year in July, it's the same time every year. And this last year we just realized that a lot of people were getting burned out because it's the same few, so we decided to do a healing and wellness camp for that eighth annual because we were feeling burned out ourselves. And it felt really good, a lot of people were really thankful to have that because they were feeling the burnout as well.

AS: I was thankful for it! One more question. A lot of the discourse around the NoDAPL movement was about water, and the rallying call was mni wiconi or "water is life." Here, on Unist'ot'en territory you've got the Wedzin Kwah [the river that runs along the border of the territory]. How do you relate to water, and what relation does water, especially the river, have to the healing work that you're doing on this territory?

FH: Water is one of the elements besides fire that is very powerful and very strong. You can't control it; that river is powerful, it's fast. It's a life giver, because it gives life to the salmon, it gives us life when we drink it, and it gives life to the plants and vegetation around it. And spiritually it's strong. Whenever you have aches and pains you can go into that river, it brings healing properties to your sore, achy muscles. And all the minerals are still intact so when you drink it you don't have to go to the health food store to get some minerals because all the waters that are cleansed and purified in the city municipalities, all the minerals are taken out for all the purification process. Water does physically give you health, life; it's one of the strongest elements. And you have to respect water the same way you respect fire. So, it's a very powerful element that we show total respect to, and that's why we hold water ceremonies and why we hold it in such high regard and want to protect it.

NOTES

1. Unist'ot'en people are C'ihlts'ehkhyu (big frog clan) of the Wet'suwet'en nation.
2. Noostel is the Wet'suwet'en word for wolverine. In the Wet'suwet'en governance system, hereditary chiefs hold names associated with the protection of different territories.
3. The name Smogelgem is a chief name held in the Laksamshu (fireweed) clan. Smogelgem has held other names, which appear in previous writing about Unist'ot'en Camp.
4. The internal politics that led to this decision are best left to Wet'suwet'en people themselves. Following Audra Simpson's "ethnographic refusal," in *Mohawk Interruptus*: Political Life across the Borders of Settler States (Durham, N.C.: Duke University Press, 2014), we note that there are some parts of this story that we know but refuse to tell.
5. Government of Canada, "Critical Infrastructure," Public Safety Canada, last modified May 22, 2018, https://www.publicsafety.gc.ca.
6. RCMP, *Criminal Threats to the Canadian Petroleum Industry*, Critical Infrastructure Intelligence Assessment, January 24, 2014.
7. The camp has hosted many urban Indigenous people, connecting them to territory and land-based traditions.

17

THE FINANCING PROBLEM OF COLONIALISM
HOW INDIGENOUS JURISDICTION IS VALUED IN PIPELINE POLITICS

Shiri Pasternak, Katie Mazer, and D. T. Cochrane

What is the financial power of Indigenous jurisdiction?

The political-economic impact of NoDAPL is enduring and expansive. In recent years, as industry and governments have scrambled to expand North American oil pipeline networks, project-by-project community-based opposition has also intensified. Repeatedly, communities have courageously resisted proposed pipelines, forcing companies to reconfigure their plans, find new routes, or cancel projects altogether. Governments are stymied in their efforts to sell access to lands they have conquered only on paper. This has resulted in instructive encounters between governments and companies that are pushing these infrastructure projects and the communities and movements working to protect lands, waters, and the world from climate change.

Importantly, this dynamic is continental in character. By attending to these struggles from a continental perspective, this chapter draws attention to the *interconnectedness* of North American infrastructure projects in both physical and financial dimensions. These connections are manifest not only through industry's constant effort to skirt resistance through the geographic reconfiguration and capital reorganization of infrastructure networks, but also through the transnational tactics and geographies of resistance to the Dakota Access Pipeline (DAPL) and other extractive projects across North America.

In this chapter, we think about DAPL from a broad perspective, both in terms of its enduring financial implications and in terms of its implications for other places and struggles. We span our analysis out from Standing Rock and the powerful opposition of the Oceti Sakowin (the Great Sioux Nation) to the pipeline to consider the broader implications for North American pipeline expansion and resistance, focusing on Secwepemc (Shushwap) resistance to the Kinder Morgan Pipeline Expansion Project as another instantiation of this struggle.

Our contribution to this collection is framed by our shared position as scholars and activists working on themes related to oil, resource extraction, political economy, and Indigenous jurisdiction in the Canadian context. Watching the events surrounding DAPL and the NoDAPL campaign from this perspective highlights the broad significance and far-reaching implications of this struggle. More specifically, our analysis pivots on two points. First, generally, DAPL and the struggle that surrounds it exist within a broader, flexible, and fluctuating environment of North American oil infrastructure expansion. While each proposed pipeline presents as a single or isolated project, we might instead think of them as flashpoints in a much larger ongoing struggle over the expansion of extractive capitalism across North America.

Secondly, and more specifically, even when the Dakota Access Pipeline is built its legacy will not be of community failure to abort construction, but about the power of Indigenous jurisdiction to intervene in the financial architecture of investment in North America and, more fundamentally, to challenge the system of valuation on which this architecture rests. The NoDAPL campaign posed a clear and fundamental threat to Energy Transfer Partners' (ETP) bottom line by conjoining disruption of pipeline construction with targeting of its financing; these combined tactics undermined the viability and profitability of the project on a number of fronts. But NoDAPL's most fundamental disruption—to which the North American oil industry and its financial backers have taken notice—was to the certainty that capital can control and dictate the rules of the game.

The assertion of Indigenous jurisdiction at Standing Rock by the Oceti Sakowin also threw into question the supremacy of North American extractive capital in a more fundamental way. By enacting geographies of Indigenous title, law, and responsibility, these assertions challenged the regime of valuation that calculates life, climate, and refusal as costs or risks that must be accounted for. Companies try to account for these risks in the language they know, but Indigenous regimes of countervaluation cannot be easily absorbed into a framework of financial calculation. Practices of accounting derived from Indigenous socioeconomic orders like those we saw at Standing Rock—for land, water, the future, and life systems of reciprocal obligation—lay down a different political-economic terrain that sits uneasily alongside industry's calculative logic. The enactment of this political economy of Indigenous authority sends extractive capital into frenzy because it challenges its most basic assumptions: relentless social and natural extraction as a source of value. By blocking construction, disrupting finances, and destabilizing the supremacy of extractive valuation, Indigenous jurisdiction poses an entwined physical, financial, and epistemological risk to the expansion of oil infrastructure well beyond the specific geographies of DAPL.

After placing DAPL and the NoDAPL campaign in continental context, we explore some of these dynamics as they are playing out in the case of the Kinder Morgan Trans Mountain project in south-central British Columbia: a pipeline expansion project that would transport tar sands bitumen across the unceded territories of several nations, including the Treaty 8 nations at the source of the oil that is set to flow to the Kwatlen, Squamish, and Tsleil Wauthuth territories on the coast, crossing through the largest part of its route (among others) on the Indigenous territory of the Secwepemc Nation (pronounced Se-KWEP-umk).

We explore the multifaceted ways that Secwepemc jurisdiction throws into question the completion of this project, and the broader ways this threat is reconfiguring the financial and geographical landscape of pipeline politics. By way of conclusion we aim to draw broader lessons across these two cases by thinking through what it means for extractive capital to confront these parallel regimes of valuation as they are enacted through assertions of Indigenous authority on the ground.

DAPL's Continental Context

The struggle over DAPL was informed by the broader scramble to get North American oil to refineries, ports, and markets, and to build the transportation infrastructure that would make this possible. This drive has been particularly intense in the context of the Alberta tar sands—but is also, as we have seen, present in the Bakken context underlying parts of Montana, North Dakota, Saskatchewan, and Manitoba—as industry and decision makers have repeatedly invoked the "imperative" of accessing new markets.[1]

In turn, capital markets have followed with great interest the expansion of North American oil transportation infrastructure across the continent. The major pipeline companies have developed complex and sophisticated ownership structures to entice investors with stable returns. They have also entered into numerous lending agreements with banks in North America as well as Europe. On the surface, this was done to attract the financing necessary for the costly projects. Beyond that, however, the attraction of a broader swath of investors increases and diversifies the beneficiaries of a project. This augments and reinforces the intracapitalist coalition supporting and advocating for pipelines and oil infrastructure.

But the economic justification for pipelines is always shifting, generally between two main poles: one, that lines are needed as a way to move oil to markets; and two, pipeline construction is needed as a form of economic stimulus. After President Obama's delay in approving Keystone XL, for example, which would have given "Canadian oil" passage to U.S. refineries and markets, the Canadian government emphasized the imperative of moving tar sands oil to tidewater to enable it to fetch world prices.

More recently, industry and governments have been focused on the economic benefits of the infrastructure itself. In Canada, since the crash in oil prices starting in 2014, industry advocates have been arguing that private pipeline expansion is an effective form of national economic stimulus. The active debate that surrounds these different claims has thrown into question the need for expanded pipeline capacity in North America. Crucially, researchers have found that new pipeline projects would only be needed under scenarios in which oil sands production were expanded to levels that would push Canada well beyond its climate obligations. As long ago as 2011, the International Energy Agency warned of the pivotal role played by energy infrastructure in the future of the climate. Investing in new fossil-fuel infrastructure, they warned, would risk locking us into a future of expanded fossil-fuel production beyond what the climate could bear.[2] It is against this backdrop that governments and industry have repeatedly appealed to the need for more pipeline capacity across North America.

North American oil pipeline projects exist in relation to one another. The conditions for one project change very quickly depending on the status of other projects, market conditions, resistance, and political climate. As noted, in 2011 U.S. president Barack Obama announced that he would delay the approval of Keystone XL by at least a year. In reaction to this, the Canadian federal government led by Prime Minister Stephen Harper aggressively asserted energy exports as a top government priority and claimed that diversifying markets away from the United States was a "strategic imperative" for Canada. Holding up Asia as the key target market, the Canadian government turned its attention to pushing forward the Enbridge Northern Gateway Pipeline, designed to transport tar sands oil from northern Alberta to the coast of northern British Columbia. From here, the oil would be loaded onto tankers, where it would have traveled through the rough, pristine, and remote waters of the Douglas Channel on its way to Asian markets.

The most controversial of domestic pipelines, the Northern Gateway drew massive resistance for its incursion into unceded Indigenous lands, its threat to environmentally sensitive areas, and its promise to expand tar sands production. As resistance mounted to Northern Gateway, two new pipeline projects were proposed to transport tar sands bitumen to tidewater: Kinder Morgan's Trans Mountain Expansion to the city of Burnaby terminal in British Columbia, and TransCanada's Energy East, which would run 4,600 km east to Saint John, New Brunswick.[3] When the Northern Gateway project was ultimately rejected by the Liberal government of Justin Trudeau in November 2016, it was on the same day that he approved two other major projects: the Kinder Morgan Trans Mountain project and the Enbridge Line 3 "replacement," the largest project in Enbridge history.[4]

The continental character of oil infrastructure is important to keep in mind. Not only does it form the basis on which particular place-based contestations unfold, but it informs the logic under which industry operates. Governments, pipeline companies, and the financial backers of pipeline projects have an eye to the shifting terrain of certainty when it comes to their perceived ability to access territory and build infrastructure free of financial or physical disruptions. Pipeline companies have generally been considered lower risk investments. That appears to be changing as capital grapples with the uncertain effects of resistance to pipeline projects. In this way, shifting local conditions related to one project have implications for the perceived viability and profitability of other proposals.

Within this context, in both Canada and the United States, companies and governments have fast-tracked, fragmented, and avoided approvals processes in an attempt to skirt public scrutiny and expedite construction. Recently companies are focusing on another important strategy for skirting resistance: the consolidation of corporate control and an increased emphasis on "pipe in the ground."[5] As industry and governments have repeatedly encountered opposition to new-build projects, companies are beginning to understand the political advantages of consolidating control over *existing* infrastructure. Canadian company Enbridge has been at the forefront of this trend. As part of an effort to build flexibility into its operations, the company has dramatically expanded its ownership of the North American network, recently merging with Houston-based pipeline company Spectra Energy in the largest deal in Canadian oil patch history. Analysts place this merger within the context of widespread resistance to pipelines in Canada and repeated delays in the approval and construction of new-build projects. Analysts predict that this sort of cross-border merger of assets—including, crucially, infrastructure assets—will become more common within this context as an alternative to building new infrastructure.[6]

Resistance to hydrocarbon expansion is continental, too, however, and it is becoming increasingly difficult to isolate local struggles against energy infrastructure as coalitions coalesce to coordinate assertions of jurisdiction that map over the temporal and geographic strategies of extraction companies. For example, the Tar Sands Treaty Alliance is a continental alliance convened to prohibit "the pipelines/trains/tankers that will feed the expansion of the Alberta Tar Sands." In May 2017, the coalition that includes 121 grassroots First Nations and Tribes committed to an integrated divestment campaign against the banks funding DAPL and tar sands pipelines including the Kinder Morgan Trans Mountain Expansion, TransCanada's Energy East and Keystone XL projects, and Enbridge's Line 3.[7]

These efforts have not gone unnoticed among investors. During ETP's earnings call for its fourth quarter results of 2016, one analyst asked the ETP executives, "Do you see any permanent damage to financing sources from the pushback that your counterparties have received on Dakota Access?"[8] The executives reassured the analyst that all was well. However, one ETP representative added that the pressure on financial backers "has been tough." He further acknowledged that the continued backing of the banks may have been dependent on contractual obligation. The fact that the question was raised means resistance tactics targeting financing have caught the attention of capital.

The coalescing movement against hydrocarbon expansion is further conjoined to the global climate justice movement. Governments have tried to separate the two movements, with Canada's Liberal government and Alberta's New

Democratic Party government both implementing carbon taxes in order to obtain "social license" for pipeline projects, particularly Kinder Morgan's Trans Mountain Expansion. As capital struggles to account for the costs of climate change, companies and projects associated with fossil-fuel use and expansion become much riskier investments. The risk is compounded by the growing efforts of social movements and Indigenous communities to intervene in financial markets, such as the bank divestment campaign mentioned above.

Indigenous Jurisdiction against Capitalism: Kinder Morgan and the Secwepemc "Standing Rock North" Standoff

The NoDAPL campaign cost billions of dollars in delays, launched dozens of bank divestment campaigns, created massive reputational risks for financial backers, and brought into stark relief the integral tie between finance and physical infrastructure.

The continental oil industry was put on notice by the massive disruptions to pipeline construction on Standing Rock Sioux territory. Now the precedent of NoDAPL disruption to business-as-usual has cast a shadow on all pipeline projects currently under review for approval or pushing forward toward construction. The Kinder Morgan Trans Mountain Expansion, for example, is set to carry tar sands oil through a number of Indigenous territories creating elevated risk and uncertainty for investors. The specter of NoDAPL provoked Canada's Natural Resources Minister Jim Carr to suggest that resistance to pipelines could be met with military force. Although Carr backed away from the statement, it demonstrates the government's line-in-the-sand where their otherwise progressive rhetoric on recognizing Indigenous rights and jurisdiction will not tread.

In July 2017, the Secwepemc Nation in south-central British Columbia released the *Secwepemc Peoples Declaration on Protecting Our Land and Water against the Kinder Morgan Trans Mountain Pipeline.*[9] The declaration states: "we hereby explicitly and irrevocably refuse its passage through our territory." According to the Secwepemc Nation, Kinder Morgan will be unable to commence and complete construction of the Trans Mountain Expansion.

Dubbed "Standing Rock North" by Canadian media, Secwepemcul'ecw in south-central British Columbia covers approximately a third of the total pipeline route. The people of this region—the Secwepemc—hold what the Supreme Court of Canada calls "Aboriginal Title" to the land, which means the land has never been ceded or surrendered or treatied, and therefore is the proprietary interest of the Indigenous nation. The Supreme Court of Canada has found that an Indigenous Nation with Aboriginal Title must give consent to development on their lands. So the legal precariousness of Kinder Morgan to obtain all necessary permits and right-of-ways and to succeed in proceeding with construction hangs dangerously in the balance of Secwepemc proprietary rights and jurisdiction.

Against the backdrop of heightened uncertainty introduced by NoDAPL, there are clear signs that the environment for pipeline investment has shifted. Desjardins Bank has suspended lending to pipeline projects. And the Dutch bank ING responded to a letter sent by a coalition of Indigenous peoples and environmentalists to banks investing in Kinder Morgan by announcing it no longer plans to finance pipelines from Canadian tar sands. The main argument in this letter sent by the Indigenous coalition called on institutions to "avoid financing Indigenous rights abuses and climate change":

> As with DAPL—a highly controversial project constructed without the free, prior and informed consent of the Standing Rock Sioux Tribe and other affected tribal nations that source their drinking water from the Missouri River—the Trans Mountain pipeline expansion also poses a grave threat to Indigenous rights. First Nations that would be directly impacted by the route and port terminal are fighting the project in the courts and leading heated protests on the ground.[10]

The failures of industry to obtain consent from the Standing Rock Sioux is held up as warning of the continuing ecological devastation that Indigenous peoples oppose and will fight on their lands. ING's announcement followed one by Sweden's pension fund AP7 that it would divest from Trans Canada and five other companies because they were incompatible with the Paris climate agreement.

The Kinder Morgan Canada prospectus identifies several risks associated with the financial operations of the pipeline. Most of these risks are transformed and amplified by the declaration of sovereignty and resolute rejection of the project by the Secwepemc. The financial risks associated with the pipeline stemming from commodity supply and demand, market volatility, capital access, and corporate debt are magnified by the increased likelihood of delays and the possibility of outright cancellation that emerge from the Secwepemc declaration.

In Kinder Morgan's 2012 annual report, it estimated the Trans Mountain Expansion would be in operation by late 2017. In its 2016 report, this had been extended to December 2019, with construction estimated to begin in September 2017. The projected completion in the company's June 2017 credit agreement with twenty-four lenders was April 30, 2020. Then, in the spring of 2018 Kinder Morgan, frustrated by unpredicted delays and investment risks, suspended all "non-essential" activities related to the pipeline. In response, touting jobs and the national interest, the Canadian government announced its plans to purchase the Trans Mountain Pipeline and its planned expansion project. Kinder Morgan shareholders approved the CDN$4.5 billion sale in August 2018. This chapter was written before the sale of the pipeline, however, and focuses on the period of Kinder Morgan ownership.

DAPL crossed about 50 km of Sioux territory, where it generated high-profile resistance that cost ETP millions of dollars. The planned route of the

Trans Mountain Expansion traverses more than four times that distance through Secwepemcul'ecw. In an affidavit filed with the B.C. Supreme Court, a Trans Mountain representative states that each month of delay costs the company CDN$5.6 million. Beyond the direct costs incurred, delays create uncertainty about future costs. The company consistently projected that building the pipeline would cost US$5.4 billion, beginning with its 2012 annual report (10-K). This remained the estimate in its 2016 annual report. However, when the Canada–U.S. exchange rate is taken into account, this estimate represents a 32 percent increase from CDN$5.4 billion to CDN$7.15 billion. In Kinder Morgan Canada's credit agreement the estimate is CDN$7.4 billion. The costs will only increase if the start of construction is delayed. They will increase further if delays occur after construction has begun. Even more recently a court challenge quashed federal Cabinet approval for the pipeline due to the lack of meaningful consultation with Indigenous peoples and poor marine studies to determine oil tanker risks.[11]

Delays in building the pipeline make projected oil prices more uncertain. Recent dramatic fluctuations, plus the suggestion of several experts that prices will fall further, create uncertainty around the future earnings of the pipeline.[12] Although the expansion is fully subscribed for the near future, and Kinder Morgan touts the stability of its customers, Alberta's oil industry is in a state of great turbulence. With falling oil prices comes falling production and falling demand for pipeline capacity. Once again, this is worsened by the Secwepemc refusal, which is not only against this pipeline in particular, but aligned with the anti–tar sands movement. The campaign against the Trans Mountain Expansion is supported by several groups opposing extraction and transportation of Alberta tar sands oil. This campaign extends further, connecting with the movement to stop climate change. Successes by these movements will make extraction of Alberta bitumen costlier, squeezing the margins of midstream operators like Kinder Morgan.

The company is scrambling to account for Secwepemc opposition and related risks. But either due to a lack of understanding or—more likely—to their desire to downplay the risk to shareholders and the public, Kinder Morgan has publicly understated the real threat posed by Indigenous jurisdiction. Kinder Morgan Canada's recent IPO prospectus engages only with the question of "Aboriginal Relationships" rather than the riskier terrain of rights and jurisdiction. Further, discussions of Indigenous rights are completely absent from Kinder Morgan's annual management discussion and analysis of the Trans Mountain Expansion. While KML's prospectus identifies potential for opposition through the permitting process and in the courts, there is no mention of blockades, encampments, or other direct action tactics. The consequences of this blinkered view come into sharp relief when considering the Secwepemc's clear statement of opposition and intention to stop the pipeline using diverse means. The Secwepemc have a well-established history of using direct action to defend their sovereignty, including the high-profile

Gustefsen Lake standoff. Inspired by actions at Standing Rock, members of the Secwepemc Nation have come together under the name Tiny House Warriors to construct homes that will be placed in the path of the planned pipeline.

In the fall of 2016, in the midst of the struggle at Standing Rock, Kinder Morgan CEO Ian Anderson reflected to the media on the possibility of similar protests against the Trans Mountain Expansion: "I'd be naive if I didn't expect that," he told a CBC reporter. "Hopefully, it's peaceful. People have the right to express their views publicly and in that regard, we will accept and acknowledge that." But, "it's when it goes beyond that that we'll have to be prepared," he said, explaining that the company had held preparatory meetings with the RCMP.[13] The criminalization and pacification of land defenders is always a weapon of weakest resort because it reflects the shallow depths of settler colonialism. These lands are not British Columbia's or Canada's to sell: calling in the military—the Royal Canadian Mounted Police that have terrorized communities for centuries—is a scare tactic of violence meant to divert the Secwepemc from asserting their inherent jurisdiction to the land.[14]

The construction of the Dakota Access Pipeline encountered various degrees of resistance along its length.[15] Within the context of growing international movements to defend the planet and Indigenous rights, there is a high likelihood of similar, if not greater, opposition to the Trans Mountain Expansion. Given the evidence that NoDAPL put the continental oil industry on notice to the power of Indigenous jurisdiction, Kinder Morgan's muted public characterization of the risk posed to the Trans Mountain Expansion is likely part of the company's attempt to account for it. As the late great Secwepemc leader Arthur Manuel used to say, "the first risk mitigation strategy is always to *deny* Indigenous economic rights."[16]

Valuation: Colonialism's Accounting Problem

The risk of Indigenous jurisdiction is both a liability and an indispensible strength in the movement to defend the land and reshape how resource extraction is authorized throughout the continent. The market capitalization of corporations must constantly re-resolve its calculation of growth and decline with realities on the ground. A process of endless adjustment keeps capitalist enterprises in a state of flux and uncertainty as shifting social and ecological landscapes can affect that bold, single, all-encompassing number: the price of share value. But when this magical price encounters Indigenous jurisdiction, how is value reestablished?

Critical political economy has long maintained a distinction between productive and finance capital, between Main Street and Wall Street. The latter was considered "fictitious," while the former was "real."[17] Based on this distinction, value theorists tried to find the measure of real productivity that bypassed financial measures. Although impressive in both scope and detail, these alternative accountings have failed to unveil a fundamental quantitative basis for nominal financial values.[18] Like economists, capitalists also try to locate a basis or determinant for market valuations. However, they remain entirely within the domain of finance, with both productivity and capitalization denominated in financial values. Capitalization is routinely checked against productivity through quarterly earnings reports that get scrutinized by analysts and defended by executives. Between reports, capitalists devour information about events on the ground in anticipation of their effects on earnings. The buying and selling of shares, which constructs and responds to the share price, translates the expectations of capitalists. The volatility of the price is an expression of capitalist uncertainty about those expectations.

In the case of pipelines, capitalist uncertainty has grown at the same time as earnings and capitalization have fallen. Between 2014 and 2015, the average earnings of pipeline companies fell by 75 percent and average market capitalization fell by 35 percent.[19] Both recovered in 2016, although they remain below 2014 levels. Of greater significance, however, is an increased volatility of share prices. Before 2015, pipeline shares displayed lower price volatility than the market in general, expressing greater certainty by capitalists about conditions on the ground and their likely effect on returns. Conversely, since 2015 the situation has reversed. Now, pipeline shares are more volatile than the market as capitalists try to grapple with the changing situation of global oil demand and the greater awareness of—and resistance to—continental oil infrastructure.[20]

The changing situation concerns an old uncertainty: What knowledge will settler states produce to authorize their extraction of resources from Indigenous land? The valuation regimes of capital are not just technical figures produced by the strict rationale of economic scientists. Bigger and Robertson define *valuation regimes* as "the rules for and models of comparison" between forms of life that bring into focus the way that *value* is measured as a political act of performance. As they write, "Understanding value as the capacity to be measured or compared, lets us see how apparently incompatible value regimes flow from foundational choices about what is to be counted, visible, and present."[21]

This look at valuation is an important step for "recognizing the co-presence of valuation regimes" toward "contesting the expansion of the logics of capital on the terrain of nature."[22] This exercise is not simply about pointing out the incompatibility between Kinder Morgan and DAPL and Enbridge with Indigenous peoples' forms of life, but rather to intervene precisely in these places where such incompatibilities are resolved "in more or less violent or absurd ways."[23] These companies that seek to render Indigenous life *value-less* or *invaluable* avoid any need for reconciliation between competing claims to jurisdiction. If Indigenous life were counted, sovereignty would need to exist as a crucial index of value. For this reason, Bigger and Robertson urge us to understand the conversion of value earlier in the process, rather than just debate the measurements themselves. "The measurement of the thing is not as important as the settlement about what measurement is and what ruler will be used."[24] This much is clear in pipeline battles.

A parallel process of valuation is simultaneously taking place alongside the capitalist valuation that is fueling the pipeline construction boom. This parallel process is deemed a "threat" because Indigenous jurisdiction endangers capitalist production: the "production of hierarchical difference is crucial to the production of value," in this case because "to accumulate capital, capitalism needs the diverse materials and creative forces of natures ordered in a variety of positions within society, not just as commodities."[25] The legal rights of Indigenous peoples and the moral authority of their socioeconomic orders and sacred obligations to their lands throw up a valuation system that forces a radical recalculation of *both* the means by which to measure the *value* of a resource-extraction project (capitalization) and the *cost* of proceeding without Indigenous consent (physical/material/financial/climate). When pipeline projects externalize risk, they do so not only onto local Indigenous communities, but also to the continental infrastructure and the global ecology.

The existing Kinder Morgan pipeline that currently goes through Secwepemc territory has not been free from spills. These spills threaten the land and the water that many of the Secwepemc land use activities depend on. Defenders of the pipeline expansion—the plan is to twin the lines—contend that it will be the safest and most environmentally sound ever built. However, even the small threat of a spill carries excessive risk for the Secwepemc opponents of the expansion. More importantly, accepting the pipeline would change the relationship of the Secwepemc with the land, including their underlying title. As Art Manuel has noted, "Sleeping on your rights is an argument that the governments have used against [Indigenous peoples] in past litigation."[26] The Secwepemc peoples' declaration against the Trans Mountain pipeline expansion states that it constitutes an "infringement" that "can never be accepted or justified."

Indigenous peoples take into account their own systems of value and principles of land use and care. Asserting their values through the physical occupation of their lands in the path of pipeline construction not only reinforces Indigenous jurisdiction through its exercise and potent expression of authority. It also confronts the foundations of capitalism. Market capitalization is the fundamental expression of power in capitalist societies. Resistance takes the form of both intervening in capitalist valuations and challenging the capitalist value regime,[27] bringing colonial capitalism to its knees.

NOTES

1. See, for example, "Joe Oliver Concerned about a Canada Divided over Energy," *CBC News*, December 30, 2014, http://www.cbc.ca.
2. The IEA's analysis indicated that 80 percent of the total carbon dioxide (CO_2) emissions permissible through 2035 under the 450 Scenario—the IEA's widely used but conservative scenario in which the rise in average global temperature is limited to

2°C—was already "locked-in" by infrastructure currently in place or under construction in 2011. The IEA's 2011 World Energy Outlook explains: "Emissions that will come from the infrastructure that is currently in place or under construction can be thought of as 'locked-in' because they cannot be avoided without stringent policy intervention to force premature retirements, costly refurbishment and retrofitting or letting capacity lie idle to become economic. They are not avoidable, but avoiding them does not make economic sense in the current policy context." International Energy Agency, *World Energy Outlook, 2011* (Paris: OECD/IEA, 2011), 229, https://webstore.iea.org/world-energy-outlook-2011.

3. "Harper Looks to Asian Energy Markets after Keystone Delay," *CBC News*, November 14, 2011, http://www.cbc.ca; Carrie Tait, "New Energy Infrastructure 'Strategic Imperative' for Canada," *The Globe and Mail*, August 27, 2013, http://www.theglobeandmail.com/report-on-business/new-energy-infrastructure-strategic-imperative-for-canada/article13990628/.

4. John Paul Tasker, "Trudeau Cabinet Approves Trans Mountain, Line 3 Pipelines, Rejects Northern Gateway," *CBC News*, November 29, 2016, http://www.cbc.ca.

5. Chris Varcoe, "If You Can't Build Pipelines, Buy 'Pipe in the Ground,'" *Calgary Herald*, September 7, 2016, http://calgaryherald.com.

6. In September 2016, Enbridge announced plans to merge with Spectra Energy, a Houston-based pipeline and midstream company. The merger renders Enbridge the largest energy infrastructure company in North America and endows it with major new gas pipeline infrastructure to add to its extensive collection of liquids pipelines. JPMorgan Chase analyst Jeremy Tonet called the combined Enbridge-Spectra entity an "energy infrastructure colossus." The $37 billion Enbridge-Spectra merger is the third-largest mergers and acquisitions deal ever involving a Canadian company and the largest deal in Canadian oil patch history. The new company is said to have a $74 billion "growth backlog" of potential new development. The merger was completed on February 27, 2017. Geoffrey Morgan, "Enbridge Inc Deal to Buy Spectra Creates 'Energy Infrastructure Colossus' with $48 Billion of Future Projects," *Financial Post*, September 6, 2016, http://business.financialpost.com; "Enbridge and Spectra Energy Complete Merger" (press release), Enbridge, February 27, 2017, http://www.enbridge.com; Varcoe, "If You Can't Build Pipelines."

7. See the Tar Sands Treaty Alliance, http://www.treatyalliance.org/.

8. "Energy Transfer Partners LP (ETP) Q4 2016 Results—Earnings Call Transcript," Seeking Alpha, February 23, 2017, https://seekingalpha.com.

9. See Secwepemcul'ecw Assembly, https://www.secwepemculecw.org/.

10. The letter is available at https://d3n8a8pro7vhmx.cloudfront.net/ubcic/pages/1512/attachments/original/1497272052/Trans_Mountain_letter_June_2017.pdf?1497272052, 2.

11. Ainslie Cruickshank, David P. Ball, and Kieran Leavitt, "Federal Court of Appeal Quashes Trans Mountain Approval, Calling It 'Unjustifiable Failure,' in Win for First Nations, Environmentalists," *Toronto Star*, August 30, 2018.

12. On oil price projections, see, for example, "Oil Prices Will Remain Flat for Foreseeable Future, Deloitte Forecasts," *CBC News*, July 5, 2017, http://www.cbc.ca.

13. Kyle Bakx, "Kinder Morgan Braces for Standing Rock–Type Protests," *CBC News*, November 5, 2017, http://www.cbc.ca.

14. See, for example, the recent actions of the RCMP on Wet'suwet'en lands north west of Secwepemc territory: "Unist'ot'en Camp Awaits RCMP after Injunction Enforced at Gidimt;en Anti-pipeline Checkpoint, Mounties Enforcing Court Order to Allow Pipeline Company Access to Northern B.C. Road and Bridge," *CBC News*, January 8, 2019, http://www.cbc.ca.

15. Gregor Aisch and K. K. Rebecca Lai, "The Conflicts along 1,172 Miles of the Dakota Access Pipeline," *New York Times*, March 20, 2017, https://www.nytimes .com.

16. Arthur Manuel used to say this often in public lectures. See, for example, "Aboriginal Rights as Economic Rights: Whose Land Is Canada Selling?" lecture, November 24, 2016.

17. Jonathan Nitzan and Shimshon Bichler, "Capital Accumulation: Breaking the Duality of 'Economics' and 'Politics,'" in *Global Political Economy: Contemporary Theories*, ed. by Ronen Palan (New York: Routledge, 2000), 67–88.

18. For an overview and critique of these efforts by both mainstream and critical political economists, see Jonathan Nitzan and Shimshon Bichler, *Capital as Power: A Study of Order and Creorder* (London: Routledge, 2009), chaps. 5–7.

19. Calculations based on data from Bloomberg.

20. Volatility is measured using beta. A beta value for the pipeline sector was constructed using Bloomberg classifications and weighting the beta of individual companies by market capitalization. A beta value of less than one indicates lower volatility than a benchmark for the market—often the S&P 500. A beta of greater than one indicates higher volatility than the market. The beta for pipeline companies crossed one in 2015. In the first quarter of 2017, the value was 1.17. The volatility of pipeline shares is highly correlated, and the correlation has increased over time.

21. Patrick Bigger and Morgan Robertson, "Value Is Simple: Valuation Is Complex," *Capitalism Nature Socialism* 28, no. 1 (2017): 69.

22. Bigger and Robertson, "Value Is Simple."

23. Bigger and Robertson, "Value Is Simple."

24. Bigger and Robertson, "Value Is Simple," 71.

25. Rosemary Collard and Jessica Dempsey, "Capitalist Natures in Five Orientations," *Capitalism Nature Socialism* 28, no. 1 (2017): 80, 78.

26. Arthur Manuel, "Report on Canada's Self-government + Land Rights Policies at the Root of Canada's Opposition to the UN Draft Declaration on Indigenous Rights," Indigenous Networks on Economies and Trade, October 1, 2006, http://www.first nations.de/links.htm.

27. Nitzan and Bichler, "Capital Accumulation."

18

WHAT STANDING ROCK TEACHES US
ABOUT ENVIRONMENTAL JUSTICE

Jaskiran Dhillon

This essay was originally published in Items, *a digital forum of the Social Science Research Council, on December 5, 2017.*

We live in a historical moment marked by grave uncertainty about the fate of planet Earth. Our children and grandchildren are inheriting a world almost singularly defined by climate change. Temperatures are rising. Oceans are experiencing acidification. Arctic polar icecaps are melting faster than they should. Small island states are being swallowed up by rising sea levels. The American Psychological Association is mapping the mental health consequences of what they are calling "eco-anxiety." And, in the midst of this planet-wide crisis riddled with debates about the Anthropocene, Indigenous peoples and their long-standing resistance to environmental devastation are clear signposts of who should guide us into the future.[1]

One of the most recent and stark representations of Indigenous peoples' leadership concerning climate change is the historic and epic resistance to the Dakota Access Pipeline (DAPL) led by the Standing Rock Sioux.[2] This pipeline, now complete and already leaking, the struggle against it, and similar acts of violence against the land, water, sky, plants, animals, and ecosystems as a whole is far from over.[3] As Trump withdraws the United States from the Paris Agreement and systematically works to dismantle the Environmental Protection Agency, it should be evident that the interests of capital are what matter most to the U.S. government. In the wake of these governmental decisions, what does Standing Rock teach us about the environmental justice movements and why they must be led by and accountable to Native peoples?

Indigenous Sovereignty Is Environmental Justice

Standing Rock, I argue, illustrates that a fight for environmental justice must be framed, first and foremost, as a struggle for Indigenous sovereignty. As I have written elsewhere, the colonial violence that fostered the ruination of the planet has, for the most part, been blurred out of focus in public dialogue. An accurate examination of the social and political causes of climate change requires a close look at the history of genocide, land dispossession, and concerted destruction of Indigenous societies and cultural practices that accompanies the irreversible damage wrought by environmental destruction. Zoe Todd asks the fundamental question: "What does it mean to have a reciprocal discourse on catastrophic end times and apocalyptic environmental change in a place where, over the past five hundred years, Indigenous peoples faced the end of the worlds with the violent incursion of colonial ideologies and actions?"[4] Colonial systems of capitalist accumulation, tied directly to the invention of private property, opened the floodgates for "natural resources" to be transported, as Glen Coulthard explains, "from oil and gas fields, refineries, lumber mills, mining operations, and hydro-electric facilities located on the dispossessed lands of Indigenous nations to international markets."[5] The economic infrastructure in settler colonies, like the United States and Canada, depends on extractive industries. Indeed, Kyle Whyte points out that "in the US settler context, settler colonial laws, policies and programs are 'both' a significant factor in opening up Indigenous territories for carbon-intensive economic activities and, at the same time, a significant factor in why Indigenous peoples face heightened climate risks."[6] DAPL, then, must be viewed as the most recent incarnation of environmental harm that has found its legitimation and footing in colonialism and occupation.

A closer look at Standing Rock reveals the Sioux Nation never ceded the 1851 treaty lands that lie at the center of their opposition to DAPL. Nick Estes and Jeffrey Ostler remind us, "There is no question about the accuracy of Standing Rock's contention that the pipeline is being constructed across lands recognized as Sioux territory under the 1851 Treaty." Following in the footsteps of a long history of violence and encroachment on Indigenous homelands, Energy Transfer Partners, with the support of the federal government, violated this treaty relationship between the U.S. settler state and the Sioux Nation even though treaties are regarded by the U.S. Constitution as the "supreme law of the land." In a similar vein, Heidi Stark offers a critical analysis of the ways that the imposition of colonial law allowed the United States to increasingly undermine Indigenous authority and assert jurisdiction over Indigenous peoples and their lands—political moves in direct violation of treaty relationships that actively produce settler-state sovereignty over the land.[7] Stark also makes evident how the imposition of colonial law paved the way for the legalization of criminal actions of emerging settler states while casting Indigenous resistance as inherently unlawful and illegitimate.[8] The criminalization of Indigenous resistance, which reinforces the power and sanctity of settler law, became glaringly apparent at Standing Rock.

For example, the horrific violence enacted upon the Water Protectors in frontline resistance camps shows the lengths to which the state will go to quell resistance against industrial development projects and shut down perceived insurgencies and

claims to territory.[9] *The Intercept*'s series on Standing Rock and police violence
revealed that counterterrorism tactics were used at Standing Rock to undertake
intrusive and aggressive surveillance of Water Protectors who were criminalized
by state authorities. According to internal documents acquired through the investigation, police across at least five states were working in close collaboration with
the international mercenary security firm TigerSwan to spearhead a multifaceted
response to the growing resistance camps at Standing Rock.[10] Following Stark, this
projection of the Water Protectors at Standing Rock and their allies as criminal and
violent—essentially as a threat to the political authority of state power—enabled
the United States to divert attention from its own illegal actions and egregious violence against the Sioux Nation.[11]

This violent suppression of resistance at Standing Rock raises an essential question: How can we expect the same colonial government that is partnered with an
international mercenary security firm enlisted to brutally halt opposition to a pipeline project to work in the service of climate recovery? We can't. Our strongest
chance of restoring balance on the planet and respecting the interconnectedness
of all things, human and other than human, is to fervently advocate for justice for
Indigenous communities and return to them the power of governance—which
was violently apprehended through war, genocide, starvation, disease, abuse, the
dispossession of land, and forced repression of Indigenous communities on reservations. The only way to upend this form of sociopolitical and economic ordering, I argue, is through the reinstatement of Indigenous authority and sovereignty.

Ending Colonial Gender Violence Is
Fundamental to Environmental Justice

Once Indigenous sovereignty becomes placed front and center within movements
for environmental justice, the links between violence against Indigenous lands and
violence against Indigenous bodies, particularly the bodies of young women and
girls, becomes painfully clear. One of the first things I noticed pulling into Standing Rock during my first visit in August 2016 was the signage erected at the active
drilling sites. Two large signs flanking either side of the construction read: NO
MORE STOLEN SISTERS and VIOLENCE AGAINST THE LAND IS VIOLENCE AGAINST
WOMEN. While violence against women is often sidelined within environmental discussions, Indigenous resistance to extractive projects, like Standing Rock,
reveals that these forms of violence work in tandem with one another. Focusing
on colonial gender violence, Leanne Simpson reminds us of the ties between the
seizure of Indigenous homelands, gender violence, and extractive processes that
accompany capitalist colonialism: "You use gender violence to remove Indigenous
peoples and their descendants from the land, you remove agency from the plant
and animal worlds and you reposition aki [Annishnabeg for "the land"] as 'natural resources' for the use and betterment of white people."[12]

My interview with Zaysha Grinnell, a young Indigenous woman from Fort

Berthold reservation and a youth leader in the political resistance at Standing Rock, illustrated the links Simpson highlights when Zaysha spoke at length about the violence against Indigenous women and girls that goes hand in hand with the extractive industry. "I was about eight when the oil companies first came here and I noticed a difference right away. It felt unsafe because oil rigs were popping up everywhere. And it makes me really sad because this is all we have left—this tiny bit of land, and the government and companies are still trying to come in and use it and take it." She went on to explain, "When these oil companies come in they bring in the men. These men bring with them the man camps and with that comes violence and sex trafficking. Indigenous women and girls near the camps are really affected by this, and we are not going to put up with it." Young women like Zaysha are signaling the importance of having Indigenous women and youth, including two-spirit youth,[13] as leaders in the movement because of their insight into how environmental injury carries violence across multiple aspects of Indigenous life and living.[14] A struggle for environmental justice is a call to end structural colonial violence more broadly, and colonial gender violence against Indigenous women and girls must remain at the center of advocacy and political strategy in this movement.[15]

Indigenous Environmental Justice Defies a Purely Localized Analysis

The struggle at Standing Rock reverberated across the world. The movement brought international attention and media coverage to the Sioux's resistance efforts against the decimation of sacred burial sites, the ongoing encroachment of the U.S. government and private corporations on Native land, and the contamination of the Missouri River. One of the reasons this resonance carried so far and wide is because Standing Rock is only one of multiple frontlines of resistance that aim to conceive of decolonization as foundational to environmental justice. Indigenous peoples are leading the fight for environmental justice not just here on Turtle Island, but all over the globe.

In North Sikkim, India, for example, Lepcha Indigenous youth went on a hunger strike to protest against the Indian Power Ministry's plan to develop seven hydroelectric dams as a means to increase energy production in the Himalayan states.[16] Citing the failure of the Indian government to foster employment opportunities in a country beset by endemic poverty and deprivation, these Indigenous youth were critically questioning a state-directed development agenda that does not serve the interests of the community. They were able to garner enough international attention that four out of the seven hydroelectric projects were canceled.

Further exemplifying the plurality of a transnational Indigenous movement at the forefront of environmental action and climate justice,[17] Indigenous peoples in Cambodia are on the frontlines of halting rampant deforestation, land grabbing, illegal logging, and the granting of mining concessions. In the remote province of Ratanakiri, Indigenous communities are making visible the impacts of climate change that have already drastically altered their livelihoods and ways of living. They are calling attention to the contamination of food and water sources caused by development projects that have come alongside globalization—projects that are often positioned by the Cambodian government as beneficial for the economic prosperity of the country. Lack of rainfall has created dire conditions in a country where 80 percent of the population relies on agriculture.

One can also turn to Ecuador, and numerous other countries in South and Central America, where Indigenous peoples are vociferously staging a battle against neoliberal economic agendas that have devastated communities, increased poverty and inequality, and threaten the very existence of the Amazon. They are the makers of a political revolution that centers the universal right to water, the protection of biodiversity, and the redistribution of lands unjustly seized.

Taken together, this window into the multiple, worldwide struggles to protect the land, water, and air unquestionably shows us that environmental justice is firmly rooted in Indigenous political strategies advancing decolonization. Resistance efforts, like the one at Standing Rock, defy purely localized analysis. Importantly, they remind us of the symbolic and political power the #NoDAPL movement has that can inspire, legitimize, and speak to future similar resistance efforts across a range of locations. As the battle over our planet plays out, this window into resistance also sends a message about who should be leading us.

NOTES

1. In this essay, "Indigenous peoples" refers to the original inhabitants that occupied the land of Turtle Island (North America) prior to colonization. I am fully aware that this term does not signify a singular common identity or lived experience among people who are marked or self-identify as such. As Alice Feldman observes of the international Indigenous movement: "In international contexts, Indigenous peoples have sought to articulate a unifying and politically operational identity emanating from their shared experiences of colonialism and goals of self-determination, as well as the diversity of their localized experiences and immediate needs. They have drawn upon cultural traditions, both intact and fragmented, to construct and empower an overarching 'Indigenousness' that is simultaneously hybrid. Recognition of their identity as peoples and nations who have legitimate claims to the rights and means of sovereignty and self-determination constitutes the foundation of this collective consciousness and the claims it animates, and serves as a central vehicle for change." For further reading, see Alice Feldman, "Transforming Peoples and Subverting States: Developing a Pedagogical Approach to the Study of Indigenous Peoples and Ethnocultural Movements," *Ethnicities* 1, no. 2 (2001): 147–78 (quote from 150).

2. Katie Mazer et al., *Mapping a Many Headed Hydra: The Struggle over the Dakota Access Pipeline*, Infrastructure Otherwise Report no. 001 (2017), http://infrastructure otherwise.org, offers an excellent synopsis of the Dakota Access Pipeline and related pipeline projects.

3. For an account of the Keystone Pipeline oil spill in South Dakota, which leaked 200,000 gallons of oil, see Robinson Meyer, "200,000 Gallons of Oil Spill from the Keystone Pipeline," *The Atlantic,* November 16, 2017.

4. Zoe Todd, "Relationships," *Cultural Anthropology*, July 21, 2016, https://culanth .org/fieldsights/relationships.

5. Glen Coulthard, "For Our Nations to Live, Capitalism Must Die," *Unsettling America: Decolonization in Theory & Practice*, November 5, 2013, https://unsettlingamerica .wordpress.com.

6. Kyle Powys Whyte, "Is It Colonial Déjà Vu? Indigenous Peoples and Climate Injustice," in *Humanities for the Environment: Integrating Knowledges, Forging New Constellations of Practice*, ed. Joni Adamson and Michael Davis (London: Routledge, 2017), 90.

7. Heidi Kiiwetinepinesiik Stark, "Criminal Empire: The Making of the Savage in a Lawless Land," *Theory and Event* 19, no. 4 (2016), https://muse.jhu.edu/.

8. "The construction of Indigenous resistance as criminal activity produced an environment where Indigenous lands could be legally stolen and Indigenous leaders could be legally murdered under the dominion of settler laws": Stark, "Criminal Empire."

9. Kyle Powys Whyte, "The Dakota Access Pipeline, Environmental Justice, and U.S. Colonialism," *RED INK* 19, no. 1 (Spring 2017): 154–69.

10. These methods of deliberate political suppression took the form of aerial surveillance and radio eavesdropping, infiltration of camps and activist circles, and the reaping of information from social media—all of which fed directly into FBI and local police tactics of violent containment (e.g., water cannons, armored vehicles, rubber bullets, tear gas, attack dogs, the deployment of snipers, and physical road blockades). As the article explains, "the leaked materials not only highlight Tiger-Swan's militaristic approach protecting its client's interests but also the company's profit-driven imperative to portray the nonviolent water protector movement as unpredictable and menacing enough to justify the continued need for extraordinary security measures": Alleen Brown, Will Parrish, and Alice Speri, "Leaked Documents Reveal Counterterrorism Tactics Used at Standing Rock to 'Defeat Pipeline Insurgencies,'" *The Intercept*, May 27, 2017, https://theintercept.com.

11. For an excellent exposition of the hypersurveillance technology and tactics of criminalization used by settler states like the United States and Canada, including the positioning of Indigenous peoples as "extremists" and "domestic terrorists," see Shiri Pasternak, *Grounded Authority: The Algonquins of Barriere Lake against the State* (Minneapolis: University of Minnesota Press, 2017).

12. Leanne Betasamosake Simpson, "Not Murdered, Not Missing: Rebelling Against Colonial Gender Violence," March 5, 2014, https://www.leannesimpson.ca/.

13. According to Wilson, the term "two-spirit" is drawn from a traditional world view that affirms the inseparability of the experience of Indigenous peoples' sexuality from the experience of their culture and community. For further reflection, see Alex Wilson, "How We Find Ourselves: Identity Development and Two Spirit People," *Harvard Educational Review* 66, no. 2 (1996): 303–18.

14. See http://rezpectourwater.com/ for more information on the youth-led Rezpect Our Water campaign.

15. Erin Marie Konsmo and A. M. Kahealani Pacheco, *Violence on the Land, Violence on Our Bodies: Building an Indigenous Response to Environmental Violence* (Berkeley: Women's Earth Alliance; Toronto: Native Youth Sexual Health Network, 2016).

16. Mabel D. Gergan, "Precarity and Possibility: On Being Young and Indigenous in Sikkim, India," *Himalaya, the Journal of the Association for Nepal and Himalayan Studies* 34, no. 2 (2014): 67–80.

17. Indigenous People NGO Network, *The Rights of Indigenous Peoples in Cambodia* (UN Committee on the Elimination of Racial Discrimination, 2010).

V.
EDUCATION AND CRITICAL PEDAGOGIES

"Tipi." Photograph by Jaida Grey Eagle.

19

RED PRAXIS
LESSONS FROM MASHANTUCKET TO STANDING ROCK

Sandy Grande, Natalie Avalos, Jason Mancini,
Christopher Newell, and endawnis Spears

What affects one, affects all, so we stand together united.
—Nakai Clearwater Northup, Mashantucket Pequot, Youth Council

Our women have given our wombs, our breast milk, our whisper-
sung lullaby prayers, our ceremony and our community for this day:
to follow our youth as they lead us into a sustained future. From our
corner of the world in Mashantucket, this has given us the means
to talk more urgently about empowerment, land and fishing rights,
sovereignty, and the inherent power of our women called forward to
protect mother earth.
—endawnis Spears, Mashantucket Pequot Museum and Research Center

We write as a diverse group of scholars and cultural workers who work both in
and outside the academy. In the fall of 2016, against the shadow of Standing Rock,
we came together around our mutual work and concern for Native communities,[1] Indigenous sovereignty, water, land, and each other to convene a teach-in on
#NoDAPL at Connecticut College, a central location among us in New London,
Connecticut.[2] In the spirit of the prayer camps, we aimed to (re)create a communal,
collaborative, and educational space inclusive of youth, elders, scholars, and community members that was intentionally diverse at the same time it stayed grounded
in the history, knowledge, and experience of Indigenous peoples.

The teach-in provided a space to present a history and context for Standing
Rock and to hear how local Indigenous peoples were affected by it. The diversity
of perspectives and experiences created an entry point to discuss the interconnected web of dispossession as well as the kind of transformative resistance that is
possible by working in coalition. For example, Christopher Newell's testimony on
Passamaquoddy land disputes and endawnis Spears's call to recognize the earth as

our mother remind us that these settler projects continue to affect Native nations across the United States and the Americas. The overarching goal was to develop collective understanding of the parallel mechanisms of settler dispossession faced by Indigenous peoples locally, nationally, and even globally.

It has been over a year since the teach-in and questions regarding the significance and impact of Standing Rock have continued to circulate in our circles and the broader public discourse: What did the "victory" at Standing Rock teach us? What are the most effective means of intervention: Peaceful protest? Direct action? Ceremony and prayer? As the Trump administration takes greater aim at existing environmental protections while also emboldening corporate tricksters such as Energy Transfer Partners,[3] such questions have taken on greater urgency. Across the nation, peoples have rallied against what is perceived as a rise in authoritarianism: the abuse of executive power, the disregard for human rights, the enforcement of arbitrary borders and boundaries, and the ongoing treatment of land and water as corporate commodities.

For us, however, such developments are understood not as an aberration but rather as an extension of the settler colonial project. The campaign for "Native elimination" has always been waged through the collective actions of presidents, statesmen, generals, university officials, and church leaders.[4] For more than two hundred years, the settler state has relentlessly worked, through strategies of religious conversion, child abduction, forced assimilation,[5] and the rule of law, to "kill the Indian and save the man." This context informs our collective understanding of the colonial present as well as our ongoing struggles to defend Indigenous land and ways of life. That said, in the time that has passed between Standing Rock and now, we have all felt compelled to reexamine the myriad ways in which the most recent expressions of "Native elimination" impact our work and communities.

While, as Native and non-Native peoples, we are differently situated in our relationships to Indigenous communities, we are all educators. And, as educators, we each engage pedagogy as both land based and place specific, literally grounding our teachings in the history and context of where we work: the traditional territories of the Pequot or "people of the shallow water."[6] What is now known as southeastern Connecticut were once Pequot villages dotted along the coastline, including a place called Nameag. In 1646, the English settled at Nameag and shortly afterward relocated five villages, renamed Nameag as New London and the Pequot River, the Thames. Now the college occupies this place/space, and the majority of students, faculty, staff, and townspeople who walk its grounds have no knowledge that they walk on Pequot land.[7]

Beyond this common ground, we undertake the questions and issues raised by Standing Rock from different perspectives and disciplinary fields. Specifically, as a scholar of Native American and Indigenous religious traditions, Natalie Avalos (Chicana/Apache descent)[8] thinks about the metaphysical dimensions of Native resistance and how to translate this dynamic to students as one that shapes earth and human relationships. As museum educators, Jason Mancini, endawnis Spears (Diné, Ojibwe, Chickasaw), and Christopher Newell (Passamaquoddy) look to influence social change by making the lived experience of Native peoples—historical and contemporary—integral to the ways in which Indigenous educational institutions engage the broader public. And, as a scholar of Native studies and education, Sandy Grande (Quechua) pushes us to consider the pedagogical implications of Indigenous social and political life. Our collective work evidences the ways in which the issues central to Standing Rock are not limited to a geographic location.

The spirit and teachings of the movement have penetrated and reinvigorated our ongoing work to connect peoples with the spaces and places they inhabit, reanimate hidden histories and cultural landscapes, and amplify the effective leadership and voices of Native peoples. As we work beyond the teach-in we focus more expressly on challenging the structures and politics of Indigenous erasure. We begin by drawing parallels between the history of Native dispossession among the Pequots and Standing Rock, drawing forth historical continuities of Indigenous resistance. Next, we offer two examples of how Standing Rock has informed and animated our respective efforts to teach about Native peoples and issues. Finally, we end with discussion of how the teachings of Standing Rock are relevant well beyond the issue of the pipeline, speaking to the more generalized concern of a settler state still intent on the eliminative logics of accumulation and extraction.

Making Native Histories Present

> What the Standing Rock movement provided Indigenous peoples, not just in the United States, but around the world, is an opportunity, a foot in the door, a spotlight, a chance to engage in a conversation about Indigenous issues in a meaningful way. We are often denied the opportunity to talk about any kind of topic that has resonance to our shared experiences and daily lives. "Americans" love to ask Indians about their jewelry, their spirituality, their long black hair and high cheekbones, their dances and "costumes." What they are more ignorant of or more reluctant to talk about, is their actual lived experience. The meaningful. The deep. The colonization. The denied access to our sacred lands, to our languages, to healthy bodies. The exploitation of our dead. What the Water Protectors and the social movement they sparked gave us was an opportunity to talk about something real.
> —endawnis Spears, Mashantucket Pequot Museum and Research Center

Glancing back from Standing Rock to Jacksonian America, the struggle to protect and retain unceded Native land was in full effect in the north as Indian removal was

SANDY GRANDE, NATALIE AVALOS, JASON MANCINI, CHRISTOPHER NEWELL, AND ENDAWNIS SPEARS

being brutally undertaken in the south. By 1822 New England's tribes had already been enumerated by the U.S. War Department and were being "managed" by state governments through appointed "guardians." Among other affairs, guardians oversaw the division and leasing of tribal lands to non-Natives, a corrupt process that opened the floodgates of settler access to tribal lands and resources. It was against this backdrop in 1833 that a young Methodist minister and Pequot Indian, Rev. William Apess, and members of the Mashpee Wampanoag Tribe attempted to regain legal and political control over Mashpee lands in Cape Cod, Massachusetts.

In their efforts to reclaim land and jurisdiction, Apess and the Mashpee peacefully confronted a group of white men who were stealing timber. For this action, the men were arrested and imprisoned for "assault and trespass" as well as "tried and convicted . . . for riot" on tribal lands (O'Connell 1992, 193, 200). The events were reported in the news in decidedly uneven terms. For example, while one local paper described the Indians as "troublesome" and engaging in "war-like movements," another account underscored the issue of Indian sovereignty writing, "we are still at a loss to know under what law these Indians were found guilty of riot, in preventing their own wood from being carried off their own land" (O'Connell 1992, 198, 202).

In response, Apess also produced his own chronicle of events published in 1835 as "Indian Nullification of the Unconstitutional Laws of Massachusetts Relative to the Marshpee Tribe; or, The Pretended Riot Explained" (O'Connell 1992, 163–274). His account detailed the abuses of white settlers against their "red brethren," the encroachment on Indian lands and rights, and the misrepresentation of Native peoples and issues in the media. Apess's analysis noted the ways in which the nonviolent protest of the Indians was manipulated in the Massachusetts press writing, "our affairs got into the public prints, and it was reported through the whole land that there were hostile movements among the Indians at Cape Cod. . . . All the editors were very willing to speak on the favorite topic of Indian wrongs; but very few of them said anything about redress" (O'Connell 1992, 190).

The parallels between the incident at Mashpee (1833) and Standing Rock are noteworthy insofar as they indicate how little has changed in terms of the (mis)representation of Indian resistance in nearly two hundred years. That is, nonviolent actions to (re)claim Indigenous land and sovereignty are still being met by swift and violent state suppression that is both under- and misreported by the media. As discouraging as this might seem, the trials of Apess and the Mashpee also evidence how Indigenous resistance and agency have been unrelenting in the face of settler violence. Their example not only points to historical continuities among forms of Native resistance—including nonviolent action and ceremony—but also suggests a praxis of Indigenous protest that, if drawn upon, may be instructive for contemporary movements.

For instance, from the Ghost Dance to the American Indian Movement, Native peoples in the United States have consistently operationalized religious practice by employing ceremony as a form of resistance and protest (Irwin 2008; Kelley 2014). In the Indigenous-led movements of Decolonize Oakland and (Un)Occupy Albuquerque (sister movements to Occupy Wall Street), for example, prayer and ceremony were employed as integral components of a broader critique of economic exploitation and empire. Similarly, the Idle No More (INM) movement in Canada staged public ceremony as a means of drawing attention to the ongoing violations of Native treaty rights and sovereignty,[9] wherein round dances transformed malls and town squares into spaces of decolonial contention. Indigenous peoples in the United States acted in solidarity with their relatives to the north, staging similar gatherings aimed at publicly decrying the continued abuses of settler states. Prayer and ceremony were salient features within and across these movements, serving as one of the central means by which Native and non-Native peoples came together around the shared goal of decolonization.

The grounding of Indigenous resistance in spiritual practice has been a persistent feature of Indigenous protest and social movement building. When the #NoDAPL warriors positioned themselves as "protectors," they were foregrounding their responsibility to be good relatives, which, in part, means to protect and nurture the life force of the earth as a spiritual entity. Similarly, Standing Rock emerged as a "prayer camp" because the grounds in question are sacred, a site of ceremony and ancestral knowledge. The lands and water of the Oceti Sakowin have their own teachings and are understood as both essential and instructive to life. Thus, to protect them is to protect life.

Indigenous peoples from all over the world gathered at the prayer camps to collectively honor their relations, supplicating the spirit world for guidance as they assumed their roles as protectors of the land. In such contexts, ceremony is often enacted as a means of coalescing power; song, dance, and prayer become part of a decolonial practice of stewardship. Those gathered prayed protection into being, not only to protect the treaty lands of the Oceti Sakowin but also for humanity's collective need for water, and for the water itself. Through this decolonial reclamation of sacred place and purpose, they assert their right and responsibility to serve as protectors. These assertions inhere both ontological claims—this is who Indigenous peoples are and what they need to do to remain Indigenous peoples—and epistemological claims: the land has knowledge that is instructive and guides Indigenous peoples to live in a good way.

Lakota scholar Vine Deloria Jr. marked the chasm of difference between "Western" and Native peoples as being partly rooted in their distinct metaphysics, the first ordered through time and the latter through place (Deloria 1994). This understanding helps to illuminate the incommensurability between Indigenous world views that perceive land as relation and "Western" conceptions of land as inert matter (not alive and therefore without rights). Which raises the question: How do we as educators challenge not only pedagogical approaches that serve to erase, marginalize, and misrepresent Native American peoples and histories but also the more deeply held belief systems that endanger Indigenous lifeways?

In the next section we discuss how we undertake this question within our distinct yet overlapping roles and professional fields. Specifically, we provide two examples of how the complex politics of Standing Rock resonate with but also deepen our approaches to teaching. The first provides an example of teaching in the public sphere, the Mashantucket Pequot Museum, and the second in a more traditionally academic one, Connecticut College. Both of these institutional spaces have historically served projects of white supremacy and Native dispossession. We demonstrate how the inverse is possible. Considered together the examples illustrate the importance of historical context, the centrality of Native ethics and religious lifeways, and the increased salience of Indigenous or Red Pedagogies (see Grande 2015). In this way, history, ideology, and immaterial life provide ways to contextualize the Native present.

Red Pedagogy and Praxis

The Museum as Site of Decolonial Praxis

> As an educator, I have witnessed the anger of many college students after they learn the real history of Native peoples. They demand to know why they were never taught this history before. Americans don't necessarily choose to be ignorant about Native America; the system of education sets them up for it.
> —Christopher Newell, Mashantucket Pequot Museum and Research Center

When the youth from the Mashantucket Pequot Tribal Nation began making plans to travel to North Dakota to join the Standing Rock camp, they did so with the knowledge that the present is entwined with the past. They understood that this war against Native peoples and expressed desire of colonizers to possess Native resources and homelands began with their ancestors and the Pequot War of 1636–37. Understanding that this narrative of conflict, dispossession, and erasure has repeated itself ceaselessly over the centuries, the young warriors took to the road, traveling together with the support and allyship of the museum director, Jason Mancini.[10]

While the youth understood how their histories were connected, Standing Rock provided a backdrop against which the depth of American ignorance was revealed. That is, before Standing Rock, the plight of continued Native dispossession was virtually unknown to most of the nation. As museum educators we often contend with the ways in which U.S. history is structured and taught to confine Native peoples to the past, making the Native present appear impossible. Moreover, because southeastern Connecticut was a point of first contact, many museum patrons have never met an Indigenous person. They base their knowledge on what they have learned in school: the story of the first Thanksgiving, manifest destiny, and westward expansion and the "discovery" of America, all of which are fundamentally rooted in the mythical claims of *terra nullius* and white supremacy.[11]

Such false narratives function to normalize Indigenous dispossession. The emergence of Standing Rock suggests that teaching U.S. history accurately, with intellectual integrity and an eye toward Indigenous erasure and misrepresentation, is more important now than ever. The experience and witnessing of the Mashantucket Pequot delegation inspired and served as a catalyst for the museum to develop new programming and partnerships more directly aimed at accurately narrating the history of southeastern Connecticut as not only Pequot land but also occupied territory.[12] The broader public awareness and curiosity engendered by Standing Rock provided the latitude that staff needed to more pointedly draw attention to the colonialist nature of school curricula (e.g., the erasures from history texts, the prevalence of Indian mascots in schools) and to the ongoing denial of access to traditional lands (and therefore lifeways) for Native nations in Connecticut, Rhode Island, Massachusetts, New York, and beyond.

For most visitors, a trip to the Pequot Museum is their first opportunity to learn about Native history and culture from Indigenous peoples and perspectives. Indeed, the museum was established to tell the Pequot story from a Pequot point of view, designed to speak truth to power and act as a voice of advocacy to change the narrative of Native histories, peoples, and cultures. Moreover, as a tribally owned and operated facility, the museum not only has a responsibility to promote more accurate tellings of history but also to underscore that "American History Starts Here!" on Pequot land.[13] That is, Pequot territory is ground zero in the ongoing struggle between Native peoples and settler society with the Pequot War standing as one of the most definitive moments in the formation of the United States. Thus, while Standing Rock may have called the world's attention to the ways in which colonization is ongoing, the Pequot War marks the beginning of the unrelenting march of settler colonialism across the nation. For this reason among many, museum staff hold that the teaching of pre-Revolutionary American history—in Connecticut public schools and beyond—should begin with and center Pequot history.

Specifically, the Pequot War (1636–37), the Treaty of Hartford (1638), and the creation of the first "sequestered" or "reserved" lands in Connecticut—Golden Hill (1639), Noank (1651), and Mashantucket (1666)—should be taught as decisive moments in the history of Indigenous dispossession that not only alienated Native peoples from their homelands and each other but also cleared the path for white settlement. By 1856 when the Pequot came to the stunning realization that seven hundred (of around nine hundred) acres had been auctioned off, the tribe petitioned the state of Connecticut against the "Land Sale" imploring, "We have been bereved of our native land, we have been torn from the breast of our mother Country which has nursed our generations for many a century, yet notwithstanding all this, our bosom treasures has been torn from our arms without our consent and our bread has been torn from our mouths without any Justification whatever" (Connecticut General Assembly Papers).

The strategy of "remove to replace" as theorized by Patrick Wolfe (2006), lies at the heart of the settler colonial "logic of elimination" (388).[14] Played out over five hundred years through strategies of accumulation and extraction, eliminatory logics have resulted in the loss of over nine million acres of Indian land in what is now the region of southern New England. And for Native peoples, the loss of land results in the loss of life. Thus, teaching about the Pequot War, especially in Connecticut schools, not only challenges historical narratives that champion settler aggression as American exceptionalism but also explores how the violence of colonization unfolded and continues to impact the local Native communities. Students should know that "history" begins long before the arrival of the first settlers and that this land was home to Indigenous peoples for at least twelve thousand years prior.

The significance of these historical continuities is the reason why museum staff organize exhibits and events around broader themes and "key issues in Indian Country" as opposed to chronological orderings that reify false narratives of American progress. Programs invite audiences to reflect on their own presence on and occupation of Indigenous homelands, peeling back the layers of settler implication while also simultaneously revealing the rich cultural space of Native peoples and traditions hidden in their plain sight. While museum staff have long considered ways to engage the broader public in issues of contemporary significance to Native peoples, Standing Rock allowed these efforts to be reinvigorated in extraordinary ways that deepened not only public awareness but also our own commitments and relations with local Indigenous communities, scholars, and educational institutions. Together we are working with local teachers to rethink and revise school curricula, moving away from decontextualized notions of "culture" and focusing on history, human rights, and social justice. Through such efforts, the museum is leaning into a future that honors Indigenous sovereignty, which is a way of saying land, water, and all of their relations.

The Metaphysics of Resistance: Teaching Native American and Indigenous Religious Traditions

Dr. Natalie Avalos teaches several courses on Native American and Indigenous religious traditions at Connecticut College. The goal of these courses is to understand a Native American and Indigenous philosophical present, given overlapping histories of colonialism. Her approach provides another example of making Native voices, world views, and resistance visible but in a traditional classroom setting. In one course, Earth Justice: Indigenous Stewardship around the Globe, she focuses on environmental dispossession as another effect of settler logics of elimination. Indigenous philosophies of land/living serve as the foundation for challenging dominant assumptions about land as inert and for understanding earth justice as an existential goal tethered to human and other-than-human survival. Native-centered narratives about the responsibility to maintain good relations with the spiritual forces immanent in the land help students understand Indigenous views of land as having a sacred dimension that is morally instructive. For example, some readings explore Indigenous views of plants as persons and teachers, such as the Three Sisters: corn, beans, and squash. As understood by the Pequot, the familial relationship of these sister plants asks that they be grown together, and science has confirmed that the coplanting produces a natural nitrogen cycle that fertilizes the soil, preventing depletion.[15] As students consider the ethical instructions provided by these three sisters, they begin to recognize the value and mutually beneficial outcomes of interdependence broadly construed.

Integral to understanding Indigenous perspectives is exploring how the universe is perceived as alive and sentient. That is, the material world is understood to be a physical expression of the immaterial, a distinct expression of life force or "spirit," referred to as wakan tanka by the Lakota, usen by the Apache, and manutoo by the Pequot (Deloria 1994; Deloria and Wildcat 2001; DeMallie and Parks 1987; Cordova 2007). Since all persons, human and other-than-human (i.e., plants, animals, rivers, winds, mountains), are expressions of spirit, they are understood to be interconnected and contingent. Here, the individual is understood as coextensive with a larger social body that is at once material and immaterial. In times of need, the people use prayer and ceremony to propitiate the spirit world, asking for strength and guidance. In return for all that the land provides, the people act as good stewards, protecting and nurturing the life force within it. In short, the land looks after the people and the people look after the land in a mutually self-sustaining, reciprocal relationship.

While spirit is understood to be a fundamental characteristic of the greater universe, it is also particular to place, as illustrated in peoples' origin stories. Through prayer, ceremony, and other communications, Native peoples come to learn and honor the proper protocols for living on their land (Deloria and Wildcat 2001; Kelley 2014). These religious lifeways are revelation based, emerging through ongoing conversations between the people and the spirit world. Maintaining reciprocal relationships to sacred lands of cultural significance to the tribe—as a place of origin, revelation, and/or collective memory—is central to everyday life. In this way, Native religious practice is dynamic, always changing to meet the needs of the community.

Given the (literally) grounded nature of Indigenous religious life, teaching about it not only requires transmission of tribally specific religious views and ethics but also a context for understanding the persecution of Native religion by settler colonial forces. The devoutly monotheistic pilgrims, conquistadors, and various Christian missionaries framed Indigenous metaphysical worlds as flawed and "primitive" knowledge systems, which, in turn, justified Native dispossession. Like the criminalization of Native protest referred to above, Native religion was systematically outlawed through the Religious Crimes Code of 1883. What settlers did not realize was that because Native religious practice is experiential and the spirit world is an immanent dimension of land, it can never be destroyed.[16]

Course texts and films help students explore how Indigenous religious life continued in secret or veiled ways among many tribes as well as how contemporary efforts for religious continuity help to strengthen relationships within communities, supporting mobilizations of anticolonial resistance. By making the relationship between the criminalization of Native religions and cultural genocide more salient, students begin to understand religious continuity as a profound form of Indigenous protest. Such teaching is, thus, by definition, not just "interdisciplinary" or justice oriented but rather tethered to the deepest questions of meaning, the sacred, and ultimate concern.

By putting the metaphysical insights that come from and with teaching Native American religious traditions in conversation with local/national Native histories, we are able to counter the profoundly limited views of the universe as inert matter so normativized in settler society. If we want to effectively address climate change and other forms of environmental destruction, we have to consider how such a materialistic view abets the malevolence of empire: unsustainable growth, reckless development, human rights violations, and extractive economies. The dispossession of conquest in the Americas is born out of the same set of ethics that bore unmanaged resource extraction. If we want to fight climate crises then we need to reevaluate our ethics, not only in terms of human-to-human relationships but also human-to-land and human-to-water relations.

Standing Rock teaches us that understanding the value of interdependence among peoples and the nonhuman world is critical. The metaphysics of Indigenous stewardship force us to reckon with the ways in which the land is both spirit and sovereign, exposing the limits of settler logics. When we accept that land is sentient, alive, and watching us, we better understand its significance as a place of revelation; land is conversant with human life and not a passive object for use and abuse. We learn to contemplate the possibility that immaterial forms of power transcend human authority and that the land itself may actually be a space for listening, guidance, and divination. Students, moreover, are left with the realization that the burden of environmental justice cannot fall to Indigenous peoples alone; the teachings implore them to reflect on how the health and well-being of all peoples is interdependent with the health and well-being of the planet. In this way, the centering of Indigenous religious life through prayer and ceremony at Standing Rock wages a metaphysical war against settler colonialism.

> Indigenous struggles against the settler state, against capitalist accumulation and extraction represent the front line of critical praxis. The struggle calls all of us to stage and register our collective voices and bodies against Native elimination. Against corporate and capitalist greed that is bleeding the earth dry. That is raping our grandmother. That is intent on normalizing a state of precarity for peoples and beings made most vulnerable by the false promise of an America that never was.
> —Sandy Grande

Beginning with the teach-in, the Standing Rock movement both reenergized and ignited new collaborations among our various work sites: the museum, the college, local schools, and the Mashantucket Pequot reservation community. The overwhelming and positive response to our collective teachings across these spaces suggests a deepening desire among the broader public to learn and to learn more accurately about Native peoples, histories, and cultures. It is, however, a constant challenge that requires an exhausting level of vigilance as the desire to make "the Native" disappear—to forget, deny, and disavow Indigeneity—is so deeply ingrained as the default setting of settler logics. Even in moments when the nation's history of racial terror returns to haunt the present, Native peoples are erased. For example, in the wake of the "Unite the Right" rally (2017) staged by white nationalists in Charlottesville, Virginia, "race talk" once again dominated public discourse. For the most part, however, talk turned around the familiar and false binary of race and Black–white, wherein slavery is discussed as the "original sin" of the nation and the civil rights movement as the horizon of democracy. While such issues are of grave importance, erased from this version of history is the nation's centuries' long war against Native peoples, the prior and enduring sovereignty of Indigenous peoples, and the continued occupation of their lands.

Such omissions and misrepresentations, if addressed at all, are most often "corrected" by inviting Indigenous peoples into the fold, adding their perspectives and voices to the multicultural narrative of "America." Strategies of recognition and inclusion do little to address the more fundamental question of Indigenous sovereignty. That is, Native peoples have long demonstrated that their central desire is not to be included into the settler state, but rather to have their prior and enduring sovereignty abided and acknowledged.

Toward this end, we advocate critical Indigenous pedagogies grounded in the fundamental connections among place, power, and knowledge that require educators to take interruptive aim at the settler logics that pervade schools and society. Making such conceptual and pedagogical shifts requires a contestation of settler logics, particularly as transmitted through multicultural discourses of inclusion

SANDY GRANDE, NATALIE AVALOS, JASON MANCINI, CHRISTOPHER NEWELL, AND ENDAWNIS SPEARS

that privilege a "tolerance for difference" over analyses of power. For example, Trump's now infamous claim that the Charlottesville rally evidenced "blame" and "bad people" on "both sides" cast a spotlight not only on his own convictions, but also on the dangers of a politics that refuses to acknowledge relations of power and domination. That is, one that parodies justice through (false) claims to impartiality, moral equivalence, and "diversity." Actual resistance demands an understanding of history through relations of power. Without such a commitment, young people will continue to be enlisted into "the great lies of America: that we are a nation of laws and not random power, that we are governed by representation and not executive order; and that we stand as a self-determined citizenry and not blood or aristocracy" (Grande 2015, 50).

Standing Rock demonstrates the persistence of these settler logics. Through their actions and inactions, the United States violated the treaty rights of the Oceti Sakowin as well as denied their religious freedom, their right to protect what is sacred. In this sense, Standing Rock also demands a reconsideration of how we teach about the (im)material world. Even if some peoples do not have experiences of the sacred and its power, others do. And while we might not be able to reconcile these competing experiences, we can acknowledge that when the earth and its inhabitants are treated with respect and dignity, we all benefit. Everyone depends on the earth for food, clothing, and shelter and relies on its cycles of days, months, and years to carry us through life. One need not perceive the world as sacred in order to see that we are sustained by the plants, the animals, the trees, the mountains, and the waters. They give us life. We need them in order to live.

From the Pequot's refusal to relent to the New England colonists, to the Oceti Sakowin's refusal of Lewis and Clark, Native peoples struggle against settler descendants in New England, Bismarck, and across this land who are given license to enact white supremacy every day. Among our own efforts to address these aims, Sandy Grande continues her work through her support of the *Defenders of the Water School*,[17] started by Alayna Eagle Shield on the ground at Standing Rock, Natalie Avalos continues to develop critical Indigenous pedagogies that not only articulate earth-centered ethics but also Native voices and epistemologies as generative sites of resistance in the classroom, and Jason, endawnis, and Chris continue their work on "narrative change" with their new partnership (the Akomawt Educational Initiative) through a growing set of new alliances with the University of Connecticut, Connecticut College, and the Upstander Project, revising and Indigenizing K–12 Native studies curricula across the region.

All of the above underscores how Standing Rock was and is so much more than a people's struggle against a pipeline. For us the struggle is about:

> The refusal of alternative facts—that we need more fossil fuel, more extraction, more oil; that climate change is a myth; and that we should trust a multibillion dollar industry to tell the truth about renewable energy.

The reclamation of history and the acknowledgment of Indigenous peoples'
centuries' long service on the front lines of settler encroachment.

The rule of law and this nation's obligation to not only abide by Native treaties
but also their own laws and policies (e.g., the Paris agreements).

The refusal of state violence such as the use of hired mercenaries to serve and
protect the interests of corporations and property, not peoples.

The future of this so-called democracy and the right to speak freely, protest,
demand, resist, and protect, outside of zones, walls, and perimeters.

The recognition of the power of the people and strengthening solidarities
between Black and Indigenous communities that remain in the sight lines of
settler desire. This is about liberation.

Finally, the struggle is about land and water. It is about the Mini Sosi, the Missouri River that gives life to so many. We struggle for her life and the right to practice our collective responsibility to protect her for all that she provides. Which is to say, it is about ceremony, prayer, and Native women as carriers of water who also give life. We work in honor of them, the waters of the Quinnitukqut, and the lands of Nameag.

Water Is Life.

NOTES

1. For the purposes of this chapter, the terms Indigenous and Native peoples will be used interchangeably. The UN Special Rapporteur, José Martínez Cobo (1981, 1) initiated the following working definition of Indigenous peoples: Indigenous communities, peoples, and nations are those that, having a historical continuity with preinvasion and precolonial societies that developed on their territories, consider themselves distinct from other sections of societies once prevailing in these territories or parts of them. They form at present nondominant sectors of society and are determined to preserve, develop, and transmit to future generations their ancestral territories, and their ethnic identity, as the basis of their continued existence as peoples, in accordance with their own cultural patterns, social institutions, and legal systems (as cited in Dhillon 2017, 41–42).

2. Across the time of Standing Rock and the writing of this chapter there have been three teach-ins on the campus of Connecticut College. The first teach-in, on which this chapter is loosely based, included college faculty Natalie Avalos (religious studies), Sandy Grande (education), Michelle Neely (English), and Rijuta Mehta (English); Mashantucket Pequot Museum and Research Center staff Jason Mancini (director/archaeologist), Christopher Newell (educator), and endawnis Spears (educator); and multiple members from the southeastern Connecticut Indigenous community.

3. "Trickster" figures in Indigenous literatures and oral traditions are seen as actors

that seek to either undermine or challenge protagonists, foiling, "tricking," or causing them harm. Symbolically, they may represent the thwarting forces present in daily life that we must continually struggle with.

4. See Wolfe (2006).

5. Forced assimilation was enacted through a variety of means including mission and boarding schools and imposed citizenship. Both functioned to replace Indigenous understandings of land and kinship with settler capitalist notions of private property and liberal notions of individual human/civil rights.

6. The Pequot are a coastal tribe that has maintained rich maritime traditions centered on the estuaries of eastern Long Island Sound. Today Pequot territory is inhabited by three distinct, but related, polities: the Mashantucket Pequot Tribal Nation, the Eastern Pequot Tribal Nation, and the Mohegan Tribe.

7. As noted by Patrick Wolfe (2006) "renaming" is a central feature of the "remove to replace" logics of settler colonialism.

8. My mother was born in Mexico to a Nahua Indian father from Veracruz and French/Spanish mother from Jalisco. My father was born in California to a Mescalero Apache mother and mestizo father, both of whom were from New Mexico. Because I was raised in the Bay Area away from both sides of my Indigenous roots and communities I identify as a "Chicana of Apache descent," to note that I am not an enrolled citizen of this Native nation. I include these details to mark how contemporary Native identity, particularly mixed and urban Indian identity, is fraught in diaspora.

9. Idle No More is a woman-led grassroots movement rooted in Native sovereignty that seeks to protect the land and waters against abusive forms of environmental development. The call to rally Indigenous communities in this fight was initiated by Nina Wilson, Sylvia McAdam, Jessica Gordan, and Sheelah McLean in response to a Canadian bill that would strip Native tribes of their rights to decide how energy corporations would use tribal lands.

10. While to the outside world, the director with a PhD may outrank the young traditionalists, in the world of Native social movements that Standing Rock helped to illustrate, the youth were both the originators and leaders.

11. For example, see the work of Shear et al. (2015). *Terra nullius* is a Latin term that means "land belonging to no one" or "no man's land." The construct was used to frame land in the Americas as "empty" in order to justify settler colonization.

12. Multiple trips from the Mashantucket Pequot Reservation to Standing Rock occurred in the fall of 2016. Travelers included Mashantucket Pequot Tribal members Nakai Northup, Clifford Sebastian, Shaquanna Sebastian, Mylasia Thomas, Dominique Beltran, Lisa Reels, Wayne Reels, Jeremy Whipple, and Joshua Carter as well as tribal employees Jason Mancini, Sherry Pocknett (Mashpee Wampanoag), Annawon Weeden (Mashpee Wampanoag), Chenae Bullock (Shinnecock), and Mashamoquet Myles (Diné, Mohegan).

13. "American History Starts Here!" is a new initiative by the museum intended as a

not-so-subtle reminder that the "American" narrative is not solely the domain of European settlement. It also serves to make explicit the historical connection of Native peoples to the land that at Mashantucket spans at least twelve thousand years.

14. Wolfe explains further, "The positive outcomes of the logic of elimination include officially encouraged miscegenation, the breaking-down of native title into alienable individual freeholds, native citizenship, child abduction, religious conversion, resocialization in total institutions such as missions or boarding schools, and a whole range of cognate biocultural assimilations" (2006, 388).

15. This is an example of companion planting where the plants' properties support one another's growth. For instance, the corn stalk acts as a pole upon which the beans can grow; the shape of the squash leaves, broad in form and low to the ground, provide shade and maintain soil moisture.

16. Even in instances where traditions have become disrupted due to colonial forces (e.g., missionization, compulsory schooling) recovery is possible through concerted, humble efforts to regenerate communication with the land and spirit and associated protocols; see Crawford O'Brien (2013); Afred (2005); and Kelley (2014).

17. See Grande (2017).

REFERENCES

Afred, Taiaiake (Gerald). 2005. *Wasáse: Indigenous Pathways of Action and Freedom.* Peterborough: Broadview Press.

Connecticut General Assembly Papers. Rejected Bills, Native Americans.

Cordova, A. F. 2007. *How It Is: The Native American Philosophy of A. F. Cordova.* Edited by Kathleen Dean Moore, Kurt Peters, Ted Jojola, and Amber Lacy. Tucson: University of Arizona Press.

Crawford O'Brien, Suzanne. 2013. *Coming Full Circle: Spirituality and Wellness among Native Communities in the Pacific Northwest.* Lincoln: University of Nebraska Press.

Deloria, Vine, Jr. 1994. *God Is Red: A Native View of Religion, the Classic Work Updated.* Golden, Colo.: Fulcrum Publishing.

Deloria, Vine, and Daniel Wildcat. 2001. *Power and Place: Indian Education in America.* Golden, Colo.: Fulcrum Resources.

DeMallie, Raymond J., and Douglas R. Parks. 1987. *Sioux Indian Religion.* Norman: University of Oklahoma Press.

Dhillon, Jaskiran. 2017. *Prairie Rising: Indigenous Youth, Decolonization, and the Politics of Intervention.* Toronto: University of Toronto Press.

Grande, Sandy. 2015. *Red Pedagogy: Native American Social and Political Thought.* Lanham, Md.: Rowman and Littlefield.

———. 2017. "The Future of US Education Is Standing Rock." Truthout. July 4. http://www.truthout.org.

Irwin, Lee. 2008. *Coming Down from Above: Prophecy, Resistance, and Renewal in Native American Religious Traditions.* Norman: University of Oklahoma Press.

Kelley, Dennis. 2014. *Tradition, Performance, and Religion in Native America*. New York: Routledge.

O'Connell, Barry. 1992. *On Our Own Ground: The Complete Writings of William Apess, a Pequot*. Amherst: University of Massachusetts Press.

Shear, Sarah B., et al. 2015. "Manifesting Destiny: Re/presentations of Indigenous Peoples in K–12 U.S. History Standards." *Theory and Research in Social Education* 43, no. 1: 68–101.

Wolfe, Patrick. 2006. "Settler Colonialism and the Elimination of the Native." *Journal of Genocide Research* 8, no. 4: 387–409.

20

FOR STANDING ROCK
A MOVING DIALOGUE

Tomoki Mari Birkett and Teresa Montoya

This exchange of letters between two friends reflects on their trip to Standing Rock in November 2016 from their respective Diné/Indigenous and nonbinary mixed-race subjectivities. Given the media saturation and sensationalization of Standing Rock, this dialogue responds to the violence at its edges, the affects it inspired, and the refusals it asserted through an Indigenous movement that produced new practices of solidarity and intimacy to sustain anticolonial resistance. The exchange grapples with myriad forms of historical narrative, toxicity, environmental contamination, erasure, and solidarity from the authors' locations, from the occupied Indigenous Southwest to Japan. They narrate Standing Rock as both grounded place and circulating set of concerns, affects, and memories carried with them through time and space. The photography traces threads of thought and feeling around Standing Rock, holding its promise for reinvigorating our relationships to land, territory, water, each other, and all our nonhuman relations.

Dear Tomoki,

I struggle to begin writing, not for lack of inspiration or understanding the significance of the movement galvanized at Standing Rock. Instead, I grapple with my attempt to locate an entry point. This is not just an analytical or conceptual shortcoming but rather an affective one. When state agencies and the federal government revive standard tactics of removal and erasure, we experience the compounded trauma of multiple massacres. I remember the Trail of Tears, the California Gold Rush, then the Pikes Peak Gold Rush, Inyan Ska (Whitestone), Sand Creek, Washita, the Long Walk, the theft of the Black Hills, and also, Wounded Knee. As historian Roxanne Dunbar-Ortiz argues, "the history of the United States is a history of settler colonialism—the founding of a state based on the ideology of white supremacy, the widespread practice of African slavery, and a policy of genocide and land theft."[2] To comprehend the significance of Standing Rock is to not merely acknowledge but to reorient the

Signs from Water Protectors who came to Oceti Sakowin, November 2016. Photograph by Teresa Montoya.

dominant historical narratives that undergird every media tagline or agency press release. We have seen how these assaults are often framed as regrettable but necessary sacrifices for the prosperity of a nation built on our erasure and then, assimilation. To us, this processing of history can be traumatic in and of itself. How our education in Western institutions has required a cultivation of special coping mechanisms and strategic delusion, of knowing when to speak up and when to remain silent, if only to protect our own energy and sanity. Standing Rock demands a new orientation not only of social movements or environmentalism, as has been frequently discussed in so-called ally politics, but also of history-making itself. How will we narrate these events? To what other histories and solidarities does Standing Rock incite?

In the aftermath of these assaults I am reminded of how our ancestors and relatives have continued to gather and resist: Greasy Grass, Ghost Dance, the other Wounded Knee, Alcatraz, Kanesatake, and Idle No More.[3] Each of these names not only situates itself in a particular Indigenous time and space, but also indexes an origin of a larger movement, a catalyst. For every attempted decimation, we have found new ways to survive. And so, let us not forget how those survived before us and the ways that these historical flash points of settler violence beget other ongoing manifestations of violence.

With a fast approaching winter at the camps, I remember hearing about the haunting occurrence of nightmares. Not just imagined, but real trauma. Because of the heightened sense of collective vulnerability, ever more so under the normalized aggressions of a Trump presidency, I now feel compelled to share with you a nightmare I had the night before you and I drove to Standing Rock.

It was a warning then as much as it is a reminder now to remain vigilant to the shifting forms settler trauma takes.

When we first heard the reports of water cannons being deployed on Water Protectors in subfreezing winter conditions, we were both holed up in Minneapolis following a conference. It was cold there, but nothing compared to the frigid temperatures in North Dakota. Huddled under the temporary warmth of our fleece blankets in an Airbnb rental, we were busily preparing our travel plans to head to Standing Rock early the following morning. Between car rental reservations and supply checklists we watched Facebook livestreams and reacted with horror, though not necessarily surprise, at the escalated violence on the ground. Even firmer in our resolve to bring supplies and protective gear for Water Protectors, we wondered what chaos we would soon be entering.

Later, after offering prayers in those early morning hours, I tried to sleep. I tossed and turned. I cried too. And somewhere between my anxiety and anger, fear and worry, I finally felt my consciousness melt away. But restful slumber did not come easy. In my dream state, I emerged into a desert landscape. There, I noticed sage and low brush surrounding my feet. I looked down at the sandy earth and surmised that I was back home in Diné Bikéyah, our Navajo homelands. In this arid place, the sun was high and bright. I welcomed the warmth upon my skin, allowing myself to embrace this feeling of home. But such comforting nostalgia was soon displaced by a sudden shift in the ground below me. An earthquake? No. I looked closer. From beneath the sand surfaced a large black creature whose scales moved quickly and methodically, almost in a digitized fashion. It was a large snake of monumental proportions, something like those dinosaur illustrations you see in museums brought to life. As I glanced around me to gain some bearings, I saw not just one creature, but several more emerging from the desert floor. Multiple shadowy heads emerging through crimson sand. In the distance, I saw a platform extending from the edge of a shallow cliff. Suddenly I'm walking on the platform with a large crowd of people gathered all around me. They have cameras and phones ready as they glance down at the creatures from the imagined safety of their viewing point. Some take selfies and express excitement and awe at the spectacle below. But for me this wasn't a spectacle. It was horror. Why don't they recognize the danger of the situation? None of us were safe, but everyone around me is blissfully oblivious. They see but cannot comprehend.

In my waking mind, I interpreted this message as a condition of Indigenous political subjectivity. That our histories, our territories, and our existence are not merely overlooked but have been and continually sought to be violently displaced and erased; how "settler colonialism destroys to replace."[4] Thus, the image of the black snake, and the toxicity it all but guarantees for our waterways haunts us in our dreams and our wakefulness. This is not a reality any living being can escape from as a biological fact. However, there is another form of

Mural depicting Gold King mine spill and #NoDAPL on an abandoned building in Shiprock, New Mexico, August 2016. Photograph by Teresa Montoya.

toxicity that the black snake animates. It is this nightmare toxin that embodies the uncertainty and anxiety wrought by intergenerational trauma we dwell within but *also* from where regeneration can occur. There is productive potential here. It is critical action that both Glen Coulthard and Leanne Simpson speak of as rage;[5] that Audra Simpson asserts as refusal;[6] or Rachel Flowers understands as resentment.[7] These speak back to liberal placatory politics of recognition and reconciliation that maintain the integrity of the settler state, rather than disrupt it. In many ways I find I'm still learning how to allow these feelings to articulate my attempts to understand and most importantly, to act.

I am reminded anew of Kim TallBear's assessment of how kinship may be "a partial and productive tool to help us forge alternatives to the settler colonial state. Making kin is to make people into familiars in order to relate." TallBear urges us to consider how such an arrangement seems "fundamentally different from negotiating relations between those who are seen as different—between 'sovereigns' or 'Nations'—especially when one of those nations is a militarized and white supremacist empire."[8] In this way I see making relations is also about forming networks of accountability and responsibility. To seek relationality isn't the performance of a sort of intertribal or even multicultural utopia, but it is about demanding and upholding the Indigenous terms of our existence. We exist because we have maintained enduring relations. Tribal sovereignty may align with this assertion, but in many other ways it has not yet. We know that kinship and relationality are not legible to state politics, at least in so far as a claim of our preexisting power, authority, or livelihood. Rather federal policies of quantifying blood have relied on the expectation of dilution. So when we

Oceti Sakowin, November 2016. Photograph by Teresa Montoya.

affirm relationality, we reject this material assumption. And so I ask, in what ways does Standing Rock call us to bring new forms of relating and accounting forward? How can our own friendship speak to these solidarities and urgencies?

Dear Teresa,

I am struck by what you wrote about the toxicity of the black snake and your dream as expressing the state of Indigenous political subjectivity. When you wrote about the need for new history-making and what settler colonial toxicity actually means, I was reminded of how Zoe Todd has discussed oil extraction as the weaponization of fossilized kin. What is toxic is not the oil, but "the machinations of human political-ideological entanglements that deem it appropriate to carry this oil through pipelines running along vital waterways."[9] These entanglements become a justification for further escalating settler colonial possession and occupation. It becomes an excuse to deepen and expand the invasion, as we saw at Standing Rock. So as you wrote, we should not repeat that original settler colonial erasure on which all of this infrastructure is based.

I also want to think more about what you pointed out about Indigenous sovereignty. Audre Lorde's concept of the erotic is something I turn to often because it has sustained me through some of the violences you named in American educational institutions. Lorde encourages us to seek out the depths of our "unexpressed or unrecognized feeling" and to recognize them as a source of strength.[10] For two-spirit Cherokee scholar Qwo-li Driskill, there is also a "Sovereign Erotic," "an erotic wholeness healed and/or healing from the historical trauma that First Nations people continue to survive, rooted within the histories, traditions, and resistance struggles of our nation."[11] For Driskill, relating to the erotic is an act that resists and heals from colonial violence by "relat[ing] our bodies to our nations, traditions, and histories."[12] Living as two-spirit is part of a practice of a sovereign erotic because it means reclaiming and remaking their body in ways that evict "the specters of conquistadors, priests, and politicians" and reconnect their body to creation.[13] By thinking about the erotic, Driskill is also foregrounding how the work of sovereignty is also about care and defense of Indigenous bodies, and how important this is, especially for women and two-spirit people who bear the brunt of colonial assaults. They are also writing from their position as "a Red-Black person" when they say, "I have not only been removed from my homelands, I have also been removed from my erotic self and continue a journey back to my first homeland: the body."[14] Similar to the Red Nation's point about the need to defend Indigenous rights both on and off reservation, Driskill is making the critical point that the colonial gender system, which has been an important tool to try to make Indigenous erasure and assimilation a reality, creates the additional labor of finding their body by reconnecting to the sovereign erotic. Sovereignty from this perspective is also about this work of making Indigenous existences prohibited by colonial gender.

Audre Lorde also helps me because she provides a compass to recognize and relate to these severings. She tells me what to hold dear and how to recognize the difference between the self-gratification of sensation and the shared joy of the erotic, which is about everyone's liberation.[15] Thinking about decolonization with her tells me that decolonization is a truth and a response to our deepest needs. And it allows me to connect with the work of reproducing Indigenous sovereignty, even if the concept of the erotic before Driskill's theorization was not specifically about that. Because transforming social reproduction—how we care for each other; how we determine which beings deserve what kind of care—is necessary for decolonization, which is about reproducing Indigenous sovereignty.

I am thinking about how Audra Simpson discusses Indigenous sovereignty as labor, even if it is not recognized as such by capitalist valuation:

> This is the labor of living in the face of an expectant and a foretold cultural and political death. As such it is the hard labor of hanging on to territory, defining and fighting for your rights, negotiating and maintaining governmental and gendered forms of power. Much of this labor I am talking about is tied up with a care for and defense of territory.[16]

This definition goes beyond sovereignty as confrontations between two sovereign nations, because it is emphasizing the constant reproduction of self and life on Mohawk terms. Settlers should also be doing similar work from the positions we are in. Like Nick Estes has said, it is not hard.[17] In practice, this could look like fighting for the realization of the Red Nation's ten-point program.[18] And it would look like no longer recognizing the sovereignty of the United States or thinking we somehow belong to it. If we really lived as though we believed that this is stolen land, we would cease to be citizens or to respond to the United States when it calls our name; we would call places by their proper names; we would ask permission for using resources; we would teach the history of settler colonialism; we would stop acting as though we have property; we would show up when Indigenous rights are violated on and off reservations. If Mohawk people are Mohawk and refuse the toxic "gifts" of settler recognition,[19] if Indigenous sovereignty is a current reality—which it is—then I am an out-of-place question mark. I think it makes no sense for us to dream of inclusion—the fantasy of adoption and so on.[20] Settlers should accept that we actually do not belong anywhere or have a claim to anything. This is not the same as settler anarchism, which still has a colonial understanding of freedom that is also often about becoming a fully entitled man (hence the rampant sexual violence also present in many anarchist spaces). It is based on the erotic, based on embracing as fully as possible the desire to not live like this, to share the desire to be free. And while the liberatory possibilities of body-work are often contained through assumptions of racialized safety and domesticity, I find a guide for how to make it part of decolonization in the lives of Harriet Tubman, Chrystos, Kaneko Fumiko, and other militant women.[21]

This labor is also about material redistribution through the care for territory. Tokata Iron Eyes, one of the leaders of the Indigenous youth campaign Rezpect Our Water that helped begin #NoDAPL, said "think about all the things you can do to help, it would help Mother Earth and *she would be built back up.*"[22] Her words speak to me of the material thickening that happens through labor,[23] of the strength we can create by committing to and renewing everyday practices of care for Indigenous sovereignty—*not* for the moral rehabilitation of settlers or "atonement," as some settlers who came to camp framed their participation, but out of recognition and acceptance of the truth. To build her back up, Indigenous people and sovereign institutions must also matter. This is something that was reiterated in so many different ways in NoDAPL. *The land and its people are not separate.* Or as Kim TallBear writes, "This isn't about indigenous peoples being incorporated into your world. It's about you learning how to live here in relation with this place and with peoples who were long co-constituted in relation to these lands and waters and skies. You clearly did not learn how to do that very well."[24]

Maria Lagones and Audra Simpson have demonstrated that gender was a colonial imposition that hierarchically reorganized social relationships based on racialized conceptions of biology, and was instrumental to the attempted destruction of Indigenous political orders through the targeting of Indigenous womxn.[25] This means that cis people are not people whose "gender matches

Bank of Cannonball River, Oceti Sakowin, November 2016. Photograph by Teresa Montoya.

their sex"; they are people who are made legible and defensible by this colonial gender system. They get to make sense because we are not allowed to exist. This means that trans identity is not about biology, but about the fact that we are a form of existence also targeted by colonial gender (though this does not mean there are not trans people who remain quite colonial in practice). We are affected by settler colonial gender by being publicly exhibited and desired as pieces of meat to destroy.[26]

It is from this perspective that nonbinary poet Alok Vaid-Menon writes about their existence as being staked on a politics of vulnerability and inter-subjectivity. They always write, "I need you."[27] But they are not inhabiting liberal vulnerability, which is about aestheticizing suffering to accrue racialized entitlements, access, and security.[28] It is about the recognition and care for themself and others in their depths as we are harmed by gender, and insisting that we claim our own bodies, *now*.[29] And it recognizes that we need others to actually be able to do this. I think this is actually a recognition of erotics as body-work, which is also suggested by Driskill. I remember the moments when I found new relationships to my body as a nonbinary person, how other trans people made that possible by how they related to me. In part, this is what Alok's words "I need you" mean to me. Part of making sovereign erotics matter can mean carrying universes in your hands as much as protecting the sacred places and histories that people need to heal.

Winona LaDuke has said, "When our ancestors went into battle, we didn't know what the consequences were going to be. All we knew is that if we did

Navajo Nation flag with message DOODA OIL (translation: NO OIL) at Oceti Sakowin, November 2016.
Photograph by Teresa Montoya.

nothing, things would not go well for our children."[30] I think a solidarity
centered on the erotic can be similar—a process of searching for our bodies,
sensing them, throwing them out farther than we know how to go, finding them
snag where they might have passed cleanly before.

This is also something happening in time and in the many places we inhabit
and carry with us. When first thinking of this exchange, we had talked about
Standing Rock as a set of affects and concerns. How do you carry it with you?
Where do you carry it? Does it tell you to move differently than you did before?

Dear Tomoki,

I am moved to consider how you invite us to think about solidarity and
intimacy in times, such as now, that makes us feel increasingly vulnerable.
In response to your evocations of the sovereign erotic, a sort of parceling of
Indigenous bodies from the land and from oneself (as well as labor), I would
like to share Mishuana Goeman's literary exploration of "settler colonialism as
an enduring form of gendered spatial violence." In her book *Mark My Words:
Native Women Mapping Our Nations*, Goeman foregrounds Indigenous feminist
voices as "alternatives to heteropatriarchal representation of national space"
or what she also terms "geographies of imperialism."[31] For Goeman, the act of
poetic evocation is a sort of remapping of Indigenous territory and space such
as when she references Diné poet Esther Belin, "I always forget L.A. has sacred
mountains." By invoking Diné conceptualizations of geography, which also
frame temporal ontologies, Belin imagines California coastal features as Diné

Bikéyah (traditional Diné homeland defined by the four sacred mountains). This transcendence of geography is expressed through Goeman's incitement of "directional memory" to mediate the multiple relationships, geographies, and histories that define contemporary Indigenous experience. And it is the discontinuity of these experiences that is a direct result of termination policies that effectively severed the ties between many Indigenous peoples and their ancestral territories, even as new urban communities were born. Nevertheless, there are sacred spaces all around us even when they are no longer recognized as such by colonial cartographies. What incredible power then that Indigenous place-naming projects have to disrupt settler spatial imaginaries and to denaturalize their a priori claims. There is strength in our breath, in naming, in speaking territory.

Whenever I travel to a new place, I always make a point of learning whose territory I am visiting, to whom I can recognize and make appropriate offerings. When possible, I also try to learn place names, though I admit this endeavor isn't always easy and more often than not, remains a goal unfulfilled. And so, prior to our arrival to Oceti Sakowin I remember reading a story told by LaDonna Bravebull Allard about the Inyan Ska (Whitestone) Massacre.[32] Through her narration I became drawn to these lands and more so because Indigenous women/womxn have always been the heart of our struggles.[33]

In her telling, Allard emphasizes that the *true* name for the Cannonball River is Inyan Wakangapi Wakpa, which means "River That Makes the Sacred Stones." This name refers to a once active whirlpool whose movement shaped "large, spherical sandstone formations" in the river's bed. Back in the 1950s, however, the U.S. Corps of Engineers severed this flow when they flooded the area for the construction of Oahe Dam. The project resulted in a loss of 150,000 acres for the Cheyenne River Indian Reservation. But the greater loss was not quantifiable or limited to one Nation or another. Allard writes, "They killed a portion of our sacred river. I was a young girl when the floods came and desecrated our burial sites and Sundance grounds. Our people are in that water. This river holds the story of my entire life."

And it is this opening, a deep reckoning with the wounds severed through generations of settler violence, that I recognized at Oceti Sakowin. The water continues to carry those histories.

And so, we search for a way to relate. Or at least we should be. Kim Tall-Bear's indictment of settler colonialism, "you clearly did not learn how to do that very well," takes on especially crucial significance here.

A loved one back home taught me that our prayers are more powerful through water—whether on the banks of Inyan Wakangapi Wakpa, Sá Bitó, or what is currently called the Hudson River in Lenapehoking, the Lenape territory on which New York City was built.[34] I've prayed to all these waters as one body, so I've been told, because they are all connected. This is as much a material

NYC Stands with Standing Rock action in Washington Square, New York, September 2016. Photograph by Teresa Montoya.

reality as a symbolic one. Water *does* connect us. This understanding goes beyond environmentalist assertions of justice, not because they are wrong but because they are incomplete. It is why, time and time again, our relatives have felt so implored to defend this being.

When you ask, where do I carry this knowledge, I contemplate instead, where does *it* carry us?

This knowledge carries me to consider the impacts of resource extraction on our Diné homelands. Uranium mining and its associated discharges.[35] Radioactive atmospheres and new biopolitical subjectivities known as "downwiders"—those who were unknowingly exposed to ionizing radiation from nuclear weapons testing.[36] The largest nuclear disaster in U.S. history that is obscured and forgotten: the Church Rock uranium mill tailings spill of 1979.[37] The systematic anxiety and uncertainty manifest in our relatives who wait for the diagnosis of a mysterious disease followed by the framing of said disease as moral failure rather than the expected result of rampant extraction. It is the toxicity from the contamination itself and the toxicity of denial at the hands of state regulatory agencies and federal programs that haunts us. This is as much of a reality at Standing Rock as it is on the Navajo Nation.

From the mid-1940s until the 1980s several million tons of uranium ore were extracted from Diné Bikéyah. Because of this wanton "development," there now remains over 500 abandoned uranium mines on the Navajo Nation. Concerns for public health and environment were mitigated in service of "national interest." Back then it was munitions development for the Cold War and now, the supposed security of a domestic oil market. It is no wonder that the combined keywords "hydrocarbon" and "frontier" produce hundreds of thousands of online search results. Oil extraction forges through an imagined sub–terra nullius where groundwater becomes both aid and casualty to this process.

For Diné, it is the color of Yellow that indexes many ongoing causalities of extraction—both from in-situ uranium mines and from upstream Rocky Mountain hard rock mine waste.[38] Front lines formed on the banks of our sacred rivers, from Shiprock to Standing Rock, therefore carry a momentum of urgency. The contamination of Diné lands, as a result of myriad forms of extraction, is symbolically and materially linked to the literal contamination of our bodies.[39]

Despite the passage of a Navajo Nation moratorium on uranium mining in 2005,[40] the toxic effects of this industry are dispersed everywhere but their omnipresent location evades serious accountability. Instead, settler projects of extraction have a way of manifesting into a sort of sublime spectacle, that the scale of their infrastructure or feat of their manufacture overshadows the corporal violence of their technologies.[41] I'm thinking here of Hiroshima and the Cold War crisis that originally legitimized the extraction of Navajo-sourced uranium. These are the entanglements of militarized violence and energy extraction that haven't ceased. Oil is the lubricant for modern colonial violence.

While these concerns are the heart of my academic research, they also inform a responsibility to cultivate new forms of knowledge alongside relatives working to break these extractive cycles and structures.[42] We cannot continue to act like the uranium contamination in Diné Bikéyah is somehow removed from Standing Rock, or Flint, or even Fukushima. The assault on our integrity as Indigenous people—as human beings—demands a reorientation of history that Standing Rock reminded us *is* possible. This is certainly not our first resistance, but it is one that has galvanized action across other front lines. Here we find the opening and the relation that compels us to act. Standing Rock, to me, is like that whirlpool momentum, moving and pushing you in unanticipated ways. I ask now in return; how does Standing Rock compel you to act? What do you carry through this metaphorical and literal movement and where does it take you?

Dear Teresa,

Thank you so much for your letter, and for sharing Goeman's writing on the power of the Indigenous remapping of space as part of the sovereign erotic. You ask me about where I am carried. I think I have been pulled toward clarifying how to decolonize from all my histories. Once we have boiled away settler colonial and colonial knowledge production, how can I see the relation between me, Japan, America, and Chinook territory where I grew up? What is the channel that is actually connecting us? I have been trying to think about this in examining Japanese antinuclear politics from an anticolonial perspective.

NYC Stands with Standing Rock action in Washington Square, New York, September 2016. Photograph by Teresa Montoya.

What you are saying about the sublime spectacle of settler colonial violence is so central in that. It is like we are looking into different ends of a tunnel—part of nuclear spectacle was the monumental scale of production you talked about, and part of it was a moment of corporeal violence that has been remembered as a uniquely Japanese event. This has reproduced the erasure of Indigenous injuries and of colonized atomic bomb victims: "Japan is the only country to suffer atomic bombings," I hear.[43] *Burakumin* (outcaste) and colonized Korean and Chinese victims of the atomic bombings are also materially excluded from this memory, allowing "full" Japanese to become an innocent and singular victim.[44] *Hibakusha* (atomic bomb victims) paid for this complicity by being turned into a disposable labor force, some of whom were paid a pittance to build the very museum that memorialized some of their seared flesh, but not their lives.[45] This erasure also kept antinuclear activists from recognizing the truth, weakening the movement. In 1954, a publicity campaign run by the CIA and Yomiuri newspaper redirected antinuclear sentiment toward supporting the construction of nuclear power plants for "peace."[46] By ignoring the colonial death required by nuclear production, mainstream Japanese "antinuclear" progressives erased Japanese colonialism and came to support ongoing American settler colonization, and their own domination by the same.[47]

This afterlife continues today in the liberalism of antinuclear politics in the wake of the Fukushima nuclear disaster, which often casts victims as innocent citizens being sacrificed for the nation. While it is necessary to indict the state and capital, this narrative leaves little room for meaningfully facing issues of class, nuclear colonialism, imperialism, or gender in Japan's nuclear present. It keeps Japan safely removed from needing to concern itself with decolonization, despite the ongoing settler colonization of Ainu Mosir and the ongoing colonization of the Ryūkyū Islands. It also expresses the complicity of Japanese wartime memory and antinuclear politics with the very settler colonial regime that decimated Japanese cities, placed Japanese Americans as well as Aleut people in internment camps, and treated atomic bomb survivors as mere objects of study.[48] As such, the continued commitment to liberal discourses of "democracy" and "peace" in "progressive" Japanese and American discourse—like resonating magnets that constitute a field of American imperialism based in settler colonialism—needs to be completely shattered. We need to stop acting like whiteness has anything to offer us, and instead decolonize and learn to speak directly to each other.

Japanese publications on Standing Rock often mention that three Japanese megabanks (Mitsubishi, Mizuho, and Mitsui Sumitomo) were among the top ten investors in TransCanada, Enbridge, Energy Transfer Partners, and Kinder Morgan, responsible for the Dakota Access, Line 3, Keystone XL, Energy East, and Trans Mountain pipelines.[49] Again, the reconfiguration of Japanese colonial structures within U.S. imperialism made this possible. Japanese corporate conglomerates (*zaibatsu*) were never really dismantled because the occupying American government was interested in retooling Japanese colonial structures to aid its imperialist expansion during the Cold War.[50] These *zaibatsu*—the same companies invested in DAPL—got rich making weapons for the Korean War.[51] Japan's post–World War II rise is also due to neocolonial extraction in Southeast Asia, suggested by the CIA to replace extraction from former colonies.[52] By refusing to deal with these colonial reconfigurations, we are complicit in ongoing settler colonization.

Now, Japanese and American imperial intertwining is trickling back to occupied Chinook territory where I grew up as fallout from the Fukushima Daiichi nuclear disaster. Though the source of uranium has changed, the forms of coloniality on which it depends are the same—much of the uranium in the Daiichi reactor cores was extracted from the Olympic Dam mine on Kookotha land claimed by Australia.[53] As Todd urges us to recognize, it is the settler colonial processes of severing relationships, violating Indigenous sovereignty, and then exporting the toxic fruits of that process abroad through imperialist occupation and militarism that have spit the fallout from Fukushima Daiichi across the world and built the Dakota Access Pipeline. Our resistance to these processes needs to be on these grounds. Liberating the terms of body-work through erotics will be central to that.

The movement to protect the water at Standing Rock spirals out in so many directions, through seeping groundwater, as evaporated atmosphere, through ocean currents. As you wrote, having enduring relations, despite losses and through victories, has sustained Indigenous practices of decolonization for hundreds of years. In interviews since the camps at Standing Rock were emptied,

Circular rainbow in Yayoi, Nayoro, in colonized Ainu Mosir (Hokkaidō),
August 5, 2017. Photograph by Tomoki Mari Birkett.

leaders of the NoDAPL movement have emphasized this continuity. Holy Elk Lafferty has said, "For me it's been a continuum. It has never stopped. We're all continuing to fight. Now, camp is the globe. Camp is everywhere."[54]

There is as much possibility for decolonization in the defense of places where the water is still drinkable as in the care for people and places into whom settler toxins have settled—in the provision of healthcare, basic necessities, conducting health studies,[55] continuing relations with contaminated animals and plants, and more. This is why I find Alok Vaid-Menon's words sustaining: "i do not believe we will win. i do not believe hope should be a prerequisite for trying anyway."[56] We are living with so many losses, and the enduring qualities of toxicity bring into serious question what "victory" or what accomplishing decolonization can mean. But following Alok and, for me, following the philosophy of Japanese anarchist Kaneko Fumiko, we should continue: "Whether it was successful or not was not our concern; it was enough that we believed it to be a valid work."[57] Maybe decolonization is a relation, not an event. Let us continue to carry it and be carried by it, to weave in and strengthen those veins that are always being buried.

In the spring of 2017, an Ainu delegation went to visit the Lower Elhwa Klallam and Makah tribes. They learned about how the ecosystem was reviving after the removal of the Elwha dams, which had destroyed the salmon and other forms of life on the Elwha River. May such a rebirth come for Inyan Wakangapi

Wakpa—may the whirlpool only be carried for a time in dispersed, evaporated form as people; may it return to the river. May it have returned to it the fullness of a homecoming.

> We were stolen from our bodies
> We were stolen from our homes
> And we are fighters in the long war
> To bring us all back home
> —Qwo-li Driskill, "Stolen from Our Bodies: First Nations Two-Spirits/Queers and the Journey to a Sovereign Erotic"

NOTES

1. We recognize the inspiration and knowledge shared with friends/comrades/colleagues of our informal toxicity collective: Anne Spice, Kristen Simmons, and Sonia Grant. This collaboration developed after the panel "States of Entanglement: Embodying Toxic Futures under Settler Colonial Regimes" at the 2016 American Anthropological Association annual meeting. We thank the following people for their support, conversations, and collective prayers: Nozomi Birkett, Yukari Birkett, Andrew Curley, Lais Duarte, Margaux Kristjansson, Yuko Tonohira, Manu Vimalassery, and Janene Yazzie. We offer gratitude for the sharing of knowledge around trans and Black feminisms, ethics, settler colonialism, and toxicity across Dine Bikéyah, Japan, and Asian and queer America, and for the forms of transformative love you have taught through your ways of living. Many thanks to Ogawa Sanae and Kuzuno Tsugio for long discussions about Japanese settler colonialism despite their exhaustion, and to Yoshihiko Tonohira. Lastly, an emphatic *ahe'hee* (thank you) to Nick Estes and Jaskiran Dhillon for the invitation to contribute to this volume, a manifestation of their collective support and labor for the project of Indigenous liberation.

2. See *An Indigenous Peoples' History of the United States* by Roxanne Dunbar-Ortiz (Boston: Beacon, 2014) for an excellent primer on settler colonial historiography and the dominant ways Indigenous histories have been diminished and erased, much like the genocidal policies of the state itself. Centering settler colonialism as a critical framework radically challenges and undermines the narrative of American supremacy.

3. See Leanne Betasamosake Simpson and Kiera Ladner, eds., *This Is an Honour Song: Twenty Years since the Blockades* (Winnipeg: ARP Books, 2010). Also the Kino-nda-niimi Collective, ed., *The Winter We Danced: Voices from the Past, the Future, and the Idle No More Movement* (Winnipeg: ARP Books, 2014).

4. See Patrick Wolfe, "Settler Colonialism and the Elimination of the Native," *Journal of Genocide Research* 8, no 4 (2006): 387–409. Also, Kēhaulani Kauanui provides a useful discussion of the origin and limits of settler colonialism as a discourse: see

J. Kēhaulani Kauanui, "'A Structure, Not an Event': Settler Colonialism and Enduring Indigeneity," *Lateral* 5, no. 1 (2016).

5. Glen Coulthard, *Red Skin, White Masks: Rejecting the Colonial Politics of Recognition* (Minneapolis: University of Minnesota Press, 2014). Leanne Simpson, "Indict the System: Indigenous & Black Connected Resistance," November 28, 2014. https://www.leannesimpson.ca.

6. Audra Simpson, *Mohawk Interruptus: Political Life across the Borders of Settler States* (Durham, N.C.: Duke University Press, 2014).

7. Rachel Flowers, "Refusal to Forgive: Indigenous Women's Love and Rage," *Decolonization: Indigeneity, Education & Society* 4, no. 2 (2015): 32–49.

8. Kim TallBear, "Annual Meeting: The US-Dakota War and Failed Settler Kinship," *Anthropology News* 57, no. 9 (September 2016), https://doi.org/10.1111/AN.137.

9. Zoe Todd, "Fish, Kin and Hope: Tending to Water Violations in amiskwaciwâskahikan and Treaty Six Territory," *Afterall* 43 (2017): 107. https://www.afterall.org/journal.

10. Audre Lorde, "Uses of the Erotic: The Erotic as Power," in *Sister Outsider: Essays and Speeches by Audre Lorde* (New York: Crossing Press, 1984), 53.

11. Qwo-li Driskill, "Stolen from Our Bodies: First Nations Two-Spirits/Queers and the Journey to a Sovereign Erotic," *Studies in American Indian Literatures*, series 2, 16, no. 2 (2004): 52.

12. Driskill, "Stolen from Our Bodies," 52.

13. Driskill, "Stolen from Our Bodies," 54–55.

14. Driskill, "Stolen from Our Bodies," 53.

15. Or as Édouard Glissant writes, "Our boats are open, and we sail them for everyone." *Poetics of Relation* (Ann Arbor: University of Michigan Press, 1997), 9.

16. Simpson, *Mohawk Interruptus*, 3.

17. Christina Heatherton, "Policing the Crisis of Indigenous Lives: An Interview with the Red Nation," in *Policing the Planet: Why the Policing Crisis Led to Black Lives Matter*, ed. Jordan T. Camp and Christina Heatherton (London: Verso, 2016), https://nycstandswithstandingrock.files.wordpress.com/2016/10/heatherton-2016.pdf.

18. "10 Point Program," The Red Nation, https://therednation.org.

19. Simpson, *Mohawk Interruptus*, 1, 7, 12. See also Leslie Sabiston and Didier Sylvain, "Give and Take," *Savage Minds: Notes and Queries in Anthropology*, September 27, 2016, https://savageminds.org/2016/09/27/give-and-take/.

20. See Eve Tuck and K. Wayne Yang, "Decolonization Is Not a Metaphor," *Decolonization: Indigeneity, Education & Society* 1, no. 1 (2012): 1–40.

21. Cf. Butch Lee, *Jailbreak out of History: The Re-biography of Harriet Tubman* (Chicago: Stoopsale Books, 2000); Chrystos, *In Her I Am* (Vancouver: Press Gang Publishers, 1993); Kaneko Fumiko, *The Prison Memoirs of a Japanese Woman* (London: M. E. Sharpe, 1991).

22. "Voices from Standing Rock: Tokata Iron Eyes," YouTube, December 6, 2016, https://www.youtube.com, emphasis added.

23. Cf. Marx's poetics of labor, "the spindle and cotton, instead of resting quietly side by side, *join together in the process, their forms are altered*, and they are turned into yarn." Karl Marx, *Capital* (New York: Penguin, 1976), 1:294, emphasis mine.

24. Kim TallBear, "Failed Settler Kinship, Truth and Reconciliation, and Science," Indigenous Science, Technology, Society, March 16, 2016, http://indigenoussts.com /failed-settler-kinship-truth-and-reconciliation-and-science.

25. Maria Lagones, "Heterosexualism and the Colonial / Modern Gender System," *Hypatia* 22, no. 1 (2007): 186–209; Audra Simpson, "The State Is a Man: Theresa Spence, Loretta Saunders and the Gender of Settler Sovereignty," *Theory and Event* 19, no. 4 (2016).

26. Thinking with Vaid-Menon's words, "EXHIBIT ME. TO PROHIBIT ME." From "Street Tax," in *Femme in Public* (New York: Alok Vaid-Menon, 2017), 8.

27. "i need your help in creating a world that celebrates gender non-conforming people of color. we cannot do this alone. it's terrifying out here. i cannot do this alone." Instagram post, May 22, 2018.

28. See Aileen Moreton-Robinson, *The White Possessive: Property, Power, and Indigenous Sovereignty* (Minneapolis: University of Minnesota Press, 2015), and Cheryl Harris, "Whiteness as Property," *Harvard Law Review* 106, no. 8 (1993): 1707–91.

29. "i begin to wonder if. i. have. a. body. anymore." From "Street Tax," in *Femme in Public*, 7.

30. "Mni Wiconi: The Stand at Standing Rock," YouTube, November 14, 2016, https:// www.youtube.com.

31. Mishuana Goeman, *Mark My Words: Native Women Mapping Our Nations* (Minneapolis: University of Minnesota Press, 2013).

32. LaDonna Bravebull Allard, "Why the Founder of Standing Rock Sioux Camp Can't Forget the Whitestone Massacre," *Yes! Magazine*, September 3, 2016, http://www .yesmagazine.org.

33. We have chosen the orthography "womxn" over alternatives such as "womyn" because of the latter's association with TERF (trans-exclusionary radical feminist) politics at the Michigan Womyn's Music Festival, which excluded trans women from participating based on a transphobic definition of gender where only cis women were acknowledged as truly female. "Womxn" is associated with POC queer feminisms in a variety of ways. Most notably, it calls to mind the emergence of "Latinx" as a gender-neutral term for people of Latin American descent in the early 2000s, which counters the de facto man=human equation with a term inclusive of all gender identifications, including nonbinary and agender. The use of "x" in feminist orthography is also associated with indigenous Xicanx feminisms, which reclaim language through the incorporation of the Nahuatl use of "x." Crystal Stella Becerril, "What's with the 'X' in 'Xicanisma?'" Latino Rebels, June 24, 2015, http:// www.latinorebels.com/2015/06/24/whats-with-the-x-in-xicanisma/.

34. Sá Bitó means "old or ancient river" in our Diné language but many would call this

male entity by its English name, the San Juan River. As a practice I endeavor to prioritize Indigenous place names to challenge Euro-American epistemologies of place.

35. See Doug Brugge, Timothy Benally, and Esther Yazzie-Lewis, *The Navajo People and Uranium Mining* (Albuquerque: University of New Mexico Press, 2007).

36. See Sarah Alisabeth Fox, *Downwind: A People's History of the Nuclear West* (Lincoln: University of Nebraska Press, 2014). Also Kristen Simmons, "Settler Atmospherics," Member Voices, *Fieldsights*, November 20, 2017, https://culanth.org/fieldsights/settler-atmospherics.

37. See Marley Shebala, "Poison in the Earth: 1979 Church Rock Spill a Symbol for Uranium Dangers," *Navajo Times*, July 23, 2009, http://navajotimes.com.

38. See Teresa Montoya, "Yellow Water: Rupture and Return One Year after the Gold King Mine Spill," *Anthropology Now* 9 (2017): 91–115.

39. Ongoing research through the Navajo Birth Cohort Study, for instance, reveals the existence of elevations of uranium in a generation of Diné woman that has never had direct contact with uranium mining. Preliminary findings suggest, according to researcher Chris Shuey, that uranium has the ability to cross the placental barrier. Finalized data and analysis are forthcoming. For more information consult the Southwest Research Information Center webpage: http://www.sric.org/nbcs/index.php. See also Elizabeth Hoover's environmental justice work that critically engages the toxic legacy of industrial contamination with the Mohawk Nation of Akwesasne. Elizabeth Hoover, *The River Is in Us: Fighting Toxics in a Mohawk Community* (Minneapolis: University of Minnesota Press, 2017).

40. Associated Press, "Navajos Ban Uranium Mining on Reservation," *NBC News*, April 22, 2005, http://www.nbcnews.com/id/7602821/ns/us_news-environment/t/navajos-ban-uranium-mining-reservation/#.WZN-UtPytE4.

41. Consider the National Museum of Nuclear Science & History located in Albuquerque, New Mexico. I visited the institution a couple years ago curious to see how nuclear disaster was narrated and to what extent health impacts were represented. To my surprise, there was not one mention of the 1979 Church Rock uranium mill tailings spill, despite it being larger than the Three Mile Island spill *and* occurring in western New Mexico. I did find exhibit panels dedicated to the uranium industry on the Colorado Plateau titled with puns such as "enriching your future." The "Pioneers of the Atom" exhibition was no better where the same American prerogative and legitimization for settler colonial violence comes into sharp relief with the linear path of technoscience.

42. In addition to important work being done on the ground by relatives in Diné grassroots groups such as Tó Bei Nihi Ziil, Ké Info Shop, Puerco Valley Uranium Remediation Coalition, and the Little Colorado River Watershed Chapters Association, I am inspired by the models of fellow Diné scholars: Jennifer Denetdale, Melanie Yazzie, Andrew Curley, and Angelo Baca. Their respective work is especially

crucial in critically engaging the various ways that U.S. settler nationalism permeates Navajo governance, from energy development and "public lands" debates to gender and border town violence.

43. "Nihon wa sekai yuiitsu no hibakukoku."

44. See Lisa Yoneyama, *Hiroshima Traces: Time, Space, and the Dialectics of Memory* (Berkeley: University of California Press, 1999); Tomoko Otake, "Nagasaki's 'Providential' Nightmare Shaped by Religious, Ethnic Undercurrents," *Japan Times*, August 7, 2015, https://www.japantimes.co.jp.

45. The exhibit on them was even temporarily displaced to make way for Eisenhower's "Atoms For Peace" exhibit. See Maya Todeschini, "Illegitimate Sufferers: A-Bomb Victims, Medical Science, and the Government," *Daedalus* 128, no. 2 (1999): 67–100.

46. Muto Ichiyo, "The Buildup of a Nuclear Armament Capability and the Postwar Statehood of Japan: Fukushima and the Genealogy of Nuclear Bombs and Power Plants," *Inter-Asia Cultural Studies* 14, no. 2 (2013): 171–212.

47. Todeschini, "Illegitimate Sufferers"; Yoneyama, *Hiroshima Traces*. See Joseph Masco, "Age of Fallout," *History of the Present* 5, no. 2 (Fall 2015): 137–68, for more on the bifurcation of radioactive contamination into sublime event and "fallout."

48. Tuck and Yang, "Decolonization Is Not a Metaphor."

49. See https://mazaskatalks.org/thebanks/#banks and Jo Miles and Hugh MacMillan, "Who's Banking on the Dakota Access Pipeline?" Food & Water Watch, September 6, 2016, https://www.foodandwaterwatch.org.

50. Giovanni Arrighi, "States, Markets, and Capitalism, East and West," *positions* 15, no. 2 (2007): 251–84.

51. Arrighi, "States, Markets, and Capitalism, East and West."

52. Giovanni Arrighi, *The Long Twentieth Century: Money, Power, and the Origins of Our Times* (New York: Verso, 2010), 375.

53. "Peter Watts: Uranium Should Stay in the Ground," *Green Left Weekly*, January 30, 2012, https://www.greenleft.org.au.

54. Dennis Ward, "Standing Rock: One Year Later," APTN National News, April 6, 2018, http://aptnnews.ca.

55. Cf. *Violence on the Land, Violence on Our Bodies: Building an Indigenous Response to Environmental Violence*, http://landbodydefense.org/uploads/files/VLVBReport Toolkit2016.pdf; "International Indigenous Women's Environmental and Reproductive Health Symposium Declaration," Incite! (blog), August 19, 2010, https://incite-national.org.

56. "Confessional," in *Femme in Public*, 16.

57. Fumiko, *The Prison Memoirs of a Japanese Woman*, 237.

21

A LESSON IN NATURAL LAW

Marcella Gilbert

I thank Nick Estes for inviting me to participate in this important work. I will start my experience by first sharing that I come from a family of Native activists. My mother, Madonna Thunder Hawk, and my aunts, Mabel Ann Eagle Hunter, Phyllis Young, and many others, have a long history of taking a stand against injustice for all people, not only Native people of this land. My uncles on my mother's side have led, and continue to lead, intelligent resistance based in American Indian Movement principles set fifty years ago by Lakota elders who were immersed in the true discipline of our spirituality and Oceti Sakowin lifeways. These elders were eighty years old or more in the early 1970s and evoked the free-thinking processes of their parents and grandparents who lived in and survived the nineteenth century. As a very young person, I was fortunate to witness these remarkable relationships and the influence these elders had on the movement and the people.

As I grew up with these strong women, in and among my family, community organizing was the example. My mother played a significant role in the Wounded Knee standoff of 1973; she was a young fearless mother and sister who fought alongside her brothers and many others in the stance against the injustices of this government. Along with many other women at Wounded Knee, Madonna helped organize food rationing and medic services all while caring for her ten-year-old son, who was trapped there along with everyone else. Following Wounded Knee, she went on to form the first survival school for young Native children in Rapid City, South Dakota, in 1974. As a teenager, I personally participated in and witnessed more than two hundred young people come through our school during a period of over six years. My aunt Mabel Ann sat on the local all-white public school board in Rapid City during the early years of the survival school. This resulted in our school receiving the hot meals program for school children, as well as the placement of certified math and reading teachers at our alternative school. In 1977, our school moved to the Pine Ridge Reservation and became the We Will Remember Survival Group living in the Porcupine community for four years.

"March on Backwater Bridge." Photograph by Vanessa Bowen.

In 1978 my mother Madonna and aunts Mabel Ann and Phyllis formed Women of All Red Nations (WARN) to organize community support against forced sterilization acts of genocide against Native women on the Pine Ridge Reservation in the 1970s. This resulted in an exposé of radiation contamination of the drinking water on the reservation and the covert medical acts of sterilization. Phyllis Young assisted Russell Means in organizing meaningful relationships at the national and international levels, thus leading to the formation of the first North American Indigenous delegation to the 1977 Geneva Convention on Human Rights. I was selected as a representative of the delegation and also was the youngest to attend from our survival group.

The examples given here are only a very few of the many, many projects and organizations that these women initiated and continue to organize to this day. Their commitment to our people and justice is their life work. As I watch my mother and aunts become great-grandmothers and great-great-grandmothers, and they continue to work for justice, I see that their legacy lies in all of us who love and support them, and we have a responsibility to carry their work forward. I take pride in being able to witness this kind of strength built and maintained through their love for the people. These were and continue to be my life instructors on the political stage of Indigenous existence and resistance. I am fortunate to have had a lifelong experience and education of this magnitude that continues to guide my life and inspiration so personally. These women named here, and many others who were active during the Red Power Movement of the sixties and seventies, were also active in organizing and strategizing at Standing Rock. I was fortunate, once again, to witness the power and commitment of these extraordinary women as they easily fell back into the roles of community organizers, leaders, educators, diplomats, elders, mothers, and grandmothers. The love for our people and our way of life as Oceti Sakowin Oyate drives their commitment and integrity to be Lakota. Their example is my life goal.

Standing Rock represented the conscience of this nation and the world. People of all ages from many nations, cultures, belief systems, and prayer circles came together to support the life of water and the earth. The futures of all human beings lie in the health and well-being of the earth. This represents our ability to connect to the earth and to each other, as well as our spiritual selves. Standing Rock provided expressions of hope, examples of human responsibility, and an uncompromising return to the discipline of natural law, which fully supports being a good relative and protecting justice on all levels. When we are allowed to express our humanity through a lifestyle of justice, family, generosity, and prayer without prejudice or hate, we thrive in the love and caring of each other and our mother, the earth. These are lessons that lie in the fabric of Indigenous principles once shared by all people, as all people once were truly indigenous to their lands, foods, prayers, families, and the natural laws that protected us. The fact that spirituality was the most important aspect of life at Oceti Sakowin resistance camp situated the people directly within our daily cultural expectations of generosity and respect. When thousands of people are living in a spiritual manner of the mind, from all corners of the world, the true meaning of life is easily understood and easily lived. Indigenous people of North America have struggled to return to this way of life, and Standing Rock provided a tangible experience to regain our own Indigenous spirituality and to believe once more in our own gift of prayer and true generosity.

Decolonization grew from the space of humanity thrust upon by our reclamation of our responsibility to our true mother, the earth, and life-giving water. Oceti Sakowin Camp became its own world where families and individuals thrived in their own space with the freedom to be a good relative and to express justice as we saw it.

With Indigenous leadership built on ancestral teachings, basic natural laws were set forth allowing every person from every nation the opportunity to become a true human being, thus allowing the expression of our spiritual selves to live in the joy of protecting our birthright, the earth. Standing Rock premiered an example of social success built on spirituality, safety, common ground, and trust. The fact that there were rules to live by set in place immediately at Oceti Sakowin resistance camp allowed for people to behave at a higher standard, based on spirituality and respect, and to expect that from themselves and each other. These rules may seem ordinary, but set in a context of prayer and resistance, standing up for justice for life-giving water, the world's spiritual commitment to life flowed toward Standing

Rock, allowing all who came there or looked in that direction to feel the power of the simple desire for justice and to support each other in our right to exist on this earth. Everyone, every person, every family, held an important role and contributed to the success of the community at Oceti Sakowin. The world expressed its generosity by supporting the needs of the camp, and that expression is a true contribution to humanity. As groups of people and families worked together for the good of the camp community, the decolonization of daily lives became evident.

Within the first few weeks at camp, the Oceti Sakowin people immediately began to resurrect our original systems of governance, and each tribal band was instructed to select one individual as a representative to the Council of Seven Fires, which met almost every day to discuss strategy, camp conduct, and peaceful action based on discipline. Individuals were selected according to their character and ability to lead by example and humility. One such person represented the Ihanktonwan band of Nakota and was the youngest man on that council. He brought his family to Standing Rock to support the people, to pray with the world, and to stand on the front lines for our water. This young man, along with his wife and eight-year-old son, camped at Standing Rock until the very end.

Daily life at camp provided opportunities to be a good relative, and that is the first step in building a mindset toward decolonization. Every individual camp needed firewood, and that firewood needed to be cut and delivered, so young men came together to cut wood as young boys stacked it and older men loaded it into trucks for delivery. This action took place out of community need, and each person involved visited with another, the older ones looked out for the younger ones, and everyone helped each other. On that particular day, cutting wood was an example of intergenerational excellence. As one of the kitchen's cooks and helpers tore husks off the corn from the local community gardens, others loaded the husks and delivered them to the camps where horses were living. When the school sprouted, the education of the children evolved around the daily happenings of the camp and the generosity of the adults in their knowledge of plants, horses, water, art, music, and truth. Meanwhile, young men and women built shelves for school supplies that poured in continuously for the first few weeks of school.

This basic natural law of being useful and living a spiritual life is part of the glue that builds discipline and success. Success became evident when young people became a vital component of the community and received the attention that they long deserved and their voices were heard by the world. In this age of violence against young people, Oceti Sakowin Camp provided a sense of safety that young people expressed as "home." Most young people living at camp had decided that they were not leaving until "we win," and thoughts of after that, they envisioned a new community where they could thrive, a community where the more vulnerable populations such as youth and young people, disabled, elderly, LGBTQ, recovering, and women could feel safe. Safety is most important for social success in any community. The ability for a community to self-regulate positive behavior through equality and justice builds trust among the masses and puts everyone on even ground no matter where they come from.

Young people considered Oceti Sakowin Camp home only days after arriving, since there they found safety, food, shelter, and protection. They knew that the older people around them would do whatever they could to protect them and keep them safe—for young people, this is paramount. Our young people became contributing members of the camp community, and adults looked to them for their vibrant expressions of life. As they ran across Turtle Island in prayer and sacrifice, the awakening within themselves became empowered by the awakening of the world. Our young people had found their purpose and the desire to live without question while adults took pride in them and offered to help and provide direction in whatever ways we could. When a nation's young people thrive, the community thrives, and adults, parents, grandparents, and relatives can revel in our jobs well done. Such security among the young people provides assurance to the larger community that they will grow into their future with confidence and therefore our nation will survive. Human beings are instinctively kind and loving, and in this place of safety and spiritual memory we were able to be that human being that the creator intended us to be.

As groups of white people organized daily orientation for newcomers, the topic of the day was white privilege. Respect for the Indigenous people of the Oceti Sakowin lands was paramount, and many of us Native people experienced for the first time in our lives the respect of being considered first. It is a powerful and humbling experience to be put first for the first time in all aspects of life. Even more powerful is to watch white people create discipline among their own people for the benefit of another people. That, too, was a first for many Native people to see, and that created hope among everyone. Hope that maybe white people working for justice for Native people and all people will soon create a mechanism of discipline for white men who work within the corporations that are bent on destroying our planet—or, more important, to create discipline that is worth their honor and integrity based on humanity and generosity.

The medic camp provided healing methods from the world: massage, acupuncture, crystal and stone healing, herbal remedies, and much more. The lines were long to get the opportunity to receive such gifts, and those who provided this loving service worked throughout the day to provide peace and healing for everyone. Native people needn't stand in line; we were moved to the front of the line to receive such gifts. The medic camp also provided midwives for pregnant women to receive care and prepare for childbirth. In this environment, women could feel confident in their bodies and decisions about childbirth, a gift that has long been removed from many Native communities. Young women engaged in conversations about nutrition, vitamins, healing teas, exercises, mother–child relationships, and on and on, geared toward having healthy babies as we are meant to, through home birth methods with help and direction from women. As many

Native women relearned the sacredness of pregnancy and birth, our Native nations' rebirth became an apparent responsibility—a responsibility that involves trusting our own Indigenous knowledge embedded in our DNA. The future of our existence relies on our responsibility to uphold natural laws by teaching our young and supporting their future.

Young women initiated the resistance at Standing Rock; grandmothers put out the call to the Oceti Sakowin and organized the people to prepare for the influx of supporters. Women from many nations accepted the call for justice and to assist fellow tribal relatives. Their roles fulfilled every aspect of the resistance, provided leadership on many levels in many arenas, and led actions at the front lines. The highways of this country are filled with the sacrifices of young women running for justice, for water, and for life. Daily camp life led by women involved managing seven community kitchens; staffing the donation and food centers; managing social media and press; coordinating school activities; managing communication between camp, tribal councils, and international dignitaries; and advising groups and individuals on camp business. A sewing center was set up to make skirts for women in need, and camps were made aware of items available for children. A legal defense committee for Water Protector arrestees was organized by elder women who had experienced similar situations in their younger years. Oceti Sakowin allowed Native people to return to our original methods of governing, where women held positions of equality and their input was sought and respected. Our Native grandmothers held positions of respect and honor within individual camps and within the overall resistance camp. Women exhibited great value on many levels, and our people welcomed them back into their historic roles without question or doubt. As women thought about the future, our water, and the gift of life, the love for our grandchildren became the greatest motivator of all. As women came from the front lines to seek medical care or regain their strength, some were asked how they could keep fighting. Many simply answered, "I do this for my grandchildren."

Much of camp was led by example. Everyone picked up trash as they went about their daily business, and daily announcements were made at the sacred fire and everyone took those messages home. Young Native men stepped into their official traditional role as providers and protectors without any fanfare and took pride in being a man performing any task required. They also supported their peers on the highways of this country, running and sacrificing for all of us who depend on water. As young men stood in the front lines, adrenaline surged within their veins urging them to act out physically; however, the discipline of our prayers and nonviolence held them fast. Many young men learned discipline on a higher level—a test of the strength of mind and heart to remain peaceful when under attack. Many have earned their feathers at Standing Rock. Standing guard at the security gates, the induction into responsibility to and for the people was evident: this is where young men and women could test their resolve and enter the space of protecting the people. Men organized the building of floors for camp tents in preparation for colder weather, and wood stoves were delivered to community tents for people to stay warm on very cold nights. Many tasks were shared between women and men, and camp needs were met on all levels, including having a veterinarian on site. The needs of the camp community were assessed through the eyes of relatives; each person ready to serve the community did so without limitations on gender roles and responsibilities or age. As the last days of camp approached and a few holdouts remained, men took on all roles without question. They monitored the security gates, helped cook meals and clean up kitchens, dump trash, cut wood, check on those younger or more vulnerable. *Everyone* became useful in ways that served the wellness of the camp community.

Oceti Sakowin resistance camp swelled into the fourth largest "town" in North Dakota, built from resistance, sustained through hope for justice, and thriving on prayer and generosity. A "town" like no other, and as the cold winds blew and snow covered the earth, many Water Protectors from all across Turtle Island were contemplating the future of the camp after we win. Plans for a permanent community began to formulate based on the natural laws of humanity where all who live there can thrive in their own discipline and responsibility, hope, justice, and prayer. This is an example of free thought, holding freedom in our hands and minds in ways that protect our birthright, the earth. Ironically, this is also a glimpse of the history of white America. Within their freedom they took land and built their homes and communities with the same motivations. Yet in white America, Native people do not have the right to free thought, to create a community on their own lands stolen by white America, to hope for a better future, and sadly our allies at Standing Rock became criminalized along with us by their own government.

Standing Rock magnified the historical attitude of the United States toward Indigenous people of this planet and the fact that greed remains their greatest god of all. Native people have been resisting for many generations, so this powerful act of resistance is not new to us (Native people): this is a continuation of Native struggles. In 1973, the Wounded Knee takeover on Pine Ridge Reservation awakened the world to our existence; much of the world did not know that the Oceti Sakowin people still existed. The world knew about Wounded Knee but the world didn't come to Wounded Knee; thanks to social media, the world came to Standing Rock. Due to corporate domination worldwide, Standing Rock provided common ground for all people to express themselves by supporting a movement focused on our right to live and to stand against the corporate machine of destruction and the shock of this country being officially turned over to oligarchic rule. American citizens witnessed the validity of their laws, as the Constitution drifted out the window of justice; anyone standing up for water, for life, was deemed criminal. Constitutional laws were broken without remorse, making them as meaningless as the paper they were written on, and simple public laws became criminal laws with felony convictions attached. Lies, deceit, infiltration, bribery, kidnapping, attempted murder, battery, betrayal, and more were the tools used against Water Protectors and justified through hate, racism, privilege, and greed. The true power of America rested in the hearts and minds of the veterans who supported Standing Rock. These amazing women and men became true warriors, as defined in my culture, and I will always hold them in a place of honor and remember the day that the U.S. veterans came to the aid of my people against their own government and corporations for sake of life and water.

The world of humanity hopes for proof: proof that life will sustain itself in the face of recklessness. When a people forget their god and the teachings of a spiritual life, they forget the natural laws, they forget themselves, their children, and their children's futures within a natural world in which to live. A future cannot be a purchase guaranteed, nor can the future be perceived only for a few. The earth is our mother and we are all her children; we are responsible for her health that in turn will secure our own.

Water Protectors and our allies proved to the world that this life and this earth is sacred, but, most of all, we want to LIVE. Life is our greatest gift from the creator, and our right to life as human beings depends on our ability to live according to natural laws. Standing Rock provided a place for life to thrive within a world of war, violence, and hopelessness. The expression of humanity and discipline through prayer, peace, and unity provided a powerful spiritual army, one that no military could stand against without risking its own humanity. Spirituality is key in this time of uncertainty, and its power is inevitable. As the Water Protectors at Standing Rock stood with the world's prayers in our hearts and held the power of grace and love as our shields, we witnessed the transformation of minds and hearts across the world. Our voices could be heard across the planet, and our prayers focused in one direction. That is power! This expression is everlasting and will continue, as long as there are human beings that value life in the face of ego, greed, and destruction.

As we move forward from Standing Rock, we remain inspired despite the ugliness of corporate greed and false gods. The people of Oceti Sakowin still live at Standing Rock, Cheyenne River, Pine Ridge, Rosebud, Crow Creek, Lower Brule, Flandreau, Yankton, and Sisseton, and we still face the onslaught of corporate terrorism and the inevitability of another fossil fuel standoff. Many of the Water Protectors who were arrested remain tied to confinement through trumped-up charges and official changes within North Dakota laws that have criminalized them even further. The struggle is not over. The cameras and celebrities have left, and social media has calmed visions of bandanna faces and fists in the sky while the Native people of the Dakotas now face emboldened racism, outright criminalization, and even murder. Native struggles continue. Many Water Protectors have moved on, but many more have remained inspired. Allies work to promote divestment, and that work is important. Corporations are dependent on currency, and the people can control currency if we participate on common ground. Water Protectors all over the world now hold Mni Wiconi in their hearts and are working to build new conversations and better communities by being generous and continuing to pray for our planet, our mother the earth. Through the generosity of Water Protectors and our allies, many Native communities have support to make meaningful changes in their lives and the lives of their relatives and the earth. This is evidence of an organic lesson in natural law, in humanity through resistance, and the desire to protect life. It is okay to be good to one another, to support each other, and to keep each other inspired to continue on, and it is definitely okay to want to live!

Wamaskanskan Oyasin.

22

STANDING ROCK
THE ACTUALIZATION OF A COMMUNITY AND A MOVEMENT

Sarah Sunshine Manning

We waited for this. Our blood memory yearned for Standing Rock. We yearned for the health and well-being of generations past, the days of healthy families, healthy communities, and a healthy land to walk and live upon.

Our blood memory yearned for deep purpose and connection, again— connection so lacking in a world addicted to material things, a world moving so fast that it forgets the most basic elements of just being human.

It was early August when I was alerted to the rapidly building momentum in Standing Rock. I was at a powwow in my southern Idaho homelands with family, enjoying the last days of summer before we returned to our residence in northeast South Dakota on the Lake Traverse Indian Reservation. From the screen of my smartphone, I watched on as, one by one, Standing Rock tribal members and their allies were arrested on North Dakota Highway 1806 just north of the reservation, the original front lines of the unarmed standoff against Energy Transfer Partners and the Dakota Access Pipeline.

By way of social media, I learned that Dr. Sara Jumping Eagle, Hunkpapa Lakota mother and medical doctor, was arrested by Morton County Sheriff's Department officers while defending the waters of her children and the sacred lands of her ancestors. I watched on as Standing Rock Sioux Tribal Chairman David Archambault II pushed through a crowd of law enforcement to reach tribal elders who were swept away in the crowd, only to be arrested within seconds and charged with disorderly conduct. I watched on as Tito Ybarra, Anishinaabe comedian, and Scotty Clifford and Juliana Brown Eyes-Clifford, musicians from the Oglala Lakota band Scatter Their Own, locked their arms, side by side, onto a big green iron gate leading to the easement of the Dakota Access Pipeline. The trio was also arrested.

Like thousands of others watching from their smartphones, I was shaken so intensely, so viscerally, that I was drawn into the movement almost instantly. Within a week, I was there, breathing in the air of hallowed ground rumbling with possibilities.

Indian Country: Who We Are, Where We've Been

Indian Country. Noun. The socio-cultural-political landscape shaped by generations of Indigenous existence, disenfranchisement, and resilience. The interconnected community of Indigenous peoples throughout Turtle Island—so-called North America.

I grew up on the Duck Valley Indian Reservation located in the high desert of northern Nevada and southern Idaho, home to the Shoshone–Paiute Tribes. Life as a young girl was relatively carefree. I played in the open fields of my family's ranch with my sisters, I ran the dirt roads, swam in the river and canals, made forts in the tall weeds and trees, and pretended to be grown, doing grown people things. I attended ceremonies and gatherings, and listened to adults and elders speak in our Native tongue. I watched picturesque sunsets and vibrant stars light up the night sky without the interference of harsh city lights. Childhood was beautiful on the reservation.

With each passing year, my naïve awareness of the world transformed into the painful recognition of our unique position as Indians, as disenfranchised, often forgotten, and struggling people. I participated in my first political demonstration at the age of ten, as the Shoshone–Paiute Tribes and its membership protested a U.S. Air Force practice bombing range just north of the reservation that endangered sacred sites and sent a barrage of sonic booms throughout the reservation.

I did not know it at the time, but at the core of our demonstration was the most innate impulse to protect ourselves—to simply continue to exist as Indigenous people with physical and spiritual ties to the land. I was "protesting" to live without intrusion as a Shoshone and Paiute girl, as Newe' and Numu, who was, by virtue of ancestry, responsible for protecting her homelands, the beloved land of ancestors, and the future home of our grandchildren yet to be born. At the age of ten, during that influential moment in time, I learned to take a stand.

Taking a stand, I later learned, was in our blood.

Throughout my upbringing, I remember my parents occasionally chanting the phrase "Water for Life," and stickers and posters with the phrase were hung throughout our home as part of a local campaign on the reservation to defend the water rights of the Shoshone and Paiute Tribes during the late 1970s and 1980s. My late aunt, Tina Manning Trudell, led the fight on our reservation to ensure that residents and ranchers in Duck Valley did not suffer from the damming of the Owyhee River, a major water supply on the reservation.

I never had the privilege of meeting my auntie Tina, as she was taken tragically in a mysterious house fire of unknown origin in 1979 on the Duck Valley Indian Reservation, less than twenty-four hours after my uncle John Trudell, her husband, burned the U.S. flag on the steps of the FBI headquarters in Washington, D.C. Our uncle John was a staunch Indigenous rights activist at the time, and Tina and John together were a dynamic couple, grounded by a love for land, water, and their people. The suspicious fire took the lives of my auntie Tina, her mother Leah Manning Hicks, and Tina and uncle John's three children, Ricarda Star, Sunshine Karma, and Eli Changing Sun. Tina was also pregnant with a son, who was later named Josiah Hawk.

After Tina's passing, John fell into despair, and the community of Duck Valley was utterly stunned and heartbroken. My parents were heartbroken not just as relatives but as close friends with Tina and John. John continued Tina's work for the water in Duck Valley by organizing the Water for Life benefit concert in 1981 in Boise, Idaho, with performers Jackson Browne, Bonnie Raitt, Cris Williamson, Floyd Westerman, and Carole King. I was born in 1982, with a middle name in honor and memory of my late cousin, Sunshine Trudell.

In many ways, my story is not entirely unique for a young girl growing up on the reservation or for any Indigenous young person growing into the awareness of the complicated position we occupy as the original people of a land violently invaded by settler colonists—a land where we must fight for basic human rights. At an early age, we learn that we are "Indian," and yet not *Indian* because we are not from India. We learn that we had it all and then lost virtually all of it, only to be left with broken pieces of our communities and our lands. We learn that we must fight and take stands, and that doing so can mean putting ourselves and our family in danger. We learn that we are beautiful, resilient people, rich with culture yet resented by our invaders and silenced by corporations, the federal government, and institutional racism. We are initiated into young adulthood enduring emotions of anxiousness, anger, sadness, and confusion. Life is unjust, we learn, and Indians somehow ended up with the short end of the stick.

Outside the reservation, we see cities sparkle with affluent neighborhoods, sidewalks, streetlights, and parks. White ranchers and farmers thrive on prime land—lands taken from our ancestors as a result of broken and scuttled treaties. On the reservation, we run back down our dusty dirt roads, and suddenly those dirt roads and our forts in the weeds seem deficient. Our collective and relative poverty becomes obvious against the white norm of comfort and luxury.

On the reservation, we read from secondhand textbooks in school, stamped with the emblems of schools of white children. We read about George Washington and Anne Frank, seeing no reflection of our brown faces or our brown story. We attend the funerals of relatives lost to suicide, homicide, or alcohol-related accidents. We watch our relatives stumble drunk into walls, crying themselves to sleep, anguishing over loved ones lost. While we see incredible beauty and strength in our indisputable tenacity, the magnificent landscape, and our enduring culture, we also see tragedy and despair all around us.

We hope and even anguish, much like our addicted loved ones, for better days—days where we just don't have to hurt, days where we can have it all again.

The Rise of a Movement

In early August 2016, tribal nations throughout North America passed resolutions in support of the Standing Rock Sioux Tribe in their stance to protect the waters of the Mni Sose, Missouri River, against threats from the Dakota Access crude oil pipeline. This, after Standing Rock Sioux Tribal (SRST) Chairman David Archambault II put out an official call to tribal nations for support. The Standing Rock Sioux youth runners and founder of the Sacred Stone Camp, LaDonna Bravebull Allard, put out calls of their own via social media, also for allied support. Their messages to Indian Country and beyond went viral, reaching the masses worldwide. Within days, in early August, caravans of cars and delegations from throughout Turtle Island made their way to the Sacred Stone Camp and to the newly erected Red Warrior and Oceti Sakowin Camps just across the Cannonball River.

During my first visit to the Oceti Sakowin camp in mid-August with a young relative, the grass was still high and a small number of camps stretched across the plain. Upon our arrival to camp late one night, we were greeted by security and then assisted by a volunteer who helped us set up our tent in the rain. The next morning, we woke up to sights and sounds of happiness and community. People were so eager to help one another, to contribute supplies, and even just to offer a warm smile. Together, that morning, approximately two hundred of us walked to the Cannonball River for a water ceremony. We prayed and cheered together, and the energy was palpable. In that moment, there was no sign of despair or sadness, only purpose and cooperation—something of our ancestors' time.

After spending the weekend at the resistance camps, I returned home. Back at my residence on the Lake Traverse Reservation in South Dakota, a five-hour drive from camp, I felt lonely and sad. As I walked back and forth in my box, in my two-bedroom duplex, I felt the utter separation from the sense of community and hope that was overflowing at the Oceti Sakowin Camp. I immediately began to recognize the stark contrast between the energy of the Western world we are consumed by in our daily lives versus the energy of an Indigenous world of true communal living, which was manifesting rapidly back in camp.

During my second visit to the Oceti Sakowin camp the following weekend, I took my son and three teenaged nephews along. We left on a Friday afternoon right after they all got out of school. The boys were excited and anxious, especially after completing their second week back in school, where the growing movement in Standing Rock was being discussed in many of their classes.

"Auntie, what do you have to do to be an arrestable?" asked one of my nephews on our five-hour drive to Standing Rock, already imagining offering himself up for the cause. This young man was, by nature, very quiet and, in many respects, an introvert. As a high school senior, he was not involved in extracurricular activities in school, and he was generally a C student, content with doing just enough to get by.

My youngest nephew, age thirteen, an A student and frequent recipient of Student of the Month awards, was bursting with energy. A budding digital storyteller, he eagerly anticipated making and producing a video of the resistance camp using apps on his iPod.

We arrived at the resistance camps late at night and set up our tent in the dark. The next morning, the boys sprang from bed with eyes wide open. In the daylight, I quickly noticed that camp had grown exponentially in just one week. Not long after breakfast at the main kitchen, the boys set about delivering supplies to the camps, which were now thickly spread across the plain. They jumped on the back of a truck with other young men, most of them complete strangers, dropping off cases of water, sleeping bags, and miscellaneous camp gear throughout Oceti Sakowin in the hot August sun.

They joined hundreds of others from camp on foot to the original front line during a prayer walk, walking nearly three miles in total, the most walking that at least one of them had done in quite a long time. They war whooped and held up their fists. They joked and smiled, and late into the night they sat around the fire, feeling good.

When it came time to leave camp on Sunday evening and head back home, the boys unanimously asked to stay just one more night. "Maybe I can just be homeschooled and stay in camp," said my thirteen-year-old, Student of the Month nephew. He called his mom and made the case for staying a little bit longer. To no avail: we ended up going home anyway, earlier than he wanted, earlier than they all wanted. All of them were undeniably imprinted with an experience that would stay with them forever. They were drawn in, much like the countless others who answered the call to support Standing Rock, and they savored every moment, standing for something—in fact, many things—that simply made them feel whole.

Self and Community Actualization in the Resistance Camps

In the world of psychology and education, academics are schooled in Abraham Maslow's Theory of Motivation, which outlines the most basic needs of human beings required to reach a state of motivation and self-actualization, or one's own personal and greatest potential in life. As an educator of Native youth for six years on the Lake Traverse Indian Reservation, I regularly considered Maslow's theory, also known as Maslow's Hierarchy of Needs, recognizing the many obstacles in place for Native American students who often struggled to reach a state of motivation, as their most basic needs were just not being met.

The first and most basic need of human beings, according to Maslow, is our need for food, water, warmth, and rest—our physiological needs. Then we must fulfill our needs of security and safety. If those most basic needs are met, then we can begin to focus more directly on our psychological needs—our need for love and belonging—and our esteem needs, which derive from feeling a sense of accomplishment. Once all of our needs are met, we are free, in a sense, equipped to set about the process of self-actualization, where we achieve our full potential in any given moment. But without any of those most basic physiological and psychological needs being met, human beings cannot even begin to focus on anything else but those absent needs, which, in turn, inhibits their ability to self-actualize.

As a secondary education social studies teacher, I was tasked with teaching Native American students the basics of the social sciences. I taught courses in geography, social studies, psychology, sociology, American Indian history, and Tribal Government. Many students often showed up to class tired, unprepared, without their books or even a pencil to write with. Some were incredibly unmotivated and/or emotionally disconnected, going through the motions of compulsory education, unable to receive the full benefits of the opportunities that lay before them.

Many Native American students drop out of school, and in higher proportion than any other demographic in America, as they are too often lacking institutional support, direction, and inspiration from the schools that serve them. Native youth also suffer tragically from mental health disparities, some of them going into substance abuse treatment in their teenage years, others cutting and even taking their own lives.

As a teacher of American Indian history and Tribal Government, in these courses with culturally relevant content where the material regularly reflected Indigenous experiences, tribal communities, and all of the goodness, resolve, and intelligence of Indigenous people, students were noticeably more motivated to learn. In those classes, students were inspired, at the very least, to lift their heads from the desk and pay attention. They participated in class discussions, asked important questions, and wanted to know more. They were invested and present. They learned and they hungered for more—even the kids otherwise perceived as defiant. In those two culturally relevant courses, the students' esteem needs and their needs of love and belonging were being met. Their existence, as Indigenous young women and men, was being validated and affirmed, simply by virtue of the content studied. I also loved my students dearly and worked hard to deliver material in a way that communicated my love and concern for them.

Still, as a teacher back then, I wasn't able to change the fact that many students came to school late, often due to family and personal issues, or they missed school altogether as a result of a whole range of tragedies, from the most serious matters of family death to the lack of family stability and support. I had no control over their home life or the vast majority of their most basic physiological or psychological needs, yet I was supposed to teach them and, somehow, communicate content to their clouded and confused, yet fertile and impressionable, young minds. I had hoped so deeply that they would ultimately begin to think and imagine their own magnificent thoughts and soon speak powerfully from a place of self-awareness, having learned their history as Indigenous people. I wanted them to become motivated, and then create a good life for themselves and their communities through the opportunities of a Western education. This was so much easier said than done.

Compared to the standard classrooms of contemporary American education, the camps at Standing Rock produced an environment substantially and holistically more supportive for Native youth. During my regular visits to Standing Rock, which became weekly, and in stretches of three to eight days at a time while working as a journalist and correspondent for Indian Country Media Network, I began noticing many of my former students sprinkled throughout various volunteer stations in camp. One young man, a recent graduate and a student who was suspended numerous times from school, was staying up late into the night at Oceti Sakowin, working the security gate. Before long, he took to riding horse bareback and was often seen trailing along with the Spirit Riders, a group of young men and women on horseback, as they patrolled in and around the outskirts of camp and near pipeline construction sites. He had a newfound purpose and a community that met his most basic physiological and psychological needs in ways that school, or life on the reservation, did not quite accomplish.

At Oceti Sakowin, for so many youth and adults alike, virtually every one of their most basic needs was being met and, consequently, individuals were motivated, prompting them to offer up their best skills and talents for the good of the community. This was a community that each individual relied on, for food, shelter, safety, love, and belonging, and, conversely, the community relied on them too. Each individual was valuable and necessary, and they knew it. And while there were, in fact, variations and sometimes sharp divisions in tactics and ideologies in camp throughout the duration of the resistance against the Dakota Access Pipeline, the underlying goal was the same: protect the water, protect the land, and protect the future of tribal nations.

That common goal and tremendous communal support motivated many campgoers and Water Protectors to push beyond their limits and expand their skill sets by stepping out of their comfort zones and onto a well-lit path of self-actualization. Thousands were growing, healing, and becoming, constantly. Relatives who battled depression beamed with energy in camp, and youth who were otherwise withdrawn suddenly operated with an obvious sense of purpose. There was truly a job and a place for everyone. You simply had to show up and then give it your best.

Children, youth, and adults learned phrases and songs in the Lakota and Dakota language. Some participated in their first ceremonies, while others learned to ride horse, bareback, with fearlessness. Many women, as first-time seamstresses, learned how to sew ribbon skirts. Kitchens overflowed with expert cooks, and novice cooks who shadowed them and soon became skilled in the kitchen too. Carpenters came and created new carpenters, and structures began emerging all throughout camp. Organizers mobilized new organizers, many of whom refined their oratory and communication skills along the way. Both seasoned artists and courageous new artists contributed their artwork in "Action Art" stations throughout camp. Nonviolent direct action trainings, offered regularly, transmuted the energy, anger, and anxiousness of the disenfranchised into focus and commitment. Elders came with knowledge and history, and thousands showed up to listen and learn. All the while, truckloads of donations poured into camp, creating mountains of wood, food, medicines, clothing, camp gear, and miscellaneous personal items.

In the camps and on the front lines, individuals became a necessary part of the whole, as they each became tightly woven into a reciprocal relationship with community that would sustain them through even the harshest conditions. As frontline Water Protectors organized dynamic frontline actions, the atmosphere grew increasingly more dangerous, and still they pushed on. Dog attacks, mace, freezing water in the black of night, blizzards, and hundreds of arrests were not enough to deter the many who came to protect the water, the land, and the health and well-being of future generations. New tactics constantly emerged to stop construction of the pipeline, keeping the Morton County Sherriff's Department and Dakota Access security on their toes. Actualization was constant.

In all corners of camp, thousands of ordinary people became committed protectors, emboldened with collective confidence. Together, they found their voice, if not amplified it, deepening their commitments to protecting the land, waters, and their own communities. Individuals of all ages actualized—and, in fact, spontaneously in many synergistic moments. With thousands of actualizing individuals spread throughout camp and on the front lines, the entire community inevitably actualized, too. What began as a small camp of fewer than a dozen at Sacred Stone in April 2016 blossomed to nearly twenty thousand at the height of camp occupation, which expanded into Oceti Sakowin, Red Warrior, and Rosebud Camps.

During that time, roads were well worn into the grass, culture-based schools for children were established by volunteer teachers, kitchens sprang up, structures for living and gathering were built, legal teams organized, and medic tents with massage therapists, Reiki practitioners, and even acupuncturists took care of the health and well-being of Water Protectors. There were supply areas and enough clothing donations to clothe everyone for several seasons over. Sweat lodges were erected all throughout camp, and ceremonies took place daily. Solar panels and small wind turbines produced energy, while composting toilets eventually replaced port-a-potties in early winter. Security stations remained in various places throughout camp, and what became known as media hill served as a hub for communication.

In virtually just weeks, an entire city of thousands was born out of the hopes, cooperation, and imaginations of healthy and motivated individuals yearning for something more in this world, while aiming, ultimately, to stop the Dakota Access Pipeline. Moments of community actualization sometimes ebbed, to a degree, but at the same time continuously flowed, as the community makeup transformed and expanded day by day.

Yet from the earliest and most uplifting phases of camp life, there were logistical and ideological challenges. New arrivals poured into camp daily, while many others left to return to their jobs or to their families. Some stayed for the weekend, and others for stretches of a few weeks or even months at a time. Leadership was fluid, horizontal, and varied from camp to camp, while the SRST government continued to engage with the federal government in their usual government-to-government relationship outside of camp.

With national attention mounting, and camp population rapidly expanding, it wasn't long before talk of infiltrators and agitators alerted Water Protectors to the lurking threat of internal sabotage. And even amid the fear of infiltrators, a greater threat to the movement, and beloved camp life, was looming.

The Culmination and Diaspora of the Standing Rock Movement

Throughout the duration of the legal battle between the Standing Rock Sioux Tribe and Energy Transfer Partners, the federal government continued to send mixed messages about its position. From the perspective of Water Protectors, even partial legal victories seemed like red herrings devised to send them home.

On December 5, 2016, the outgoing Obama administration announced that the U.S. Army Corps of Engineers would not grant the final easement to complete the Dakota Access Pipeline. It seemed like a victory. In a YouTube video posted later that day, Standing Rock Sioux Tribal Chairman David Archambault II thanked the Water Protectors for their sacrifice, then asked them to go home, citing concern for safety during harsh North Dakota winter storms. While thousands of Water Protectors celebrated victory on the ground, others, more skeptical, held back their cheers. With a Trump presidency approaching, many prepared for the worst. Despite the message to return home, approximately two thousand Water Protectors dug in their heels, vowing to stay until the very end.

On January 20, 2017, Donald Trump was inaugurated as the forty-fifth president of the United States, having won a highly controversial election with campaign promises including energy and infrastructure development. As winter continued through the month of January, discussion on the state, tribal, and federal levels concerning clearing the camps became a major subject. Talk of camp eviction brought unease to Water Protectors not only in light of the Trump presidency but also due to the continued presence of Dakota Access machinery on the drill pad to bore under the Missouri River. In the end, the remaining residents in camp were given a deadline of February 22, 2017, to leave camp. On that day the last remaining

Water Protectors were forcefully evicted, with a total of forty-seven arrests made. What became a spontaneous, profound, and rapidly growing movement was being suffocated aggressively by a Trump presidency and other governmental forces.

As the Sacred Stone Camp, the original resistance camp consecrated in April 2016, was the last to be cleared, Water Protectors on the ground and those who had already returned home expressed great sadness at the end of what seemed so much like a dream full of momentous victories. That beautiful and otherworldly community created from the hearts and visions of thousands was leveled out by machinery in late February 2017, and soon thereafter taken back by the elements. What must be thoroughly appreciated and remembered, though, is the confluence of conditions that created such a hope-filled movement and community in the first place.

Indian Country yearned for this, above all, and at long last the conditions were ripe for a movement of this scale. While seeking to stop the Dakota Access Pipeline, there was a massive Indigenous return to community, and as a corollary a return to the successful communal learning model that sustained tribal nations for millennia. This return to our original Indigenous living conditions and pedagogies was largely responsible, then, for creating the conditions most conducive to healthy living, learning, and motivation in the camps—conditions so lacking in American society today.

For those dreamlike months in the resistance camps at Standing Rock, scores of Indigenous people and their allies grew, healed, expanded, and actualized together. An entire community actualized, giving life to a movement unlike anything ever known in recorded history. Every day in the camps and on the front lines, great feats of courage were displayed. Women and men cared for each other and took stands courageously like their ancestors. They built community like their ancestors and empowered children like their ancestors. And all who answered the call of their hearts to protect the water in Standing Rock, in some capacity, became stronger and wiser in the end. Emboldened.

As a mother, an educator of Native youth, a journalist, and an Indigenous woman, I was personally pulled into a space that I, too, longed for. A place where Indigenous people were happy and healthy again, telling our own stories again. In being present there at the resistance camps and during frontline actions, I was given the incredible opportunity to bear witness and to tell the stories of Indigenous resilience through the mechanism of Indigenous journalism, to ensure that this time an Indigenous perspective was told and remembered.

Like so many others, I left deeply inspired. I can also say with confidence that my loved ones, former students, and new allies made were equally impacted, as we were each markedly infused with a taste of what precolonial, healthy community actualization must have looked and felt like before generations of historical trauma and suppression. Through our collective efforts, as protectors, organizers, builders, and storytellers, it was proven possible that tribal nations can, in fact, mobilize thousands of people in a short amount of time. Indigenous people can defend the water and defend the land, and collectively defend anything, so long as all are unified by a common goal, so long as the conditions are right. Community health can be realized, again, and people can heal and become motivated, again, so long as there is a trust in and reliance on what worked most within precolonial models of community building. We saw it all in Standing Rock.

While there is still great ambiguity on the legal front in the fight against the Dakota Access Pipeline, on the societal level there is no question as to the enormous wins that continue to bear fruit. Global consciousness expanded, and exponentially, because of Standing Rock, as light was cast on a plethora of environmental issues, global injustice, Indigenous rights, and human rights. Seeds of consciousness were planted in camp and far beyond camp, as onlookers throughout the globe observed the movement while learning and being inspired from their electronic screens. Only time will tell how those seeds of consciousness will continue to grow and manifest in the face of growing threats to the environment, to tribal nations, and to all marginalized communities. In the meantime, the movement born in Standing Rock endures in the hearts, minds, homes, and communities of every single person who participated, or even just watched on, as a historic stand was taken for water and for life.

23

#NoDAPL SYLLABUS PROJECT

The New York City Stands with Standing Rock Collective

As Indigenous and non-Indigenous scholars and organizers who engage in studies of Indigenous life, politics, and education, settler colonialism, and decolonization, we stand in solidarity with the Indigenous struggle to stop the 1,172-mile Dakota Access Pipeline. Projected to transport hydraulically fractured (or "fracked") natural gas from the Bakken oil fields in North Dakota to the Gulf Coast, DAPL violates the Fort Laramie Treaties signed in 1851 and 1868 by the United States and bands of the Sioux and other tribes, as well as recent U.S. environmental regulations.

The dangers to the natural environment and local Indigenous communities are grave. While the pipeline was originally planned upriver from the predominantly white border town of Bismarck, North Dakota, the new route passes immediately above the Standing Rock Sioux Reservation, running under Lake Oahe and tributaries of Lake Sakakawea, crossing the Missouri River twice and the Mississippi River once. Not only may this pipeline contaminate a vital water source for Standing Rock, and millions of people in the surrounding area, but it also threatens one of the largest subterranean water tables in the world, the Ogallala aquifer. In the past two years, more than three hundred pipeline leaks and spills have damaged irreparably land, water, and animal life—ecosystems as a whole. It is also clear that the benefits of this construction project are tied to the prosperity of a very few—in particular, a private energy corporation, Energy Transfer Partners, based in Dallas, Texas, and their financial backers.

At present, the Water Protectors in the resistance camps hold the line against immanent environmental disaster that goes well beyond Standing Rock. The thousands of people convened at camps in North Dakota in solidarity with the Standing Rock Sioux and their allies hold the line for *everyone, every being, and everything* around them. Their selflessness and courage in deploying their very bodies to block construction demands our support; the mounting state police and military response sparks our outrage. Yet the mainstream media has failed to offer sufficient coverage of the Standing Rock Collective's nonviolent, peaceful resistance or of the demonstrations of solidarity all across the United States and Canada. Journalists and filmmakers are being arrested for reporting on daily life in the camps.

Now is the time to stand with the Standing Rock Sioux against catastrophic environmental damage and to publicly support Indigenous sovereignty and the protection of their land and water.

With this document, we, the New York City Stands with Standing Rock Collective, proclaim our intent to advance the historic work of the Sacred Stone Camp, the Red Warrior Camp, and the Oceti Sakowin Camp to resist the construction of the Dakota Access Pipeline (DAPL), which threatens traditional and treaty-guaranteed Great Sioux Nation territory. We pursue three goals:

1. To heighten awareness of the Dakota Access Pipeline in New York City and the surrounding region.
2. To support the Water Protectors at the camps with material supplies, money, and publicity.
3. To launch a syllabus project to contextualize DAPL within Sioux and settler history so that those who seek a deeper understanding of the territory and the conflict might learn and teach.

Already we have organized a rally of more than two thousand people, in collaboration with Decolonize This Place, at Washington Square Park on September 9 to collect donations for the resistance camps and to raise awareness about a ruling that day by the U.S. district court judge in favor of Energy Transfer Partners, denying the Standing Rock Sioux's claim for an injunction. Our letters of support to Chairman David Archambault at Standing Rock, professing both scholarly concern and solidarity from our universities, may be viewed on our website. Teach-ins continue at Connecticut College, Columbia University, and the New School.

Our decision to design and write a syllabus centering on the Dakota Access Pipeline is driven by the urgency of the situation and a desire to offer intellectual and curricular support to the ongoing resistance efforts. *But most important, we are interested in supporting and contextualizing the Standing Rock struggle within literatures that can help those new to Sioux history and contemporary Indigenous politics and criticism to understand this issue within history, within the literature on toxicity and its dangers to the environment, and within gender and police violence within settler states.* We were inspired by the Black Lives Matter Syllabus, the Trump 101 Syllabus, and the TRUMP 2.0 Syllabus that responded to social events and political phenomena with contextualizing, methodical, revisionary, and critical curricular suggestions. We aim to be part of the answer to "How did this happen?"; "What do I need to read to get a handle on what's happening?"; and "What can we now do?"

Our methodology (which we believe is important to share) involved collaborating closely with each other through meetings and through Google Docs. A group of us is working on the project, but Matthew Chrisler, a doctoral student at CUNY in anthropology, started the syllabus with a timeline of events that contextualizes DAPL within treaty history in the Plains, but specifically Sioux treaty history. He immediately started drafting a rationale for the syllabus as well. We invited Maria John, a historian now on a postdoctoral fellowship at Wesleyan University, to add to the timeline and to join the syllabus project. Other New York City–based contributors provided feedback on the timeline, made corrections, and suggested possibilities for inclusion. We then started posting what we considered key readings on the shared Google Doc. We asked each other to read the texts to confirm their significance and put specific inquiries out to American Studies scholars Nick Estes and Alyosha Goldstein at University of New Mexico and Manu Vimalassery at Barnard College and asked for their recommendations. Identifying scholarship by Sioux scholars, other Indigenous scholars, and allied settler scholars became a deliberative curatorial exercise in radical accountability to Indigenous thought and politics.

We individually *read all the materials* for various sections to arrange them into emergent thematic areas (fifteen in total). What we thought was going to be a one-week project took almost two months as we saw new themes pop up. The New York City Stands with Standing Rock Collective then met again, and we talked at length about the syllabus and how to curate emergent sections. We want our readers and future teachers to understand that we take Sioux notions of history seriously but came to impasses with certain materials that we wanted to include but felt inadequate to interpret. So we direct educators and students to the crucial archives of Lakota Winter Counts. One of the founders of the resistance camps at Standing Rock, LaDonna Bravebull Allard, has devoted her life to the interpretation of these counts, and any responsible curriculum will point to them and invite students to think about and with them. Recognizing, then, our limitations, we volunteered to work with our strengths and to curate specific sections of the syllabus, to take charge of, so to speak, the content and the form. Matthew Chrisler managed the group and ordered the text with Jaskiran Dhillon, New School assistant professor of global studies and anthropology, who stepped in at certain points to read entries. Along with Matthew Chrisler, Sheehan Moore, a doctoral student in anthropology at CUNY, organized all of the PDFs to attach to our website for syllabus readers to view and download. Multiple eyes reviewed each section as it took shape. We also asked curators to narrow their selections to book chapters and specific articles to further focus the syllabus and keep it accessible for people who would read and download it in short amounts of time. We wanted people to read the syllabus and teach the material but also have access to the readings for themselves and their students and/or community members.

Although a work in progress, the current #StandingRockSyllabus places what is happening now in a broader historical, political, economic, and social context going back more than five hundred years to the first expeditions of Columbus, the founding of the United States on institutionalized slavery, private property, and dispossession, and the rise of global carbon supply and demand. Indigenous peoples around the world have been on the front lines of conflicts like Standing Rock for centuries. The syllabus foregrounds the work of Indigenous and allied activists and scholars: anthropologists, historians, environmental scientists, and legal scholars, all of whom contribute important insights into the conflicts between Indigenous sovereignty and resource extraction. It can be taught in its entirety, or in sections depending on the pedagogic needs. We hope that it will be used in K–12 school settings, community centers, social justice agencies training organizers, university classrooms, legal defense campaigns, social movement and political education workshops, and in the resistance camps at Standing Rock and other similar standoffs across the globe. As we move forward, we anticipate posting lesson plans on our website that will be derived from individuals and communities who are using the syllabus in their respective locales.

Our primary goal is to stop the Dakota Access Pipeline, but we also recognize that Standing Rock is one front line of many around the world. This syllabus can be a tool to access research usually kept behind paywalls, or it can be a resource package for those unfamiliar with Indigenous histories and politics. Please share, add, and discuss using the hashtag #StandingRockSyllabus on Facebook, Twitter, or other social media. Like those on the front lines, we are here for as long as it takes.

NOTE

The NYC Stands with Standing Rock Collective contributors are Audra Simpson (Kahnawake Mohawk), Crystal Migwans (Anishnaabe of Wikwemikong Unceded), Elsa Hoover (Anishnaabe), Jamey Jesperson, Jaskiran Dhillon, Margaux Kay Kristjansson, Maria John, Matthew Chrisler, Paige West, Sandy Grande (Quechua), Sheehan Moore, Tamar Blickstein, and Teresa Montoya (Diné). The NYC Stands with Standing Rock Collective thanks the following people for suggestions and guidance: Alyosha Goldstein, Cynthia Malone, Dean Saranillio, Jerry Jacka, Jessica Barnes, Karl Jacoby, Kim TallBear (Sisseton–Wahpeton Oyate), Manu Vimalassery, and Nick Estes (Lower Brule Sioux).

VI.
INDIGENOUS ORGANIZING AND SOLIDARITY IN MOVEMENT BUILDING

"Camp." Photograph by Jaida Grey Eagle.

24

LESSONS FROM THE LAND
PEACE THROUGH RELATIONSHIP

Michelle Latimer

This TedX talk was delivered by Michelle Latimer in Toronto, Canada, on October 27, 2017.

I would like to begin by acknowledging that the land on which we gather is the traditional territory of the Haudenosaunee, the Anishinaabe, the Métis, and most recently the territory of the Mississaugas of the New Credit First Nation. The territory was part of the Dish with One Spoon Wampum Belt Treaty, an agreement between the Iroquois Confederacy and the Ojibwe and allied nations to peaceably share and care for the resources around the Great Lakes.

Today, the meeting place of Tkaronto is still the home to many Indigenous people from across Turtle Island, and I am grateful to have the opportunity to speak with you on this territory.

So why do I acknowledge this land we stand on?

Almost exactly one year ago to this day, I was living and working inside a war zone. The war zone I was in was probably something like you might imagine. There was razor wire demarking boundaries you dare not step foot over. If you do, you are met by armed police decked out in riot gear—guns and shields, their faces masked in balaclavas. There is a constant feeling of threat. It feels heavy and, over time, it made me feel slightly paranoid.

There are militarized check points where army tanks are parked. If you try and pass, you are questioned by guards holding weapons. Your movements are tracked, and you are always aware that you could be detained and questioned at any moment.

There is the constant and pervasive sound of surveillance planes and helicopters. This is probably the thing I remember the most—the endless hovering of aircraft overhead morning and night. Always present. It's a sound I never got used to.

There were the flood lights that shone white light through the night. Imagine a dozen full moons shining down on you, but accompanied by snipers, lurking in the shadows, trained to kill. Always watching.

"Bobbi Jean Three Legs." Photograph by Michelle Latimer.

And then there were the people—the people living on the front lines and in the camps. Rows upon rows of tents and shelters where men and women, children, strangers, friends, and families slept side by side. It was a small village: medical tents, schools, kitchens where mass meals were prepared. There was camaraderie and accountability. We survived through the help of one another, and this connected us vitally.

You might think I am describing the conflict in Syria or Gaza or any one of the war zones we see reported over the news. But I did not have to travel so far to be in *this* war zone. The place I am describing was inside the United States of America— Standing Rock, North Dakota, to be exact. It could have been anywhere. It could have just as easily been here.

I had arrived there to document the nine-month standoff that saw unarmed civilians occupying land in protest of the Dakota Access Pipeline, a large-scale oil pipeline project that would cut across four states and threaten the drinking water supply of millions. Originally, the pipeline was set to be built near the state capital, but when people took offense to the possible environmental harm it would cause, they lobbied to have the pipeline rerouted. And just like that the pipeline was moved. Moved to within half a mile of the Standing Rock Sioux Indian Reservation. Moved without consultation with the tribe and without proper environmental assessments done.

And just like that, the repeat button of history was pressed. The repeat button was pressed.

When settlers first came to North America, they employed many tools to extract control over the land and, by extension, the First Peoples who lived here.

The fur trade and the gold rush are just two examples of industry that used the land in the service of "progress." Indigenous women were attacked through acts of violence and forced marriage in order to procure landownership. Buffalo, which once roamed free in the thousands and were an important food source to Indigenous people, were mass slaughtered to induce famine, dependency, and forced relocation, thus freeing land for settlement. And residential schools, which separated children from their parents and community, were state-led tactics to decimate Indigenous spirituality and language.

Time and time again we've learned lessons about the value of land, the meaning of Indian lives, and the language that connects them both.

At Standing Rock we had state-sanctioned armed forces standing in retaliation against unarmed civilians, all in order to protect the corporate interests of a private company.

No one expected that a few dozen Native people would balloon into tens of thousands to make this the largest Indigenous-led protest in more than a century. Who would have thought that people occupying land peacefully would incite so much force?

I spent months, in and out of Standing Rock, documenting the occupation there. And I could share many things because I saw many instances of beauty during my time there, but today there's a particular memory I'd like to share with you.

I was filming on a crisp day in November when the warriors from the camp were called to the front lines. The construction crews were advancing, and we were being called to stop them from crossing a small river. Tensions were high, and the media was beginning to take note of what was going on there. People from the camp rushed to the water and waded out to form a line facing the riot police, who stood on a hill above them. The police stared back. They rarely looked at you; it was more like they were looking through you. Never direct eye contact, just the imposing threat of their bodies clad in armor, weapons in hand.

One woman who stood near me began to sing. She was beautiful, standing there, waist-deep in cold water. She was midsong when she suddenly stopped and pointed her finger at a police officer—she looked him straight in the eye and said, "I see you. And I see that you see me." She held his eye and he tried to look away but his eyes kept coming back to her. She held him there—in that space.

And she began to sing to him, holding his gaze. She sang as the enforcement started spraying tear gas into the faces of the protestors. A white cloud of smoke overtook the crowd, and the police officer she was singing to broke rank and yelled out to her, "Run, please run, save yourself." But the woman stood there as they gassed her at point blank range, her body a weapon of protest.

What I had witnessed was a rare moment of connectivity. An officer disarmed by a singing woman. A singing woman emboldened because she had been seen. Two people recognizing each other's humanity inside a moment of violence—one doing his job as an officer sent to protect the interests of an oil company, the other an Indigenous woman fulfilling her traditional role as a Water Keeper by standing up to protect the river. The land that holds their bodies connects them, their shared language connects them, and the recognition of one another connects them. In this moment of violence, there was harmony within the dissonance.

And so when I stand before you and acknowledge our ancestors and the land we are on, I'm acknowledging our shared humanity—our connection to one another. I'm also acknowledging decades upon decades of colonization that has sought to control, own, and destroy our relationship to this land. Not just my relationship as an Indigenous person, but your relationship to this land.

When I acknowledge the land, I do so in a language that is not my People's. And this may seem like a small detail. *However, I believe the erasure of Indigenous language is key to why we are where we are today.* You cannot separate our languages from the land. Language is the connective tissue that allows our relationships to flourish and evolve. Erasing the way we communicate affects how we relate to everything around us.

First Nations peoples have always operated within an oral culture. Our culture and traditions are passed on through storytelling, and these stories embrace a world view where the natural world—both human and nonhuman—is a relative. And when you see your relatives all around you, it suddenly becomes much harder to enact violence toward that which you love.

Indigenous language is derived from listening to the land. Through listening we came to know the names of things. When our children come into the world, we wait for them to show us their names. And more often than not, a word will suggest a relational meaning. For example, the Ojibwe word for "Wind" is "Noodin"; this means "the wind blows," "it is windy," and "there is wind." The human relationship to wind is inherent in its meaning. It does not exist alone—we are present in its meaning, existing only in relation to everything else. It is a delicate balance.

So when you hurt the land, you hurt yourself.

I wanted to take time today to speak aloud these ideas because I believe that words have power. The ideas I present to you are not new; they are not mine. They are as old as the rock we come from and as far-reaching as the Four Directions. They are shaped by the ancestors who have come before.

When we acknowledge our history, we hold space for all of our relations, we make room. When we cultivate a relationship with the Earth, we can become the stewards of the land we are meant to be. And when we listen we can foster hope and understanding. We can foster peace.

I don't speak my language. No one in my family does anymore. But I learned these words to bring them here to you today.

Kak-kin-a-geen-wit Et-shay-ake Mina-shtodan Kakina-gegwa Ken-tow-gook.

"Be gentle with all things of nature, for everyone."

Chi Miigwetch.

25

WAKE WORK VERSUS WORK OF SETTLER MEMORY
MODES OF SOLIDARITY IN #NoDAPL, BLACK LIVES MATTER, AND ANTI-TRUMPISM

Kevin Bruyneel

The November 8, 2016, election of Donald Trump to the U.S. presidency came as a shock to most of the country. The vast majority of polls and pundits predicted that the xenophobic, misogynistic Republican candidate who took pleasure in being "politically incorrect" could not garner the necessary votes, beyond his enthusiastic base of supporters, to win a national election against Democratic nominee Hillary Clinton. Right after the election, starting the next day and continuing on for months, massive demonstrations took place, as millions of people took to the streets to #Resist, with many asserting that Donald Trump was #NotMyPresident. On January 21, 2017, the day after Trump's inauguration, the Women's March on Washington and in locales across the country turned into possibly the largest demonstration in U.S. history, with some estimates of over four million participating nationwide and more than five million worldwide.[1] A random survey of attendees at the Washington, D.C., march, which had an estimated half million people in attendance, found that one-third of them were participating in their first ever protest and 56 percent had not been to a demonstration in five years. Ninety percent of those surveyed said they voted for Hillary Clinton.[2] Thus, in the wake of Trump's victory, many Americans, especially white liberal Americans although not entirely or exclusively so, engaged in forms of political activism unlike anything they had ever done before or that they had not done in a number of years. Radical scholar and activist Angela Davis even referred to the 2016 election as a "wake-up call for Americans."[3] A new day seemed to have dawned for millions of Americans by the morning of November 9, 2016—the morning after—marking a clear break between the past and present of their nation.

A new day for some, however, was a familiar one for others. In particular, given the rise of and significant public attention garnered by Indigenous and Black radical political movements in the preceding years, it is safe to say that the distinct past/present break that millions of Americans may have experienced after the 2016 election likely did not resonate with the organizers and activists of #NoDAPL/ Standing Rock and Black Lives Matter (BLM). Rather, to draw upon Christina Sharpe's insightful conceptualization, these activists were more likely to experience that the "past that is not past reappears, always, to rupture the present."[4] Sharpe refers to this as being "in the wake," which is "to occupy and be occupied by the continuous and changing present of slavery's as yet unresolved unfolding."[5] Sharpe's focus is on the afterlife of slavery not on settler colonialism, but her notion of the "unresolved unfolding" of past oppressive and dehumanizing structures, practices, and ideologies in the present speaks to that which the #NoDAPL and Black Lives Matter movements stand against in refusal and radical resistance. As LaDonna Bravebull Allard, Lakota activist and historian of the Standing Rock Sioux Tribe, stated in September 2016 in the midst of the standoff against the development of the Dakota Access Pipeline that threatens her people's sovereignty, land, and water: "We must remember we are part of a larger story. We are still here. We are still fighting for our lives, 153 years after my great-great-grandmother Mary watched as our people were senselessly murdered. We should not have to fight so hard to survive on our own lands."[6] Allard's words call forth the pain and political persistence that are shaped by a clear sense of history, the "larger story," within which she and her community exist and fight. Her words convey "a sense of place made strong through intergenerational memory" that, to quote Mishuana Goeman's discussion of the memory work of Indigenous visual art, "avoids reaffirming notions of vanishing Indians or stagnant traditions."[7] This sense of strength that comes through a deeply embedded, intergenerational politics of collective memory stands in contrast with the wave of national mnemonic dysfunction and contestation, across the political spectrum, compelled by the Trump candidacy and election. This contrast points to the importance of the politics of collective memory for shaping the terms of solidarity work and the aims of resistance. In this regard, I see Indigenous and Black radical movements in the U.S. context as engaged in what Sharpe calls "wake work," whereas liberal political formations (as well as those to the right) fall back on what I call settler memory that reproduces the oppressive formations that emerge from the "past that is not past." The balance of this chapter offers a consideration of each modality and its implications for politics and the meaning of solidarity.

Indigenous and Black radical politics in the U.S. context have their distinct histories, formations, and claims that can be traced back centuries right on up to their most notable contemporary forms in the emergence of #NoDAPL and Black Lives Matter. One cannot and should not collapse these histories and movements as identical, and I suggest it is also not productive politically nor intellectually defensible to prioritize one subject position, Indigenous or Black, or form of structure and practice of domination, settler colonialism or slavery, as prior to or more urgent than the other. For one, these histories are deeply interwoven; distinctive, but also fundamentally interconnected. Enslavement of African people in the United States does not occur without dispossession of Indigenous territory, and a major motivation for dispossession was the economic and political prospects of the implantation and expansion of such slavery. As Tiffany King argues, "Black fungibility represents this space of discursive and conceptual possibility for settler colonial imaginaries. Black fungible bodies work beyond the metrics and 'metaphysics of labor' in White settler colonial states."[8] African people were dispossessed from their home territories in the course of becoming enslaved, and while the enslavement of African and African descended peoples was institutionalized, legal and central to the U.S. political economy, there also existed the "other slavery" of Indigenous people in the so-called New World.[9] As well, colonialism and slavery were/are fundamentally heteropatriarchal formations and modes of rule, in which colonizers and enslavers (not rarely one and the same persons) utilized sexual violence and the destruction of family structures as a mode of conquest, domination, and exploitation of and upon human bodies and territory.[10] Thus, the familiar scholarly and political binaries of land/labor, dispossession/enslavement, and Indigenous/Black do not play out so neatly in history once one takes heed of the fact that it was and is a messier interconnection and coanimation. To speak of interconnections is also to consider tensions and conflict, and here we can recall that Indigenous people such as those of the Cherokee Nation and of other nations owned Black slaves, while after the U.S. Civil War, Black U.S. soldiers, who came to be known as buffalo soldiers, were deployed to the western frontier of the United States to assist in the violent dispossession of Indigenous nations for an expanding American nation.[11]

With this in mind, and speaking and writing as someone who is of white settler lineage born and raised on the unceded lands of the Musqueam, Squamish, and Tsleil-Waututh Nations (also known as Vancouver, British Columbia), I find it imperative to refuse to fall back on familiar, even comfortable, intellectual and political narratives, scholarly sources, pathways, concepts, barriers, binaries, or accepted truths in the effort to understand the meaning and possibilities of Indigenous and Black radical politics on their own and in collaboration, and how this informs the practices of collaboration and solidarity work for those who are not Indigenous or Black. This leads me to the radical potentiality of Sharpe's notion of "wake work," which she defines as "a mode of inhabiting *and* rupturing this episteme with our known lived and un/imaginable lives. With that analytic we might imagine otherwise from what we know *now* in the wake of slavery."[12] While Sharpe's work is *on blackness and being* in slavery's afterlife, not settler colonialism or Indigeneity directly, her notion of "inhabiting *and* rupturing" prevailing world views via "our known lived and un/imaginable lives" speaks poignantly to how many Black and Indigenous radical activists and thinkers speak to and practice resistance as that which is rooted in an acknowledged inhabiting—or what I call in collaborative terms a *coinhabitation*—of a white settler colonial context that one engages and resists through a deeply informed politics of memory about the interconnected oppressive structures of enslavement, colonialism, and heteropatriarchy that continue to shape the present. This politics of memory accords with the practices of wake work, which during a February 2017 panel on her book, *In the Wake*, Sharpe set out as "a reading practice, a critical practice, a practice of care, a practice of thinking, and of attempting to see and look . . . [and] community response work as a type of wake work."[13] In drawing out wake work to speak to Black and Indigenous radical politics in collaboration and the practices of solidarity in general, I take heed of Sharpe's hope that "wake work might have enough capaciousness to travel and do work that I have not here been able to imagine or anticipate."[14] This traveling involves looking back centuries in time to expressions and terms of Black and Indigenous collaborations and coinhabitations, and then looking present and forward.

Cedric Robinson's study of the long history of Black radicalism, *Black Marxism: The Making of the Black Radical Tradition*, is peppered with references to Indigenous and Black political and social comingling, such as "in Hispaniola, Blacks had joined the native uprising of 1533," "several plots involving first Indians and Blacks, and then Blacks separately were reported discovered in 1709, 1722 and 1723. And in 1727, a maroon community of Indians and Blacks, which its inhabitants called des Natanpelle, was betrayed by a former resident."[15] In *Black Movements in America*, Robinson carries this historical narrative forward and with attention to the emergent U.S. context, as he discusses the distinct yet also intertwined, coinhabitative radical struggles of Indigenous and Black peoples that can be traced to and beyond the American Revolutionary period:

> Like the Native American nations that sided with the British, the Black Loyalists sought to employ the British army to serve their own interests, for their own ends. Long after the defeated British had departed, their allies, the Native Americans and the Blacks, continued the struggle for liberty. For generations to come, Native Americans recognized America as a colonial power, and Blacks read the new nation as tyrannical. Their suspicion of and opposition toward American society survived in the political cultures of Blacks and Native Americans for the next two hundred years.[16]

As well, he notes that in the seventeenth, eighteenth, and nineteenth centuries, "in the Southeastern United States, Black Indians and Black–Indian alliances had pursued liberty through anticolonial struggle and under the authority of Indian nations."[17] The point here is that on their own and in tandem Black and Indigenous people have never not been resisting settler colonialism, enslavement, and the rippling consequences of both. While Indigenous politics has a minor role in the political history he sets out, as a rigorous political historian and radical scholar Robinson shows that any thorough grasp of the Black radical tradition has to account for colonialism, globally and in the United States, and the coinhabitation and collaborations of Black and Indigenous people. In other words, there is no Black radical tradition as a separate distinct pathway—separate from settler colonialism and Indigeneity—just as there is no Indigenous radical tradition in the U.S. context (for this case) distinctly cleaved off from enslavement, its afterlife, and Blackness. Two major contemporary formations of these radical traditions, #NoDAPL and Black Lives Matter, reflect the coinhabitation of un/imaginable lives as a type of wake work that we can discern in the way these movements and activists define that which undergirds their mutual understanding, collaborations, resistance, and efforts to engage in the "critical practices"—of care, of thinking, and of attempting to see and look—that lead to imagining otherwise than that which dominates the present; that being white settler colonial rule, neoliberal capitalism and governance, and heteropatriarchy.

Miski Noor, an "organizer with Black Lives Matter Minneapolis" who visited the encampments at Standing Rock in August 2016 with other BLM organizers, provided her take on what connects the movements:

> This isn't just an Indigenous issue; water is life for all of us and we have a responsibility to the Earth and future generations to protect it. While at the camp, I heard over and over again from Native folks how they have shown up in their cities across the country for Black lives. As BLM, we have built power and we have a platform. And as a movement, we have a duty to uplift and amplify the stories and struggles of all marginalized folks, as our liberation is intertwined. The history of genocide and stolen land and stolen labor in America will forever link Black folks and Indigenous folks (and let us be clear that the two are not mutually exclusive), as there can be no Black liberation without Indigenous sovereignty.[18]

Noor emphasizes the importance of interconnection, intergenerational memory, and a refusal to abide "mutually exclusive" demarcations—such as land and labor or Black and Indigenous—as the basis of collaborations over time. These sorts of claims build out of the coinhabitation of the white settler colonial system as a form of wake work whose disruptive threat to the dominant episteme comes in the critical practice of refusing to abide the containment of identities, movements, claims, and concerns into discrete matters, as say Indigenous or Black issues alone. When such containment succeeds, collaborations and disruptive coinhabitations that are at the heart of solidarity work are undermined, or never get off the ground. In this spirit, Noor refuses the idea that environmental concerns are solely or primarily an Indigenous issue. We see the same sentiments in the #BlackLivesMatter Organization's official statement of solidarity with Standing Rock, posted in early September 2016:

> Black Lives Matter stands with Standing Rock. As there are many diverse manifestations of Blackness, and Black people are also displaced Indigenous peoples, we are

clear that there is no Black liberation without Indigenous sovereignty. Environmental racism is not limited to pipelines on Indigenous land, because we know that the chemicals used for fracking and the materials used to build pipelines are also used in water containment and sanitation plants in Black communities like Flint, Michigan.[19]

Again, we see the refusal of contained categories and an embrace of coinhabitation without collapsing experience, identities, and claims. The assertion of "no Black liberation without Indigenous sovereignty" does not deny the tensions that may arise. For example, what forms do Black liberation and Indigenous sovereignty take in relation to each other, what defines one's relationship to these subject positions, and to what degree are Indigenous liberation and "Black sovereignty"—a historical topic Robinson explores in his work[20]—themselves at stake here too, and in what form? The answer to these questions about the meaning of the intertwined aims of Black liberation and Indigenous sovereignty are addressed more concretely in the process of bringing about this vision through collaborative resistance and the critical practices of wake work.

We see this collaboration in Indigenous solidarity practices that seek to engage and support the movements and concerns most directly associated with and mobilized by Black Americans. For example, in April 2016, as the Standing Rock encampments and standoff against the Dakota Access Pipeline were just beginning and thus before #NoDAPL was in the public eye, Kyle Mays, Black/Saginaw Anishinaabe historian, noted that "his Michigan Native cousins, the Little Traverse Band of Ottawa Indians, gave $10,000 U.S. dollars to support the residents of Flint." As well as financial assistance, Mays observed solidarity practices in artistic expression, here by Christy Bieber, an Anishinaabe singer performing with the Dream Keepers Native American Youth Group in Detroit. One song, which includes the lyric "let's meet up by the water / Nakweshkodaadiiidaa Ekobiiyag," Mays describes "as the sounds of drums and rattles—sacred sounds to Indigenous people—poetry, and rapping. It is a protest song, preparing people for a ceremony to bring healing to the residents of Flint, suffering under the yoke of Governor Rick Snyder's decision to deliberately poison its citizens with water from the Flint River."[21] While the urgency of resistance stems from the crisis in a specific community, understandably, once one refuses the constraints of the dominant episteme, wake work as a practice of care and coinhabitation widens the vision and experience regarding whose concern, cause, and fight this really is.

In this regard, consider Miski Noor's earlier reference to "Native folks" showing up to BLM demonstrations in the cities, often to protest police violence, in which they are doing so not only to support Black communities but also with the knowledge that police brutality is a concern not only for Black people. In fact, studies show that Indigenous people suffer proportionally even higher rates of police violence and abuse, and as an article on this matter phrased it, "nobody is talking about it" as an Indigenous issue too.[22] Leanne Simpson, Mississauga Nishnaabeg, reminds us that police violence is not random but is rather a product of historically rooted forms of structural domination and exploitation that have shaped the contemporary episteme: "Indigenous and black people are disproportionately attacked and targeted by the state, and, in fact, policing in Turtle Island was born of the need to suppress and oppress black and Indigenous resistance to colonialism and slavery."[23] The long history of colonialist and racist policing continues in many forms, such as in the violent state attacks upon and repression of the Water Protectors at Standing Rock.[24]

The defining #NoDAPL affirmation, "Water Is Life—Mni Wičoni," that resonated from Standing Rock to Flint and beyond was in a literal sense about the water itself, the threat presented to water and the life it sustained by oil pipelines and poisoned city water systems. Water Is Life is also about refusing and challenging governmental and corporate structures, practices, and ideological presuppositions that end up turning water, that which should be a source of life for all, into a weapon against those who resist the dictates of institutions and actors representing capital and the settler state. This refusal is nothing new, and neither is the weapon. The water hoses turned on Black civil rights activists in the 1960s became the "past that is not past" when water hoses were turned on Water Protectors in the freezing cold of Standing Rock in the winter of 2016.[25] Sharpe's evocative notion and title of her book, "in the wake," stems from the image of the water that forms the wake of a slave ship cutting through the Middle Passage. Here water is a source of death, not life, another one of the weapons of enslavement and thus also dispossession. A wake is also a mode of grieving for the dead, "to defend the dead," and in so doing calls forth the weight and the commitment produced by the collective memory of those who came before, who resisted and sacrificed, and the fight carried on in the present day that lives up to their legacy.[26] In this regard, I think again of the politics of collective memory in LaDonna Bravebull Allard's remembering how her "great-great-grandmother Mary watched as our people were senselessly murdered," and that this intergenerational memory of the long story emboldens the claim that "we are still fighting for our lives." We also see that in wake work one form of wake stimulates another form. Defending the dead prods one to wake as in to be conscious, to open one's eyes and be aware.

This is not mere word games, for in Sharpe's notion of "wake work" what I find compelling is that it is a mode of resistance, or reimagining, that is deeply embedded in "inhabiting" the long story of the "known lived and un/imaginable lives"— which I take to be that of the dead and the living—as a politics of collective memory committed to radical practices of thinking, care, and community response that do not cleave the past off from the present and also are not constrained and defined to and by the past. The "rupturing" of the dominant episteme—the world view and way of knowing of white settler heteropatriarchy—can only occur through such a serious and often painful inhabitation, and for collaborators a coinhabitation, that grounds resistance and is the basis of alternative, liberating imaginaries.

This is a major lesson for potential collaborators who are neither Black nor Indigenous, and in particular but not exclusively I mean for white people who may see ourselves as *allies*, as it is popularly phrased. To be a collaborator via the mode of wake work does not and should not mean claiming the experience of Black and Indigenous people as reflective of one's own, or ventriloquizing as such. Rather, we—and I mean *we* as in white settler subjects—have to be accountable to and embedded in the long story of white settler nation and state building, in which we construct our commitments and practices based upon engaging in the critical practices of thinking, care, and seeing that leads to acknowledging "the past that is not past." To acknowledge is about more than knowing this history, as important as that is. It requires individual and community action to turn this knowledge into transformative practice. Those of us who are white settlers cannot and should not claim to be *in the wake* of slavery and settler colonialism in any way that claims to know/empath the experience of this inhabitation. We are obligated to wake work, but in a slightly different direction. Here I mean it as a form of radical engagement premised on one's defined commitments to dismantle and decolonize the white settler state as an outcome that would be best for all; all except the small percentage who most concretely benefit. This work requires critical engagement with and resistance against other white settlers as a core principle and practice of our fight for and pursuit of a better world, and it should not be contained as someone else's problem for whom we can serve only as allies. It must be understood and acted upon as our problem too. For example, it means being on the front lines of confronting white supremacists such as those who marched in Charlottesville, Virginia, in August 2017 and killed one of the protesters standing bravely on those front lines, Heather Heyer, and injured many others.[27] The wake work of white settler subjects requires seeing, advocating, organizing, and being active in transformative and likely confrontational politics that pursues an imaginary in which white settler-ness is abolished as a status and subject position. Here we see how abolitionist and decolonization politics are deeply intertwined, or should be seen as such, as the dismantling of racial hierarchy and colonial capitalism go hand in hand, for as Natsu Taylor Saito puts it, "whiteness has been constructed and defended as a rigidly exclusive category precisely because it is not a descriptor of national origin but a marker of entitlement to colonial power, privilege and property."[28]

I contrast the notion of wake work, that which reflects a deeply embedded politics of collective memory that generates radical practices and imaginaries, with the idea of the "wake-up call" experienced by those for whom the 2016 election marked the dawn of a bad new day and a stark past/present break for the nation. My concern is not people taking to the streets to protest the white authoritarian imperatives of the Trump administration, as this is a needed resistance that must continue against this administration and those that follow it. Rather, my focus involves taking a deeper look at what many Americans are being woken up to, and

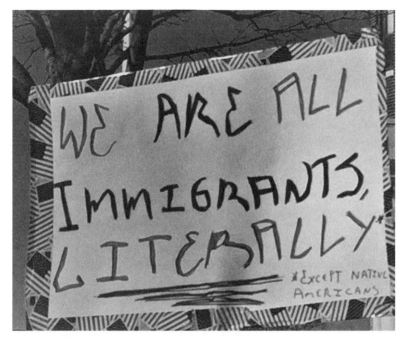

"Somerville, Massachusetts," February 4, 2017. Photograph by Kevin Bruyneel.

what sort of politics of memory is at work here. To draw this out, I examine something I witnessed at a demonstration in early 2017, which I deem representative of a type of solidarity politics that reflects the work of settler memory, not wake work.

On February 4, 2017, I attended a pro–sanctuary city rally held at City Hall of Somerville, Massachusetts, the city in which I live. Politically, Somerville is a decidedly liberal-left city, where Hillary Clinton won 85 percent of the vote in the 2016 presidential election. This rally occurred in the wake of the Trump administration's proposed "Muslim Bans" and general anti-immigrant rhetoric, policies, and state practices. The people who attended the rally, the city's mayor Joe Curtatone, and the city's elected representatives are all strong advocates in support of Somerville being a sanctuary city, as it has been for more than thirty years. In fact, Curtatone has become a nationally famous mayor for his defiant stance on this position and against Trump.[29] As I was walking home from the rally, I saw a sign held up amid the departing crowd.

Framed entirely by images of the U.S. flag, with the red, white, and blue reproduced in the color of the text posited on a white background, the sign's visual aesthetics on their own convey an overtly positive evocation of the American nation. The words then provide a liberal, and in some forms left, trope of national identification, constructing and asserting solidarity with immigrants and refugees under the premise that "we"—that being American citizens—"are all immigrants, literally." Then there is the smaller printed text, positioned in the lower right corner, which offers a corrective, an addition, an asterisk to the theme of America as a nation of immigrants: "*Except Native Americans." As if ripped from the pages of Indigenous critical theory, this * addition is an example, literally, of Eve Tuck and K. Wayne Yang's claim that Indigenous people are often positioned as "asterisk peoples . . . footnotes in the dominant paradigms" of the United States. As they put it: "the asterisk is a body count that does not account for Indigenous politics, educational concerns, and epistemologies."[30]

Building on Tuck and Yang's notion as it concerns the dynamics of political struggle in the United States, I see this sign not as an exception but as acutely representative of a dominant mode of collective memory production that, from the left to the right side of the political spectrum, reinforces the status and boundaries of the American settler nation and its episteme as regenerative fuel for making political claims and shoring up contained alliances. In this case, what is at work here is settler memory, a mode of collective memory that places Indigeneity in the background of race and other politics discussions in the United States by simultaneously remembering and disavowing, seeing and not seeing, marking as both present and absent Indigenous people and the history of colonialism. This positioning is also fundamentally anti-Black for not being able see and theorize the reach and forms of practices of white supremacy in settler contexts in the afterlife of slavery.

Taking heed of this dynamic matters because in U.S. politics Indigenous people and their political struggles are too easily footnoted, and the #NoDAPL resistance and struggle by Water Protectors at Standing Rock compels us to dig deeper as to the ways in which the dominant American public (mis)understands and (dis)locates contemporary Indigenous struggle in the national imaginary. Understanding and resisting the political work that settler memory does in the U.S. context is critical in this effort to refuse blindness to, disavowal or exoticization of radical Indigenous political struggles such as that of #NoDAPL. My focus here is primarily on the liberal to left side of the political spectrum, although I note consistencies in U.S. collective memory across the spectrum too. Those on the liberal to left politically too often and easily succumb to the soporific power of settler memory that undermines the capacity to generate wider political connections and imaginaries for liberation. Next, I assess the sign in the context of contemporary U.S. politics, define and elaborate on the concept of settler memory, and consider what this tells us about what many people should but often are not awake to about the history and present of Indigenous and Black radical struggles.

I try to imagine the creation of this sign for the Sanctuary City Rally. A liberal effort at a message of unifying, inclusive multicultural patriotism is complete, when someone in the sign-making party realizes their oversight: "Uh, but what about Native Americans? They're not immigrants." A solution is quickly devised, and the * points to the "exception" of Native Americans who are nevertheless still positioned within the frame of the American nation—and the sign is good to go, with just a few more U.S. flag stickers wrapped around the sign-post to hold it and its message firmly in place. Whether accurate or not regarding this exact instance, my imagined scenario hits on a likely truth, which is that Indigenous people were an afterthought in this political moment, a product of settler memory in the remembrance and disavowal (seeing and then footnoting) of Indigenous people. In that way, this particular rally reproduced a wider liberal trend in contemporary U.S. politics.

In the context of their #NotMyPresident denial of the fact that Trump was, indeed, their president and that the historic and present state of U.S. white settler nationalism played no small part in bringing Trump to power—a form of nationalism that one can trace back to noted Indian-killer and slaveholder Andrew Jackson whom Trump sees as such an ideal U.S. president that he had Jackson's portrait placed in the Oval Office[31]—a familiar liberal response to the 2016 election results involved constructing an imaginary where the America that elected Trump was not really their America, not "literally." For example, in response to Trump's mnemonic reference to the nation's lost national greatness in his defining slogan and promise to "Make America Great Again," many liberals asserted that such greatness was not at all lost but rather quite present, best exemplified in the words of presidential candidate Hillary Clinton in her acceptance speech at the Democratic National Convention: "America is great—because America is good."[32] Such a statement and others like them throughout the campaign reflect, if anything, anti–wake work, with no sense of the past, no defense of the dead, and no consciousness of what it means for the present and future. In the years, months, and weeks leading up to the DNC convention in late July 2016 highly public acts of police violence against Black Americans continued as did the Black Lives Matter mobilization to address this issue.[33] As well, during the exact days in which the DNC took place the U.S. Army Corp of Engineers approved easements for Dakota Access, lawyers representing the Standing Rock Tribe filed injunctions against these decisions, and the #NoDAPL encampments and protests gained greater public attention.[34] In light of these events occurring just before and during the Democratic Convention, Clinton's statement of American greatness/goodness reads as, at best, a practice of neither care nor critical thinking and, at worst, a cruel disavowal of white settler violence, an all too familiar disavowal in U.S. liberal discourse. Beyond the usual nationalistic banalities of campaign messaging, these words also reflect an imaginary of an America otherwise than that which millions of people inhabit.

We see this dynamic as well in the way in which the "We Are All Immigrants, Literally" sign constructs the *we* around the idea of migration as a transgenerational experience and memory that links immigrants of the past and their descendants to the immigrants, and potential immigrants, of the present day. The use of "literally" signals the refusal to abide any other interpretations of what defines the identity of all Americans, save the * exception. No other imaginary or construction of the nation's collective memory is tolerated but that of the immigrant narrative. As Roxanne Dunbar-Ortiz persuasively argues, the idea of the United States as a "nation of immigrants" is a "convenient myth developed as a response to the 1960s movements against colonialism, neocolonialism, and white supremacy."[35] At a time of intense political resistance and crisis over the history and meaning of America in the 1960s, a reactionary turn to the immigrant narrative sought to suture the wounds of national identity. In our time of movements and crisis, this narrative has once again become the only acceptable "past that is not past." However, when we shine the light of the exception back on the rule an elision reveals itself, as "we are all immigrants" references movement to and arrival upon the land whereas the exception of Native Americans speaks to the reality of non-Indigenous conquest, colonization, and settlement of the land itself. In short, the sign refers to immigrants and Native Americans, but not the settler. "We Are Immigrants, Literally" is about the arrival, not the staying—as Patrick Wolfe put it, "settler colonizers come to stay"[36]—and the * exception noted on the sign simultaneously points to and elides the historical and contemporary implications of this staying; that being colonization, settlement, enslavement, and the afterlife of slavery. This double movement is the work of settler memory, which is more than a simple denial of U.S. history but is rather a form of remembrance and disavowal that undermines radical political possibilities, solidarities, and imaginaries by shoring up settler nationalist commitments, boundaries, identity, and myths.

Settler memory is not a forgetting of Indigenous people, and thus of settler colonialism. It is a cycle of disavowal that replays and reproduces settlement on a mnemonic loop, such as in annual celebrations of Thanksgiving and Columbus Day, the use of Indigenous names and symbols in military nomenclature, popular culture, and U.S. topography, and many other examples of appropriation. Settler memory habituates settlement as the legitimate inhabitation of the land by those who were once long ago but are no longer settlers who acquired and took land from once long ago but no longer active Indigenous people. No longer settlers, but now immigrants, no longer active Indigenous people, but rather * exceptions. At the same time, given the deeply intertwined relationship of colonialist dispossession of Indigenous territory with slavery in the United States, settler memory elides the deeper history, development, and impact of white supremacist structures, practices, and world views. The work of settler memory reinforces white settler identity by disavowing and masking the centrality of settler identity for whiteness as a political identity, status, and experience. This occurs not only in mainstream political discourse, but even in contexts and with those attuned to matters of race in the United States. In our time, those concerned with race talk a lot about whiteness but almost never about white *settler*-ness. Across the political spectrum, settler memory serves the white settler capacity to remember and not remember, to see and not see, to know and not acknowledge its settler-ness as a status produced through and benefited by the historical and contemporary practices of white supremacy, slavery, its afterlife, and settler colonialism. Critical attention to settler memory is not only about attending to Indigeneity and settler colonialism historically and in our time, but also draws light on deeper forms of anti-Blackness that are masked when settler narratives are remembered as otherwise.

In all, the sanctuary city sign is a representative form of U.S. settler memory work that sees and does not see Indigenous people/settler colonialism as it also turns the history of the capture, transport, and enslavement of African people and their descendants into a narrative that would fit quite well with Housing and Urban Development Secretary Ben Carson's March 2017 claim that slaves were the "other immigrants who came here in the bottom of slave ships, worked even longer, even harder for less."[37] Black Americans do not even get an * footnote in this construction, as they are incorporated into the immigrant story. Given its constitutive relationship to securing by masking white settler-ness, settler memory is at work in Carson's statement in the way in which he remembers and at the same time disavows slavery by subsuming it within an immigration narrative that elides—under the guise of it being a matter of terrible labor conditions, working "longer . . . for less"—the forced displacement and violence of U.S. enslavement of African and African-descended people. As Christina Sharpe reminds us "the bottom of slave ships" is also known as "the hold," which is the place on a ship where cargo—here captured people transported across the Middle Passage—is stowed below deck. From the hold of a ship during enslavement to the holding cell of prison in the afterlife of slavery, the role of "the hold repeats and repeats and repeats in and into the present."[38] The intergenerational repetition of these practices produce and reinforce dominant world views about racial hierarchy, among other dynamics, which can become accepted passively as somehow the unchangeable work of history, as just the way things are, and in this sense "the hold is what is taken as given; it is the logic, it is the characterization of a relation in that moment."[39] Wake work seeks to resist this hold on the given, whereas the work of settler memory sustains it. This chapter has argued that there are contrasting "givens" that have shaped the urgency and solidarity practices of the major political movements that emerged in the years leading up to and in response to the 2016 election. A major source of this difference between radical and liberal forms of resistance is how these movements place themselves and their concerns in history, in the hold of contrasting collective memories.

Without doubt, there is considerable crossover in the people who actively support #NoDAPL and Black Lives Matter and those who actively oppose the Trump administration's policies and state practices. These are not self-contained and mutually exclusive movements. This convergence, in some regard, was evident in the thousands who attended the Rise With Standing Rock, Native Nations March on Washington on March 10, 2017.[40] This march was planned before but was also catalyzed by the Trump administration's directive to approve the continued construction of the Dakota Access Pipeline on February 7, 2017, which had been halted in December 2016 under the Barack Obama administration.[41] As successful and important as this D.C. march was, it did not capture the imagination and participation of millions as did the Women's March on Washington in January 2017, which is a result of many causes. I have argued that one way to discern the difference in political mobilizations and forms and meaning of solidarity is to take note of the contrasting politics of memory between the #NoDAPL/#BlackLivesMatter movements and the liberal anti-Trump movements, in which the former practices wake work and the latter too easily relies on the work of settler memory. This is not to say that #NoDAPL and radical Indigenous movements will always be on the same page with Black Lives Matter and radical Black movements, and vice versa, or internally among and within their own movements. As political theorist Jane Gordon aptly notes about the nature of collaborations that comprise political movements, "alliances are contingent and forged, contingent and forged again."[42] Any collaboration is a persistent working through of compatibilities and tensions as the movement develops, acts, and sets out key commitments and goals. I denoted forms of wake work in the practices of coinhabitation, critical thinking, care, and the community response of these movements that provide the basis for collaborations that have been forged historically and will likely continue moving forward. I have contrasted this with, in particular, liberal political movements in the United States that see and oppose, for very good reasons, the policies of the Trump administration, but which end up articulating a constrained imaginary of the past, present, and future of the United States, thereby narrowing the scope of collaborative possibilities and snuffing out radical potentiality. These efforts are embedded in and reflect the work of settler memory.

In this light, I turn one final time to Sharpe to consider a fundamental question for all potential collaborators engaged in solidarity work, one that she devises from another sense of the hold: "How are we beholden to and beholders of each other in ways that change across time and place and space and yet remain?"[43] The wake work of radical political movements and the work of settler memory of liberal political movements end up with different answers to this question of our beholden-ness, our obligations. Wake work provides the basis to widen the frame of coinhabitation to imagine otherwise than is at present, and thereby demand of collaborators a greater level of critical thinking, care, response, action, and beholden-ness. The work of settler memory narrows the scope of one's sense of obligations to others and to the world around us. This lack of beholden-ness diminishes the capacity to radically reimagine what the world might look like beyond this moment, and thereby puts our world into greater danger.

1. Erica Chenoweth and Jeremy Pressman. "This Is What We Learned by Counting the Women's Marches," *Washington Post*, February 7, 2017, https://www.washington post.com.

2. Tim Wallace and Alicia Parlapiano, "Crowd Scientists Say Women's March in Washington Had 3 Times as Many People as Trump's Inauguration," *New York Times*, January 22, 2017, https://www.nytimes.com. Nancy Benac, "Survey: DC Women's March Drew Many First-Time Protestors," *AP News*, January 26, 2017, https://apnews.com/712f88ea46aa40babae99702514b3344.

3. "Angela Davis: Trump Is a Wake-up Call to Americans," *Newsmax*, February 27, 2017, http://www.newsmax.com. To be clear, Davis is making an observation about the country, not herself. Davis, of course, does not need a wake-up call regarding the past and present of oppression and authoritarianism in the United States.

4. Christina Sharpe, *In the Wake: On Blackness and Being* (Durham, N.C.: Duke University Press, 2016), 9.

5. Sharpe, *In the Wake*, 13–14.

6. LaDonna Bravebull Allard, "Why the Founder of Standing Rock Sioux Camp Can't Forget the Whitestone Massacre," *Yes! Magazine*, September 3, 2016, http://www.yesmagazine.org.

7. Mishuana R. Goeman, "Disrupting a Settler-Colonial Grammar of Place," in *Theorizing Native Studies* (Durham, N.C.: Duke University Press, 2014), 245.

8. Tiffany King, "Labor's Aphasia: Toward Antiblackness as Constitutive to Settler Colonialism," *Decolonization: Indigeneity, Education & Society*, June 10, 2014. https://decolonization.wordpress.com. For further insight on this dynamic, King helpfully draws our attention to Shona Jackson, *Creole Indigeneity: Between Myth and Nation in the Caribbean* (Minneapolis: University of Minnesota Press, 2012).

9. On this topic, see Andrés Reséndez, *The Other Slavery: The Uncovered Story* (Boston: Houghton Mifflin, 2016).

10. Among the important scholarship and sources on these topics are Maile Arvin, Eve Tuck, and Angie Morrill, "Decolonizing Feminism: Challenging Connections between Settler Colonialism and Heteropatriarchy," *Feminist Formations* 25, no. 1 (Spring 2013): 8–34; Andrea Smith, *Conquest: Sexual Violence and American Indian Genocide* (Cambridge, Mass.: South End Press, 2005); Sarah Deer, *The Beginning and End of Rape: Confronting Sexual Violence in Native America* (Minneapolis: University of Minnesota Press, 2015); Gregory Smithers, *Slave Breeding: Sex, Violence, and Memory in African American History* (Gainesville: University of Florida Press, 2012); "On Slaveholders' Sexual Abuse of Slaves: Selections from Nineteenth- and Twentieth-Century Slave Narratives," in *The Making of African American Identity*, vol. 1, *1500–1865* (National Humanities Center, 2007), http://nationalhumanities center.org/pds/maai/enslavement/text6/masterslavesexualabuse.pdf.

11. There are many works on these topics, but to start see Annie Heloise Abel, *The American Indian as Slaveholder and Secessionist* (1915; repr. Lincoln: University of Nebraska Press, 1992); and William H. Leckie and Shirley A. Leckie, *The Buffalo Soldiers: A Narrative of the Black Cavalry in the West*, revised ed. (Norman: University of Oklahoma Press, 2007).

12. Sharpe, *In the Wake*, 18.

13. "In the Wake: A Salon in Honor of Christina Sharpe," hosted by the Barnard Center for Research on Women, Barnard College, February 2, 2017, http://bcrw.barnard .edu/event/in-the-wake-a-salon-in-honor-of-christina-sharpe/.

14. Sharpe, *In the Wake*, 22.

15. Cedric Robinson, *Black Marxism: The Making of the Black Radical Tradition* (London: Zed Books, 1983), 183, 196.

16. Cedric Robinson, *Black Movements in America* (New York: Routledge, 1997), 20.

17. Robinson, *Black Movements in America*, 53.

18. Kelly Hayes, "Where Movements Meet: Black Lives Matter Organizers Visit #NoDAPL," *Truthout*, September 2, 2016. http://www.truthout.org.

19. "Black Lives Matter Stands in Solidarity with Water Protectors at Standing Rock," Black Lives Matter, September 2016, http://blacklivesmatter.com/solidarity -with-standing-rock (no longer available on the BLM site, but the text can be accessed at http://www.holyangels.com/node/300).

20. Robinson, *Black Movements in America*: see "Black Sovereignty," 53–58.

21. Kyle Mays. "Song 'Let's Meet by the Water' Invites Support at Indigenous Water Ceremony in Flint," Indian Country Today, April 14, 2016. https://newsmaven.io/ indiancountrytoday.

22. Matt Agorist, "Police Are Killing Native Americans at Higher Rate Than Any Race, and Nobody Is Talking about It," The Free Thought Project, August 2, 2015, http:// thefreethoughtproject.com.

23. Leanne Simpson, "An Indigenous View on #BlackLivesMatter," *Yes! Magazine*, December 5, 2014. http://www.yesmagazine.org.

24. For the historic and present of colonial state violence leading up to and including Standing Rock, see Nick Estes, "Indian Killers: Crime, Punishment, and Empire," The Red Nation, January 11, 2017, https://therednation.org.

25. Alan Taylor, "Water Cannons and Tear Gas Used against Dakota Access Pipeline Protesters," *The Atlantic*, November 21, 2016. https://www.theatlantic.com.

26. Sharpe, *In the Wake*, 10.

27. Maev Kennedy, "Heather Heyer, Victim of Charlottesville Car Attack, Was Civil Rights Activist," *The Guardian*, August 13, 2017, https://www.theguardian.com.

28. Natsu Taylor Saito, "Race and Decolonization: Whiteness as Property in the American Settler Colonial Project," *Harvard Journal on Racial and Ethnic Justice* 31 (Spring 2015): 62.

29. Sameer Rao, "Mass. Mayor to Bobby Jindal: 'Come and Get Me,'" *Colorlines*, August 4, 2015, https://www.colorlines.com.

30. Eve Tuck and K. Wayne Yang. "Decolonization Is Not a Metaphor," *Decolonization: Indigeneity, Education & Society* 1, no. 1 (2012): 22, 23.

31. Max Greenwood, "Trump Hangs Portrait of Andrew Jackson in Oval Office," *The Hill*, January 25, 2017, http://thehill.com.

32. Hillary Clinton, "Full text: Hillary Clinton's DNC Speech," *Politico*, July 28, 2016, http://www.politico.com/story/2016/07/full-text-hillary-clintons-dnc-speech-226410.

33. As just a couple of stark examples of police violence in the weeks prior to the Democratic National Convention: on July 5, 2016, Alton Sterling was killed by police in Baton Rouge, Louisiana, and on July 6, 2016, Philando Castile was killed by police in a suburb of St. Paul, Minnesota. The shooting and death of both men were recorded on video and became the source of increased Black Lives Matter demonstrations in these locales and nationwide in the following weeks.

34. The 2016 Democratic National Convention in Philadelphia was held July 25–28. On July 25, 2016, "the U.S. Army Corps of Engineers approved three easements for water crossings for the Dakota pipeline at Sakakawea, the Mississippi River, and the ancestral site for the Standing Rock Sioux tribe, Lake Oahe." Two days later, lawyers for the Standing Rock Nation filed injunctions against the Army Corp of Engineers. See "#NoDAPL: Full Timeline of Dakota Access Pipeline Protest," *TruNews*, December 1, 2016, http://www.trunews.com/article/nodapl-full-timeline-of-dakota-access-pipeline-protest.

35. Roxanne Dunbar-Ortiz, "Stop Saying This Is a Nation of Immigrants!" *Monthly Review/MROnline*, May 29, 2006, https://mronline.org.

36. Patrick Wolfe, "Settler Colonialism and the Elimination of the Native," *Journal of Genocide Research* 8, no. 4 (2006): 388.

37. Liam Stack, "Ben Carson Refers to Slaves as 'Immigrants' in First Remarks to HUD Staff," *New York Times*, March 6, 2017, https://www.nytimes.com.

38. Sharpe, *In the Wake*, 90.

39. Sharpe, *In the Wake*, 97.

40. Nika Knight, "'We Exist, We Resist, We Rise': Thousands March for Native Nations," *Common Dreams*, March 10, 2017, https://www.commondreams.org.

41. Valerie Volcovici and Ernest Sheyder, "Controversial Dakota Pipeline to Go Ahead after Army Approval," Reuters, February 7, 2017, http://www.reuters.com.

42. Jane Gordon, *Creolizing Political Theory: Reading Rousseau through Fanon* (New York: Fordham University Press, 2014), 201.

43. Sharpe, *In the Wake*, 101.

26

THREATS OF VIOLENCE
REFUSING THE THIRTY METER TELESCOPE AND DAKOTA ACCESS PIPELINE

David Uahikeaikalei'ohu Maile

This is an expanded version of an essay that was originally published December 22, 2016, on the Cultural Anthropology *website as part of the Hot Spots series.*

What is a threat of violence? Who gets to say who is threatening violence? In particular, how are protectors of Indigenous life, land, and water labeled violent threats? These are central and pressing questions. In this essay, I investigate how the discursive formation "threats of violence" is produced and dispersed by the U.S. settler state across two struggles: the Thirty Meter Telescope (TMT) on Mauna a Wākea in Hawai'i and Dakota Access Pipeline (DAPL) at the Mni Sose in Standing Rock. I explore the ways in which the U.S. settler state, with its multiple institutional forms, geographic locations, and individual agents, talks about violence when Kānaka Maoli (Native Hawaiians) refuse construction of TMT and when the Oceti Sakowin (Great Sioux Nation) refuses development of DAPL. As Kia'i (guardians and protectors) of Mauna a Wākea and Water Protectors of Mni Sose defend Indigenous life, land, and water, their actions and mere presence have been called violent. Defense gets coded violent. The defensive position, against projects like the TMT and DAPL that are violent in the first place, is reconfigured as hostile, dangerous, and terrorizing. In this cacophony, stakes are high. What are the material consequences for Indigenous-centered movements for liberation when they are marked threats of violence? How does such a marking rationalize and defer concrete forms of violence? In what ways have Mountain and Water Protectors exposed the precariousness of U.S. settler-state sovereignty by collectively refusing TMT and DAPL?

I argue threats of violence is a discursive formation manufactured by the settler state with a dual function. First, suggesting protectors of Indigenous life, land, and water threaten violence, or simply are violent threats in and of themselves, justifies violent interventions against them by the settler state. In other words, (symbolic) threats of alleged violence condone real (material) violence. Second, threats of violence tries to conceal not only the colonial violence animating the settler state, and its brutal interventions against protectors of Indigenous life, land, and water, but also how TMT and DAPL have always already been violent to Indigenous life, land, and water. Co-constitutive of settler colonial capitalism, TMT and DAPL perform diverse forms of violence, from the desecration of sacred sites to resource extraction, environmental racism, and ecological genocide. My thesis here is simple. I elaborate in this essay on threats of violence. I hope to demonstrate that threats of violence might be upended by Mountain and Water Protectors asserting radical Indigenous sovereignties to blockade the TMT and DAPL, which highlight and challenge the precariousness of U.S. settler sovereignty in performances of policing. I show how the refusals of TMT and DAPL articulate transoceanic alliances, forging solidarities in anticolonial and anticapitalist resistance. This is a crucial objective since the violence we experience as unique Indigenous peoples and nations is indeed similar. But rather than claim it to be universally the same, our specific refusals to similar structures of violence are, in fact, what binds us together. To conclude, I discuss that it is an aligned goal to end such violence that unites and strengthens us against the real threats: the settler state, settler colonialism, and capitalism. The intertwining futures of Mauna a Wākea, Mni Sose, and many others depend on this.

Kū Kiaʻi Mauna

Mauna a Wākea—known also as Mauna Kea—is a sacred mountain to Kānaka Maoli that is located on Hawaiʻi island. In her study of hoʻomana Hawaiʻi (Indigenous beliefs and belief-related practices of Hawaiʻi), Marie Alohalani Brown suggests the sacredness of Mauna a Wākea is a fundamental characteristic in the movement to protect the mountain from TMT. It is a movement organized around the call to Kū Kiaʻi Mauna, which means stand and protect the mountain. Brown writes, "It is our kuleana (set of rights and responsibilities) to care for and protect our island world. We believe that upholding this kuleana is crucial to our physical, spiritual, and intellectual wellbeing. The struggle to protect Mauna a Wākea from further desecration is our kuleana."[1] This responsibility to protect the sacred in Hawaiʻi is tied to Kānaka Maoli (Native Hawaiian) epistemology and ontology. Because of our particular ways of knowing and being, we must defend Mauna a Wākea at any cost. For example, in "Hanau-a-Hua-Kalani," the birth chant authored for Kamehameha III Kauikeaouli, Mauna a Wākea is the genealogical kin of Papahānaumoku and Wākea. Papahānaumoku is our Earth Mother, and her name translates to "foundation that births islands," whereas Wākea is our Sky Father and can be translated as "expansive sky." Examining Kānaka Maoli geographies of exploration, David A. Chang contends, "The birth chant of Kauikeaouli evokes an identification between the newborn chief and the land," in which, "these identifications sacralized the ali'i and also the land."[2] We come from and thus are intimately related to Mauna a Wākea. It is the piko (navel, umbilical cord, and blood relative) of our lāhui (people, nation, and nationhood). Leon No'eau Peralto aptly explains, "Born of the union between Papahānaumoku and Wākea, Mauna a Wākea is an elder sibling of Hāloa, the first ali'i [chief]. As such, both the Mauna and Kanaka are instilled, at birth, with particular kuleana to each other. This relationship is reciprocal, and its sanctity requires continual maintenance in order to remain pono, or balanced."[3] This is why we stand to protect.

There are other examples of how the mountain is a wahi kapu (sacred place). At almost 14,000 feet in elevation, the northern summit is the wao akua (realm of the gods) that connects Papahānaumoku to Wākea. After all, Mauna a Wākea literally means Wākea's mountain. One mo'olelo (story and history) discusses that Poli'ahu, the snow goddess of the mountain, was sought after by the god Kū in his form of Kūkahau'ula, or Kū of the red-tinted snow.[4] In this mo'olelo, Kūkahau'ula's pursuit is thwarted. His kinolau (physical manifestation) is the rising sun, and Poli'ahu, in her kinolau of frost, snow, and freezing rain, stops him from pursuing her. Eventually, Kūkahau'ula and Poli'ahu do embrace each other, and Poli'ahu's heart melts along with the snow on Mauna a Wākea. This mo'olelo elaborates on the sacredness of the mountain in two important ways. On the one hand, it describes the mountain as a wahi pana (celebrated place) not just where our more-than-human relatives reside but also where our akua (gods) dwell in the physical world. When development of TMT was slated to begin, construction crews attempting to ascend to the northern plateau were stopped in their tracks by frost, snow, and freezing rain.[5] Refusing her consent to the project, Poli'ahu prevented construction. On the other hand, the mo'olelo illustrates how snow, creating and sustaining life for Hawai'i island, can accumulate and melt into water on Mauna a Wākea in terms of ho'omana Hawai'i. It is an account of the end of the ice age, which provides an alternative history to dominant and naturalized narratives from Westernized science. The point I am trying to make is that Mauna a Wākea is a wahi kapu, and it is our kuleana to protect it from being desecrated and destroyed.

The Thirty Meter Telescope International Observatory (TIO) organized in 2014, after having been the Thirty Meter Telescope Observatory Corporation, to construct an industrial telescope complex on Mauna a Wākea. Advanced by TIO, the TMT would be a wide-field, alt-az Ritchey-Chrétien telescope with a thirty-meter diameter segmented primary mirror. In turn, the complex to house it requires a significant amount of space and land. According to KAHEA: The Hawaiian-Environmental Alliance, proposals for TMT estimate that it would be eighteen stories tall at 184 feet in height, extend twenty feet down into the mountain, and create a construction footprint of eight acres with a final footprint of five acres. Furthermore, the development of TMT would excavate 64,000 cubic yards at the northern plateau and also add a 3,400-foot road.[6] TIO suggests this would be the largest telescope in the world. With twenty-one telescopes and thirteen complexes already built on Mauna a Wākea, TMT would add to growing amounts of waste by producing 120–250 cubic feet of solid waste every week, which will be stored, along with hazardous chemical materials, in a 5,000-gallon storage tank underground.[7] Despite these pernicious ecological implications, constructing TMT at Mauna a Wākea is rationalized because of the mountain's scientific value.

For Westernized science and its industry to produce knowledge about astronomy, Mauna a Wākea is a preferred build site. The mountain offers "the best window on the universe."[8] TMT's General Information Brochure states, "To capture the sharpest images and produce the best science, astronomers need more than an extraordinary telescope; they also need an equally extraordinary location with just the right atmospheric qualities."[9] Our sacred mountain is an "extraordinary location" because of the value it adds to knowledge about science. Astronomers desire the mountain for its "atmospheric qualities," as if akua like Poli'ahu can be reduced to scientific commodity. The elevation, climate, and overall environmental conditions of the mountain are marked as ideal and exceptional, if not quantifiably perfect. Consider the terms in which TIO delineates rationale for selecting Mauna a Wākea:

> After a rigorous five-year campaign that spanned the entire globe, TMT scientists found such a site, Mauna Kea, a dormant volcano in Hawaii that rises nearly 14,000 feet above the surface of the Pacific Ocean. This site, which is above approximately 40 percent of Earth's atmosphere, has a climate that is particularly stable, dry, and cold. All of which are important characteristics for clear seeing. This mountain in Hawaii is also home to some of today's most powerful telescopes, including the Gemini North Telescope, the Canada-France-Hawaii Telescope, the Subaru Telescope, and TMT's forerunners the twin Keck telescopes.[10]

Additionally, the passage suggests that since there are other telescopes already built at the northern plateau of Mauna a Wākea, the newer, larger, and more powerful TMT ought to be manufactured. The goal and promise is to "unlock new frontiers."[11] This conjures up an allegedly successful conquest of Hawai'i—an old frontier, they allude. But it also imagines the potential to open new frontiers in the universe. It is a timeworn logic and trope of Euro-American exploration that Jodi A. Byrd names "imperial planetarity,"[12] or what we might refer to as planetary imperialism. Such a promise invokes Fredrick Jackson Turner's infamous "frontier thesis"—published in 1893, which happens to be the same year as the illegal U.S. military overthrow of the Hawaiian Kingdom, to encourage settlement of the American Southwest—that has been weaponized for the dispossession, elimination, and replacement of Native American peoples and nations.[13] Transiting U.S. empire,[14] frontier violence extends from the American continent to Hawai'i at Mauna a Wākea and against Kānaka Maoli. "We're searching for truth and knowledge, the kinds of things that have motivated countries for centuries," opines professor of astronomy at California Institute of Technology Richard Ellis. He proclaims, "We don't need to apologize."[15] This is the environmental impact, astronomy industry development, and science we are up against.

The total cost to build TMT is estimated at $1.5 billion, and funding has been pledged worldwide.[16] The Gordon and Betty Moore Foundation, California Institute of Technology, University of California, National Astronomical Observatory of Japan, National Astronomical Observatories of the Chinese Academy of Sciences, Indian Astronomy Research Institutes, and Canadian government are all financing the project. This motley crew of funders, from U.S.-based universities to national astronomy organizations and even the Canadian crown, are paying the expenses to construct TMT. Ironically, some claim the financing will benefit Kānaka Maoli via expenditures, jobs, and educational scholarships.[17] The claim has also been used to argue alleged benefits to Hawai'i and thus Kānaka Maoli to prove that TMT does not contribute to colonization: "From my vantage," Kelly Dickerson writes, "colonialism is a separate issue from TMT."[18] Dickerson's analysis is shortsighted and condescending, emblematic in the title of her article: "This Giant Telescope May Taint Sacred Land. Here's Why It Should Be Built Anyway." Frankly, her argument simply is not true. If my readers take anything away from this essay, I hope you will see that TMT is a project structured by and reifying settler colonial capitalism. For instance, the international funding of TMT demonstrates how global capital finances the desecration and destruction of Mauna a Wākea in a process that furthers the dispossession of Hawai'i and elimination of Kānaka Maoli. It is a form of settler capitalism that brings together U.S. and Canadian settler states as well as Japan, China, and India. Colonialism and capitalism are core issues of TMT.

Financial support for TMT is aided by legal advocacy from the U.S. settler state. In 1968, Hawai'i's state land board issued a general lease to the University of Hawai'i (UH) for the purpose of building only one telescope complex at Mauna a Wākea. After receiving this initial lease, multiple telescope complexes began developing, and public protest emerged with claims that new development violated terms of the general lease. In 2011, the UH submitted an application for a Conservation District Use Permit (CDUP) in order to acquire the proper permitting to build TMT. A petition was filed then with the Board of Land and Natural Resources (BLNR) for a contested case hearing. However, the BLNR steamrolled ahead and approved the CDUP before holding the contested case hearing. But on December 2, 2015, the Hawai'i Supreme Court ruled this violated due process by "putting the cart before the horse."[19] The decision invalidated the building permit and remanded the case back to the BLNR to hold a new contested case hearing. The new contested case hearing concluded on July 26, 2017, with the hearing's officer recommending that the BLNR approve TMT's building permit.[20] On September 28, 2017, the BLNR voted in favor of granting a CDUP for TMT.[21] Although the supreme court ruled against TMT, this brief legal history shows how the U.S. settler state in Hawai'i has played a significant role in authorizing land leases and building permits for the project. The settler state mediates and facilitates astronomy industry development while simultaneously being produced from it. On this point, Byrd contends:

> Transit refers to a rare astronomical event, the paired transits of Venus across the sun, that served in 1761 and again in 1769 as global moments that moved European conquest toward notions of imperialist planetarity that provided the basis for Enlightenment liberalism. The imperial planetarity that sparked scientific rationalism and inspired humanist articulations of freedom, sovereignty, and equality touched four continents and a sea of islands in order to cohere itself.[22]

In the pursuit to track the transit of Venus and universalize Enlightenment science, astronomy industry development emerged through the dispossession and elimination of Indigenous people by imperial nation-states. When the so-called fiftieth state of the union sanctions the TMT, it does not just mark how the state entity constitutes itself on stolen lands. It also demonstrates that advocacy of astronomy industry development proliferates settler colonial power so as to secure its institutionalization in the formation of Hawai'i as a U.S. settler state.

Although legal actions have proved to be a successful strategy for stalling development of TMT, the corporeal blockades directly stopped construction of TMT on the 'āina (land, that which feeds). Currently, legal authority to begin building is still wrapped up in court. But the threat is not over. This is abundantly true since the Supreme Court's main reason to invalidate TMT's building permit was premised on due process. If the court recognizes that due process subsequently is followed, there is concern that authorization may be granted for TMT to proceed with construction, once and for all. It is the U.S. settler state that maintains so-called power in Hawai'i to deny or grant these projects—a prescient reminder. And it is also the settler state producing and dispersing discourses that suggest Kia'i protecting Mauna a Wākea are threats of violence.

Kia'i protecting Mauna a Wākea have halted TMT from being built but, in doing so, been labeled violent. On July 14, 2015, Hawai'i governor David Ige signed an emergency rule passed by the BLNR to criminalize and remove Kia'i. Settler-state officials argued in favor of the emergency rule by claiming that Kia'i "harassed" visitors and staff and even perpetrated numerous "hostile incidents," "other threats of violence," and a bomb threat.[23] However, no evidence has come forth to substantiate these claims. This is an echo chamber the settler state shouts into. Furthermore, their arguments referenced a June 24, 2015, blockade of TMT construction crews in order to suggest the rocks, boulders, and ahu (altars) placed on the road to the northern plateau caused "hazardous conditions." Ige insisted, "We cannot let some people put others at risk of harm or property damage."[24] The language that he uses here argues that Kia'i who placed rocks in the road, so that construction crews could not ascend to begin building the TMT, risked harming state workers and tourists and risked damaging settler property. When BLNR passed the emergency rule, Kia'i were called an "imminent peril to the public health or natural resources."[25] Perhaps this discursive maneuver is not simply ironic but something more. This is how flagging Kia'i as threats of violence does work to grant and defer violence exacted by the settler state as well as TMT. A few weeks after passing the emergency rule, in the early morning of July 31, 2015, on a Hawaiian national holiday celebrating Lā Ho'iho'i Ea (Sovereignty Restoration Day), police from the Division of Conservation and Resource Enforcement crept up the mountain and arrested seven Kia'i who were reoccupying Mauna a Wākea. The administrative power of the emergency rule provided executive authority to make these arrests, passed by the BLNR and signed into law by the governor. Therefore, accusing Kia'i of violence allowed the settler state to do two things: (1) criminalize, detain, and incarcerate Kia'i and (2) conceal the desecration and destruction of Mauna a Wākea by TMT. This is the work that threats of violence performs. Since 2015, it has operationalized fifty-nine different arrests of Kia'i protecting the mountain, practicing and taking care of our kuleana to guard what we hold sacred.

Another example illuminates the imaginative speculation in threats of violence. On June 7, 2015, reports alleged that a bullet hole was found on a door at the Subaru Observatory, one of the many telescope complexes already erect upon Mauna a Wākea.[26] Police investigated the claim, and Kia'i were quickly blamed for the incident. Mountain Protectors reoccupying that wahi kapu haunted observatory employees and their telescope complexes, and their relatively close proximity was reason enough to place blame. What is interesting about this case is the allegation was immediate, as if the threat of such violence—a loaded gun fired at an observatory—was unsurprisingly expected. Ben Gutierrez and Chelsea Davis noted, "Mauna a Wakea protector Kahookahi Kanuha said he has no idea where the damage came from. 'We do not condone that kind of action by anybody for any reason at any time, especially on Mauna a Wakea, the place that we know is sacred,' Kanuha said."[27] In a follow-up report a few days later, an observatory spokesperson clarified that the hole was not caused by a bullet but, instead, damage from an adjacent bolt fixture. Another plot twist, police confirmed that "the damage had been there for about six months."[28] The bullet hole was only reported, and its image circulated through news media, during a time when blockades amped up. Tom Callis observed, "TMT opponent Kaho'okahi Kanuha said he was glad to see the matter resolved but also was disappointed that protesters, a few of whom remain camped on the mountain, were being accused on social media of being responsible."[29] In what should be in clearer focus, the depiction of Kia'i as violent is a racist fabrication that sidesteps and attempts to erase the violence of TMT and its champion the settler state. It is a colonial violence enacted through the settler state's existence, advocacy of TMT, and exercise of force against Kia'i.

Whether it is the imagined threat of violent acts or violent bodies, threats of violence rationalizes police brutalization of Kia'i. David Correia and Tyler Wall posit, "Declaring *something* or *someone* a threat is one of the most normalized of all powers internal to the police function."[30] When Kia'i defending a different mountain sacred to Kānaka Maoli blockaded development, this became abundantly clear. On August 2, 2017, more than one hundred Kia'i attempted to block the delivery of a three-ton primary mirror for the Daniel K. Inouye Solar Telescope (DKIST) upon Haleakalā on Maui island. Applying new techniques for detainment and removal, adapted from lessons learned on Mauna a Wākea, police arrested six Kia'i. Settler-state policing is not unique to the case of TMT. Astronomy development is an industry, not one telescope. In fact, on July 30, 2015—the night before emergency rule arrests on Mauna a Wākea—heavily militarized police arrested twenty Kia'i demonstrating against the DKIST on Haleakalā. David "Kai" Prais was arrested then. Subsequently, on August 2, 2017, he was arrested again, but this time in a spectacular display of violence. Prais was viciously detained and lost consciousness while in custody. A police officer pressed his knee into Prais's skull. He shrieked in pain for help, but the cop "continued to keep his knee on his head."[31] The knee jammed into his skull, says Kaukaohu Wahilani who was next to Prais during the blockade, "was overkill."[32] Kāko'o Haleakalā, a coalition organizing the blockade, commented that they called an ambulance while police "just stood there and did not assist."[33] The coalition and Kia'i claim police used excessive force, whereas police suggest Prais "resisted arrest" and "officers did what they're trained to do."[34] Labeling Kia'i as threatening acts of violence and violent threats rationalizes and defers this visceral violence.

From Mauna a Wākea to Haleakalā, the discursive formation I have tracked here justifies police brutality to secure settler capital for astronomy industry development in Hawai'i. Conversely, settler capital bolsters the policing of our Mountain Protectors, especially in a recent moment wherein former Hawai'i attorney general Douglas Chin compared Kia'i to the fascist, alt-right white supremacists that marched on Charlottesville in the Unite the Right rally to request $2.5 million from the state legislature for "respond[ing] to potential mass violence or civil disobedience, possibly atop Mauna a Wākea."[35] Although threats of violence is conjured in an abstract realm, the implications drawn are dangerously concrete.

Mni Wiconi

Over 3,500 miles away from Hawai'i, the discursive formation threats of violence has been deployed at Oceti Sakowin (the Great Sioux Nation) against Water Protectors of the Mni Sose (Missouri River) to build DAPL. The parallels between how these movements are cast are no coincidence. They are Indigenous-centered struggles for liberation against projects of settler capitalism that the United States deeply desires. I contend that both movements—one protecting the mountain, one protecting the water—encounter this discursive formation as a transit of empire. Put differently, threats of violence transfers across these sites in order to cohere

U.S. control over Indigenous people and nations. For instance, whereas chants of Kū Kiaʻi Mauna have been policed at Mauna a Wākea, at the Standing Rock Sioux Indian Reservation police have attempted to quell cries of Mni Wiconi. A Lakotayapi phrase, Mni Wiconi means "water is life." More accurately, according to Jaskiran Dhillon and Nick Estes in the introduction to this volume, it means water is alive. Animate and alive, Mauna a Wākea and the Mni Sose are our more-than-human relatives and sacred, storied places. Relations with them, in fact, are responsibilities to refuse their desecration and destruction. In this volume and elsewhere, folks other than myself are expertly positioned to speak on #NoDAPL and criticize the political economy of DAPL. In this section, I am interested in examining how discourses of violence circulate when Water Protectors guard the Mni Sose from DAPL. As a Kānaka Maoli scholar, I launch my analysis of the threats of violence from Hawaiʻi. But, as I aim to show, what has been taking place in my ancestral homeland shares unfortunate similarities with what is occurring in the territories of other Indigenous peoples and nations. These are relationships that cross oceans, mountains, and rivers. In my writing here, I hope to cultivate such relations not just in solidarity but with ethical sincerity.

On June 1, 2017, Energy Transfer Partners (ETP) completed construction of DAPL.[36] Almost 1,200 miles in length, this gargantuan pipeline begins in the Bakken fields of North Dakota, drags down through South Dakota and Iowa, and empties into a depot in Patoka, Illinois. The Energy Transfer Crude Oil Pipeline then moves oil from Patoka to storage farms in Nederland, Texas. There is big money in this. It is a $3.8 billion project, but $2.5 billion are financed through loans. Capital has been lent by seventeen banks, such as TD Securities, the Bank of Tokyo-Mitsubishi UFJ, and Mizuho Bank who are primary lenders of the key DAPL loan.[37] At the time of writing this, DAPL is transporting approximately 470,000 barrels of crude oil each day, with promises that it could reach up to 520,000 barrels per day.[38] Half a million barrels of oil pass every day underneath the Mni Sose, specially at Lake Oahe reservoir in Cannon Ball, North Dakota, where the Standing Rock Sioux Indian Reservation is located. Notably though, Amy Dalrymple reported, "an early proposal for the Dakota Access Pipeline called for the project to cross the Missouri River north of Bismarck, but one reason that route was rejected was its potential threat to Bismarck's water supply."[39] In a blatant display of environmental racism, the possibility for contaminating water supplies of the Standing Rock Sioux was a risk worth taking by the U.S. settler state and corporations to protect the lives and water of Bismarck, the capitol city of North Dakota with an overwhelming white majority population—putting the white supremacy of settler capitalism on full display. So, the Standing Rock Sioux and Cheyenne River Sioux Tribes sued the U.S. Army Corps of Engineers. They brought suit on the basis that the corps granted permits for DAPL before sufficiently considering the project's environmental impact. On June 14, 2016, District Court Judge James Boasberg ruled in favor of the tribes, arguing under the premise of the National

Environmental Policy Act (NEPA), "Although the Corps substantially complied with NEPA in many areas, the Court agrees that it did not adequately consider the impacts of an oil spill on fishing rights, hunting rights, or environmental justice." Despite stalling DAPL, the decision did not erode its easement. Months later on October 11, Boasberg made another ruling, which authorized that DAPL could continue operations, pending an environmental review by the corps. Later in December, he imposed interim measures for spill response plans at Lake Oahe, in the wake of a 210,000 gallon oil leak from the Keystone Pipeline in South Dakota.[40]

Judicial and corporate powers, the settler state and finance capital, and law and oil have congealed in favor of DAPL at the expense of the Mni Sose and Oceti Sakowin. Sharing affinities with TMT in Hawai'i, DAPL is conditioned through settler colonial capitalism while also contributing to it. In unique yet overlapping operations of violence, settler capitalism permeates telescopes and pipelines. But they are forms of violence that have been refused steadfastly.

When construction approached Lake Oahe in the beginning of 2016, thousands upon thousands of people gathered in Standing Rock to stop DAPL and protect the Mni Sose. Multiple camps formed, and Water Protectors organized their refusal on-the-ground. However, talk began to surface that Water Protectors were planning violent actions. Morton County Sheriff Kyle Kirchmeier played a substantial role in proliferating these ideas. For example, Kirchmeier in particular "has been largely responsible for law enforcement at the site and he has accused protesters of shooting guns, carrying weapons and even threatening to use pipe bombs against his officers."[41] He once alleged, "We have had incidents and reports of weapons, of pipe bombs, of some shots fired."[42] However, Jon Eagle Sr., the Tribal Historic Preservation Officer for the Standing Rock Sioux Tribe, responded to accusations of pipe bombs being constructed in camps near the Mni Sose. He exclaimed, "When we say we're loading our pipes, that's our chanupa. That's a sacred object that we carry to communicate with everything within creation. It's not a weapon."[43] Discussing this with Eagle, Kate Grumke added, "Eagle thinks law enforcement misinterpreted what people were saying on social media. He said they were talking about sacred pipes, not pipe bombs."[44] Reports about crafting and detonating bombs, much like those circulating about protectors of Mauna a Wākea, were yet another speculative fiction. They are imagined for symbolic maximization with minimal material evidence. Yet, such accusations were produced by agents of the U.S. settler state as a way of establishing threats of violence.

Threats of violence exacted physical damage to the Water Protectors. On September 4, 2016, Water Protectors rallied to a construction site adjacent to Lake Oahe where bulldozers, making room for the pipeline, dug up sites sacred to the Oceti Sakowin. A private security force was contracted by ETP to manage the situation. Trained dogs and dog handlers from Frost Kennels in Ohio were employed and present during this time. After seeing DAPL crews tear up the earth, Water Protectors broke through a wire fence and attempted to shut down bulldozers. Six bulldozers pulled back from the site, and additional security arrived to push back Water Protectors. Security forces then deployed pepper spray as well as dogs. Some handlers charged Water Protectors, releasing their hold on dogs so that they could attack freely without restraint. A modern version of Deborah Miranda's "dogs of conquest,"[45] large German shepherds sank their teeth into the bodies of Water Protectors to the point at which blood could be seen dripping from the dogs' mouths.

However, the story told by private security and local police forces centered on how escalating protester violence needed to be subdued. "It started out peaceful," said Frost Kennel owner Bob Frost, "but as soon as you tear a fence down, come in charging and screaming and throwing stuff, that's not peaceful."[46] Representatives from the security detail identified "there were no intentions of using the dogs or handlers for security work. . . . However, because of the protest events, the dogs were deployed as a method of trying to keep the protesters under control."[47] In other words, these were tactics necessitated because Water Protectors were allegedly not peaceful and acting lawlessly. The Morton County Sheriff's Department observed that "within five minutes the crowd of protestors, estimated to be a few hundred people became violent. They stampeded into the construction area with horses, dogs and vehicles."[48] Not lacking irony, the statement by the Morton County Sheriff's Department flags that Water Protectors attacked with dogs, before private security did. Sheriff Kirchmeier suggested the action "was more like a riot than a protest."[49] The language of protest became supplanted by more inflammatory rhetoric: rioting. Therefore, the U.S. settler state fashioned ideas that Water Protectors of Mni Sose were not protectors or even protesters. For the settler state, they were rioters who represented threats of violence.

The following month, in October, police presence increased, as did their vicious interventions. Road blocks on highways strengthened. Police from outside of Morton County were called in for back-up. The National Guard also arrived. Sheriff Kirchmeier continued to speak, in press conferences and media interviews, about the absolute danger of protestors and their camps. On October 26, days after Water Protectors created a new frontline treaty camp, claimed from sovereign territorial authority detailed in the 1851 Treaty of Fort Laramie, police ameliorated their rationale to intervene. The sheriff of Cass County in Minnesota, Paul Laney, noted live to press, "We don't want a confrontation . . . we're having our hand forced." On that same day, Kirchmeier was interviewed by the press where he stated a large group of police and military forces gathered to "end this peaceful." Reminiscent of earlier dog attacks by private security, police at Standing Rock carefully forged a narrative that suggested violent confrontation was desired by Water Protectors and that militarized police response was forced, as a result, in order to promote peace and manifest resolution. This was a cunning rhetorical strategy that promulgated threats of violence as a form of gaslighting, an institutionalized practice whereby the settler state weaponizes uneven relations of racialized colonial power to manipulate material realities for abusive ends that prop up its own legitimacy and free the flow of capital. It is clear that the U.S. has sought to bind and trap Indigenous peoples and nations within such an abusive relationship.

What happened next on October 27 was nothing short of spectacularly violent. Upward of three hundred officers from various law enforcement agencies, more than 30 percent of which came from outside of North Dakota, descended on the frontline treaty camp.[50] Settler-state police collaborated with ETP's private security, with reports indicating sniper teams were positioned in various locations using all-terrain vehicles operated by security.[51] Accompanied by a fleet of Humvee vehicles, police forces advanced on Water Protectors at two barricades of the frontline treaty camp, at North Dakota highways 1806 and 134. They were equipped with assault rifles, sound cannons, concussion grenades, rubber bullets, bean bag rounds, tasers, pepper spray, tear gas, and batons, and used them in shocking force. Purposed to remove and detain Water Protectors, the massive battalion broke through barricades and invaded the camp, arresting 142 people. Many of those arrested were drawn on with identification numbers, stripped of their clothes, and crammed into dog kennels. At least one Water Protector had a hood placed over their head.[52] Afterwards, the United Nations special rapporteur on the rights of freedom of association and assembly, Maini Kiai, claimed, "Law enforcement officials, private security firms and the North Dakota National Guard have used unjustified force to deal with opponents of the Dakota Access pipeline."[53] "This is a troubling response," he went on to say, "to people who are taking action to protect natural resources and ancestral territory in the face of profit-seeking activity. . . . The excessive use of State security apparatus to suppress protest against corporate activities that are alleged to violate human rights is wrong." Kiai's statement powerfully illustrates, quite explicitly, that police and private security forces combined to mete out spectacular forms of violence against Water Protectors in an unjustified and flagrant manner, demonstrating clear violations of human rights that functioned in the name of ongoing colonialism and capitalism.

Transoceanic Solidarities

Although the discursive formation threats of violence has been utilized by settler-state forces to rationalize and defer concrete violence against protectors of Indigenous life, land, and water from Mauna a Wākea to the Mni Sose, collectively sustained refusals of TMT and DAPL expose the precariousness of U.S. settler sovereignty. In both movements, the policing of Mountain and Water Protectors, fighting in Indigenous-centered movements for liberation, is a performance. The settler state attempts to perform territorial control and juridical authority to counter claims that lands have been stolen and laws and policy are actually unlawful—claims that Kānaka Maoli and Oceti Sakowin have made in and out of courts. In this equation, policing offers a unique function. The institution of police and techniques for policing try to concretize U.S. settler sovereignty. When Kiaʻi reoccupied Mauna a Wākea to defend it from the desecration and destruction of TMT, the BLNR and governor of Hawaiʻi institutionalized emergency rules to criminalize and remove Kiaʻi. When Water Protectors established the frontline treaty camp premised on the 1851 Treaty of Fort Laramie, the Morton County Sheriff's Department mobilized a massive militarized police force to break up barricades and dismantle the camp. These were performances that, in and of themselves, demonstrated a lack of control. When Kiaʻi were blamed for a hole in the door of the Subaru Observatory atop Mauna a Wākea, it was confirmed that the hole was not a bullet hole but, instead, pierced from an adjacent bolt fixture. When Water Protectors were accused of making bombs, it was confirmed that police mistook sacred chanupa pipes for what they imagined to be pipe bombs. These were performances of speculation proven to be untrue.

The imperfections and limits of U.S. settler sovereignty have unraveled. The assault at Standing Rock clarifies, as Byrd laments, "in the United States, the Indian is the original enemy combatant."[54] For Lisa Ford, the criminalization of Indigenous populations, from America to Australia, is an original feature of settler sovereignty. She suggests, "The exercise of jurisdiction over indigenous crime performs the myth of settler sovereignty over and over."[55] What Ford refers to as legal myth, Mark Rifkin calls an empty sign of settler sovereignty,[56] which, when performed over and over again, reveals a hollowness in settler-state power to be antagonized.

The refusals of TMT and DAPL have amplified the power of Indigenous-centered movements for liberation to antagonize real threats of violence to our mountains and lands, to our rivers and water, to our people and nations. What these collective refusals have been forged in are transoceanic solidarities. "For all the differences between American Indians and Kānaka," Chang reflects, "the most important force that made them like one another was the problem of American colonialism."[57] I would add that it is the problems of the U.S. settler state, settler colonialism, and capitalism. Kānaka Maoli and Oceti Sakowin have shown solidarity against both DAPL and TMT in the profoundly anticolonial, anticapitalist philosophies of Kū Kiaʻi Mauna and Mni Wiconi. Indeed, Water Protectors have guarded Mauna a Wākea and Kiaʻi have defended the Mni Sose. These are struggles shared against real, material, and visceral forms of violence structured in the colonialism and capital championed by the U.S. settler state. Such relationships must be sustained and cultivated so that our collective refusals of TMT and DAPL may work in concert toward unseating settler states and overturning settler capitalism, once and for all.

NOTES

1. Marie Alohalani Brown, "Mauna Kea: Hoʻomana Hawaiʻi and Protecting the Sacred," *Journal for the Study of Religion, Nature and Culture* 10, no. 2 (2016): 164.

2. David A. Chang, *The World and All the Things upon It: Native Hawaiian Geographies of Exploration* (Minneapolis: University of Minnesota Press, 2016), 203.

3. Leon Noʻeau Peralto, "Mauna a Wākea: Hānau Ka Mauna, the Piko of Our Ea," in *A Nation Rising: Hawaiian Movements for Life, Land, and Sovereignty*, ed. Noelani Goodyear-Kaʻōpua, Ikaika Hussey, and Erin Kahunawaikaʻala Wright (Durham, N.C.: Duke University Press, 2014), 234.

4. "The Story of Kukahauʻula and Poliʻahu," Mauna Kea—from Mountain to Sea, accessed August 30, 2017, http://www.mauna-a-wakea.info.

5. Tom Callis, "Icy Conditions Delay TMT Work," *Hawaii Tribune-Herald*, March 10, 2015, http://www.hawaiitribune-herald.com.

6. "Fact Sheet: Massive 18-story Telescope Complex Proposed for Mauna Kea," KAHEA: The Hawaiian-Environmental Alliance, accessed August 30, 2017, http://www.kahea.org.

7. "Fact Sheet," KAHEA.

8. "Building the Gateway to the Universe," Thirty Meter Telescope, accessed August 30, 2017, http://www.tmt.org.

9. "Building the Gateway to the Universe," Thirty Meter Telescope.

10. "Building the Gateway to the Universe," Thirty Meter Telescope.

11. "Building the Gateway to the Universe," Thirty Meter Telescope.

12. Jodi A. Byrd, *The Transit of Empire: Indigenous Critiques of Colonialism* (Minneapolis: University of Minnesota Press, 2011), xx.

13. Fredrick Jackson Turner, "The Significance of the Frontier in American History," *Report of the American Historical Association* 1, no. 1 (1893): 199–227.

14. Byrd, *The Transit of Empire*, xxi.

15. Usha Lee McFarling, "Science, Culture Clash over Sacred Mountain," *Los Angeles Times*, March 18, 2001, http://www.latimes.com.

16. Korey Haynes, "Hawaii Supreme Court Revokes Permit for Massive Telescope," *Astronomy Magazine*, December 3, 2015, http://www.astronomy.com.

17. John Stickler, "Thirty Meter Telescope Could Boost Hawaii Island's Economy," *Hawaii Business*, September 16, 2013, http://www.hawaiibusiness.com.

18. Kelly Dickerson, "This Giant Telescope May Taint Sacred Land. Here's Why It Should Be Built Anyway," *Business Insider*, November 18, 2015, http://www.businessinsider.com.

19. Catherine Bauknight, "Hawaii Supreme Court Invalidates Thirty Meter Telescope's Permit for Mauna Kea," *Huffington Post*, December 14, 2015, http://www.huffingtonpost.com.

20. "Judge: Thirty Meter Telescope Should Be Given OK to Move Forward," *Hawaii News Now*, July 26, 2017, http://www.hawaiinewsnow.com.

21. Jennifer Sinco Kelleher, "Telescope on Land Sacred to Native Hawaiians Moves Forward," *Washington Post*, September 28, 2017, http://www.washingtonpost.com.

22. Byrd, *The Transit of Empire*, xx–xxi.

23. Mileka Lincoln, "Ige Signs Emergency Rule Restricting Mauna Kea Access," *Hawaii News Now*, July 14, 2015, http://www.hawaiinewsnow.

24. Lincoln, "Ige Signs Emergency Rule."

25. Lincoln, "Ige Signs Emergency Rule."

26. Ben Gutierrez and Chelsea Davis, "Police Investigating Possible Bullet Hole in Mauna Kea Observatory," *Hawaii News Now*, June 7, 2015, http://www.hawaiinews now.com.

27. Gutierrez and Davis, "Police Investigating Possible Bullet Hole."

28. Tom Callis, "Hole in Door Not Caused by Bullet, Subaru Says," *Hawaii Tribune-Herald*, June 9, 2015, http://www.hawaiitribune-herald.com.

29. Callis, "Hole in Door Not Caused by Bullet."

30. David Correia and Tyler Wall, *Police: A Field Guide* (Brooklyn: Verso, 2018), 232, emphasis mine.

31. Wendy Osher, "Police Force Questioned during Injury to Demonstrator at Kākoʻo Haleakalā Protest," *Maui News*, August 3, 2017, http://www.mauinews.com.

32. Mileka Lincoln, "Maui Police Deny Claims Officer Used Excessive Force during Haleakala Protest," *Hawaii News Now*, August 4, 2017, http://www.hawaiinewsnow .com.

33. Wendy Osher, "Kākoʻo Haleakalā Protest: Police Force Questioned during Injury to Demonstrator," *Maui News*, August 1, 2017, http://www.mauinews.com.

34. Lincoln, "Maui Police Deny Claims Officer Used Excessive Force during Haleakala Protest."

35. Nanea Kalani, "Attorney General Seeks $2.5 Million for Security," *Honolulu Star-Advertiser*, January 11, 2018, http://www.staradvertiser.com.

36. Ali Stratton, "Dakota Access Pipeline Starts Shipping Oil," *Wall Street Journal*, June 1, 2017, http://www.wsj.com.

37. "Banks Funding DAPL," Defund DAPL, accessed June 6, 2018, http://www.defund dapl.org.

38. Blake Nicholson, "$3.8 Billion Dakota Access Oil Pipeline Begins Service," *Chicago Tribune*, June 1, 2017, http://www.chicagotribune.com.

39. Amy Dalrymple, "Pipeline Route Plan First Called for Crossing North of Bismarck," *Bismarck Tribune*, August 18, 2016, http://www.bismarcktribune.com.

40. Mitch Smith and Julie Bosman, "Keystone Pipeline Leaks 210,000 Gallons of Oil in South Dakota," *New York Times*, November 16, 2017, http://www.nytimes.com.

41. "Sheriff Mistook Sacred Pipes for Pipe Bombs at Pipeline Protest," *Indianz*, August 23, 2016, http://www.indianz.com.

42. Kate Grumke, "American Indians Stand Together to Shut Down Pipeline Project," *Newsy*, August 21, 2016, http://www.newsy.com.

43. Grumke, "American Indians Stand Together to Shut Down Pipeline Project."

44. Grumke, "American Indians Stand Together to Shut Down Pipeline Project."

45. Deborah Miranda, "Extermination of the Joyas: Gendercide in Spanish California," *GLQ: A Journal of Gay and Lesbian Studies* 16, no. 1–2 (2010): 257.

46. Sam Allard, "How Did an Ohio Kennel Get Involved in Dakota Access Pipeline Security?" *Scene*, September 20, 2016, http://www.cleverscene.com.

47. Sam Levin, "Guards for North Dakota Pipeline Could Be Charged for Using Dogs on Activists," *The Guardian*, October 26, 2016, http://www.theguardian.com.

48. Eyder Peralta, "Dakota Access Pipeline Protests in North Dakota Turn Violent," National Public Radio, September 4, 2016, http://www.npr.org.

49. Peralta, "Dakota Access Pipeline Protests in North Dakota Turn Violent."

50. Alleen Brown, Will Parrish, and Alice Speri, "The Battle of Treaty Camp: Law Enforcement Descended on Standing Rock a Year Ago and Changed the DAPL Fight Forever," *The Intercept*, October 27, 2017, http://www.theintercept.com.

51. Brown, Parrish, and Speri, "The Battle of Treaty Camp."

52. Rene Rougeau, "Mass Arrests at Standing Rock," *Socialist Worker*, October 27, 2016, http://www.socialistworker.org.

53. "Native Americans Facing Excessive Force in North Dakota Pipeline Protests—UN Expert," United Nations Human Rights Office of the High Commissioner, November 15, 2016, http://www.ohchr.org.

54. Byrd, *The Transit of Empire*, viii.

55. Lisa Ford, *Settler Sovereignty: Jurisdiction and Indigenous People in America and Australia, 1788–1836* (Cambridge, Mass.: Harvard University Press, 2010), 208.

56. Mark Rifkin, "Indigenizing Agamben: Rethinking Sovereignty in Light of the 'Peculiar' Status of Native Peoples," *Cultural Critique* 1, no. 73 (2009): 88–124.

57. Chang, *The World and All the Things upon It*, 248.

27

DECOLONIZE THIS PLACE AND RADICAL SOLIDARITY
AN INTERVIEW WITH NITASHA DHILLON AND AMIN HUSAIN

Jaskiran Dhillon

Nitasha Dhillon and Amin Husain are MTL, a collaboration that joins research, aesthetics, organizing, and action in its practice. Amin, a Palestinian American, has a BA in philosophy, a JD from Indiana University Law School, and an LLM from Columbia University. He practiced law for five years before transitioning to art, studying at the School of the International Center of Photography and Whitney Independent Study Program. Nitasha, an Indian national, has a BA in mathematics from St. Stephen's College, University of Delhi; she attended the Whitney Independent Study Program in New York and School of the International Center of Photography. Together, as MTL, Nitasha and Amin cofounded MTL+, the collective that facilitates Decolonize This Place, Global Ultra Luxury Faction, the direct action wing of Gulf Labor Coalition, Strike Debt, Rolling Jubilee, and Tidal: Occupy Theory magazine. This interview was conducted on November 5, 2017.

As the resistance at Standing Rock grew, New York City became one of the primary sites of radical solidarity and support for the movement against the Dakota Access Pipeline. In this interview, Nitasha Dhillon and Amin Husain from Decolonize This Place describe their work of politicized allyship.

JASKIRAN DHILLON: Let's start with a general question about what Decolonize This Place is and how it emerged.

NITASHA DHILLON: Decolonize This Place was first organized by MTL+. We have, as you know, many core organizers to this project. Decolonize This Place is a call to action and an ongoing construction of a "we" that materializes in opening up spaces as decolonial formations, bringing together specificities of struggle within an overall analytic of decolonization that aim for communal futures and decolonial freedom. It is necessarily unsettling, and its core is an "us" who are militants of life.

Decolonize This Place banners. Photograph by Nick Estes.

Our first action with Decolonize This Place was at the Brooklyn Museum in May 2015. I think that was also the start of our work with being in solidarity with Indigenous struggles here in the United States. We were talking about Palestine and gentrification in Brooklyn, but it was also important for us to begin with talking about the occupation of this land. And from that action we moved to 55 Walker Street, which is an artist space, and took it over. We looked at it as a movement space and that was organized around five different strands: Indigenous struggle, Black liberation, free Palestine, global wage workers, and degentrification.

So that's really where the work began, and one of the first things we did during that time was actually support one of our collaborators, NYC Stands with Standing Rock, for the first action that was organized at Washington Square Park.

AMIN HUSAIN: Yeah, I mean, the importance of the list Nitasha just described was in a way to decenter whiteness. So when we were offered a space—we were offered an exhibition, and what we said is that we don't want to do an exhibition, but we're willing to take the space from the gallery, which was two floors, a large space, its pedigree, and also its resources, and redistribute that for the groups that are not NGOs, that are doing radical work, that are trying to build, that are unsettling, and can open the possibility for different futures.

At the time that Standing Rock was happening and we wanted to take the lead from people that were doing that work, the New York City Stands with Standing Rock Collective, and so we played a supporting role. But in action. And so all the resources and space were made available, and we used all our assets, whatever we had to support that work. And also to build good faith and to recognize that we actually are throwing down for the sake of our freedom, as artists, as cultural producers, as thinkers, as doers. And from there, we continued to build our relationships together with the intention of knowing that our relationships would go on past this specific struggle.

JD: Yes, I remember how instrumental Decolonize This Place was in helping us organize that first rally and supply drive, and then so many things afterwards as well. Can you comment on how you saw Standing Rock as emblematic of some of the work that matters to the heart of Decolonize This Place and MTL+?

AH: It's the moment in which it came in the evolution of our thinking. We were also involved in what is known as Occupy Wall Street, and the failures there led us over time to understand that social justice is operating within silos. We also recognized that the word "occupy" is problematic, and it excluded some essential kind of thinking, core thinking, to how to create this different world that we want to live in. We tried doing stuff around debt, thinking that the notion of debt can get at capitalism and in a way can kind of create a different space for mapping our struggle. But we also recognize that it lacked the racial analysis that needed to happen. So when Standing Rock started, we knew of Indigenous resurgence, but we didn't really know how to incorporate it into our thinking. And so the failures led us to this moment that happened at the time of Standing Rock, with us doing an action about Palestine, and that recognition of how it was that we were talking about Palestine—which is about occupation and settler colonialism—and not talk about what does it mean to be part of, and complicit in, the settler colonialism happening here in the United States.

JD: Right. You began to see the connections.

AH: Yes. And so it's a question of timing and it's a question of failures that led us to that moment and then also just knowing people who are involved in that struggle here in the city. It was essential for us to begin to think together. And the first banner that went up in the Decolonize This Place space, the only banner that we actually made for that space, was a banner that Nitasha insisted on. It said: "de-occupy."

JD: I think that helps to clarify why you support Standing Rock at this moment. I'm wondering if you can speak just a little bit more generally here to your ideas about solidarity. It seems like you are implying that this kind of solidarity work is central to your vision for radical justice and freedom, but I'm wondering if you could reflect on this idea and what it means to work in solidarity. Clarify, in other words, your understanding and ideas about solidarity and then I think maybe some direct references to how this connects to your work in Palestine.

AH: I mean you know the thing about solidarity and a lot of words like that, is that at some point they seem to lack the vision and the commitment for how solidarity is directly related to each group's liberation, freedom, possibilities, and life. And this has been a frustrating experience. And in thinking about solidarity, people don't—our experience has been that within the circles that we traversed prior to Decolonize This Place and what led us to that point, is people don't really think of solidarity as a political choice and that it is part of a strategy. It is a political choice and a kind of identity.

And that is actually an embodiment of the kind of politics that we want to have and live by in this world. And I think that we wanted to kind of think about solidarity in terms of how our actions relate to each and every group's liberation, not to speak on behalf of others, but actually construct a new "we." In the process of doing this, in the process of showing people the level of commitment, not to help others, but actually to help ourselves in the process. That's where my solidarity thinking comes from. Now why is that important strategically? It's something that we see in Palestine. The exceptionalization of Palestine versus a specificity of the struggle in Palestine in relation to settler colonialism is something that we think about. We know that Palestinians themselves perpetuate forms of oppression against one another, and that's part of what is happening. So the new formations that we're thinking about are formations that in a way do not, are not, limited by boundaries and borders, are not limited by even an identity that is taken up as Palestinian. Though there are people who lead and people who are accomplices and people who support, right, and that we take turns at doing that, and as we—in the process of doing this—we learn from one another and undo in fact, the things that perpetuate the conditions of injustice that we exist in.

ND: To add to that I'll give a concrete example. In the context of art institutions, wherever you go, everywhere you see that there is an urgent need to actively shift the way these institutions work. They have been institutions of settler colonial power. You often see the language of "native New Yorkers." So how you shift in terms of the language was something that was very important. Also a lot of our struggles can get co-opted, but when we—and in this construction of the "we" that Amin is talking about—when we actually work together it becomes very difficult for them to actually tackle it and co-opt it. And it helps us to keep moving, it helps us to also not be stagnant at one place because that is very important for the work that we do, that we have to keep moving.

JD: I see. So a kind of coalition building and solidarity in the ways that you're describing it as a political strategy to also counter co-optation by state institutions.

AH: Yeah, it's collapsing a lot of concerns and problems together. So rather than simplify it and make it digestible, rather than it speaking to power, in the process of collaboration, we're speaking to each other. And in the process of speaking to each other, we're learning and unlearning as we do and in that kind of situation we're also cognizant of our movement's ebb and flow in time, in terms of intensities. We all have multiple concerns just like we carry with us multiple identities, and I think that doing that kind of work where it's not just focused on one thing also allows us to make the connections. So that it's not just intersectional, but it's actually moving toward this understanding, that is complex, of a world that we live in that has been made complex for our understanding.

JD: It sounds to me that relationships, building relationships are central to what it is that's required if you're trying to have these kinds of multiple axes of experience and also organizing to come together in a space like Decolonize This Place. Can you reflect a little bit on that? How you think about relationships within the context of your work?

AH: Yeah. I mean the thing about relationships is that it's the core. I mean you can talk about capitalism all you want, socialism, those kinds of things, leaving aside that they come from a Western epistemology, put that aside even, but they can feel like abstractions. But of course we live them and experience them every day of our life. So then the question is, how do we actually understand them, how do we learn to be cognizant of them in how we are living?

In that sense, relationships become almost a pedagogical experience for us. Where the failure of imagination all of a sudden is supplanted by these kinds of relationships that raise more questions. The other thing about doing this kind of work is that most people think of activism, or think of teaching, or think of organizing as specific modes of operating, when in fact most of the organizing in our experience happens over coffee, over food, over shared space, in ways that a meeting for two hours facilitated by the best facilitators won't actually produce the kind of experience that people need to continue doing the work. Or the imagination that is needed to continue on. So by creating the space, by focusing on relationships, we actually recognize where our powers are, and we recognize not the abstraction but actually how this thing is embodied in our relationships.

JD: Absolutely. I couldn't agree more. I think it's absolutely so key, and you see this when you try to teach political education. You can teach history, rewrite history, counter narratives to imperialist and colonial history, but people without access or access points in terms of developing connections to the way it's lived in the everyday, really it's easy for them to back away from the critique once they learn it, because there's nothing to sustain it.

ND: Yes. The other thing I think we've encountered a lot in terms of trajectories of people being involved is once they understand the critique, there's also a sense of paralysis. There's either guilt, there's either shame, there are all these things but it doesn't mobilize people, or it doesn't get people to think of what they can actually do in terms of action. So a lot of people will do programming around these things but they won't know how to actually change it in their institutions. And that is where these relationships come in and help us figure it out together.

JD: This is a great segue to having you speak a little bit about the kind of concrete and material political work that you engaged in to foster these relationships. Can you offer a sampling of the range of the kinds of things that you did? This seems to be one of the really key distinguishing features of the work of Decolonize This Place, at least in my view as an organizer.

ND: I think I would give the example of the most recent action that we did, which was at the Museum of Natural History. It was the second Anti-Columbus Day Tour, and we produced a brochure for this one. There were numerous organizations involved: Decolonize This Place and NYC Stands with Standing Rock, BYP100 which is Black Youth Project 100, Eagle and Condor House, American—sorry—Eagle and Condor Center, and American Indian Community House. And also the South Asia Solidarity Initiative and Chinatown Art Brigade. And many more. And the knowledge came together with this brochure where different movements were challenging the different halls in the museum. So again the same idea of having specificity of the struggle but then being able to move together. It was more than twenty or thirty people who worked on that brochure, and it took us almost a month to actually come together to make that. People visited the museum; they saw what was screwed up in relation to the exhibit they were talking about, came back, wrote the text, and then we put it all together.

AH: Yeah, and I think that one way—I mean part of the reason we call it a tour is so that we can make it family friendly. And we also kind of live up to that promise. Because what's important for us is also the generational knowledge that's shared. And this is a transgressive act. We took over the museum. We de-occupied it with our voices, with our bodies, in formations that they actually are not used to seeing come together.

Largely people of color. Many Indigenous. Each having a role and each having a leading role in the process of doing this. And this is the kind of work that's important. Like how do we construct the "we"? Well, the brochure is an example. Everyone went to their hall of interest, their hall of concern, the hall that seems, that claims, to represent them and actually sat with it and thought what kind of history is it telling? What kind of knowledge is it perpetuating? And then having to sit with their community outside of the museum and talk about it. Then having to translate it into words. Then for us to collaboratively work on it in the process of making the brochure, from the visual to the language and now it's being translated to Spanish and other groups who are actually only Spanish speaking are running tours through the museum. So we open up the space, we collaboratively work on it, multiple different groups take over the museum, make it for the people; in the process these formations are merged to the outside where we had a community gathering where people heard about each other's struggles, and that's important.

Now, we could've done something to the museum that day, something to the statue that day but we chose not to because it's important for us to feel strong and good together. Then autonomous groups you know, went at night and did something to the statue because it was necessary to also point out how the statue at the front of that museum perpetuates settler colonialism. Now that's just one example. We need to actually recognize that if we don't build together we're not effective. And so how do we do that? We show up. We do social media. We build good faith and trust. And over time friendships. These gestures are necessary, they're part of being generous but they're part of embodying a certain politics. With that, people started coming together. And if we can share a space and see things together, something can emerge.

ND: Something very tangible.

AH: Something very tangible. And also you further demands in that process. So we have concrete demands, some of which are probably considered unachievable. But there are other demands that are very tangible: renaming the day for example, for the museum to come out to say that we want the day renamed. And another thing is to say that this statue shouldn't be at the front of the most highly funded museum and most frequented by youth and children in this city.

ND: And so it was important for us to start with Indigenous struggle because we are on Lenape land, and then move to all these other struggles.

AH: Just one more comment, Jaskiran.

JD: Go ahead, of course.

AH: It often blindsides people as to why Palestine. But really it's an extension of the same logic. You know Palestine is this—it's almost—it kind of collapses different histories and futures together. And it's supported by the empire of the United States, as an external colony of this country in the same way Puerto Rico functions but more so. And the reason I bring Palestine up is because, unlike decolonization struggles of the past that we're more familiar with, Algeria, Libya, you know you take your pick, Palestine is a country that even the right to self-determination didn't materialize in a nation-state. Not that that's the goal. But so you have a situation where a lot of what Fanon writes about, it actually gets visualized in Palestine right now. A lot of the biopolitics gets visualized in Palestine right now. This idea of late capitalism, neoliberalism, and what are the conditions of the people to exist in this kind of Western-centric world, are things that we experience all like, rather than in time, like other people may have, all together. And in a way, it kind of highlights—because it's a smaller territory, it makes us understand how these things interrelate. And the complicity that extends beyond us here.

JD: Those connections are so important.

AH: I know it's tempting to isolate it to a specific geography, but it's actually not helpful in our experience. We have to be as bold as power is oppressive. And what is the solution? Well the solution isn't the state. States are one of the most oppressive structures that we know to exist. So then how does a Palestinian imagine, under these forms of oppression, a different future? We know it's hard to imagine. So then what does this mean? It's these connections that we are describing and interlinking in how we struggle. Just when you feel like the world has closed in, to actually see someone reaching out for you.

JD: That's a great way to end this piece and a clear indication of why this kind of solidarity work matters so much.

28

DEATH OF HYDRA

Joel Waters

it is eel-like
the reach of corporations
who worm their way thru
loophole after loophole
to take imminent domain
over the landscape
for the sake of some coal
or even black gold
and often we are told
it will be good for the nation
but this is a nation
of encroaching corporations
who have sky-scraped
through Mount Olympus
to control the laws that
govern us
and corrupt the ones who swore
to protect us
this land is no mans land
when it can be seized by a court order
stolen by bureaucracy
by proxy of a bank
it was only a matter of time
before a new hydra was born
out of the entrails of a dead plutocracy
whose oily tentacles

have now reached across our waters

across our reservations
selling a pipe dream
to an awakening nation
it is time to fight oil for water
it is time to fight oil with blood
for we have countless ancestors
fighting through us
fighting with us
let their voices slay
the many heads
of the black snake
let our words be the scythe
let our prayers be the fire
that cauterizes the wounds
of this greedy beast of an empire

"The Black Snake." Photograph by Michelle Latimer.

29

MAPPING A MANY-HEADED HYDRA
TRANSNATIONAL INFRASTRUCTURES OF EXTRACTION AND RESISTANCE

Katie Mazer, Martin Danyluk, Elise Hunchuck, and Deborah Cowen

The planet is in a state of social and ecological crisis that is anchored in infrastructure. Standing Rock is about many things, as this very collection suggests: Indigenous sovereignty and the reassertion of treaties, water protection and environmental coalition, extractive industries and settler colonial violence, privatized and militarized security forces. But alongside all of this, Standing Rock is also a flashpoint struggle in a broader frenzy over infrastructure. Public and private authorities at every scale are currently investing unprecedented amounts in the collectively assembled systems that are said to reproduce human life. Mainstream debates frame the current crisis as one of an "infrastructure deficit" and locate the solution to this quantitative shortage of infrastructure in its financialization. In this context, infrastructure is governed as a technical matter of economic security, foreclosing broader political engagement. This financialization coalesces with the securitization of critical infrastructure over the last decade that has seen states and corporations surveille and criminalize those who contest infrastructure plans, development, and management.[1]

Water Protectors challenged a particular piece of pipe—the Dakota Access Pipeline (DAPL)—but they also challenged mainstream conceptions of infrastructure and enacted alternatives. They revealed that the crisis of infrastructure lies not simply in its failure or absence, but sometimes in *its presence*—as DAPL suggests. Standing Rock exposes how problems of infrastructure are more than merely technical; it is at the heart of the making of in/justice, and the stakes of infrastructure are more than just the bottom line. In the work of the Water Protectors, other kinds of infrastructure are also visible—alternative or fugitive forms that sustained a transnational solidarity movement and that reproduced large communities who gathered on site.

Infrastructures crisscross the two-dimensional puzzle pieces of national sovereignty that constitute the settler state system. Infrastructures have distinct form—they require attention to the particular places that they stitch together—whether through pipes, cables, or cement. Network architectures take the form at scales above and below the nation-state and traverse borders. The nascent infrastructures of the protection camps were organized across Indigenous lands that themselves underlie national borders (both geographically and historically).

This chapter is based on a report we produced collaboratively that attempted to trace the changing contours of these infrastructural networks.[2] This work, intended for public education and community use, took detailed stock of the broader North American oil pipeline network, using a time-series of maps to accessibly illustrate the dynamic state of both extractive infrastructure expansion and the growing social networks that are challenging it. What becomes clear from the perspective of the broader network is that the impacts of individual flashpoints like Standing Rock ripple through the rest of the system. This networked, relational dynamic is reflected not only in industry strategies, but also in the tactics and geographies of solidarity and resistance to DAPL and other pipelines across North America. This was on clear display when water defenders resolutely refused to abandon the camps after the Army Corps of Engineers denied the easement for the final portion of the pipeline in December.[3] By maintaining that the fight was not over until the project was cancelled, protesters invoked the extensive social and ecological geographies surrounding and impacted by the pipeline that defy the boundaries of the company's tidy maps.

By highlighting some of the networks surrounding DAPL and the struggle at Standing Rock, this chapter illustrates that the Dakota Access is fundamentally transnational not only for its entrenchment in transnational networks of infrastructure, commodity flows, and finance, but also in a much more basic way. This transnationalism is manifest through the local, international, and global ecologies on which we all rely and that are at stake in the expansion of this and other pipeline infrastructure. It is clear in the geographies of Indigenous territories and assertions of Indigenous sovereignty that defy and supersede the international boundaries of Canada and the United States through which the pipeline passes. And it is perhaps most evident in the social infrastructures and solidarity efforts that have coalesced around the fight at Standing Rock. Importantly, this social infrastructure has been built on the acknowledgment that the ecological and social geographies that surround the site are in no way contained to the site itself. That is, the continental geographies of North American energy infrastructure are apparent not just in the threats posed by the pipeline and the ongoing expansion of petro-capitalism, but also in the strategies employed by industry and in communities' responses.

This analysis and the title of this chapter are inspired by the work of historians Marcus Rediker and Peter Linebaugh.[4] In their riveting history of the rebellious Atlantic, these authors invoke the metaphor of Hercules and the Hydra to describe the unruly commoners—slaves, sailors, laborers, and others—who rebelled, together, against brutal conditions of exploitation and their enrollment in the colonial expansion of North America. As the authors explain, the Hercules–Hydra myth was commonly used by rulers to convey the challenge of imposing order and discipline on this globalizing system of labor. While transatlantic networks of trade and exploitation were assembled to serve the interests of empire, these networks also built social connections and common cause among the exploited and dispossessed, allowing commoners to join together in rebellion across spatial distance and social difference. To the rulers, the Hydra represented this seemingly mutable mass of variously dispossessed peoples: near impossible to slay, when one of her many heads was severed, new ones would grow in its place. In this way, transnational networks of resistance haunted the expanding geographies of empire.

This is precisely the type of dynamism that runs through contemporary North American pipeline politics. From the pipeline pushers, we see the ever-changing geographies of industry's expansion plans and the fragmentation of approval processes so as to obscure these networks. But these continental networks are reflected right back in the transnational and organizing tactics that communities are using to stop this growing network of pipe.

Finally, the situation with North American energy infrastructure is changing quickly, and increasingly so under the Trump administration. This is not intended to be a real-time account; the information in this chapter is current as of fall 2017.[5] By contextualizing the Dakota Access Pipeline within the broader social and spatial relations of North American oil pipeline politics, our aim is to propose tools to support ongoing analysis and the broader efforts to protect waters and lands against the seemingly incessant expansion of North American extractivism.

DAPL Basics

First made public in July 2014, the Dakota Access Pipeline (DAPL) is a $3.7 billion, 1,172-mile underground oil pipeline that runs from six sites in the Bakken and Three Forks oil-producing regions of North Dakota, through South Dakota and Iowa, to southern Illinois.[6] In Patoka, Illinois, DAPL's terminus and a key Midwest transportation hub, the pipeline links into a network of other lines that are connected to refineries in the Midwest and along the Gulf Coast.[7]

DAPL has the capacity to transport up to 570,000 barrels per day (bpd) of crude oil—equal to about half of current Bakken production.[8] The pipeline carries this light sweet crude across 209 rivers, creeks, and tributaries, including the Missouri River, which is one of the cleanest river tributaries in the United States today.[9]

In North Dakota, which has seen the fiercest resistance to DAPL, documents filed as part of the permitting process indicate that Energy Transfer Partners (ETP) had originally planned to route the pipeline to the north of its current route, crossing the Missouri River just north of the state capital, Bismarck, and the town of Mandan.[10] After opposition from the area's mostly white residents, based on concerns about water contamination, the proposed water crossing was moved south to its current location just upstream from the Standing Rock Sioux Reservation.

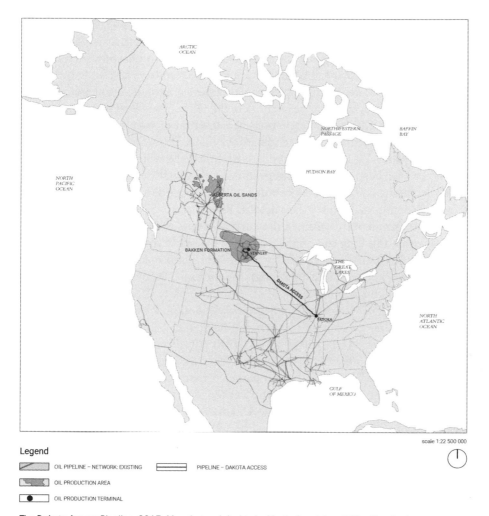

The Dakota Access Pipeline, 2017. Mapping and design by Martin Danyluk and Elise Hunchuck.

The new route crosses Lake Oahe, tributaries of Lake Sakakawea, the Missouri River twice, and the Missouri River once.[11] In late July 2016 the Army Corps of Engineers approved permits for the project without approval from the Standing Rock Sioux Tribe.[12]

The Dakota Access Pipeline violates the Fort Laramie Treaties of 1851 and 1868. The first Fort Laramie Treaty, signed in 1851 between the United States and representatives of the Arapaho, Arikara, Assiniboine, Cheyenne, Crow, Hidatsa, Mandan, and Sioux Nations, recognized and defined bounded national territories and guaranteed safe passage through the territory for settlers heading west in exchange for goods and services. Many nations who signed the treaty never received payment. The 1868 Fort Laramie Treaty created the Great Sioux Reservation, which included all of South Dakota west of the Missouri River, including the Black Hills, and protected hunting rights in Montana, Wyoming, and South Dakota. Note that in neither of these treaties did the Sioux cede the land in question surrounding the DAPL route. Since this time, in its rush to seize resources and secure access to land, the United States has repeatedly violated the terms of the Fort Laramie Treaties, including by occupying the territory of the Great Sioux Reservation such that today's fragmented reservations represent a fraction of what is stipulated in the treaty.[13] As the chairman of the Standing Rock Sioux Tribe (SRST), David Archambault II, explains, DAPL represents the third time that the Sioux Nation's lands and resources have been taken without permission: the first time was the Black Hills gold rush in the late nineteenth century, and the second in 1958, when the Army Corps of Engineers dammed the Missouri River, creating Lake Oahe.[14] While it is beyond the scope of this chapter, the current events at Standing Rock should be placed within this long and ongoing colonial history.[15] To this end, the #StandingRockSyllabus is an invaluable resource, providing conceptual background, treaty and territorial histories, and a thorough timeline of U.S. settler colonialism.[16]

The ownership and financing of DAPL is complex. The Dakota Access portion of the Bakken system was being built by Dakota Access, LLC, a subsidiary of Dallas-based Energy Transfer Partners, LP. Bakken Holdings Company, LLC, is a joint venture between ETP and Sonoco Logistics (itself a subsidiary of ETP), which owns a 75 percent interest in both Dakota Access, LLC, and Energy Transfer Crude Oil Company, LLC (ETCO), the companies responsible for developing, owning, and operating the two segments of the Bakken system.[17] Seventeen major banks have extended $2.5 billion in loans to Dakota Access, LLC, for the construction of DAPL.[18] In August 2016, Enbridge Energy Partners and Marathon Petroleum announced plans to buy a $2 billion stake in the project. Energy Transfer Partners and Sunoco Logistics are using some of the proceeds from this deal to pay back some of the resulting debts.[19]

The Bakken Context

North Dakota contains some of the United States' largest oil fields and, since 2012, has been the second-largest crude-oil-producing state, after Texas. The Bakken and Three Forks production areas are part of the Williston Basin, a deposit of several hundred thousand square miles that straddles the medicine line, spanning North Dakota, South Dakota, Montana, and the Canadian provinces of Saskatchewan and Manitoba.[20] In 2013 the U.S. Geological Survey estimated that there were more than seven billion barrels of technically recoverable oil in the Bakken and Three Forks deposits.[21] While the formation was discovered in the 1950s and some amount of early oil production occurred, the deposit remained largely technically inaccessible until the early 2000s, by which time advances in hydraulic fracturing and horizontal drilling techniques made exploitation of these reservoirs commercially viable. Since that time, production has exploded, with crude oil production in North Dakota increasing thirteen times between 2003 and 2014, by which time the state accounted for 12.5 percent of total U.S. crude oil production.[22]

The oil in the Williston formation is what the petroleum industry calls "tight oil": oil that is extracted from sandstone or shale and therefore considered to be "low permeability." Tight oil is extracted using combined horizontal drilling and hydraulic fracturing (or "fracking") methods similar to those used to extract shale gas. This involves injecting wells with water, sand, and slickwater chemicals at high pressure in order to fracture the rock.[23] Tight oil is difficult, resource intensive, and dangerous to extract. U.S. oil production has recently reached levels not seen since the 1970s, and this increase is largely due to the rise of oil fracking: in 2015 tight oil accounted for more than half of U.S. oil production.[24]

Much like with the Alberta tar sands, the rapid expansion of oil fracking has changed the geographies of oil production in the United States. Beyond the actual site of production the oil boom has also spurred changing practices and demands when it comes to the transportation of oil as industry and governments have worked to get this oil, first, to refineries and, second, to domestic and, importantly, international consumers. To this end, DAPL is the first part in the larger Bakken system: while DAPL transports Bakken crude from North Dakota, to the hub in Patoka, Illinois, from there, the Energy Transfer Crude Oil Pipeline (ETCOP) would run to the U.S. Gulf Coast, offering Bakken crude access to significant refining capacity and international export markets.[25] Announced in 2013, ETCOP is a joint venture of Energy Transfer and Canadian energy delivery company Enbridge.[26] The main part of ETCOP is comprised of an existing 678-mile natural gas Trunkline Pipeline that runs between the Gulf Coast and Illinois and Indiana. This pipeline would be converted to oil and extended by sixty-six miles.[27] This conversion would create the first pipeline transportation option for getting crude oil from the Midwest U.S. to the eastern Gulf Coast, providing access to refineries and ports in this "highly desirable market" for both Canadian and Bakken crude.[28] Adjoining the two halves of the Bakken System is the Patoka tank farm, in south-central Illinois.

In August 2016 Enbridge announced an agreement to acquire equity interest in the Bakken system as a whole. A more detailed exploration of Enbridge's role in this story is offered below, but suffice to say for now that Enbridge's involvement in this project signals the continental character of the events unfolding at Standing Rock, not only when we follow the money, but also when we follow the pipe. Enbridge's investment in the Bakken system indicates not only that the company intends to expand its business in the Bakken industry; it also points to Enbridge's interest in working around the public scrutiny that accompanies high-profile major new-build projects. By buying into already-existing pipeline, the company positions itself to expand on this infrastructure, hoping to build more piecemeal continental networks in a more expedited and low-profile way.

The Broader Pipeline Context: Windigo Economics and Continental Contingency

Despite the dubious grounds on which pro-pipeline arguments are built—explained below—Canadian and American politicians remain committed to the relentless expansion of oil and gas production and transportation. As oil workers and communities embedded in the industry have suffered job losses, underemployment, and real hardship as prices and production have declined over the past three years, especially in Canada, pipelines have been heralded as the solution to this social devastation.

The explanation for why new pipelines are needed is a confusing cocktail of economic arguments. In the case of tar sands bitumen, this so-called imperative has been framed, on the one hand, as a solution to the problem of Western Canada having exceeded its pipeline capacity—which is said to keep prices low. On the other hand, by facilitating access to international markets, it is presented as a way to close the price gap between North American and global oil markets. Because the infrastructure is not there to transport this crude to marine ports, pipeline boosters claim, Canadian producers have been beholden to the U.S. market and, as a result, unable to get world prices for their product.[29] By getting oil to tidewater, we are told, companies will be able to access world oil prices, boost sales, and reinvest in increased production.[30]

More recently, industry and governments are heralding the economic benefits of the infrastructure itself: most notably, infrastructure expansion, including pipelines, has formed a central part of U.S. president Trump's agenda. In Canada, since the crash in oil prices starting in 2014, industry advocates have also been drumming up an argument that—despite its terrible performance as a job creator—private pipeline expansion is an effective form of national economic stimulus.[31] The active debate that surrounds these different claims has thrown into question the "need" for expanded pipeline capacity.[32] But after months of study, the main conclusion we drew from scrutinizing these arguments and debates was that *this is the wrong conversation.*

First, these technical and market-based arguments are opaque, inconsistent, and factually suspicious. After sifting through them, we have been unable to discern a clear or convincing consensus as to why new pipelines are needed. But, more importantly, there is a problem with the fundamental terms on which these arguments are based: economic and technical arguments for pipeline expansion are predicated on an assumption of continued expansion of oil production. This declared *need* for incessant economic growth limits the debate, steering the conversation away from the urgent need to *question* this assumption.

Crucially, researchers have found that new pipeline projects would only be needed "if significant future expansion of oil sands production were to occur at levels that would push Canada well beyond established climate pollution limits and Alberta's emission cap."[33] Back in 2011, the International Energy Agency (IEA) flagged the centrality of energy infrastructure to the fate of the climate, warning that investing in new fossil fuel infrastructure (buildings, plants, pipelines, etc.) risks locking us into a future of expanded fossil fuel production beyond what the planet can bear.[34] The IEA's analysis indicated that 80 percent of the total carbon dioxide (CO_2) emissions permissible through 2035 under the 450 Scenario—the IEA's widely used but conservative scenario in which the rise in average global temperature is limited to 2°C—was already "locked-in" by infrastructure currently in place or under construction in 2011.[35]

Anishinaabe writer and leader Winona LaDuke diagnoses this violent and destructive political economy of extractive greed as the "Windigo economy."[36] For years she has been fighting its expansion through pipelines, as she also invests in building alternative infrastructures and economies.[37] Indeed, while pipeline boosters have been widely—and rightly—critiqued on the basis of their *factual* accuracy, findings like these highlight the degree to which the pipeline question is ultimately a key *political* question about the vision of the future we are willing to accept. We need to reclaim this crucial conversation from a narrow economic rhetoric that assumes incessant growth and externalizes the real social and ecological consequences of this agenda.

Below, we offer a brief round-up of the key pipelines that have been proposed for transporting Alberta and Bakken crude to tidewater for export and to key sites of concentrated refining capacity. This is by no means a full picture of the North American crude pipeline network; rather, it represents the major oil pipeline projects that have come under great public scrutiny. The routes to the Gulf of Mexico that have served as alternatives to the Keystone XL have been completed in a piecemeal fashion and have been subject to expedited approval processes; together this has enabled TransCanada and Enbridge to usher in these new networks without the level of public scrutiny these other lines have seen. As becomes clear from reading the following synopses, in the face of barriers to expanding their networks, the energy delivery industry, backed by governments, has been extremely adaptable. As people have risen up across North America in defense of land, water, and the future, pipeline companies have repeatedly worked to circumvent these geographies of resistance. Despite the long approval processes, huge geographical expanses, and massive capital investment characteristic of these projects, the result of this dialectic has been a high degree of *connectivity* and *dynamism* throughout the industry.

Especially in the wake of the election of U.S. president Donald Trump, at the time of writing, the fate of several key pipelines remains unclear. This environment of uncertainly encompasses not only DAPL, but also the Keystone XL Pipeline, which President Trump has tried to revive, despite its 2015 rejection by then president Barack Obama. But what this chapter aims to make clear is that this contingency is not contained to these individual projects. Rather, North American pipelines comprise a network with a series of moving and flexible parts; a single development on a single project—say, the revival of the Keystone XL—has effects that ripple through the rest of the system. Approvals, rejections, and movements to resist U.S. pipelines reorganize the incentives and viability of other U.S. projects, but also pipeline projects in Canada. The current contingency is continental.

The Fate of Canadian Tar Sands Pipelines

Here we provide a brief round-up of the key pipelines that have been proposed for transporting bitumen from Alberta to tidewater, through both Canada and the United States.

Enbridge Northern Gateway (Rejected)

The proposed Enbridge Northern Gateway Pipeline would have shipped 525,000 bpd of tar sands crude 1,177 kilometers from near Edmonton, Alberta, to Kitimat, British Columbia. From here, the oil would have been loaded onto tankers, where it would have traveled through the rough, pristine, and remote waters of the Douglas Channel on its way to Asian markets. The most controversial of domestic Canadian pipelines, the Northern Gateway drew massive resistance for its incursion into unceded Indigenous lands, its threat to environmentally sensitive areas, and its promise to expand tar sands production.

In June 2016, the Canadian Federal Court of Appeal ruled that the project approval granted in 2014 must be set aside because the government had failed in its duty to consult with Indigenous peoples who would be impacted by the project. In September 2016, proponents and the federal government both announced that they would not appeal the decision.[38] Two months later the federal cabinet finally and ultimately rejected the proposed project.[39]

Kinder Morgan Trans Mountain (In Limbo)

Built in 1953, the Trans Mountain Pipeline is currently the only line that carries oil from Alberta (Edmonton) to the British Columbia coast (Burnaby), where it can access ports for export across the Pacific. In April 2012, Kinder Morgan Canada proposed to expand the capacity of the 1,150-kilometer line from 300,000 to 890,000 bpd.[40] The Trans Mountain expansion was the subject of the "battle of Burnaby Mountain" in the fall of 2014. As surveying for the pipeline began, protests and civil disobedience on the mountain prevented crews from carrying out work for a time. After the company sought an injunction to direct the Royal Canadian Mounted Police to prevent protesters from interfering with drilling, in a huge show of opposition to the pipeline, crowds continued to grow, hundreds risked arrest, and the protests stayed in the public eye.[41] After the British Columbia Supreme Court rejected an injunction extension, the company was eventually forced to withdraw from the mountain.[42]

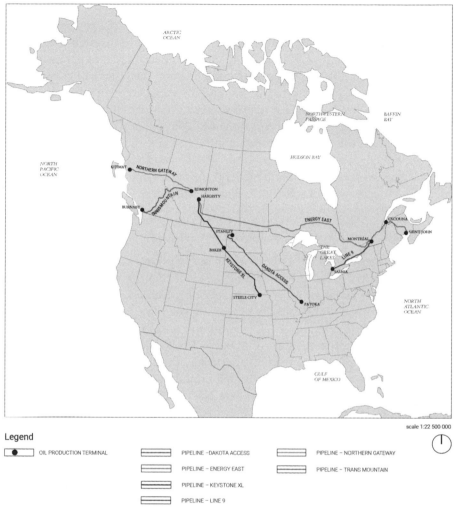

The continental context: key North American pipelines, 2017. Mapping and design by Martin Danyluk and Elise Hunchuck.

The National Energy Board (NEB) conditionally approved the expansion in May 2016, naming 157 conditions. After the approval, in response to widespread concern that the review process had been biased, the federal government tasked a three-member panel to provide further questions for the cabinet to consider. In its report, released in November 2016, the panel responded to outstanding questions about federal commitments on climate change and Canada's relationship with Indigenous peoples. At the time, Vancouver mayor Gregor Robertson warned, "I think you'll see protests like you've never seen before on this one," should the federal government approve the pipeline.[43] Prime Minister Justin Trudeau and his cabinet gave final approval to the project on November 29, 2016.[44]

Since then, protests and legal delays have continued to threaten the project and, in the spring of 2018, Kinder Morgan suspended work on the pipeline. In response, adamant that the expansion would be built, the Canadian government announced plans to purchase the pipeline and the expansion project. On the same day Kinder Morgan shareholders approved the CAD$4.5 billion sale, the Federal Court of Appeal overturned the government's 2016 approval of the project, citing shortcomings in the NEB's environmental review and the government's failure to meaningfully consult with First Nations.[45] The NEB has since reassessed and, again, endorsed the project. But no federal approval can occur until the government meets its duty to consult with Indigenous peoples.

TransCanada Keystone XL (Rejected and Revived)

TransCanada submitted its application for the Keystone XL Pipeline to the U.S. government in 2008. The proposed pipeline would transport tar sands oil 1,897 kilometers from Hardisty, Alberta, to Steele City, Nebraska, picking up Bakken crude along the way. Total capacity of the proposed line would be 730,000 bpd. From Steele City, the Keystone XL would hook into the broader Keystone network, which extends to the Gulf of Mexico. The Keystone XL is a high-profile proposal: unlike DAPL and the other sections of the Keystone system, because the Keystone XL crossed an international boundary, it required approval from the U.S. State Department. The Canadian National Energy Board approved the Canadian portion of the project in 2010.[46] But after a seven-year review process and widespread resistance, President Obama rejected the Keystone XL Pipeline in November 2015.[47] In January 2016, TransCanada launched a US$15 billion challenge under the North American Free Trade Agreement. It has also launched a separate federal lawsuit seeking a declaration that Obama overstepped his constitutional power.[48]

The election of Donald Trump, with his promise to invest in major infrastructure projects alongside his commitment to rolling back climate policy, reinvigorated the debate about the pipeline.[49] In his first week in office, President Trump signed an executive order expediting the review and approval of the Keystone XL Pipeline, and in April the project entered its final review.[50]

The Keystone XL Pipeline is part of the broader Keystone system, a network meant to run from Hardisty to the Gulf Coast. In 2014 TransCanada built phase three of the system: the Gulf Coast Project from Cushing, Oklahoma, to Nederland, Texas, on the Gulf Coast as an attempt to relieve the glut of oil in the Midwest. The Keystone XL Pipeline is meant to be phase four, connecting the Gulf Coast extension, through the Keystone–Cushing extension, directly to Hardisty.[51]

Enbridge Line 9B (Operational)

Approval for the reversal and expansion of Enbridge Line 9B was issued in March 2014. Four decades old and originally constructed to run west to east, the line had been reversed in the late 1990s. The most recent re-reversal and expansion allows for the shipment of 300,000 bpd of Western crude, through densely populated southeastern Ontario, to Quebec refineries. Construction on the project began in the fall of 2014, and the line is now operational.[52]

TransCanada Energy East (Cancelled)

The proposed Energy East line was the longest and highest capacity of the proposed tar sands pipelines. Energy East would have run 4,600 kilometers from Hardisty, Alberta, transporting 1.1 million bpd of oil to the Irving Oil refinery and export terminal in Saint John, New Brunswick. Along the way, it would have crossed through six provinces, under 2,963 identified waterways, and through or near fifty-one First Nations.[53] About two-thirds of the route was to consist of a repurposed old natural gas line, while new pipe would have been built through Alberta, Quebec, and New Brunswick, including through Wolastoqiyik and Mi'kmaq territories covered by Peace and Friendship Treaties and recognized as unceded by the Supreme Court of Canada.[54] While the pipeline was billed as a nation-building project that would bring jobs and more affordable oil to Eastern Canada, refineries along the pipeline's path never had the capacity to refine this oil, suggesting that the oil would have been loaded onto ships in the Bay of Fundy and exported.[55]

Energy East was first announced publicly in August 2013, in the midst of debates about Keystone XL and Northern Gateway. National Energy Board hearings on the project were delayed in the summer of 2016 when it was revealed that two board members had met privately in 2015 with former Quebec premier Jean Charest, who was a consultant for TransCanada at the time.[56] In October 2017, citing "changed circumstances," TransCanada announced that it would no longer be proceeding with either its Energy East Pipeline or Eastern Mainline projects.[57] The announcement came months after Trump expedited the review and approval of the Keystone XL Pipeline and just weeks after the NEB expanded the parameters for its review of Energy East to include emissions from extracting and refining the oil shipped through the pipeline.[58]

The Enbridge Network: Completing the Route to the Gulf Coast

While all eyes were on TransCanada's proposed Keystone XL project, between 2012 and 2014 Enbridge was quietly assembling and expanding an alternative network that would give Alberta and Bakken producers increased access to the U.S. Gulf Coast. The Enbridge GXL system—the network that spans the Great Lakes and U.S. Midwest before reaching for the Gulf Coast—cumulatively, represents an alternative route to the Keystone XL for transporting both Alberta and Bakken crude to Gulf refineries and ports.[59] In their detailed study of this network, Bruno et al. argue that together, the pipelines in the Enbridge GXL system can carry 2.5 million bpd.[60] Like each segment of the GXL, the Dakota Access Pipeline also sits within this broader context of the growing oil transportation networks that crisscross North America, the sum of which is much greater than its individual parts. By buying into the Bakken system, Enbridge continues to expand its networks that connect increasing amounts of Alberta and Bakken crude to refineries and global markets.

The Enbridge Network: The Superior Terminal

Constructed in 1950, the Superior Terminal in Superior, Wisconsin, has increased in significance in recent years with the expansion of tar sands and Bakken pipe networks through the Midwest United States.[61] The Superior Terminal sits at a key junction in Enbridge's alternate route to the Gulf, connecting Hardisty, Alberta (through the Alberta Clipper line), with Midwest refineries and storage (through the Southern Access Extension Project) and, ultimately, the Gulf Coast (through the Flanagan South and Seaway Pipelines). In 2012 Enbridge, through its partial ownership of North Dakota Pipeline Company, LLC, also began permitting for the Sandpiper Pipeline Project, which would connect Bakken crude into the Clearbrook, Minnesota, and Superior, Wisconsin, hubs.[62] The Sandpiper was eventually cancelled.

The Enbridge Network: Line 67 Expansion

Often known as the Alberta Clipper Pipeline, Line 67 runs about one thousand miles along Enbridge's mainline corridor between Hardisty, Alberta, and the Superior Terminal in Superior, Wisconsin, transporting Alberta oil to the U.S. market for refining and export. Because this line crosses the international border, it required approval from the U.S. State Department, and when it approved the Alberta Clipper in 2009, the department limited Enbridge to importing 450,000 bpd. But in a sneaky move that involved rerouting the oil into another older line for the border crossing, and then back to Alberta Clipper on the other side, Enbridge was able to skirt these limitations on the line's expansion.[63] By adding and modifying pump stations along the line, in a two-phase expansion, Enbridge increased the capacity of this line to its full design capacity of 800,000 bpd.[64]

The Enbridge Network: Line 61 Upgrade

Referred to as the Southern Access Pipeline Project during construction, Line 61 runs from the Superior Terminal to Enbridge's Flanagan Terminal near Pontiac,

Illinois, where it networks with the Gulf-bound Flanagan South–Seaway system. Line 61 became operational in 2009 and has since been subject to a two-phase expansion involving the construction of new pump stations. This expansion, which will bring Line 61's capacity to 1.2 million bpd, was set to be completed in 2016.[65] The second phase of the expansion was deferred in February 2017. The company explained that based on current supply projects, the plans to expand Line 3, and the expandability of other lines, the added capacity of the Line 61 Phase 2 expansion is no longer needed.[66]

The Enbridge Network: The Flanagan South and Seaway Pipelines

In 2012 Enbridge and Enterprise Products Partners completed a project to reverse the flow of the Seaway Pipeline, which runs from Cushing, Oklahoma, to Freeport, Texas. Two years later, the Seaway was twinned, more than doubling its capacity.[67] In late 2014, Enbridge completed the Flanagan South line, which runs 593 miles from Pontiac, Illinois, to the massive tank farm in Cushing, where it can pump crude from Alberta and the Bakken region into its Seaway connection to the Gulf.[68] As then premier of Alberta Jim Prentice explained, "The completion of these pipelines creates the first large-volume, direct link of Canadian crude to the U.S. Gulf Coast, where North America's largest concentration of heavy oil refineries is located."[69] In early 2015, Canadian crude began to flow through this network, doubling the shipments reaching the Gulf Coast.[70] Like DAPL, the Flanagan South line was approved using Nationwide Permit 12.[71]

The Enbridge Network: Line 3 "Replacement"

The original Line 3 was constructed in 1960 and entered into operation in 1968. It begins in Edmonton and, like Line 67, runs along the Enbridge Mainline corridor to the Superior Terminal. Because of its fragility (due to age and poor practices at the time of construction), the line is under pressure restrictions and unable to operate at capacity.[72] Rather than replace the aging line, as the project name suggests, Enbridge is seeking to abandon the line in place and build a new, higher-capacity line that would run along the same route as the original Line 3 (the Mainline corridor) between Hardisty, Alberta, and Clearbrook, Minnesota. Between the Clearbrook Terminal and the Superior Terminal, the route veers to the south of the original line, where it would follow the same route as the proposed Sandpiper line (see below).[73] According to Enbridge, this rerouting is due to the fact that the right of way that currently runs from Clearbrook to Superior is full as it already contains Lines 1, 2, 3, 4, 67, and 13.[74] But the southern route would pass through Minnesota's lake country, farmland, 1855 treaty territory, and an area of abundant wild rice—an important source of food, income, and meaning for the Anishinaabe people whose traditional territory this is.[75]

The $7.5 billion Line 3 "replacement" program is the largest project in Enbridge history.[76] But by characterizing this replacement and relocation of the line as simply maintenance, Enbridge managed to convince the State Department that no review is needed for what is, in essence, a new project. The Canadian government, meanwhile, approved the project in November 2016.[77]

The expansion of the Alberta Clipper line will free up this new Line 3 to transport 790,000 bpd, expanding Enbridge's capacity to transport tar sands crude across the border (Lines 3 and 67) from 840,000 to 1.6 million bpd—about twice the capacity of the proposed Keystone XL.[78] Of course, the abandonment of the original Line 3, which the company promises to seal, raises a host of other questions about safety and contamination.

The Enbridge Network: The Sandpiper Project (Cancelled)

Originally proposed in 2013, the Sandpiper Pipeline Project aimed to increase Enbridge's capacity to move Bakken oil. The Sandpiper was a proposal to construct a new 616-mile, 375,000 bpd crude oil pipeline from Enbridge's Beaver Lodge Station, near Tioga, North Dakota, to the Superior Terminal.[79] On September 1, 2016, after almost three years of regulatory delays, Enbridge Energy Partners withdrew its applications with the Minnesota Public Utilities Commission for the Sandpiper Pipeline Project.[80] In a news release the company explained that "the project should be delayed until such time as crude oil production in North Dakota recovers sufficiently to support development of new pipeline capacity. Based on updated projections, EEP believes that new pipeline capacity will not likely be needed until beyond the partnership's current five-year planning horizon."[81] One month earlier, the company had indicated its intention to focus on the Bakken system by announcing its $1.5 billion investment.[82]

The Enbridge Network: The Energy Transfer Crude Oil Pipeline (ETCOP)

In 2013, Enbridge struck a deal with Energy Transfer Partners on what is now the southern part of the Bakken system. In a fifty–fifty joint venture, the companies proposed to convert the more than seven-hundred-mile Trunkline natural gas system to oil, allowing for the transport of crude from the Patoka, Illinois, hub to the eastern Gulf Coast. Energy Transfer said that what was then called the Eastern Gulf Crude Access Pipeline Project would be the first line to carry crude from the Midwest to the eastern Gulf Coast.[83] Vern Yu, vice president of business development and market development for Enbridge, said of the deal: "It should help producers with their pricing because it opens up a significant new market for both Bakken and Canadian heavy."[84] As we have already seen in reviewing the expansion projects, at this time Enbridge was investing in a lot of projects that networked through the Patoka hub; the Trunkline conversion constituted an important part of that network expansion. Now this line constitutes the southern part

of the Bakken system and is called the Energy Transfer Crude Oil Pipeline. The
line will terminate in Nederland, Texas, and was originally projected to be in service by the end of 2016.[85]

Approving DAPL: Nationwide Permit No.12

Because the Keystone XL would cross an international boundary, it triggered a
State Department analysis, thereby leaving the approval decision with the U.S.
president. Being a domestic pipeline, the Dakota Access project, conversely, was
subject to a much different—less robust and much faster—approval process. Unlike
most other major energy projects, domestic pipelines built largely on private land
in the United States do not usually require overarching permits from the federal
government.

Increasingly, these projects are assessed using something called Nationwide
Permit 12 (Section 404 of the Clean Water Act and Section 10 of the Rivers and
Harbors Act), which is designed to increase efficiency for the approval of projects
that are anticipated to have minimal environmental impact. Rather than assess
these pipelines as major projects, the U.S. Army Corps of Engineers, which issues
permits for construction on and near waterways, approaches them as a series of
fragments. As such, each line is assessed as a series of individual projects, with a
focus on the individual water and wetland locations rather than the overarching
or cumulative effects of the project. This process grants exemption from the environmental reviews that are required under the Clean Water Act and the National
Environmental Policy Act. These exemptions are granted on the basis that the
pipeline is treated as a series of small construction sites.[86]

The controversial Nationwide Permit 12 was widely used under the Obama
administration. Parts of both Enbridge's Flanagan South and TransCanada's Gulf
Coast Pipelines were expedited under Nationwide Permit 12.[87] According to comments submitted to the Army Corps of Engineers from a collective of environmental organizations in August 2016, it is only since 2012—following the rejection of
the first application of the Keystone XL pipeline—that the corps has used Nationwide Permit 12 to approve major pipeline projects.[88]

The Dakota Access Pipeline was fast-tracked from the beginning using the
Nationwide Permit 12 process. In the case of DAPL, reviewing the project under
Nationwide Permit 12 relieved it from being subject to other forms of evaluation
including broader public review, evaluation through the National Environmental
Policy Act and the Endangered Species Act, and other regulations.[89] Nationwide
Permit 12 was not designed to streamline major projects, like the Dakota Access,
that have broad environmental impacts. But by dividing these projects into smaller
segments, companies have been able to access this expedited approval process and
skirt the type of scrutiny to which the Keystone XL was subject.

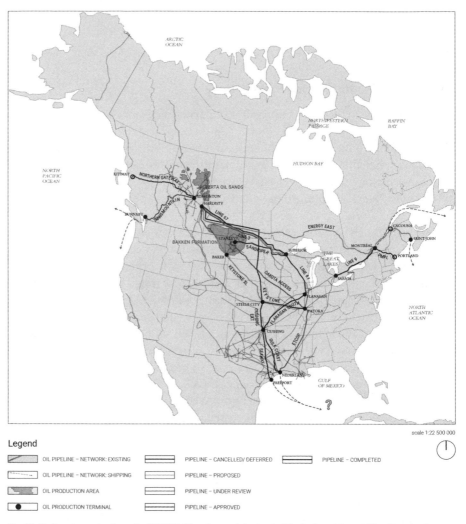

Key North American pipelines, April 2017. Mapping and design by Martin Danyluk and Elise Hunchuck.

Consolidating Control: The Enbridge Example

In addition (and related) to the fast-tracking, fragmentation, and avoidance of approvals processes, companies are focusing on another important strategy for skirting public scrutiny: the consolidation of corporate control and an increased emphasis on "pipe in the ground."[90] As industry and governments have repeatedly encountered opposition to new-build projects, companies are beginning to understand the political advantages of consolidating control over *existing* infrastructure. Enbridge offers a clear example of this trend: over the past year, the company has been focused on expanding its ownership of the North American network. This is part of an effort to neutralize opposition and to build flexibility into Enbridge's operations.

On August 2, 2016, Enbridge announced that Enbridge-held company Enbridge Energy Partners would acquire a 27.6 percent interest in the full Bakken system, consisting of the Dakota Access Pipeline and the Energy Transfer Crude Oil Pipeline. The acquisition is part of a joint venture with Marathon Petroleum Corporation, which entered into an agreement to acquire a 49 percent equity interest in the holding company that owns 75 percent of the system from an affiliate of Energy Transfer Partners, LP, and Sunoco Logistics Partners, LP.[91]

In the press release, the president of EEP, Mark Maki, explained the advantages of the Bakken System: "This acquisition is an attractive opportunity to participate in a pipeline system that will transport crude oil from the prolific Bakken formation in North Dakota to markets in eastern PADD II and the U.S. Gulf Coast ('USGC') providing another important link in our market access strategy that is driven by improving netbacks and access to the best markets for our customers. . . . Potential also exists for expansion of the pipelines should customer demand warrant."[92]

Then in September, Enbridge announced plans to merge with Spectra Energy, a Houston-based pipeline and midstream company. The merger renders Enbridge the largest energy infrastructure company in North America and endows it with major new gas pipeline infrastructure to add to its extensive collection of liquids pipelines. JPMorgan Chase analyst Jeremy Tonet called the combined Enbridge-Spectra entity an "energy infrastructure colossus."[93] The $37 billion Enbridge-Spectra merger is the third-largest mergers and acquisitions deal ever involving a Canadian company and the largest deal in Canadian oil patch history.[94] The new company is said to have a $74 billion "growth backlog" of potential new development.[95] The merger was completed on February 27, 2017.[96]

Analysts place this merger within the context of widespread resistance to pipelines in Canada and repeated delays in the approval and construction of new-build projects. In a quote to the *Calgary Herald*, Harrie Vredenburg of the University of Calgary School of Business explained, "They're trying to grow and build their business and they've been frustrated because they've become a lightning rod for environmental opposition—climate change opposition to oil pipelines particularly—and they're looking for alternative growth strategies. They're not alone in doing this."[97] Analysts predict that this sort of cross-border merger of assets—including, crucially, infrastructure assets—will become more common within this context as an alternative to building new pipeline.[98]

Indeed, Enbridge's chief financial officer emphasized the company's drive to diversify geographies, commodities, and regulatory jurisdictions in explaining the Enbridge-Spectra merger. "Pipe in the ground is worth a lot these days," he explained, "and the ability to expand and extend existing systems . . . is a lot easier sometimes than building one-off, large mega-projects"—the reason being, of course, that these megaprojects have been met, again and again, with resistance from communities.[99]

Looking Forward: Continental DAPL, Continental Fight

Enbridge's interest in "pipe in the ground" is a new approach to slaying the many-headed hydra, the thickening network of resistance that has mimicked the expansion of pipeline infrastructure across North America. At Standing Rock, networks of solidarity spanned diverse social struggles and also extended far beyond the site of the protest camps.[100] Efforts to target the project's funders through the #DefundDAPL campaign, for example, invoked global financial networks, inspiring action across the countries that are home to these institutions.[101] In a more grounded example, in early February 2017, land defenders and Water Protectors from Canada and the United States met in Secwepemcul'ecw (Kamloops, British Columbia) to build alliances against tar sands and pipeline expansion. At the gathering, called Standing Rock to Secwepemcul'ecw: Pipeline Resistance North and South of the Medicine Line, Indigenous leaders shared lessons from Standing Rock and drew links between DAPL and the recently approved Kinder Morgan Trans Mountain pipeline. The gathering led to a declaration that included an avowal to stand with Water Protectors at Standing Rock and across Mother Earth. Hundreds of Indigenous nations traveled to the site from locations around the world, and new relations were formed that persist. In these cases, the transnational network has been deployed as an explicit strategy to stand against industry's own dispersed character: its vast international linkages and tendency to shift territorially in search of the path of least resistance.

The fact that industry is strategically turning to "pipe in the ground" signals not only the success of this widespread resistance to pipeline projects, but also the fundamentally *transnational* nature of both the threat and the response. At the most literal level, DAPL could divert Bakken oil and free up space in Enbridge's other networks for Alberta crude to flow south to the Gulf Coast. But beyond this, examining the networks of energy infrastructure that snake across North America highlights that the pipeline fight is inherently transnational in a much deeper way. At the end of the day, contaminated waterways and a warming climate have little respect for international borders. In many ways, the resistance at Standing Rock mirrors these fluid geographies: Indigenous nations, whose land these growing networks traverse and threaten to contaminate, predate, transcend, and defy the colonial U.S.-Canada border, and the support that surrounds Standing Rock and other pipeline resistance are transnational illustrations of solidarity across causes, borders, and social locations. In this way, too, the Dakota Access Pipeline is a transnational issue: through both the *threat of* and the *resistance to* projects like DAPL, our relations get redefined not along the arbitrary contours of national boundaries, but along lines of infrastructure—lines of social and ecological interdependence and connection.

The final map in this chapter is part of a broader time series available in Katie Mazer et al., *Mapping a Many Headed Hydra: The Struggle over the Dakota Access Pipeline*, Infrastructure Otherwise Report no. 001 (2017), http://infrastructureotherwise .org/. The maps in the series were developed using information from company communications, media coverage, and regulatory filings and decisions. Grey lines indicate the existing network of oil pipelines. Colored lines indicate stages of approval for the projects over time. Some are new-build projects (DAPL), while others are expansions and/or reversals of existing lines (Kinder Morgan) or a combination (Energy East). In all cases these projects represent a contribution to the expansion of oil transport capacity.

A project was generally considered "proposed" once the company officially announced plans to pursue it. In some cases "proposed" refers to announcements made at industry conferences or to the media or, with the Portland–Montreal Pipeline, the community's early anticipation of the project. Projects were considered "under review" when applications were filed to the respective regulatory bodies. When projects had multiple phases, we used the earliest application date. Projects were considered "approved" once the final stage of the project received final approval. In Canada, after the NEB recommends approval of a project, it ultimately requires approval by the federal cabinet. In the case of transnational lines (Keystone), the map shows the separate approval processes in Canada and the United States.

The maps also show terminals, including construction or expansion of ports affiliated with these pipeline projects. As with the lines themselves, we indicated where proposed terminals were canceled or deferred as a result of community pressure (Cacouna) and/or project cancellations (Kitimat).

1. See Deborah Cowen, *The Deadly Life of Logistics: Mapping Violence in Global Trade* (Minneapolis: University of Minnesota Press, 2014), and Shiri Pasternak and Tia Dafnos, "How Does a Settler State Secure the Circuitry of Capital?" *Environment and Planning D: Society and Space* 36 (2018): 739–57.

2. Katie Mazer et al., *Mapping a Many Headed Hydra: The Struggle over the Dakota Access Pipeline*, Infrastructure Otherwise Report no. 001 (2017), http://infrastructureotherwise.org/.

3. Julia Carrie Wong, "Standing Rock Activists Stay in Place, Fearing Pipeline Victory Was a 'Trick,'" *The Guardian*, December 5, 2016, https://www.theguardian.com.

4. Peter Linebaugh and Marcus Rediker, *The Many-Headed Hydra: Sailors, Slaves, Commoners, and the Hidden History of the Revolutionary Atlantic* (Boston: Beacon Press, 2000).

5. For timelines and archived information about the struggle against DAPL see the #NoDAPL Archive and the Sacred Stone Camp: #NoDAPL Archive, https://www.nodaplarchive.com; "Sacred Stone Camp—Iŋyaŋ Wakháŋagapi Othí", accessed February 8, 2017, http://sacredstonecamp.org/.

6. William Petroski, "Oil Pipeline across Iowa Proposed," *Des Moines Register*, July 10, 2014, http://www.desmoinesregister.com.

7. Most important, the Nederland, Texas, crude oil terminal facility of Sunoco Logistics Partners. See "Crude Oil," Sunoco Logistics, accessed November 16, 2016, http://www.sunocologistics.com/Customers/Business-Lines/Crude-Oil/253/. On the Patoka tank farm, see "Infrastructure Map," Enbridge, accessed December 30, 2016, http://www.enbridge.com/map.

8. Dakota Access Pipeline Facts, http://daplpipelinefacts.com.

9. Winona LaDuke, "What Would Sitting Bull Do?" *L.A. Progressive*, August 25, 2016, https://www.laprogressive.com; William Yardley, "With Echoes of Wounded Knee, Tribes Mount Prairie Occupation to Block North Dakota Pipeline," *Los Angeles Times*, August 27, 2016, http://www.latimes.com; Brian Ward, "Standing Up at Standing Rock," *The Bullet*, Socialist Project, August 31, 2016, http://www.socialistproject.ca/bullet.

10. A link to this document is at Catherine Thorbecke, "Why a Previously Proposed Route for the Dakota Access Pipeline Was Rejected," *ABC News*, November 4, 2016, http://abcnews.go.com.

11. "#StandingRockSyllabus," NYC Stands with Standing Rock Collective, 2016, https://nycstandswithstandingrock.wordpress.com.

12. "Frequently Asked Questions DAPL," U.S. Army Corps of Engineers, Ohama District, May 3, 2016, http://www.nwo.usace.army.mil; David Archambault II, "Taking a Stand at Standing Rock," *New York Times*, August 24, 2016, http://www.nytimes.com.

13. "#StandingRockSyllabus," NYC Stands with Standing Rock Collective; Jeffrey Ostler and Nick Estes, "The Supreme Law of the Land," *Public Seminar*, February 3, 2017, http://www.publicseminar.org.

14. Archambault, "Taking a Stand at Standing Rock."

15. Nick Estes, "Fighting for Our Lives: #NoDAPL in Historical Context," The Red Nation, September 18, 2016, https://therednation.org.

16. "#StandingRockSyllabus," NYC Stands with Standing Rock Collective.

17. "Energy Transfer and Sunoco Logistics Announce Sale of Minority Stake in Bakken Pipeline Project to Enbridge and Marathon Petroleum" (press release), August 2, 2016, Business Wire, http://www.businesswire.com/news/home/20160802007081/en/Energy-Transfer-Sunoco-Logistics-Announce-Sale-Minority.

18. "New Investigation Names Wall Street Banks behind $3.8 Billion Dakota Access Pipeline," *Democracy Now!*, September 6, 2016, http://www.democracynow.org; the full report is available here: Hugh MacMillan, "Who's Banking on the Dakota Access Pipeline?" LittleSis, August 17, 2016, https://littlesis.org/maps/1634-who-s-banking-on-the-dakota-access-pipeline.

19. MacMillan, "Who's Banking?"

20. North Dakota Geologic Survey, "Overview of the Petroleum Geology of the North Dakota Williston Basin," ND.gov: Official Portal for North Dakota State Government, accessed March 9, 2017, https://www.dmr.nd.gov/ndgs/resources/.

21. "North Dakota State Energy Profile," U.S. Energy Information Administration, February 18, 2016, https://www.eia.gov/state/print.cfm?sid=ND.

22. "North Dakota State Energy Profile," U.S. Energy Information Administration.

23. "The Truth about Tight Oil," Union of Concerned Scientists, April 2016, http://www.ucsusa.org.

24. "The Truth about Tight Oil," Union of Concerned Scientists.

25. For details on the distribution of refining capacity in the United States, see "Petroleum and Other Liquids: Refinery Utilization and Capacity" (numbers released monthly), U.S. Energy Information Administration: Independent Statistics and Analysis, https://www.eia.gov/dnav/pet/pet_pnp_unc_a_(na)_YRL_mbblpd_m.htm.

26. "Enbridge and Energy Transfer Join to Provide Crude Oil Pipeline Access to Eastern Gulf Coast Market" (press release), Energy Transfer, February 15, 2013, http://ir.energytransfer.com/phoenix.zhtml?c=106094&p=irol-newsArticle&ID=1785681.

27. "Fact Sheet: Energy Transfer Crude Oil Pipeline Project (ETCOP)," Energy Transfer LP, September 2014, http://www.energytransfer.com/documents/ETCOP_Fact Sheet10.pdf.

28. "Enbridge and Energy Transfer Join," Energy Transfer.

29. In 2014, 97 percent of Canadian crude exports were destined for the United States, comprising 39 percent of total U.S. crude imports and 18 percent of U.S. refinery crude oil intake. In contrast, only 3 percent of Canadian crude oil exports went to Europe and Asia. "Crude Oil Industry Overview," Natural Resources Canada, Government of Canada, July 7, 2016, https://www.nrcan.gc.ca.

30. Michael Holden, "Pipe or Perish: Saving an Oil Industry at Risk," Canada West Foundation, February 7, 2013, http://cwf.ca.

31. See, for example, Canadian Association of Petroleum Producers, "The Case for Change," submission to the federal government's 2016 pre-budget consultation (March 15, 2016); Joe Oliver and Youri Chassin, "The Most Efficient Way to Stimulate the Economy: Private Pipelines or Public Infrastructure?" Montreal Economic Institute: Ideas for a More Prosperous Society, June 9, 2016, http://www.iedm.org.

32. Around 2012 world oil market conditions began to change in a number of ways that would depress prices and, ultimately, challenge the idea that new Canadian pipelines would allow Canadian oil to fetch a higher price. In the North American context, the construction of new pipeline capacity between Illinois, Oklahoma, and the Gulf Coast in 2013 and 2014 functioned to relieve the regional transportation bottleneck in the U.S. Midwest. Expansions in shale production, alongside this increased transportation capacity, led to a glut in the Gulf refineries and a drop in prices. As a result of these conditions, some have argued that what was once a wide gap between Western Canada Select and U.S. (West Texas Intermediate) oil prices closed significantly after 2014. The price gap that remained was a result of the oil's quality and geography, not pipeline capacity. According to this argument, even from a strictly economic perspective, without a significant price differential between domestic and world markets, the construction of new pipeline capacity

would be unlikely to increase crude prices. Even those in the industry began saying that expanded transportation infrastructure would not solve the problem and, in the spring of 2016, the CBC obtained a secret government memo, dated December 2015, that said exactly this: addressing the specific case of the Energy East Pipeline, the finance department document explained that given the declining price differential since 2012, the economic benefits of the pipeline had been largely curtailed. Drew Anderson, "Energy East Pipeline Benefits Questioned in Secret Government Memo," *CBC News*, May 31, 2016, http://www.cbc.ca.

In February 2016 D.C.–based nonprofit Oil Change International released a report challenging the claim that Canada is running out of pipeline capacity. According to its findings, the "need" for expanded capacity is predicated on expanded production. Research conducted by the Canadian Centre for Policy Alternatives has arrived at the same conclusion. In economic terms, there was a pipeline bottleneck in 2012–13, which resulted in a transport-related price gap; the construction of pipelines to transport Alberta bitumen to Canadian tidewater was meant to capitalize on this price differential. This research concludes that any price discount that could be relieved by building pipeline capacity to Canada's east and/or west coasts no longer exists. Hannah McKinnon et al., "Tar Sands: The Myth of Tidewater Access," Oil Change International, March 17, 2016, http://price ofoil.org; Adam Scott and Greg Muttitt, "Briefing: Canada Not Running Out of Pipeline Capacity," Oil Change International, October 18, 2016, http://priceofoil .org; J. David Hughes, "Can Canada Expand Oil and Gas Production, Build Pipelines and Keep Its Climate Change Commitments?" Canadian Centre for Policy Alternatives, June 2, 2016, https://www.policyalternatives.ca.

33. Scott and Muttitt, "Canada Not Running Out of Pipeline Capacity," 1; see also Hughes, "Can Canada Expand Oil and Gas Production."

34. The IEA's 2011 World Energy Outlook explains: "Emissions that will come from the infrastructure that is currently in place or under construction can be thought of as 'locked-in,' because they cannot be avoided without stringent policy intervention to force premature retirements, costly refurbishment and retrofitting or letting capacity lie idle to become economic. They are not unavoidable, but avoiding them does not make economic sense in the current policy context." International Energy Agency, *World Energy Outlook, 2011* (Paris: OECD/IEA, 2011), 229, https://webs tore.iea.org/world-energy-outlook-2011.

35. The report explains: "The 450 Scenario, by definition, achieves a long-term atmospheric concentration of 450 ppm CO_2-eq (resulting in average warming of 2°C). Such a temperature increase (even without allowance for additional feedback effects) would still have negative impacts, including a sea-level rise, increased floods, storms and droughts.

"The new evidence has led some researchers to conclude that even keeping the temperature rise to 2°C may risk dangerous climate change, and that an even lower temperature threshold and corresponding stabilisation target (such as 350 ppm) should be set (Anderson and Bows, 2011; Hansen et al., 2008; Rockström et al., 2009; Smith et al., 2009). The uncomfortable message from the scientific community is that although the difficulty of achieving 450ppm stabilisation is increasing sharply with every passing year, so too are the predicted consequences of failing to do so."

Looking forward to 2017, the report warns: "If internationally co-ordinated action is not implemented by 2017, we project that all permissible CO_2 emissions in the 450 Scenario will come from the infrastructure then existing, so that all new infrastructure from then until 2035 would need to be zero-carbon. This would theoretically be possible at very high cost, but probably not practicable in political terms." International Energy Agency, *World Energy Outlook, 2011*, 207, 205.

36. Winona LaDuke, "Cultivating Resistance and Lighting the Eighth Fire: Challenging the Fossil Fuel Industry and Restoring Anishnaabe Economics," public lecture at the University of Toronto, September 24, 2017.
37. Winona LaDuke, "Native Activist Winona LaDuke: Pipeline Company Enbridge Has No Right to Destroy Our Future." *Democracy Now!*, August 23, 2016, https://www.democracynow.org.
38. Christopher Adams, "Here Are the Major Canadian Pipelines the Oil Patch Wants Built," *National Observer*, September 22, 2016, http://www.nationalobserver.com; John Paul Tasker, "Ottawa Won't Appeal Court Decision Blocking Northern Gateway Pipeline," *CBC News*, September 20, 2016, http://www.cbc.ca.
39. John Paul Tasker, "Trudeau Cabinet Approves Trans Mountain, Line 3 Pipelines, Rejects Northern Gateway," *CBC News*, November 29, 2016, http://www.cbc.ca.
40. "Who We Are," Trans Mountain, accessed November 17, 2016, https://www.transmountain.com.
41. Mychaylo Prystupa, "Burnaby Mountain Battle: Our Notes from the Courts, the Woods and 100 Arrests," *National Observer*, November 29, 2014, http://www.nationalobserver.com.
42. Peter Morelli, "Amidst Celebrations, Activists Admit War Far from Won on Burnaby Mountain," *Vancouver Observer*, November 28, 2014, http://www.vancouverobserver.com.
43. Marc-Andre Cossette, "Expect Protests 'Like You've Never Seen Before' on Kinder Morgan Pipeline: Vancouver Mayor," *CBC News*, November 19, 2016, http://www.cbc.ca.
44. Tasker, "Trudeau Cabinet Approves Trans Mountain, Line 3 Pipelines."
45. "Shareholders Vote to Approve Sale of Trans Mountain Pipeline and Expansion Project," Kinder Morgan Canada Limited, August 30, 2018, https://ir.kindermorgancanadalimited.com; *Tsleil-Waututh Nation v. Canada (Attorney General)*, 2018 F.C.A. https://decisions.fca-caf.gc.ca/fca-caf/decisions/en/item/343511/index.do.
46. "Archived – TransCanada Keystone Pipeline GP Ltd. – Keystone XL Pipeline – OH-1-2009," National Energy Board, Government of Canada, December 30, 2016, https://www.neb-one.gc.ca.

47. Adams, "Here Are the Major Canadian Pipelines."

48. The details on both challenges are available at "About Keystone XL," TransCanada: Keystone XL, 2016, http://www.keystone-xl.com/.

49. Steven Mufson, "Now That Trump Has Won, Transcanada Wants to Give Keystone XL Pipeline Another Try," *Washington Post*, November 9, 2016, https://www.washingtonpost.com.

50. David Smith and Ashifa Kassam, "Trump Orders Revival of Keystone XL and Dakota Access Pipelines," *The Guardian*, January 24, 2017, https://www.theguardian.com; "Keystone XL Pipeline Enters Final Review," *Grand Island Independent*, April 19, 2017, http://www.theindependent.com.

51. "Gulf Coast Project Begins Delivering Crude Oil to Nederland, Texas" (press release), TransCanada, January 22, 2014, http://www.transcanada.com. Like DAPL, the Gulf Coast Project was approved using Nationwide Permit 12. Steve Horn, "Weeks before Dakota Access Pipeline Protests Intensified, Big Oil Pushed for Expedited Permitting," *DeSmog* (blog), September 8, 2016, https://www.desmogblog.com.

52. Adams, "Here Are the Major Canadian Pipelines"; "Enbridge Pipelines Inc. – Line 9B Reversal and Line 9 Capacity Expansion Project – OH-002-2013," National Energy Board, Government of Canada, December 20, 2016, http://www.neb-one.gc.ca.

53. Environmental Defence, Transition Initiative Kenora, and the Council of Canadians, "Energy East: A Risk to Our Drinking Water," April 2016, http://environmentaldefence.ca/report/energy-east-a-threat-to-our-drinking-water/; for a list of First Nations on or near the line, assembled by Shelley Kath, see "Will Your Community Be Affected by the Energy East Pipeline?" The Council of Canadians, July 8, 2015, http://canadians.org/pipelines/will-your-community-be-affected-energy-east-pipeline.

54. "Peace and Friendship Treaties," Indigenous and Northern Affairs Canada, Government of Canada, December 10, 2015, https://www.aadnc-aandc.gc.ca/eng/1100100028589/1100100028591.

55. The Council of Canadians et al., "TransCanada's Energy East: An Export Pipeline, Not for Domestic Gain," accessed December 15, 2016, http://environmentaldefence.ca/report/report-transcanadas-energy-east-export-pipeline-not-domestic-gain/.

56. Adams, "Here Are the Major Canadian Pipelines."

57. TransCanada, "TransCanada Announces Termination of Energy East Pipeline and Eastern Mainline Projects" (press release), *Marketwired*, October 5, 2017, http://www.marketwired.com.

58. Ethan Lou, "Canada to Consider Indirect Emissions for TransCanada Energy East Pipe," Reuters, August 23, 2017, https://www.reuters.com.

59. This name for the network comes from Kenny Bruno et al., "Enbridge over Troubled Water: The Enbridge GXL System's Threat to the Great Lakes," January 3, 2016, http://world.350.org/kishwaukee/files/2017/09/Enbridge-Over-Troubled-Water-Report.pdf.

60. Bruno et al., "Enbridge over Troubled Water."

61. "Superior Terminal," Enbridge, accessed December 31, 2016, http://www.enbridge.com.

62. "Sandpiper Pipeline Project—Building Energy Security," Enbridge, accessed December 11, 2016, http://www.enbridge.com.

63. For the full details see Bruno et al., "Enbridge over Troubled Water."

64. "Line 67 Upgrade Project (Phase 2)," Enbridge, accessed December 15, 2016, http://www.enbridge.com; see also Bruno et al., "Enbridge over Troubled Water."

65. "Line 61 Upgrade Project—Pump Stations Upgrade," Enbridge, accessed December 15, 2016, http://www.enbridge.com; see also "Line 61 Upgrade Project (Phase 2)," Enbridge, accessed 15 December 2016, http://www.enbridge.com.

66. Geoffrey Morgan, "Enbridge CEO Downplays Need for Competing Pipelines till at Least 2025," *Financial Post*, February 17, 2017, http://business.financialpost.com.

67. "About Seaway," Seaway Pipeline, 2012, http://seawaypipeline.com.

68. "Flanagan South Pipeline Complete," *Bartlesville Examiner-Enterprise*, December 8, 2014, http://www.examiner-enterprise.com.

69. "Enbridge's New North American Pipeline Pathway Hailed by Dignitaries," *@Enbridge* (blog), January 16, 2015, http://www.enbridge.com.

70. Lauren Krugel, "Newly Completed Pipelines to Carry More Canadian Oil to Gulf Coast," *Global News,* January 16, 2015, http://globalnews.ca.

71. Horn, "Weeks before Dakota Access Pipeline Protests Intensified."

72. Bruno et al., "Enbridge over Troubled Water," 21.

73. "Line 3 Replacement Project Summary," Enbridge, accessed December 15, 2016, http://www.enbridge.com.

74. Bruno et al., "Enbridge over Troubled Water."

75. Bruno et al., "Enbridge over Troubled Water."

76. "Line 3 Replacement Program," Enbridge, accessed December 15, 2016, http://www.enbridge.com.

77. Tasker, "Trudeau Cabinet Approves Trans Mountain, Line 3 Pipelines."

78. Bruno et al., "Enbridge over Troubled Water."

79. The Sandpiper was proposed by the North Dakota Pipeline Company, LLC, which is a joint venture of Enbridge Energy Partners, LP, and Williston Basin Pipe Line, LLC, an indirect subsidiary of Marathon Petroleum Corporation. See "Sandpiper Pipeline Project," Enbridge, accessed December 15, 2016, http://www.enbridge.com.

80. Kelly Cryderman, "Enbridge Defers $2.6-Billion Sandpiper Pipeline Project," *The Globe and Mail*, September 1, 2016, http://www.theglobeandmail.com.

81. "Enbridge Energy Partners, L.P. Announces Anticipated Joint Funding Arrangement Terms for Bakken Pipeline System Investment and Long-Term Deferral of Sandpiper Project" (press release), Enbridge Energy Partners, September 1, 2016), https://www.enbridgepartners.com/Media-Center/News.aspx?queryYear=2016&ReleaseId=2199188.

82. Cryderman, "'Enbridge Defers $2.6-Billion Sandpiper Pipeline Project."

83. "Enbridge and Energy Transfer Join," Energy Transfer.

84. Kelly Cryderman, "Enbridge Unveils Plan to Get Oil to Gulf," *The Globe and Mail*, February 15, 2013, http://www.theglobeandmail.com.

85. Patrick C. Miller, "Enbridge, Marathon Buy into Bakken Pipeline System," *North American Shale*, August 3, 2016, http://northamericanshalemagazine.com/.

86. William Yardley, "There's a Reason Few Even Knew the Dakota Access Pipeline Was Being Built," *Los Angeles Times*, November 9, 2016, http://www.latimes.com.

87. Horn, "Weeks before Dakota Access Pipeline Protests Intensified."

88. Sierra Club et al., "Comments on the U.S. Army Corps of Engineers' Proposal to Reissue and Modify Nationwide Permit 12, Docket No. COE-2015–0017," *DeSmog* (blog), August 1, 2016, https://www.desmogblog.com.

89. Yardley, "There's a Reason Few Even Knew."

90. Chris Varcoe, "If You Can't Build Pipelines, Buy 'Pipe in the Ground,'" *Calgary Herald*, September 7, 2016, http://calgaryherald.com.

91. "Enbridge Energy Partners, L.P. and Enbridge Inc. Announce Agreement to Acquire Equity Interest in the Bakken Pipeline System Establishing New Path to the U.S. Gulf Coast" (press release), Enbridge Energy Partners, August 2, 2016, http://www.enbridgepartners.com/Media-Center/News.aspx?queryYear=2016&ReleaseId=2192193.

92. "Enbridge Energy Partners, L.P. and Enbridge Inc. Announce Agreement," Enbridge Energy Partners.

93. Geoffrey Morgan, "Enbridge Inc Deal to Buy Spectra Creates 'Energy Infrastructure Colossus' with $48 Billion of Future Projects," *Financial Post*, September 6, 2016, http://business.financialpost.com.

94. Varcoe, "If You Can't Build Pipelines."

95. Morgan, "Enbridge Inc Deal to Buy Spectra Creates 'Energy Infrastructure Colossus.'"

96. "Enbridge and Spectra Energy Complete Merger" (press release), Enbridge, February 27, 2017, http://www.enbridge.com.

97. Varcoe, "If You Can't Build Pipelines."

98. "Enbridge-Spectra Deal Part of a Bigger North American Trend, Says Analyst," *CBC News*, September 6, 2016, http://www.cbc.ca; Morgan, "Enbridge Inc. Deal to Buy Spectra Creates 'Energy Infrastructure Colossus'"; Varcoe, "If You Can't Build Pipelines."

99. Quoted in Varcoe, "If You Can't Build Pipelines."

100. "Black Lives Matter Stands in Solidarity with Water Protectors at Standing Rock," Black Lives Matter, September 2016, http://blacklivesmatter.com/solidarity-with-standing-rock/ (no longer available); ICMN Staff, "Rank-and-File Union Members Speak-Out at Standing Rock Camp, Challenge AFL-CIO Leadership's Support for Pipeline," Indian Country Media Network, October 30, 2016, https://indiancountrymedianetwork.com/news/native-news/rank-and-file-union-members

-speak-out-at-standing-rock-camp-challenge-afl-cio-leaderships-support-for-pipeline/; Dennis Sadowski, "500 Religious Leaders Join Standing Rock Sioux in Opposing Oil Pipeline," Catholic Philly, November 7, 2016, http://catholicphilly.com. These are just several examples; for a more extensive list, see "Groups and Celebrities," #NoDAPL Archive—Standing Rock Water Protectors, accessed January 10, 2017, http://www.nodaplarchive.com.

101. In response to this pressure, on November 17 Norway's largest bank, DNB, announced that it had sold off all assets in the Dakota Access and Bakken pipeline companies. On February 7, 2017, the Seattle City Council voted unanimously to not renew its contract with Wells Fargo, Seattle's primary financial services provider, over its investment in DAPL. In doing so, Seattle became the first city in the United States to sever ties with a bank in protest of the pipeline. By early February 2017 the #DefundDAPL campaign had divested almost $60 million from the project. #Defund DAPL," http://www.defunddapl.org; William Yardley, "Seattle Becomes the First City to Sever Ties with Wells Fargo in Protest of Dakota Access Pipeline," *Los Angeles Times*, February 7, 2017, http://www.latimes.com; Tracy Loeffelholz Dunn, "Norway's Largest Bank Divests from Dakota Access, Launches Own Investigation," *YES! Magazine*, November 7, 2016, http://www.yesmagazine.org; "#DefundDAPL Has Divested $40 Million from Dakota Access Pipeline," Sacred Stone Camp—Iŋyaŋ Wakháŋagapi Othí, January 3, 2017, http://sacredstonecamp.org/blog/2017/1/3/defunddapl-reaches-40-million-divested-from-dakota-access-pipeline.

Acknowledgments

Standing with Standing Rock: Voices from the #NoDAPL Movement grew out of a desire to elevate some of the people, histories, and experiences that collectively tell the story of Standing Rock, the Oceti Sakowin, and the struggle against the Dakota Access Pipeline. As coeditors of this volume, we would like to share a bit about the evolution of this project and to locate ourselves within it. Nick Estes is Kul Wicasa, a citizen of the Lower Brule Sioux Tribe. He is an organizer and historian who grew up along the Mni Sose, the Missouri River, and he has spent more than a decade researching, writing, and teaching about the politics of land and water in Oceti Sakowin territory. For him, #NoDAPL was a continuation of a longer struggle to protect and caretake Mni Sose, the Missouri River. Jaskiran Dhillon is a first-generation anticolonial scholar and organizer who grew up on Treaty Six Cree and Metis Territory in Saskatchewan, Canada. As a settler of color living on occupied land in Indigenous North America, she is politically committed to supporting movements for Native freedom and liberation and has spent decades working on issues of colonial state violence, most recently examining environmental violence.

It is said that because of #NoDAPL all of Indian Country became Facebook friends and connected through social media. Vast solidarity networks also sprang up connecting movements across geography. As colleagues and comrades, we first came together in the early days of the resistance when we spoke about the Standing Rock Sioux Tribe's developing fight to stop DAPL on the *Cultures of Energy* podcast in fall 2016, at the invitation of Cymene Howe and Dominic Boyer from Rice University. Shortly thereafter, we met up on the front lines at Oceti Sakowin Camp, the largest encampment, to support the struggle on the ground and to begin to think through how to document the multiple dimensions of this Indigenous-led resistance movement—to necessarily situate it within political history and contemporary conversations about ongoing settler colonial violence and Indigenous land dispossession. Jaskiran had played a central role organizing the New York City Stands with Standing Rock Collective, Standing Rock Syllabus Project, and several New York City–based university teach-ins, protests, and rallies to generate supplies that could be sent to the front lines of the resistance, in addition to writing about the role of youth in spearheading the movement early on. Nick had been working with grassroots organizers from his own community against the Keystone XL Pipeline teaching water rights and the history of the river, and organizing #NoDAPL solidarity in Chicago and Albuquerque. He also had relations with Oceti Sakowin intellectuals, poets, and artists. Recognizing this collective work, Dominic, who coedits *Cultural Anthropology* with Cymene, graciously invited us to curate a Hot Spots series on the journal's website.

The series became "Standing Rock, NoDAPL, and Mni Wiconi," which highlighted how the struggle was about more than a pipeline, and was attentive to the movement as it was unfolding. It captured a number of emerging perspectives and insights on the encampments, and it laid the foundation for a panel on #NoDAPL and Mni Wiconi organized by Robert Warrior at the annual American Studies Association meeting in Denver, Colorado, in November 2016. After the panel, Warrior, editor of the First Peoples: New Directions in Indigenous Studies book series, approached us about the possibility of producing a book-length anthology that expanded the Hot Spots series. Warrior, the 2016 ASA president, honored Water Protectors in his presidential address at the annual meeting, which he concluded by holding a traditional Lakota blanket dance to collect cash donations, giving thanks and support to the Water Protectors who had traveled from the camps to attend ASA. Over time, and with the dedication and support of many, that possibility and support became this book.

As coeditors of this anthology, we owe much gratitude and respect to the numerous people that supported its conception and creation. In Nick's tradition, the act of giving thanks, or wopila, is a highly revered ceremony. It is about more than generosity: it is an act of survival, resistance, and resurgence. One gives wopila to relations, both human and other than human, to ensure the continuation of life. Above all, we thank the Water Protectors, those named and unnamed in this volume, and especially the courageous young Water Protectors who have lit the fire of the Seventh Generation and who continue to lead, create, and resist. Wopila. For reasons already mentioned, we extend a special thank you to Dominic, Cymene, and Robert. Without their initial support, this project would not have been possible.

The collective knowledge of the Oceti Sakowin is powerful and can never be fully appreciated by outsiders. As editors of this book, we acknowledge and honor those who have kept the faith, so to speak, who believed in our people, even in times of terrible danger and uncertainty. Marcella Gilbert, Madonna Thunder Hawk, LaDonna Bravebull Allard, Faith Spotted Eagle, and Phyllis Young, among many others, are an invaluable link between generations of knowledge-keepers, caretakers of our traditions, and, as Kim TallBear contends in this book, badass Indigenous women. Each of the contributors has also shaped and advanced this project in unique ways only editors can fully appreciate.

The comrades from the Red Nation allowed Nick the time and space away from other urgent matters to complete this project for his people. Melanie K. Yazzie, a Water Protector in her own right, gave invaluable emotional and intellectual labor to Nick; he is forever grateful. Walter Johnson from Harvard University's Charles Warren Center for Studies in American History provided Nick with the time and resources to complete this project as an American Democracy Fellow (2017–18). Nick is also forever grateful to his Tahansi Lewis Grassrope and his Ate Ben Estes for support, generosity, wisdom, guidance, and support for our people, the Kul Wicasa and the Oceti Sakowin.

Numerous comrades and friends helped Jaskiran think through the various dimensions of this book and offered support and encouragement—essential when attempting a project of this sort. Melanie Yazzie, Sandy Grande, and Michelle Latimer were tireless champions, always offering wise words and inspiration to keep this book moving forward. Jordan Camp and Christina Heatherton shared their wisdom about how to get this book out there and circulating in a good way and made the initial connections necessary for the book to be launched at the People's Forum in New York City. Jaskiran's daughters, Rekha and Larkin, also opened up space and time for their mother to be away at Standing Rock to support the struggle and undertake the labor required for this anthology.

A book project is a collective effort, with deep origins that precede production and afterlives that outlive publication. Coeditors make connections, track down, collate, track down, and collect. Behind these words and beyond these pages are the worlds of countless people, countless histories, and countless hours of labor. In your hands is such a book.

Contributors

David Archambault II was the forty-fifth chairman of the Standing Rock Sioux Tribe. While leading the struggle against the Dakota Access Pipeline, he emerged as a global leader for Indigenous peoples' rights, promoting peace, respect, tribal sovereignty, and efforts to protect tribal treaty lands and natural resources.

Natalie Avalos (Chicana/Apache descent) is an ethnographer of religion whose research and teaching focus on Native American and Indigenous religions in diaspora, the healing of historical trauma, and decolonization. She received her PhD in religious studies from the University of California at Santa Barbara and is a Chancellor's PostDoctoral Associate in the religious studies department at University of Colorado Boulder.

Tomoki Mari Birkett is a mixed-race nonbinary Nikkei person and PhD candidate in the Department of Anthropology at Columbia University, where they research the political economy of bodily banishment and radiation exposure in the Fukushima Daiichi nuclear disaster.

Vanessa Bowen (Diné) is a Native American multifaceted artist who specializes in fine art, graphic design, DJing, and photography.

Alleen Brown is a New York–based reporter who writes on environmental justice for *The Intercept*. Her work has been published by *The Nation* and *In These Times*.

Kevin Bruyneel is professor of politics at Babson College in Massachusetts. He wrote *The Third Space of Sovereignty: The Postcolonial Politics of U.S.–Indigenous Relations* (Minnesota, 2007) and is now writing *Settler Memory: The Disavowal of Indigeneity in the Political Life of Race in the United States*.

D. T. Cochrane is a father, partner, and economist. He studies processes of financial quantification and accumulation. He has worked with researchers at Ryerson University, the Blackwood Art Gallery, Indigenous Network on Economies and Trade, Mining Watch, and anexact office.

Michelle L. Cook is a human rights lawyer born of the Honagháahnii (One Who Walks Around You) Clan of the Diné (Navajo) Nation. She is a Doctor of Juridical Science (SJD) candidate at the University of Arizona's Indigenous Peoples Law and Policy Program and serves on the Navajo Nation Human Rights Commission.

Deborah Cowen is associate professor of geography at the University of Toronto and a fellow of the Pierre Elliott Trudeau Foundation. She serves on the board of the Groundswell Community Justice Trust Fund in Tkaronto.

Andrew Curley (Diné) is assistant professor of geography at the University of North Carolina at Chapel Hill. He studies Indigenous geography, resource conflicts, energy, water rights, land, tribal sovereignty, and Navajo (Diné) studies. He is a member of the Navajo Nation and an organizer with the Red Nation.

Martin Danyluk is a postdoctoral fellow in geography at the University of British Columbia. His research explores the social and ecological consequences of the global logistics industry.

Jaskiran Dhillon is a first-generation anticolonial scholar and organizer who grew up on Treaty Six Cree Territory in Saskatchewan, Canada. She is associate professor of global studies and anthropology at the New School in New York City and a member of the New York City Stands with Standing Rock Collective.

Roxanne Dunbar-Ortiz is professor emerita at California State University and author or editor of fifteen books, including *An Indigenous Peoples' History of the United States* and *The Great Sioux Nation: A Oral History of the Sioux Nation and Their Treaty.*

Elizabeth Ellis is a citizen of the Peoria Tribe of Indians of Oklahoma and assistant professor of history at New York University. She is writing a book on small Native nations of the Lower Mississippi Valley during the eighteenth century.

Nick Estes is Kul Wicasa, a citizen of the Lower Brule Sioux Tribe. He is assistant professor of American studies at the University of New Mexico and a cofounder of the Red Nation, an organization dedicated to Indigenous liberation.

Marcella Gilbert (Lakota/Dakota), an Oceti Sakowin Water Protector, was influenced by the activism of her extended family's leadership in the American Indian Movement. She has a master's degree in nutrition from South Dakota State University and educates Native communities on the importance of a decolonized diet and lifestyle. She has been blessed with three children, one grandchild, and an always loving husband.

Sandy Grande (Quechua) is a professor of education and director of the Center for the Critical Study of Race and Ethnicity (CCSRE) at Connecticut College. Her research interfaces Native American and Indigenous studies with critical theory and education. She has provided eldercare for her parents for more than ten years and is the primary caregiver for her ninety-year-old father.

Jaida Grey Eagle (Oglala Lakota) is an artist and photographer. She mixes traditional Indigenous art with contemporary mediums and is passionate about environmental justice, food sovereignty, and art as activism. She studied photography at the Institute of American Indian Arts in Santa Fe, New Mexico, and now lives in Minnesota.

Craig Howe (Oglala Sioux Tribe) is founder and director of the Center for American Indian Research and Native Studies (CAIRNS). He has written on tribal histories, Native studies, museum exhibitions, and community collaborations. He lectures on American Indian topics across the United States, has developed innovative museum exhibitions, and conducts professional development and cultural awareness training for schools and organizations.

Elise Hunchuck is a Berlin-based researcher and designer with degrees in landscape architecture, philosophy, and geography. Her work brings together fieldwork and design through collaborative practices. Facilitating multidisciplinary exchanges between representational methods to develop landscape-oriented research methodologies, her work enhances cartographic, photographic, and text-based practices, communicating the agency of material and disasters through the continual configuration of infrastructures of risk, including memorials, monuments, and coastal defense structures.

Michelle Latimer (Métis/Algonquin) is an award-winning filmmaker whose work is dedicated to the pursuit of Indigenous rights and sovereignty. She was the showrunner, director, and writer of the breakout Indigenous resistance series *RISE (Viceland)*, which premiered at the 2017 Sundance Film Festival and received a Canadian Screen Award. Her latest film, *Nuuca*, with executive producer Laura Poitras, premiered at the 2017 Toronto International Film Festival before screening internationally.

Layli Long Soldier (Oglala Lakota) holds a BFA from the Institute of American Indian Arts and an MFA from Bard College. She is the author of *Chromosomory* and *WHEREAS*, and her poems have been published in *POETRY* magazine, the *New York Times*, *The American Poet*, *The American Reader*, *Kenyon Review Online*, and *BOMB*. She received the 2018 PEN/Jean Stein Award and the 2018 National Book Critics Circle Award, as well as an NACF National Artist Fellowship, a Lannan Literary Fellowship, and a Whiting Award; she also was a finalist for the 2017 National Book Award. She lives in Santa Fe, New Mexico.

David Uahikeaikalei'ohu Maile is a Kanaka 'Ōiwi scholar, activist, and practitioner from Maunawili, O'ahu. He is a PhD candidate and instructor in American studies at the University of New Mexico, as well as an organizer with the Red Nation in Albuquerque.

Jason Mancini is executive director of Connecticut Humanities and cofounder of Akomawt Educational Initiative. During his past thirty years of collaboration with Native communities, he has researched settler-colonial archives in an effort to repatriate/rematriate Indigenous narratives to their homelands.

Sarah Sunshine Manning is an independent journalist, educator, writer, and speaker whose work centers the experiences of Indigenous communities. She is a member of the Shoshone-Paiute Tribes of Idaho and Nevada and also has ancestry from the Chippewa-Cree Tribes of Montana.

Katie Mazer is a PhD candidate in geography at the University of Toronto. Her research examines the politics of poverty and labor flexibility in Canadian resource extraction.

Teresa Montoya (Diné) is a Provost's Postdoctoral Fellow in the Department of Anthropology at the University of Chicago, where she holds a position in Native American and Indigenous studies. Her research and media production focuses on legacies of settler colonialism and environmental contamination in relation to contemporary issues of tribal jurisdiction and sovereign action in the Navajo Nation.

Christopher Newell (Passamaquoddy) is a lifelong educator working primarily in Native American studies and public education, combining these fields to create new ways to engage Indigenous histories and contemporary issues in all aspects of public education. He serves as education supervisor for the Mashantucket Pequot Museum and Research Center and is cofounder and director of education for the Akomawt Educational Initiative (akomawt.org).

The New York City Stands with Standing Rock Collective is a group of Indigenous scholars and activists and settler/POC supporters. We belong and are responsible to a range of Indigenous peoples and nations, including Tlingit, Haudenosaunee, Secwepemc, St'at'imc, Creek (Muscogee), Anishinaabe, Peoria, Diné, Maya Kaqchikel, and Quechua. We have joined forces to support the Standing Rock Sioux in their continued assertion of sovereignty over their traditional territories.

Jeffrey Ostler teaches history at the University of Oregon and is author of the forthcoming book *Surviving Genocide: Native Nations and the United States from the American Revolution to Bleeding Kansas.*

Will Parrish is an investigative journalist who focuses on the politics surrounding environmental and military issues nationally, globally, and in his home state of California.

Shiri Pasternak is the research director of the Yellowhead Institute and assistant professor of criminology at Ryerson University in Toronto. She is author of *Grounded Authority: The Algonquins of Barriere Lake against the State* (Minnesota, 2017).

endawnis Spears (Diné/Ojibwe/Chickasaw/Choctaw) is director of programming and outreach for the Akomawt Educational Initiative, a majority Native American–owned educational support and consultancy partnership. Originally from Camp Verde, Arizona, she lives in Rhode Island with her husband and three children.

Alice Speri is a reporter who writes on justice, immigration, and civil rights for *The Intercept*. She has reported from Haiti, Colombia, El Salvador, and Palestine, as well as from across the United States. Originally from Italy, she now lives in the Bronx.

Anne Spice is a Tlingit member of Kwanlin Dun First Nation, a queer Indigenous feminist, and an anticolonial organizer. She teaches and studies in Lenapehoking (New York City) as a doctoral candidate in anthropology at the CUNY Graduate Center.

Kim TallBear is associate professor in the Faculty of Native Studies at the University of Alberta. She is Canada Research Chair in Indigenous Peoples, Technoscience, and Environment and a citizen of the Sisseton–Wahpeton Oyate.

Mark K. Tilsen is an Oglala Lakota poet educator from Porcupine, South Dakota. He trained people at Standing Rock in direct action and led actions that temporarily stopped construction of the Dakota Access Pipeline. He continues this fight on the bayous of Louisiana, fighting the tail end of the Dakota Access Pipeline.

Edward Valandra is Sicangu Titunwan, born and raised in his homeland, Oceti Sakowin Oyate Makoce. He is the dean of Academic and Professional Development Studies at a chartered K–12 Native school.

Joel Waters is an Oglala Lakota writer. His work is featured in *Shedding Skin: Four Sioux Poets*, edited by the late Adrian C. Louis.

Tyler Young is a researcher at the Center for American Indian Research and Native Studies (CAIRNS). He works as an interpretive park ranger for the National Park Service.

Publication Information

A different version of chapter 1 was published as Kim TallBear, "Badass (Indigenous) Women Caretake Relations: #NoDAPL, #IdleNoMore, #BlackLivesMatter," Hot Spots, *Cultural Anthropology* website, December 22, 2016, https://culanth.org.

Chapter 3 was originally published as Jaskiran Dhillon, "'This Fight Has Become My Life and It's Not Over': An Interview with Zaysha Grinnell," Hot Spots, *Cultural Anthropology* website, December 22, 2016, https://culanth.org.

Chapter 5 was originally published in the *New York Times*, August 24, 2016. Copyright 2016 *New York Times*. All rights reserved. Reprinted by permission and protected by the Copyright Laws of the United States. The printing, copying, redistribution, or retransmission of this content without express written permission is prohibited.

Chapter 9 was originally published as "The Great Sioux Nation and the Resistance to Colonial Land Grabbing," *Beacon Broadside*, September 12, 2016.

An earlier version of chapter 10 was published as Jeffrey Ostler and Nick Estes, "Supreme Law of the Land: Standing Rock and the Dakota Access Pipeline," January 16, 2017, https://newsmaven.io/indiancountrytoday/archive/the-supreme-law-of-the-land-standing-rock-and-the-dakota-access-pipeline-25phRkI-JB0GmipEDLvPLPw/.

Chapter 13 was originally published as Layli Long Soldier, "Resolution 6," from *WHEREAS* (St. Paul: Graywolf Press, 2017). Copyright 2017 by Layli Long Solider. Reprinted with permission of Graywolf Press, www.graywolfpress.org.

Chapter 15 was originally published as Alleen Brown, Will Parish, and Alice Speri, "Leaked Documents Reveal Counterterrorism Tactics Used at Standing Rock to

'Defeat Pipeline Insurgencies,'" *The Intercept,* May 27, 2017, https://theintercept
.com/2017/05/27/leaked-documents-reveal-security-firms-counterterrorism-tac
tics-at-standing-rock-to-defeat-pipeline-insurgencies/.

Chapter 24 was originally presented as a TedX talk on October 27, 2017, in Toronto, Ontario, Canada.

Chapter 26 was originally published as David Uahikeaikalei'ohu Maile, "On the Violence of the Thirty Meter Telescope and the Dakota Access Pipeline," Hot Spots, *Cultural Anthropology* website, December 22, 2016, http://www.culanth.org.

Index

Aboriginal Title, 161, 227
Abu Dhabi Investment Authority, 122
abuse, 218, 228, 237, 339
accountability, 9, 115, 116, 128, 133, 264, 272, 308; corporate, 117; financial, 130; radical, 303
accumulation, 247, 252; capitalist, 5, 232, 236
ACOE. *See* U.S. Army Corps of Engineers
activism, 14, 63, 164, 204, 208, 348; antinuclear, 273; community, 43, 178; environmental, 17, 177; political, 311
actualization, self/community, 294–98
Adamson, Rebecca, 111
Agua Zarca hydroelectric dam, 175
AIM. *See* American Indian Movement
Ainu Mosir, settler colonization of, 274
akicitas, 35, 65, 66
Alberta Clipper Pipeline, 366, 368
Alcatraz Island, 2, 164, 262
Aleuts, 274
Allianz Group, 129, 153–54n174
American Anthropological Association, 276n1
American Eagle and Condor Center, 349
"American History Starts Here" (initiative), 251, 258–59n13
American Horse, J. R., 49
American Indian Community House, 349

American Indian Movement (AIM), ix, 95n9, 178, 248, 281; FBI and, 188; Pine Ridge Reservation and, 188; Wounded Knee and, 188, 189
American Indian Religious Freedom Act (1978), 189
American Museum of Natural History, 188
American Psychological Association, 235
American Revolution, 177, 314
Amnesty International, 127
ancestors, 39, 220, 250, 310
Anderson, Ian, 230
Anishinaabe, 307, 367
anthropocentrism, 78–79, 80–81, 84
Anti-Columbus Day Tour, 349
Apaches, 253, 258n8; struggles of, 174–75, 178
Apess, William, 247
Apple, 122
Apple Creek, 48
AP7 (pension fund), 228
Arapahos, 5, 182, 357
Archambault, David II, ix, 7, 16, 178, 290, 293, 298, 302, 358
Arikaras, 21, 44, 46, 113, 160, 182, 357; violence against, 175
assimilation, 162, 163, 262, 266; biocultural, 259n14; cultural, 178, 189; forced, 246, 258n5; political, 189